LONDON
city
of
words

a literary companion

blueisland.co.uk

LONDON
city
of
words

Westrow Cooper • David Caddy

Edited by
Michael Ellis

blueisland.co.uk

First published in 2006 by Blue Island Publishing
Studio 218,
30 Great Guildford Street,
London SE1 0HS

info@blueisland.co.uk
www.blueisland.co.uk

ISBN 0-9540802-9-7
ISBN 978-0-9540802-9-7

Editor: Michael Ellis

Consultant: Ferdie McDonald

Editorial Work & Indexing: Paul Hines

Proofreading: Val Phoenix

Photography & Design: Michael Ellis, Stephen Bere

Text © Westrow Cooper, David Caddy 2006
Images © Blue Island Publishing
Maps © Blue Island Publishing

The authors would like to thank the following for their help:
Jeremy Ashbee, Clive Bettington, Ian Brinton, Jim Burns, Peter Carpenter, Jonathan Coe, Tom
Chivers, Peter Collington, Elizabeth Cook, Michael Gray, Brian Hinton, Sarah Hopkins, Virginia
Johnson, Mike Kearney, Emma Trehane, Jonathan Ward, John Welch

contents

WESTMINSTER

SITE OF AN ABBEY SINCE THE 10TH CENTURY and a parliamentary palace since the 11th, historically Westminster has been at the centre of English (and later British) religious, political and literary life. It was also the scene of two key events in the evolution of the English language itself. In the late 14th century Richard II encouraged the development of a vernacular literature to replace writings customarily rendered in French or Latin; then in 1476 it was here that William Caxton established the country's first printing press.

Court officials and civil servants of the late 14th century were the first to write extensively in the new English language, while practitioners of its literary form also tended to gravitate to Westminster. Chaucer, for example, was Controller of the King's Works at Westminster and also a Member of Parliament; Gower, frequently cited as 'the first English poet', relied on Court patronage to pursue his literary career. The reputations of these writers, and the further establishment of the English language was achieved, in part, through the printing of their works on Caxton's press in the late 15th century, some 100 years after they had been written. In all, Caxton printed around 100 books, the majority new works written in English.

Westminster has a great tradition of writers who have mixed literature and politics, among them Sir Thomas More in the early 16th century, Sir Walter Ralegh in the late 16th and early 17th centuries, and Richard Brinsley Sheridan in the late 18th and early 19th centuries.

At the height of his powers, Sheridan used his phenomenal oratorical skills and understanding of theatrical presentation to argue forcefully in the Commons for the freedom of the press. In the Lords, Byron spoke eloquently against the death penalty for the Luddites in 1812, then later wrote a poem in support of their cause. Tennyson had a quieter time in the Upper House, having been made a peer towards the end of his life.

Joseph Addison and Richard Steele crossed the literary/political boundary, as parliamentarians and members of the literary circle of Swift and Pope. They pioneered the political magazine, launching both *Tatler*, in 1709, and *The Spectator*, two years later.

Since the 20th century the political diary is arguably the most satisfying literary form to come out of Westminster. The most accomplished practitioners, such as Henry 'Chips' Channon and Alan Clark, combine bracing indiscretion with the immediacy of a day-by-day account of the issues and personalities of their times.

Westminster

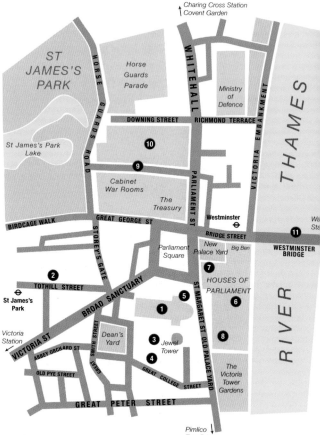

Key

1. Westminster Abbey
2. Tothill Street
3. Little Dean's Yard
4. Westminster School
5. St Margaret's Church
6. Westminster Hall
7. House of Commons
8. House of Lords
9. King Charles Street
10. Foreign Office
11. House of Commons
12. Westminster Bridge

The Birth of the Vernacular

After Edward the Confessor moved his palace to Westminster in around 1040 and built a new abbey dedicated to St Peter (Westminster Abbey), this area – at the time still mostly marshland on the banks of the Thames – attracted a greater population and became the political and religious centre of the nation.

Old English (or Anglo-Saxon) was the spoken and literary language of the day – the language used by the author of *Beowulf*, for example. However, following the Norman Conquest in 1066, 'Anglo-Norman', a dialect of Old French, was introduced. During the 12th century this became, alongside Latin (the language of the Church), the official and literary language of England. It was used at Court, in the administration of the law, to compile official documents and to write literature.

Nevertheless, far from dying out, Old English assimilated elements of Anglo-Norman and Latin, and a new form of the language, 'Middle English' evolved, becoming the spoken language of the vast majority of the population.

In 1363 Edward III's Chancellor opened the parliamentary session with a speech in English, and on his accession to the throne in 1377, Richard II adopted the European princely trend of cultivating a vernacular literature – one specific to, and expressive of, its nation. At the same time he promoted English as the official language of the state. Thus the king's entourage of career diplomats, civil servants and officials living in and around Westminster became the first writers of English. Over the course of the following century the creative and expressive powers of English were developed and stretched by London writers such as Chaucer, Lydgate, Gower, Malory and Hoccleve, and by 1430 English had become established as the 'Chancery Standard', the standard written form for official documents.

The early texts of English literature can and should be seen as defiantly political, and forged out of a demand to assert a national identity distinct from either France or Rome. The example of theologian John Wyclif (or Wycliffe) is indicative of this. He set himself the task of translating the Bible into English, in the 1380s, out of a conviction that it should be the common possession of all Christians, available in the language of the people. And when he launched an attack on the wealth of the Church, contrasting it unfavourably with the poverty of Christ, he did so in English.

Love and Rebellion
Gower and Chaucer

Court writers and poets wrote in a style appropriate for their aristocratic audience, employing deference, courtly manners and self-deprecation. One of the most famous works in this manner is John Gower's *Confessio Amantis* (1390), 33,000 lines of a lover's confession to Genius, the priest of Venus, written in English at the request of King Richard II. Gower revised *Confessio Amantis* in 1393, however, replacing his praise of Richard with a dedication to Henry of Lancaster, the future Henry IV.

Gower's *Vox clamantis* (The Voice of One Crying, 1379–81), an Anglo-Latin elegy, laments the failures of the knights, clergy and peasants in its catalogue of the nation's sins. Gower used the poet's 'crying voice' to call for repentance and social reform. *Vox clamantis* contains, however, a hastily revised response to the Peasants' Revolt of 1381 (occasioned by the third poll tax of 1380), shifting some of the blame for social ills away from the knights and clergy and on to the peasants themselves. This was a shrewd move as the knights were ruthless in their suppression and execution of the poll tax rebels. Gower died in 1408 and was buried in St Mary Overie (now Southwark Cathedral), where his tomb can still be seen.

One of the leading rebels of the Peasants' Revolt, John Ball, made use of quotation from William Langland's *The Vision of Piers Plowman* (1362) to fire his political rhetoric. This allegorical dream poem was about a poor man's search for spiritual truth, and it attacked the corruption of minor church officials. Langland, who lived on Cornhill in the City and worked as a psalter-clerk, equated the plowman of the poem's title with Christ, and juxtaposed his plight with the life of the pampered and affluent clergy. Like Gower, Langland similarly revised his poem in light of the repression of the rebels.

Geoffrey Chaucer's first major poem, *The Book of the Duchess* (1379), was an elegy on the death of Blanche, Duchess of Lancaster, wife of his patron, John of Gaunt. In 1385 Chaucer dedicated his courtly love poem *Troilus and Criseyde* to Gower, giving him the epithet 'moral Gower'. In this, we can see where Chaucer's sympathies lay, though his response to the Peasants' Revolt, made through the social satire of *The Canterbury Tales*, was more veiled than Gower's.

From 1374 Chaucer held a number of official positions, including Controller of Customs on Furs, Skins and Hides for the Port of London and Commissioner of London Embankments and Ditches. The Mayor of London had given him a rent-free dwelling over Aldgate, one of the six gates in the city wall, and it was there that he wrote *The Parliament of Fowls*, *The House of Fame* and *Troilus and Criseyde*, after finishing his daily reckonings at the customhouse. In 1386 Chaucer became a Member of Parliament, representing Kent, and in 1389 was appointed by Richard II Clerk of the King's Works at Westminster and the Tower of London.

The Canterbury Tales (see also p72), written during the 1380s and 90s and still unfinished at Chaucer's death, playfully subvert the hierarchical world of the Church and focus on many of the moral issues of the day. The work attracted the ire of the Church, most significantly in the form of Thomas Arundel who, after a period in exile under Richard II, had been re-appointed Archbishop of Canterbury by Henry IV in 1399. Not long afterwards, Chaucer disappeared from official records and, unlike other contemporary poets, did not leave behind manuscript copies of his own works.

Hoccleve Consolidates the Vernacular Tradition

By the early 15th century the clerks of Westminster had emerged as an independent civil service and at the same time established courtly English poetry as a distinct tradition that was valued, read, maintained and developed.

From about 1386 to 1426 Thomas Hoccleve was employed as a clerk in the Privy Seal Office, working as an author and scribe. He was part of an expanding group of literate and educated officials who were concerned to record and pass on vital and important manuscripts. He assembled a vast anthology of Privy Seal documents entitled the *Formulary* and in the 1420s produced an anthology of his own works. Hoccleve strove to ensure that Chaucer's and Gower's works remained in circulation and built on the vernacular tradition himself.

With patrons in the City and at Court, Hoccleve formed a link between the Westminster political elite and the London book trade, out of which The Guild of Stationers arose in 1403. His most famous poem, 'The Regiment of Princes' (1412), clearly contains an autobiographical element: the poem focuses on the life of a minor government clerk living at Chester's Inn, close to the Strand, whose life is divided between the City and Westminster. In its account of the physical and mental struggles of an ageing civil servant/poet, we may see Hoccleve's desire to assert his identity as an author and gain some measure of control over his work for future readers.

Poet's Corner • Westminster Abbey

In 1399 Chaucer had taken out a 53-year lease on a house in St Mary's Chapel Garden, Westminster Abbey, and as a result was entitled to burial in the abbey. He appears to have received a humble burial at the entrance to the Chapel of St Benedict in the South Transept. A plain slab was used (which is thought to have been sawn up when John Dryden's monument was erected in 1720), and his only memorial was a leaden plate hung on an adjacent pillar.

However, in 1556 Nicholas Brigham – poet and personal treasurer to Mary Tudor – received approval to erect a tomb in Chaucer's memory. The Purbeck marble monument probably came from a dissolved monastery. It bears a Latin inscription, which may be translated as:

> *Of old the bard who struck the noblest strains*
> *Great Geoffrey Chaucer, now this tomb retains.*
> *If for the period of his life you call,*
> *the signs are under that will note you all.*
> *In the year of our Lord 1400, on the 25th day of October*
> *Death is the repose of cares.*
> *N. Brigham charged himself with these in the name of the*
> *Muses 1556*

When Edmund Spenser was buried close to Chaucer's tomb in 1599, the concept of a 'Poets' Corner' began. Writers and poets buried in the abbey include Francis Beaumont, playwright and poet, who wrote 'Lines on the Tombs of Westminster Abbey', Ben Jonson, Dr Samuel Johnson, Richard Brinsley Sheridan, Charles Dickens, Robert Browning, Alfred Lord Tennyson, Thomas Hardy and Rudyard Kipling.

John Dryden, who had been poet laureate under James II, died in Soho in somewhat reduced circumstances in 1700. After some argument he was buried in the abbey in an unmarked grave. The Earl of Mulgrave, prompted by Pope's allusion to Dryden's 'rude and nameless stone', erected a monument *(see also p87)*.

A monument to William Shakespeare was erected in 1740. Memorials to the poets William D'Avenant (who was appointed poet laureate after Ben Jonson's death in 1638), John Milton, John Bunyan, George Herbert, John Gay, William Cowper, William

Wordsworth, Thomas Gray and Robert Burns followed. A bust of William Blake, by Sir Jacob Epstein, was erected in 1957 to commemorate Blake's bicentenary. There is a monument to Abraham Cowley that claims he was the 'Pindar, Horace and Virgil of England' in the mid-17th century. In 1737 Pope asked 'who now reads Cowley?' showing how quickly literary reputations can fade.

A memorial stone to Gerard Manley Hopkins, who was not famous during his lifetime, was laid in 1975 on the centenary of the shipwreck that inspired his famous poem, 'The Wreck of the Deutschland'. Admission to Poets' Corner has enormous prestige and can become controversial. Memorials to John Keats and Percy Bysshe Shelley were added in 1954 while the scandalous Lord Byron was finally admitted only in 1969. Writers such as Samuel Butler (for whom there had been no money to pay the abbey burial fees), Joseph Addison, Oliver Goldsmith, Jane Austen, Sir Walter Scott, William Makepeace Thackeray, John Ruskin, Charlotte, Emily and Anne Brontë, Henry James, T.S. Eliot, W.H. Auden, Dylan Thomas (following protest in his favour by US President Jimmy Carter), and Sir John Betjeman have also been given memorials. In addition, the two great Shakespearean actor-managers David Garrick and Lord Laurence Olivier are also buried in the abbey.

At the east cloister a stone marks the grave of Aphra Behn, poet, playwright, novelist, and one of the first women to earn her living as a writer. In 2002 a memorial window was installed in honour of author and diarist Fanny Burney. Outside the door to Poets' Corner a tablet was placed to commemorate William Caxton, who was buried on the site where St Margaret's Church now stands. In St Margaret's there is a memorial window to Caxton (which was severely damaged in World War II) and another to Sir Walter Ralegh, who was also buried on the site.

Caxton and the Birth of Printing • Westminster Abbey and Tothill Street
The vernacular tradition was further cemented by the establishment of Britain's first printing press, set up by William Caxton in a shop close by Westminster Abbey. Caxton had been apprenticed to Robert Large, a mercer and former Mayor of London, and in 1462 became governor of the English merchants operating in Bruges, a major trading centre for cloth, manuscripts and paintings. Caxton translated Raoul le Fevre's *History of Troy*, a popular French romance, and, having learned the art of printing in Cologne (another centre of trade), printed and published his translation in Brussels in 1474.

In 1476 Caxton returned to Westminster and on 29 September his name is recorded on the account roll of John Estency, Sacrist of Westminster Abbey, paying a year's rent in advance for premises, where he set up his press. The first known piece of printing in England – a Letter of Indulgence by John Sant, Abbot of Abingdon – issued from this press on 13 December 1476. The existence of this work remained unknown until February 1928, when it was discovered at the Public Record Office.

Here Caxton also produced the first book to be printed in England, *The dictes or sayengis of the philosophres*, translated from the French by Caxton's friend and patron Earl Rivers and completed on 18 November 1477. From this time a steady stream of work issued from the print shop, including most notably a translation of *Boethius* (1478) and the *Chronicles of England* (1480).

In 1482 Caxton moved the press to a house he rented at the southeastern end of Tothill Street (the house was demolished in the 19th century). Here he printed the first editions of Chaucer's *Canterbury Tales* (1483) and *Troilus and Criseyde* (1484), and Gower's *Confessio Amantis* (1483). He also published poems by John Lydgate, a Benedictine monk of Bury St Edmund's, and a version of Virgil's *Aeneid* (1490).

Caxton had begun incorporating woodcut illustrations in his work as early as 1480, and these are used most strikingly in Sir Thomas Malory's *Le Morte D'Arthur* (1485). In total, nearly 100 books were printed on Caxton's press, including 77 original works written in English, the majority of which he edited. He died in 1491.

After his death his press was maintained by his assistant Wynkyn de Worde who, in late 1500 or early 1501, moved the press to Fleet Street, to a house opposite Shoe Lane, at the Sign of the Sun. Fleet Street's status as a centre for printing dates from this time. Early readers, however, made little

A section of the Caxton Window, St Margaret's Church

distinction between printed books and manuscripts that were copied by hand. Indeed, they were not effectively seen as distinct until the 1620s and manuscript books existed alongside printed books well into the 17th century.

Westminster School • Little Dean's Yard
Originally attached to the Benedictine Westminster Abbey, Westminster School was reconstituted as a separate entity by Queen Elizabeth I in 1560. Among its many illustrious alumni may be counted Ben Jonson, poet George Herbert, John Dryden, the writer of hymns Charles Wesley, dramatist John Burgoyne and poet Robert Southey. The popular children's authors G.A. Henty and A.A. Milne were educated at Westminster, as was novelist Angus Wilson, writer, actor and raconteur Sir Peter Ustinov and politician and diarist Tony Benn. For one old boy, howeve, the experience proved less than wholly satisfactory, however. William Cowper wrote a long poem in

1784 entitled 'Tirocinium; or, a Review of Schools' with the aim of 'recommending private tuition in preference to an education at school'. It includes the lines:

> *There shall he learn, ere sixteen winters old,*
> *That authors are most useful, pawn'd or sold;*
> *That pedantry is all that schools impart,*
> *But taverns teach the knowledge of the heart ...*

PALACE OF WESTMINSTER
Westminster Hall
The original Palace of Westminster burnt down in 1834, leaving only Westminster Hall, which dates from 1097. The hall was used as a law court from 1130 and heard trials for treason. Sir Thomas More was brought to the hall to face charges of treason in 1535 for refusing to take the oath of the Act of Succession *(see over)*, and King Charles I was brought to trial here before a special tribunal on charges of high treason and 'other high crimes' on 2 January 1649. He refused to enter a plea, claiming that no court had jurisdiction over a monarch. Under the Act of Parliament establishing the court, this gave rise to automatic conviction and on 29 January 1649 Charles's death warrant was signed by 59 of the commissioners (judges) appointed to the tribunal. On the Restoration of the Monarchy in 1660, many of the signatories were themselves put on trial and executed, some being hanged, drawn and quartered.

From 1640 until the end of the 18th century the hall was used for bookselling.

The House of Commons
Membership of the House of Commons has sometimes forced writers into difficult literary, moral and political choices. None more so, perhaps, than Thomas More, who entered Parliament in 1504 representing the interests of the City of London wool merchants, at that time in conflict with the king.

In 1510 More was appointed under-Sheriff of London and chosen by Cardinal Wolsey to go to Antwerp as a representative of the king, whose interests now coincided with those of the wool traders. Whilst in Antwerp he wrote *Utopia* (1516), which brought him fame across Europe and established a new literary-philosophical genre. The underlying themes of *Utopia* concern identity and place, reflecting major social and political issues of the time, such as land ownership, freedom of worship and the balance between the public and private realms. Written in Latin, *Utopia* nevertheless has dialogue and dream vision sections typical of works in the English vernacular. 'Utopia' is a pun meaning 'good place' and 'no place'. More, who appears as a fictional character in the book, was king's ambassador, London lawyer and

Parliamentarian, and detached humanist philosopher. These potentially conflicting roles informed his decision to locate the perfect state in a fictional environment.

More's pre-eminence as a writer and thinker brought him high office. He became a Privy Councillor in 1518, Speaker of the House in 1523 and Lord Chancellor in 1529. However, when Henry VIII began to dismantle the Catholic Church's authority in England in order to divorce Catherine Aragon and marry Anne Boleyn, More, who had become staunchly Catholic, resigned his position in 1532.

In 1533 he was forbidden to publish, and on 14 April 1534 he was taken into the custody of the abbot of Westminster for refusing to take the oath of the Act of Succession. This included a clause repudiating the power of any 'foreign authority' in English affairs. Four days later he was transferred to the Tower of London, and executed at Tower Hill for treason on 6 July 1535. His last words as he put his head on the block were: 'I die the king's good servant, but God's first.'

More was beatified by the Pope in 1886 and canonized at a Papal Mass in St Peter's in 1935. In 2000, Saint Thomas More was declared 'heavenly patron of statesmen and politicians' by Pope John Paul II. His feast day is 22 June.

Sir Walter Ralegh, who is credited with introducing tobacco into this country among much else, was also a Court poet and member of the Commons. He was imprisoned in the Tower of London three times *(see pp51–2)* and in 1603 was implicated in the Bye Plot to oust James I. He was executed at Old Palace Yard, Westminster, on 29 October 1618. His most famous poems are 'Epitaph for Sir Philip Sidney', 'The Nymph's Reply To The Shepherd' and 'The Passionate Man's Pilgrimage', with its uplifting first stanza:

> *Give me my scallop-shell of quiet,*
> *My staff of faith to walk upon,*
> *My scrip of joy, immortal diet,*
> *My bottle of salvation,*
> *My gown of glory, hope's true gage:*
> *And thus I'll take my pilgrimage.*

The court poet Fulke Greville represented Warwickshire in Parliament and was Secretary to the Principality of Wales for forty-five years, Treasurer to the Navy (1589–1604) and Chancellor of the Exchequer (1614–22). James I made him the first Baron Brooke and elevated him to the House of Lords in 1621. He was part of the Areopagus Club *(see p27)*, an association of courtier poets concerned with prosody and the use of classical meters in English. Members of the club included Sir Philip Sidney, Edmund Spenser, Sir Edward Dyer and Gabriel Harvey. Through their work these poets defended the legitimacy of Queen Elizabeth's reign.

The great Elizabethan poets helped to consolidate the creation of a national literary, moral and religious identity. Much of Greville's work remained unpublished during his lifetime, as it dealt with sensitive matters of state, but his poems were published poshumously in *Certain Learned and Elegant Works* (1633), which included the sonnet cycle of love poems, 'Caelica', poems on philosophical and religious themes, and two tragedies. His *Life of the Renowned Sir Philip Sidney* was published in 1652.

Edmund Waller entered Parliament at the age of 16, representing Agmondesham (Amersham) in 1621. He tried to maintain a course between the royalists and their parliamentary opponents. In 1655 he wrote the poem, 'Panegyrick to my Lord Protector', celebrating Cromwell, then in 1660, 'To The King, Upon His Majesty's Happy Return', celebrating the restoration of Charles II. Upon Charles II's observation that Cromwell's was the better poem, Waller replied: 'Sir, we poets never succeed so well in writing truth as in fiction'. His contemporary Richard Lovelace, on the other hand, was an avowedly royalist poet. While imprisoned at Westminster Gatehouse in April 1642 (for calling for the restoration of Anglican bishops) he wrote 'To Althea, From Prison', which contains the famous words: 'Stone Walls do not a Prison make, / Nor Iron bars a Cage'. Imprisoned by Parliament again during 1648 and 1649 he wrote and published the *Lucasta* poems in 1649. He died in financial ruin and was buried in St Bride's, Fleet Street in 1658.

Andrew Marvell – Member of Parliament for Hull from 1659 to 1678 – is often compared to Edmund Waller, both being regarded as wits during a period of great volatility and upheaval. While Waller (though fashionable in the 17th century) is now barely remembered, Marvell is considered a major poet, though during his lifetime he was primarily thought of as a satirist. He had been John Milton's assistant as Cromwell's Latin Secretary and, after the Restoration, wrote vehement satires and pamphlets against Charles II and his ministers. He also wrote daily newsletters to his constituents for most of his parliamentary career, which were discovered and published in 1776. These provide a fascinating insight into parliamentary life.

His poems were circulated in manuscript form until the appearance of *Miscellaneous Poems* (1681). They were continually in print, admired by Hazlitt, Lamb and Leigh Hunt, and finally canonised by T.S. Eliot in 1921. His most celebrated poems include 'An Horatian Ode Upon Cromwell's return from Ireland', 'The Mower To The Glow-Worm' and the famous poem of seduction 'To His Coy Mistress':

> *Had we but world enough, and time,*
> *This coyness, Lady, were no crime.*
> *We would sit down and think which way*
> *To walk, and pass our long love's day.*

Joseph Addison and Richard Steele, co-founders of the *Tatler* (in 1709) and *The Spectator* (in 1711), were also (intermittently) members of Parliament. The highly influential magazine producers and pamphleteers were part of the literary circle of Swift and Pope. They promoted the poetry of John Milton and the philosophy of John Locke, and satirized the Tory government.

Steele was briefly M.P. for Stockbridge from June 1713 until March 1714. Both were honoured when the Whigs came to power in the autumn of 1714: Addison became a Secretary of State until poor health forced his resignation in 1718; Steele, among other appointments, was made Supervisor of the Theatre. The great friends fell out over the Peerage Bill of 1719, and Addison died the same year.

Playwright Richard Brinsley Sheridan gave up writing in favour of a political career, and was elected M.P. for Stafford in 1780. A member of Charles James Fox's Whigs, he gained the reputation as one of the greatest orators in Britain and was much admired by the succeeding generation of radical writers, such as Byron, Hazlitt and Lamb. Sheridan had met Fox and Edmund Burke at St James's Coffee House *(see p199)* after the success of his plays gained him entry into the Devonshire House set. He enjoyed a tempestuous affair with Lady Harriet Duncannon, the Duchess of Devonshire's sister, and became a leading figure in the Whig party and intimate of the Prince of Wales.

In 1806 Sheridan succeeded Fox as M.P. for Westminster, but over time became increasingly isolated as his colleagues either died or deserted to the Tories. He was in the House in February 1809 when the Theatre Royal, Drury Lane, of which he was a part owner, burned down *(see p95)*. Sheridan never recovered from this financial blow and less than a year after losing his parliamentary seat – and with it immunity from his creditors – Sheridan was imprisoned for debt. He died in poverty in 1816.

Nineteenth-century writers who were also members of Parliament include William Cobbett, who wrote *Rural Rides* (1830), and Benjamin Disraeli. Having failed to get elected as a Whig, Radical, or Independent, Disraeli was finally elected as a Tory in 1837. His satirical first novel, *Vivian Grey* (1826), sold very well, and he went on to express his political philosophy in a trilogy of novels, *Coningsby* (1844), *Sybil* (1845) and *Tancred* (1847), which showed concern for poverty and the injustices of the parliamentary system. He served as Chancellor of the Exchequer on three separate occasions and as Prime Minister in 1868 and 1874. His final novel was *Endymion* (1880).

In modern times, writers have been less inclined to seek a parliamentary career, but the path in the opposite direction has become increasingly well worn. A number of sitting (and former) M.P.s have produced works of popular fiction, often drawing on their parliamentary experiences to inform the storylines. Recent entrants to this field include William Hague, Ann Widdecombe and Boris Johnson. Douglas Hurd, Chris

Mullin (whose *A Very British Coup*, 1982, stands out) and Rupert Allison (writing as Nigel West) are thriller writers. Michael Dobbs, former Deputy Chairman of the Conservative Party and political aide to Margaret Thatcher and John Major, created the scheming Francis Urquhart, who rose to become Prime Minister (before a spectacular fall) over the course of the *House of Cards* trilogy (1989, 1992, 1995). Urquhart's catch phrase 'You might well think that; I couldn't possibly comment' has entered the language following the BBC TV adaptations, written by Andrew Davies.

The 20th-century's most celebrated Prime Minister, Winston Churchill, was a prolific historian whose works included a four-volume biography of his ancestor, *Marlborough: His Life and Times* (1933–38), a six-volume history of *The Second World War* (1948–54), and the monumental *History of the English Speaking Peoples* (1956–58). In 1953 he was awarded the Nobel Prize for Literature 'for his mastery of historical and biographical description as well as for brilliant oratory in defending exalted human values'.

Churchill made his name as a writer with *My Early Life* (1930), which takes him from school at Harrow through his period of service as a cavalry officer – during which he saw action in India, Sudan and Afghanistan – to life on the run as a war correspondent in South Africa, having made a daring escape from a Boer prison. A gripping story told with verve, it is probably his most highly regarded book today.

Many politicians, following the most significant phase of his or her careers, have been unable to resist the temptation to write (or have ghost-written) their memoirs. In recent times these have often been the subjects of enthusiastic bidding wars between publishers, the price buoyed by consideration of the newspaper serialisation rights. Frequently, however, the public reaction has more closely resembled the famous quip by Sam Goldwyn: 'Read it? I can't even lift it.'

Statue of Churchill, Parliament Square

Nevertheless, in the best parliamentary diarists – Harold Nicolson, Sir Henry 'Chips' Channon, Alan Clark and, arguably, Tony Benn – can be found a candour, wit and accomplished style that places them in the tradition of Pepys and Boswell. Of the above, Tony Benn is the only representative of the left, and the only one to have reached high office. He retired from the House of Commons in May 2001, after 50 years in Parliament, to 'devote more time to politics'. His eight volumes of diaries, covering the years 1942–2001, provide a detailed dissection of his own political character and the internal wrangling of the Labour Party.

Harold Nicolson attended the Paris Peace Conference in 1919 as a member of the Foreign Office, and served as a Conservative M.P. in 1935-45. He was married to Vita Sackville-West, a prominent member of the Bloomsbury Group, and together they created the famous garden at Sissinghurst. With extensive contacts in both political and cultural circles, his diary provides an insightful and entertaining record of the times.

The diaries of another prominent Society figure, politician and writer of the first half of the 20th century, Alfred Duff Cooper, were finally published in 2005. Duff Cooper (as he was always known) became First Lord of the Admiralty in 1937, but resigned the following year over the Munich Agreement between Prime Minister Neville Chamberlain and Adolf Hitler. He did, however, re-enter the Cabinet as Minister for Information under Winston Churchill's wartime government.

As a young man Duff Cooper established a reputation as a drinker and womaniser as well as a poet and, later, adroit politician. His diary combines a vivid first-hand account of some of the key moments in 20th-century history with details of his many infidelities during his turbulent marriage to Lady Diana Cooper, née Manners, who in her youth was often referred to as the most beautiful woman in England.

Palace of Westminster

Duff Cooper's diaries were edited for publication by his son, John Julius Norwich, who had preserved them despite advice from some members of the family, notably publisher Rupert Hart-Davis (Duff Cooper's nephew) who, shocked by the sexual revelations, suggested that it might be best for all concerned if they were burnt.

After retiring in 1947, Duff Cooper wrote a well-regarded autobiography *Old Men Forget*. The Duff Cooper Prize, awarded for the best work of history, biography, or political science published in English or French, was established in his honour.

'I sometimes wonder why I keep a diary at all,' wrote Sir Henry 'Chips' Channon in 1936. 'Is it to relieve my feelings? Console my old age? Or to dazzle my descendants?'

Born in Chicago into great wealth, Henry Channon moved to England after the First World War to study at Christ's College, Oxford, where he shared a bachelor house with a friend known as 'Fish'. As a result he acquired the nickname 'Chips'. In 1933 he married Honor Guinness, the eldest daughter of the second Earl of Iveagh, and in 1935 entered the Commons as Conservative M.P. for Southend.

Chips' diaries vividly capture the characters and style of the gilded world in which he moved, and provide tantalising accounts of major events of the period, notably King Edward VIII's love for 'jolly, plain, unprepossessing' Mrs Simpson and the ensuing abdication crisis. His entry for 1 October 1938 regarding Duff Cooper's resignation provides a flavour of his outlook:

'Duff has resigned in what I must say is a very well-written letter, and the PM has immediately accepted his resignation. But we shall hear more of this – personally my reactions are mixed. I am sorry for Diana; they give up £5,000 per annum, a lovely house – and for what? Does Duff think he will make money at literature?'

The single volume of *Diaries*, published posthumously, represents a heavily edited version of the original from which many of the spicier scandals have been removed. The original manuscript volumes, running to almost three million words, still exist, however, so the possibility remains of an unexpurgated Chips in the future.

Alan Clark was an ardent admirer of Chips' writing, noting in his diary on 27 January 1977: 'There are few things nicer than sitting in bed, drinking up strong Indian tea, and reading Chips' diaries – which loosen the mind, and cause reflection.'

The first volume of Alan Clark's diaries, *Into Power*, was published in 1993, with two further volumes published posthumously. They have a spectacular level of candour and vitality and reveal why Clark was no stranger to controversy during his years as an M.P. While famously on one occasion forced to admit that he had been 'economical with the actualité', in his diaries Clark is the very soul of indiscretion, whether offering opinions on political colleagues or foes, or recounting his many amorous adventures. This frankness, combined with acute observation and an enthralling account of the downfall of Mrs Thatcher, made his *Diaries* a great success.

House of Lords

Lord Byron gave his maiden speech in the House of Lords in February 1812 urging members to oppose a bill bringing in the death penalty for the Luddites – the Nottingham weavers who had broken the new machinery and burned the mills of their employers in protest against their poverty and unemployment. As a result of his eloquence he was included on the committee that recommended reducing the death penalty to a fine or imprisonment. When the bill went back to the Commons, however, the death penalty was restored.

The Whig politician and historian Thomas Macaulay found literary recognition with his 1825 essay on Milton published in the *Edinburgh Review*. As a parliamentarian, he was active in the anti-slavery movement and in passing the 1832 Reform Bill, and held office as Secretary of War from 1839 until the fall of Lord Melbourne's government in 1841. Out of political office, he wrote the *History of England* vols. 1 & 2 (1849) and vols. 3 & 4 (1855), which were hugely popular in the 19th century.

In the *History* series, he used a wide range of manuscript sources, celebrated the material advances of the Victorian era and sought to demonstrate that a Continental revolution was not necessary in England due the Glorious Revolution of 1688. As a result of the *History*, Lord Palmerston made him Baron Macaulay of Rothley in August 1857. He attended the Lords, refusing a government post so that he could finish writing the *History*. But when he died in 1859 he had only reached the year1697.

Alfred Tennyson was made first Baron of Freshwater in December 1883, taking his seat in the Lords in March 1884, in recognition of his contribution to English poetry. He had succeeded William Wordsworth as poet laureate in 1850 on the strength of such volumes as *The Princess* (1847) – which deals with the question of women's rights and later formed the basis of the satirical Gilbert and Sullivan opera *Princess Ida* – and *In Memoriam* (1850), an elegy to the memory of his friend, Arthur Hallam.

Enormously popular, Tennyson consolidated his fame with *Maud, and Other Poems* (1855) and the 1854 poem 'The Charge of the Light Brigade', written to celebrate the actions of a British cavalry unit in the Crimean War. He composed the first four *Idylls of the King* (1859), based on the Arthurian legends, and added to the sequence in 1885. Other notable works include *Enoch Arden* (1864), a narrative of love and self-sacrifice, and *The Holy Grail and Other Poems* (1870). A popular poet laureate, he was admired by Queen Victoria and at the centre of a literary and artistic community in Freshwater, Isle of Wight, that included photographer Julia Margaret Cameron and Thackeray's eldest daughter, Lady Anne Ritchie.

Melvyn Bragg became Lord Bragg of Wigton for services to culture in 1998, having presented and edited the TV arts programme *The South Bank Show* since 1978, written a chronicle of spoken English for BBC Radio, screenplays, biographies and novels. His semi-autobiographical novels, including *For Want of a Nail* (1965), *A Time to Dance* (1990) and *The Soldier's Return* (1999), which won the W.H. Smith Literary Award in 2000, are based on his Cumbrian upbringing.

Parliament, the King and the Diarist • Axe Yard

In the summer of 1658, having recently survived a dangerous operation for the removal of a kidney stone, and now in his third year as a clerk in the Exchequer's office under George Downing, Samuel Pepys moved to a house – or, more accurately in the first instance, half a house – in Axe Yard. A cul-de-sac just south of Downing Street, on the site where the Foreign and Commonwealth Office stands today, Axe Yard was the perfect address for Pepys, placing him in the heart of Westminster and the seat of power during one of the most tumultuous periods of English history. Eighteen months later, on 1 January 1660, he began the diary in which, over the course of the next nine and a half years, he gave the most vivid account that exists of life – both public and private – at this time.

In his youth Pepys was a strong supporter of the parliamentary cause, and was in the crowd outside the Banqueting House in Whitehall on Tuesday 30 January 1649 to see the execution of Charles I. He was also present just over 11 years later when the monarchy began to take revenge on those who had signed Charles's death warrant:

> *'I went out to Charing cross to see Maj.-Gen. Harrison hanged, drawn, and quartered – which was done there – he looking as cheerfully as any man could do in that condition. He was presently cut down and his head and his heart shown to the people, at which there was great shouts of joy ...'*
> The Diary of Samuel Pepys (entry for 13 October 1660)

The following spring Pepys joined in the celebrations for the coronation of Charles II, which ended in traditional English style:

> *'I went in with Mr Thornbury (who did give the company all their wines, he being yeoman of the wine-cellar to the King) to his house; and there we drank the King's health and nothing else, till one of the gentlemen fell down stark drunk and there lay speweing."* Pepys at this point is still feeling *'pretty well'* but *'no sooner a-bed ... my head begun to turne and I to vomitt'* waking in the morning *'wet with my spewing. Thus did the day end, with joy everywhere.'*
> The Diary of Samuel Pepys (entry for 23 April 1661)

In June 1660 Pepys was appointed Clerk of the Acts to the Navy Board, and on 27 July moved from Axe Yard to the Clerk's official lodgings in the Navy Office building in Seething Lane in the City *(see p67)*. In January 1674 Pepys achieved his ambition of entering Parliament, and so returned to Westminster, moving into rooms above Admiralty Headquarters in Derby House, situated close to Whitehall. Here Pepys remained until 1679 when he was cited in a 'Popish Plot' and briefly imprisoned in the Tower *(see p52)*. On his release, his friend (and one time clerk) Will Hewer offered Pepys a suite of rooms in his house at 12 Buckingham Street *(see p26)*. Pepys moved into a larger house at the end of the street in 1688, and there created a library to house his extensive and important book collection. With characteristic foresight and attention to detail he designed the bookcases to be demountable. Thus when, in failing health in 1701, he took up a second invitation from Will Hewer – to move to his country house in Clapham (then a quiet village) – the bookcases were dismantled and the entire library re-erected in the Clapham house.

Pepys died on 26 May 1703, leaving his library, comprising over 3,000 leather-bound books, to his old college at Cambridge. Here the six folio volumes of the *Diary*, written in shorthand with excursions into French and Spanish when recounting his sexual adventures, remained unread and virtually untouched upon the shelves for the next 100 years. In 1819 an undergraduate, John Smith, was found to take on the job of transcribing the *Diary*, a task over which he laboured for three years – without knowing that the key to the shorthand system Pepys had used was also in the library, only a few shelves away. Smith left out only a few of the sexually frank passages, but for publication the transcript was heavily edited and much of it re-written.

The *Diary* was finally published in its entirety in 1976, from a new transcription by William Matthews, almost three hundred years after Pepys's death.

Sancho's Grocery Shop • 19 Charles Street, later King Charles Street

Ignatius Sancho, the first African writer in London, lived here from winter 1773 until his death. He ran a grocery shop selling sugar, tea and tobacco. A former slave, he had received a classical education from John, second Duke of Montagu and in 1751 entered London's café society. He wrote poetry, plays and musical works and was painted by Thomas Gainsborough in 1768. He was a friend of Dr Johnson (who wanted to write Sancho's biography), Garrick and Sterne, to whom he addressed a letter in 1766 that made his intellectual mark. His *Letters* (1782), written somewhat in the style of Sterne, chronicle his daily life and share Sterne's moral vision of tolerance and philanthropy. The letters were collected by one of his correspondents, Frances Crewe, who saw their value to the Abolitionist movement. The first edition drew an astonishing 1181 subscribers, helping to establish the importance of these documents.

In Armour Complete • Westminster Bridge

James Boswell visited London for the first time in 1792 and secured affordable lodgings in Downing Street (not then the location of the Prime Minister's residence). The 22-year-old Boswell then set about exploring every aspect of the high and low life that the City had to offer – with characteristic gusto.

On 10 May 1763 he records in his journal picking up a 'strong jolly young damsel' at the bottom of Haymarket and 'taking her under the arm I conducted her to Westminster Bridge, and then in armour complete' (i.e. wearing a re-usable kid-skin condom) 'did I engage her upon this noble edifice. The whim of doing it there with the Thames rolling below us amused me much.'

William Wordsworth wrote the poem, 'Upon Westminster Bridge' (1807) with the famous opening line 'Earth has not anything to show more fair,' commemorating his crossing of Westminster Bridge, with his sister, on 3 September 1802. The old bridge has been replaced and the view of the 'ships, towers, domes, theatres, and temples' has been transformed. But 'The beauty of the morning: silent and bare,' can still be found, the Abbey still remains, and the river still 'glideth at his own sweet will'.

STRAND & FLEET STREET

THE STRAND is the main thoroughfare connecting Westminster and the City. Originally a Thames-side bridleway, it became home to aristocratic Tudor and Stuart courtiers, including Robert Dudley, Earl of Leicester, patron of Edmund Spenser and Sir Philip Sidney. Literature was supported by others, including the Earl of Essex, Fulke Greville (later Lord Brooke) and Sir Walter Ralegh, to the advantage of such writers as Ben Jonson, Michael Drayton and John Donne.

The City's old western barrier, Temple Bar, stood at the junction of the Strand and Fleet Street. Between this point and the river – in the area known as the Temple – are the Inns of Court. In the mid-14th century, the Temple became a centre for lawyers. It was their custom that sparked the relocation of printing presses from Westminster to the Strand and Fleet Street in the 16th century – a move begun by Caxton's former apprentice, Wynkyn de Worde. This increased the importance of this thoroughfare as a communications link between the Court at Westminster and the City.

The dissemination of news was initially via papers and journals and coffee-house discussions, but in 1702 the first newspaper, *The Daily Courant*, appeared. Successive newspapers provided writers with employment: Sheridan, Charles Lamb and Dickens all wrote for the *Morning Chronicle*, which was published between 1769 and 1862.

Another effect of the burgeoning print industry was the mass production of literature. A local printer, Samuel Richardson, was one of the founders of the modern novel form with his epistolary work *Pamela*.

While Fleet Street has numerous literary connections, its overriding association is with journalism. With so many newspapers, journals and satirical magazines being published in such close proximity, Fleet Street became a natural gathering point for writers, sometimes in regular weekly meetings, such as at the Punch Tavern (where *Punch* magazine was founded in 1841), sometimes in ad hoc sessions in the street's many pubs.

Rupert Murdoch's controversial move of the *Times*, *Sunday Times*, *Sun* and *News of the World* to Wapping in 1986 triggered the break-up of the newspaper publishing industry in Fleet Street. Reuters news agency was one of the last organisations to leave, in June 2005.

Strand and Fleet Street

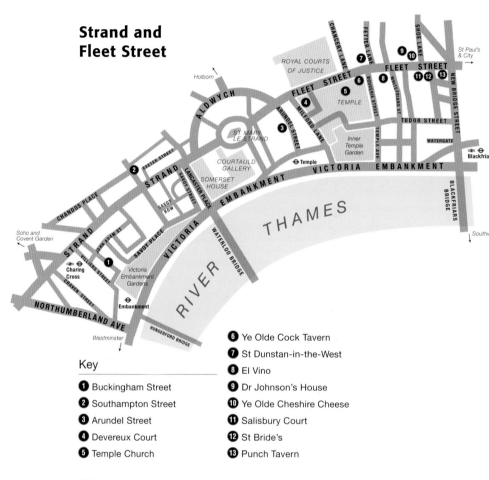

Key

1 Buckingham Street
2 Southampton Street
3 Arundel Street
4 Devereux Court
5 Temple Church
6 Ye Olde Cock Tavern
7 St Dunstan-in-the-West
8 El Vino
9 Dr Johnson's House
10 Ye Olde Cheshire Cheese
11 Salisbury Court
12 St Bride's
13 Punch Tavern

Victorian Embankment

Joseph Bazalgette, as chief engineer to the Metropolitan Board of Works, instituted the construction of the Embankment in 1870. He replaced the tidal mud with ground for riverside roads and gardens, below which a network of sewers and drains took London's sewage eastwards out of the city, as opposed to being dumped into the Thames. Prior to Bazalgette's work, the stench of raw sewage permeated central London, causing what came to be known as the 'great stink'.

The Thames used to flow to the foot of Buckingham Street, the literary residents of which have included Samuel Pepys, who lived at 12 Buckingham Street and Charles Dickens, who lived at 15 Buckingham Street in 1833. Other previous residents of No. 15 include Tsar Peter the Great in 1698 and Henry Fielding in 1753.

Jean-Jacques Rousseau, the Swiss-born author of *La nouvelle Héloise* (1761) and *Émile* (1762), arguably the most significant book on education after Plato's *Republic*, lived at No. 10 Buckingham Street in 1766 with the philosopher David Hume. He became friends with David Garrick, who in turn introduced him to Johnson, Burke and Horace Walpole – none of whom liked him. Convinced that he was being persecuted, he fell out with Hume and left for France.

However, while in London Rousseau wrote the first part of his *Confessions* which, with its intense emotional directness and emphasis on childhood and innocence, inspired the Romantic poets and also Goethe, Henry James, Tolstoy and Proust, as well as being an iconic text within the 1960s counter-culture.

253 • Embankment – Elephant and Castle

Geoff Ryman's internet novel, *253*, is set on the Bakerloo Line and describes a journey from Embankment station to Elephant and Castle. Why 253? 'There are seven carriages on a Bakerloo Line train, each with 36 seats. A train in which every passenger has a seat will carry 252 people. With the driver, that makes 253.' Each passenger is described through their outward appearance, inside information, actions and thoughts in a total of 253 words. The novel can be read in any order, passenger to passenger from one carriage to another or by pursuing any of the narrative links between passengers. The end is reached at the 'end of the line.' *253* was published in book form but the internet version, at ryman-novel.com, is more suited to the random structure.

Sweete Themmes! Runne Softly, till I End My Song
Essex House, Essex Street & Devereux Court

The Areopagus Club, named after the ancient council on the mountain near Athens, met secretly during 1579 and 1580 at Leicester House (later Essex House), the stately home of Robert Dudley, the Earl of Leicester. This association of aristocratic courtiers and poets included Sir Philip Sidney (Dudley's nephew), Edmund Spenser, Fulke Greville, Edward Dyer, Gabriel Harvey and Thomas Drant, and was concerned with the naturalisation of classical metres into English poetry. They were a literary and political group meeting to rationalise a role for the poet and sovereign within a divine Protestant universe. They saw the poet's role as essentially moral and religious, and sought to renew English as a poetic tongue. English rather than Latin poetry, they asserted, should be used to move English people to virtue and knowledge. As Spenser wrote to Harvey in 1580: 'Why a' God's name, may not we, as else the Greeks, have the kingdom of our own language?'

Dr John Dee – a philosopher and mathematician as well as the royal astrologer – advised them. He was the intellectual leader of the Elizabethan renaissance and the theorist of its imperial expansion, as laid out in his *General and Rare Memorials*

Pertaining to the Perfect Art of Navigation (1577). Dee's considerable influence can be seen in the use of Neo-Platonic and numerological schemes in the epic poems of the Areopagus Club writers, as well as in the idea that poetry and prose, by their rhythmic nature, produce a psychological effect on the reader and listener. From Petrarch they adopted the sonnet form and an interest in real human lives and loves, albeit hidden within classical references. Philip Sidney argued that poetry offered skills and moral insights for the sovereign, nation and people and a way of asserting English Protestantism within a Catholic Europe.

The poetic fruits of these meetings were Sidney's *Astrophel and Stella* (1591) and Spenser's *Amoretti* (1595), *The Faerie Queene* (1596) and *Prothalamion* (1596). The rhythms and alliterative use of language come alive when the poems are read aloud – as they would have been at the time. Indeed *The Faerie Queen*, that epic of nationhood, is often described as a dream-like work of harmony and enchanted music.

The Faerie Queene has the queen and London at its centre. Spenser describes London on the Thames as a crowded cluster of towers arranged in the form of a crown – placing the queen at the centre of the cities of London and Westminster.

John Dee's instructions in navigation and encouragement of the courtier poets to map the world became part of a wider redefinition of England in a global context. For Spenser, in *The Faerie Queene* geography is the standard by which a ruler – and perhaps poet – could measure himself.

> *So huge a scope at first him seemed best*
> *To be the compasse of his kingdom's seat;*
> *So huge a mind could not in lesser rest,*
> *Ne in small meanes containe his glory great.*

Spenser mentions Leicester House (which became Essex House in 1588 on its inheritance by Leicester's stepson, Robert Devereux, Earl of Essex) in *Prothalamion*:

> *Next whereunto there stands a stately place,*
> *Where oft I gained giftes and goodly grace*
> *Of that great lord, which therein wont to dwell.*
> *Whose want too well now feels my friendless case:*
> *But, ah! here fits not well*
> *Old woes, but ioyes, to tell*
> *Against the bridale daye, which is not long.*
> *Sweete Themmes! runne softly, till I end my song.*

The poet and dramatist John Gay also mentions the house in his poem 'Trivia, or the Art of Walking the Streets of London' (1716). He describes walking parts of London by day and night. 'There Essex stately pile adorned the shore, / There Cecil's, Bedford's, Villiers' – now no more.'

Grecian Coffee House • 19 Devereux Court

Leading off Essex Street, the Grecian Coffee House, at 19 Devereux Court, was where Richard Steele wrote his contributions to the *Tatler*. It was also patronised by fellow journalist Joseph Addison and many members of the Royal Society, including Isaac Newton and Edmund Halley. In 1709 the *Tatler* described the Grecian as, 'attracting men of learning where the arguments become so intense that swords were often drawn leading to death.'

The essayists and the coffee houses met the demand for knowledge of theology, physics, medicine, economics and the latest scientific discoveries. In issue 10 of the *Spectator* Addison hoped that he had brought philosophy out of closets and libraries and into the clubs and coffee houses. The Grecian coffee house was open from 1702 to 1813. Today The Devereux pub stands on the site it occupied.

Star Spangled Banner • Crown & Anchor Tavern

The Crown & Anchor in Arundel Street was a large building with ample conference rooms available for lectures and club meetings. Dr Johnson held club meetings there, as did the Anacreontic club of musicians and composers in the 1770s. John Stafford Smith was a member and, while there in 1780, wrote the music to which the words of the 'Star Spangled Banner' were later set.

The tavern had a long tradition of public meetings and events associated with radical and controversial causes. By dint of holding a public event at the Crown & Anchor, press coverage would follow. Richard Brinsley Sheridan spoke for the Whig club at a reform banquet to celebrate the first anniversary of the fall of the Bastille on 14 July 1790. Hosted by radical Lord Stanhope, it was attended by 652 'friends of liberty'. Sheridan proposed a resolution rejoicing in the establishment of liberty in France in an attempt to link Whig reformers with popular support for the revolution.

William Hazlitt gave four lectures here in March 1818 on poetry, Chaucer and Spenser, Shakespeare and Milton, and modern poets. Charles Lamb, the Godwin family, the Hunts, Keats, the Montagus and publisher John Taylor, of Taylor & Hussey (who later published the lectures), were all part of the large audiences.

Samuel Taylor Coleridge gave fourteen weekly lectures between 14 December 1818 and 29 March 1819 on 'Shakespeare and the History of Philosophy'. Coleridge aimed to make philosophy a living subject for his large audience, which included friends from Highgate and the City, as well as medical and art students.

Strand Magazine • **7-12 Southampton Street**

> *For three hours we strolled about together, watching*
> *the ever-changing kaleidoscope of life as it ebbs and*
> *flows through Fleet Street and the Strand. Holmes'*
> *characteristic talk, with its keen observation of detail*
> *and subtle power of inference, held me amused and*
> *enthralled.*
>
> 'The Resident Patient'

Arthur Conan Doyle was the most popular contributor to the *Strand Magazine* (founded by George Newnes in 1890 and based at 7-12 Southampton Street). This illustrated monthly periodical was sold through W.H. Smith's national network of bookstalls and had a circulation of 392,000 copies in the 1890s. Conan Doyle's Sherlock Holmes stories appealed to male readers and helped make it acceptable for men to read fiction. However, Conan Doyle had to change his character for the *Strand* as the magazine had a strong anti-drug stance. The serialisation of *The Hound of the Baskervilles* (1902) increased circulation by an estimated 30,000 copies. Conan Doyle's stories were collected and published in book form in *The Adventures of Sherlock Holmes* (1892), *The Memoirs of Sherlock Holmes* (1894), *The Hound of the Baskervilles* (1902) and other works.

Aiming for a family readership, Newnes had an illustration on every page and used a clear, simple typeface. Other contributors included P.G. Wodehouse, H.G. Wells, John Buchan, E.W. Hornung and Rudyard Kipling.

The Printed Word • **St Bride's Churchyard**
When Wynkyn De Worde, Caxton's assistant, moved his printing press from Westminster to St Bride's churchyard, Fleet Street, in 1500, he set a trend that eventually consolidated into a thriving industry. The churchyard at that time was like a small village, with taverns, inns, houses and shops. De Worde moved here to be closer to his City customers, and the business prospered as the lawyers and clergy living and working nearby became part of his clientele. Between 1491 and 1535 De Worde and his apprentices published at least 640 books, including educational books, religious books, romances and poetry, law books and chronicles.

De Worde extended the range of fonts employed in printing, introducing italics in 1524. Printers such as Richard Pynson, Julian Notary and Thomas Berthelet followed him to the Temple and St Bride's. These businesses operated not only as printers but also as booksellers and stationers and continued to deal in manuscript books as well. The Inns of Court established their own libraries in the 16th century.

Demand for printed and manuscript books remained high as the Elizabethan court poets and writers increasingly expressed a new sense of national and cultural identity. An enterprising printer, Richard Tottel, who worked at the Sign of the Hand and Star within Temple Bar from 1553 until 1594, compiled *The Booke of Songes and Sonnettes* (1557), known as *Tottel's Miscellany*, and started the Elizabethan craze for sonnets and poetry anthologies. The first edition was reprinted within two months and at least eight editions followed in the next thirty years.

Printed 'to the honour of the Englishe tongue, and for the profit of the studious of English eloquence, *Tottel's Miscellany* included the sonnets of Sir Thomas Wyatt and Henry Howard, Earl of Surrey. It contributed towards the vogue for courtly sonnets and, partly through its influence, the reading and writing of aphoristic and amorous verse became fashionable for the courtly knight.

In 1586 the Archbishop of Canterbury and Bishop of London sought to restrict the growth of printing by ordering that no new presses be opened until the then current number of printers was reduced, by death or otherwise. However, when this order was relaxed in the 17th century, poets, pamphleteers and playwrights (often educated as lawyers) took up residence near the rival printing presses and booksellers of Fleet Street and St Paul's.

On 11 March 1702 the first newspaper, *The Daily Courant*, was printed in Fleet Street. By 1724 the number of London printing presses had increased to 70. By 1819 the Strand and Fleet Street were home to eight daily morning, seven daily evening, nine irregular, four weekly, four Saturday and Monday and twelve Sunday newspapers. By 1869 these numbers had multiplied still further with a plethora of other weekly, monthly and ad hoc publications.'

St Bride's, Fleet Street

St Bride's Church

Known as the 'journalists' church', St Bride's has a long history of association with writing and journalism that can perhaps be said to have started with the printer Wynkyn De Worde, who was buried here either in late 1534 or early 1535.

Samuel Richardson *(see below)* was also buried here, as was Cavalier poet Richard Lovelace (who wrote 'To Althea, From Prison'). He is buried at the west end of the churchyard, as are the bowels of the poet Thomas Sackville. Sackville, Earl of Dorset, wrote the first English tragedy, *The Tragedie of Gorboduc* (1561) in the Temple, in collaboration with Thomas Norton.

Samuel Pepys was baptised at St Bride's in 1633. John Milton lodged in the churchyard for a time with his wife, and John Dryden wrote an ode, 'Alexander's Feast', especially for the church.

In January 1986 the rector of St Bride's held an all-night vigil praying for the future of Fleet Street as the centre of the newspaper industry after Rupert Murdoch had begun his exodus to Wapping. A church service was held on 15 June 2005 to mark the departure of Reuters news agency from Fleet Street.

The Rise of the Novel • 11 Salisbury Court

Samuel Richardson, who ran a printing and stationer's shop at 11 Salisbury Court (later called Salisbury Square) just off Fleet Street, printed the Tory periodical *The True Britain*, the newspapers *Daily Journal* (1736–37) and *Daily Gazetteer* (1738) and 26 volumes of the *Journal of the House of Commons*.

In 1739 he was invited by a group of booksellers to write a volume of model letters for unskilled letter writers. From the sequence of letters he wrote – ostensibly from a daughter in service to her father, asking his advice when threatened by her master's advances – Richardson developed the first epistolary novel *Pamela, or Virtue Rewarded*, printed in four volumes in 1740–41.

Pamela was an instant publishing success, with six editions appearing within 18 months; it was parodied, pirated, applauded and attacked, versified and dramatised – there was even a waxwork exhibition on a Fleet Street corner devoted to it.

Henry Fielding parodied Richardson's attack on rakish behaviour in *An Apology for the Life of Mrs Shamela Andrews* (1741) and in *Joseph Andrews* (1742). This led to a bitter feud between the two writers, further stimulating both controversy and sales. Richardson's response was *Clarissa, or the History of a Young Lady* (1747–48), a dark novel where the heroine is imprisoned, psychologically tortured, drugged and raped by someone she had trusted.

Clarissa concerns two contemporary issues: a single woman's right to keep inherited property after marriage, and the duplicity of men. The character of Lovelace, the seducer, was modelled on Lord Wharton, a notorious rake and former employer of Richardson. *Clarissa* upset the aristocratic notion of virtue and challenged preconceptions of what constituted a virtuous man or woman. Richardson's friend, the painter and engraver William Hogarth, satirised marriage for money in his *Marriage à la Mode* series of 1743. These works contributed to the debate that led to the new Marriage Act of 1753.

Richardson's reflections on gender roles were greatly admired in France and Germany, inspiring Laclos's *Les Liaisons Dangereuses* and Rousseau's *La nouvelle Héloise*. His writing loosened the aristocratic hold on literary values and its success led to cheaper editions of novels for an expanding middle-class reading public.

The Boy-Poet • 39 Brooke Street

Boy-poet, forger of pseudo-medieval poetry and imitator of the wits, Thomas Chatterton committed suicide in an attic in Brooke Street, Holborn and was interred in the burying ground attached to the Shoe Lane Workhouse, which was subsequently converted into a site for Farringdon Market.

Chatterton died of starvation waiting for overdue payments for his writing. His *Rowley Poems*, published posthumously in 1777, were quickly acknowledged as masterpieces. He became a hero to the Romantics, especially Keats, who dedicated *Endymion* (1818) to him. In 1856 Henry Wallis painted *The Death of Chatterton* (now hanging in Tate Britain) in the room where the poet died – novelist George Meredith posed as Chatterton. In 1987, author and chronicler of London Peter Ackroyd published *Chatterton*, a novel that interweaves the life of the poet with that of a fictional contemporary character, Charles Wychwood.

Alsatia

Between Water Lane and the Temple and leading out of Fleet Street by Bouverie Street is an area that used to be called Alsatia (after Alsace, the disputed province between France and Germany). It offered sanctuary to those on the run because it came under the liberal jurisdiction of a Carmelite monastery. The right to protect debtors from arrest had been bestowed on the Carmelites by James I in 1608. In the 17th century the area deteriorated into lawlessness and inspired Thomas Shadwell's play *Squire of Alsatia* (1688), written in a thieves' argot, and Walter Scott's *The Fortunes of Nigel* (1822).

The Temple

> *'those bricky towers*
> *That which on Thames' broad aged back do ride.*
> *Where now the studious lawyers have kept bowers;*
> *There whilom wont the Templar Knights to bide,*
> *Till they decayed through pride.'*
> *Prothalamion* (1596), Edmund Spenser

Situated at the junction between the Strand and Fleet Street, the small tranquil area now known simply as the Temple was once the home of the Knights Templar – a military and religious order established in the 12th century for protecting Christian sites and pilgrims in the Holy Land. The effigies of many knights can still be seen on the tombs in the crypt of Temple Church.

By the mid-14th century, however, the Temple had become home to the Societies of the Inner and Middle Temple, two of the four Inns of Court. Each occupied one of the halls on the site. Their status was formally recognised by James I in 1608 when they were granted the land in perpetuity for the accommodation, entertainment and education of students and practitioners of law.

In *King Henry VI Part One* (1590) Shakespeare sets the scene of the origin of the struggle between the factions of York and Lancaster in the Inner Temple Garden:

Earl of Somerset:
Let him that is no coward nor no flatterer,
But dare maintain the party of truth,
Pluck a red rose from off this thorn with me.

Earl of Warwick:
I love no colours; and, without all colour
Of base-insinuating flattery,
I pluck this white rose with Plantagenet.

Earl of Suffolk:
I pluck this red rose with young Somerset...

Shakespeare's *Twelfth Night* was first performed at Middle Temple Hall before Elizabeth I on 2 February 1602. Past members of the Middle Temple include the poets Walter Ralegh and William Cowper, diarist John Evelyn, playwrights Thomas Shadwell, John Ford, William Congreve and Richard Brinsley Sheridan, and the novelists Henry Fielding, William Makepeace Thackeray and John Buchan.

Symbolising their vow of poverty, two knights of the Order of Knights Templars share a horse outside Temple Church

Past members of the Inner Temple include biographer James Boswell, playwrights John Marston, Francis Beaumont and William Wycherley, the librettist W.S. Gilbert, *Dracula* author Bram Stoker and creator of *Rumpole of the Bailey* John Mortimer.

William Congreve lived in Surrey Street, just beyond the Temple, and was famously visited by Voltaire, while he was exiled in London. Congreve affected disdain at his visitor's admiration by saying that he was but 'a gentleman who led a life of plainness and simplicity.' Voltaire replied, 'if you were so unfortunate as to be a mere gentleman, I should never have come to see you.' Congreve wrote five successful plays between 1693 and 1700, including *The Way of the World*, 1700 *(see p93)*. Lines such as 'Heaven has no rage like love to hatred turned, Nor hell a fury like a woman scorned' (from *The Mourning Bride*, 1697) have entered the language.

Number 3 Fountain Court – one of the interconnected squares of Temple – was the final address of William Blake. Accessed via 103–4 The Strand, this was Blake's home from 1821 until his death in 1827.

Kit-Cat Club

The Kit-Cat Club began when the bookseller and publisher Jacob Tonson attracted Whig politicians and the young wits to a pie house in Shire Lane, which ran north from Temple Bar, in the 1690s. Among the Kit-Cat Club's members were William Congreve, Joseph Addison, Richard Steele, John Vanbrugh, physician and poet Samuel Garth, the artist Godfrey Kneller and politicians such as Robert Walpole, Lord Halifax and the Duke of Somerset.

Tonson was one of the first publishers of new editions of deceased dramatists and poets. He produced deluxe and cheaper editions of Spenser, Shakespeare, Milton, Beaumont and Fletcher, and by 1711 was sufficiently successful to move from the Judge's Head in Fleet Street to the Shakespear's Head in the Strand, on a site now occupied by Somerset House. He promoted Milton's *Paradise Lost* through a series of critical articles in *The Spectator*.

As club secretary of the Kit-Cat, Tonson was able to unite his most valued customers and authors. The meetings moved to the Fountain Tavern at 100 Strand, (now Simpson's-in-the-Strand) and later to his mansion at Barn Elms and in the summer to the Upper Flask Tavern, Hampstead *(see p281)*. By 1710 the group formed the centre of the Whig opposition to the Tory government, and Tonson was a leading London bookseller and publisher of Alexander Pope, John Dryden, Andrew Marvell, William Congreve, Joseph Addison and Richard Steele.

The Good Natured Man • 2 Brick Court

Oliver Goldsmith was not of the Temple, but died in Chambers at 2 Brick Court and was buried in Temple Church. He lived just off Wine Office Court in the alleyway known as Shoe Lane, and worked as a translator for the expanding book market and contributed essays to magazines. He was a prodigious drinker and self-deprecating joker, and was perennially in debt. Nevertheless, when flush he was lavish in giving money away as he walked along Fleet Street.

His fortunes changed in 1762 when Dr Johnson secured sixty guineas from a local bookseller for his novel *Vicar of Wakefield* (1766), so that Goldsmith could pay his rent. Goldsmith went on to compile histories of England and Rome and, more significantly, wrote two successful comedies – *The Good Natured Man* (1768) and *She Stoops To Conquer* (1773) – that changed the direction of English theatre by bringing laughter back to the stage, and two long poems, *The Traveller* (1764) and *The Deserted Village* (1770).

Tears of Joy • 2 Crown Office Row

The writer who best expressed delight in life in and around Fleet Street and the Strand was essayist Charles Lamb, who was born at 2 Crown Office Row, in the Inner Temple. On 30 January 1801, he wrote to his friend, William Wordsworth:

> *... The Lighted shops of the Strand and Fleet Street, the*
> *innumerable trades, tradesmen and customers, coaches,*
> *wagons, playhouses, all the bustle and wickedness about*
> *Covent Garden, the very women of the Town, the watchmen,*
> *drunken scenes, rattles; - life awake, if you awake, at*
> *all hours of the night, the impossibility of being dull*
> *in Fleet Street, the crowds, the very dirt & mud, the*
> *Sun shining upon houses and pavements, the print shops,*
> *the old Book stalls, parsons cheap'ning books, coffee*
> *houses, steams of soup from kitchens, the pantomimes,*
> *London itself a pantomime and a masquerade, all these*
> *things work themselves into my mind and feed me without*
> *a power of satiating me. The wonder of these sights*
> *impells me into night walks about the crowded streets,*
> *and I often shed tears in the motley Strand from*
> *fulness of joy at so much Life.*

Charles and his sister, Mary Lamb, are perhaps best known for their *Tales From Shakespeare* (1807), an immediate success upon publication; Charles Lamb's *Essays of Elia* (1823) are equally acclaimed *(see p162)*.

The Lambs were at the hub of the Romantic movement and famous for the literary parties they held every Wednesday at their home at 16 Mitre Court Buildings, Inner Temple between 1801 and 1809. Feasts for the mind and soul fuelled by alcohol, the parties were attended by Coleridge, Wordsworth, De Quincey, William Hazlitt, Mary Shelley, Leigh Hunt and George Dyer among many others.

As Hazlitt wrote, 'How oft did we cut into the haunch of letters, while we discussed the haunch of mutton on the table! How we skimmed the dream of criticism! How we got into the heart of controversy! How we picked on the marrow of authors!'

The Hermit of Clifford's Inn • 3 Clifford Inn

Poet, bibliophile and radical George Dyer, known as the 'hermit of Clifford's Inn', lived in chambers at 13 Clifford Inn for nearly fifty years. Famously absent-minded and disorganised, he once returned home from dinner at Leigh Hunt's in Hampstead before realizing that he had left his shoes under his host's table.

FLEET STREET
Taylor & Hussey • 93 Fleet Street

John Taylor and James Hussey started a bookshop, binders and publishing business at 93 Fleet Street in 1806. They became the leading liberal literary publishers in London at a time of acute social and political unrest. The passing of the Corn Laws in 1815 (imposing duty on cheap wheat from the Continent in order to protect the profits of English farmer-landowners) had seen the Houses of Parliament defended with troops by menacing crowds. There was unemployment, increased taxation and civil unrest, such as the Spa Fields demonstration when a crowd of six to eight thousand gathered to hear speeches calling for parliamentary reform in December 1815.

There was a concomitant increased interest in poetry, as many of the leading poets of the day were advocates of liberalism and social and political reform. One of the most eloquent spokesmen for liberty was Lord Byron, and he helped generate considerable interest in poetry and poets, and was handsomely recompensed by publishers. In this climate, Taylor & Hussey published *Poems* (1817), *Endymion* (1818) and *Lamia, Isabella, Eve of St Agnes and Other Poems* (1820) by John Keats. But, despite glowing recommendations and a healthy market for poetry, the books did not sell, and were roundly attacked by the Tory press. The Tories sneered at Keats's 'Cockney' poetry and used the poet and his work as a convenient punchbag to hit at the liberal reform movement.

William Hazlitt's *Lectures on the English Poets* (1818), based on his four talks at the Crown and Anchor, received similar treatment. The *Quarterly Review* – based at No. 32 Fleet Street and founded in 1809 as a Tory alternative to the Whig *Edinburgh Review* – described the lectures as meaningless, verbose, vague and unintelligible. Other Tory periodicals, such as *The British Critic* and *Maga*, followed their lead.

Hazlitt hit back in *The Examiner* with a forty-page pamphlet, 'Letter to William Gifford Esq', the *Quarterly's* editor. In this sustained essay he incisively dismembered Gifford's inferior critical abilities and position as leader of the literary police with a persistent fury. It partially silenced the Tory critics, and instead they turned to Taylor's own work as the author of *The Identity of Junius* (1818).

Taylor and Hussey consolidated their resources by holding monthly dinner parties at 93 Fleet Street involving Hazlitt, Lamb, the lawyers Thomas Noon Talfourd and Richard Woodhouse, art critic Thomas Wainewright and others. They purchased the *London Magazine*, which Taylor began editing, with Thomas Hood as deputy editor, in April 1821. They had some success publishing John Clare's first book *Poems Descriptive of Rural Life and Scenery* (1820) and Henry Francis Cary's translation of Dante's *Divine Comedy* (1819). However, their surprise bestseller was Thomas De Quincey's *Confessions of an English Opium-Eater* (1822). Clare's second book, *The Village Minstrel and Other Poems* (1821), despite being superior to the first, sold less well and, amid a worsening economic situation and increased taxes on periodicals, they were forced to sell *London Magazine*. During Clare's third visit to Fleet Street in 1824 he met Coleridge, Hazlitt, Lamb and De Quincey, but found Taylor nervous as he felt the poetry boom was ending – a feeling compounded by the news of Byron's death, which had arrived 'like an earthquake', as reported in *London Magazine*.

The Dean of Westminster refused to bury Byron in the abbey, and his body was taken to Nottinghamshire for burial. Clare was in Oxford Street among the large crowds that came out to see the hearse, and the coach with the urn containing Byron's heart and brain, followed as far as Highgate Hill by a procession of sixty-three empty carriages sent by Byron's fellow aristocrats.

Taylor & Hussey managed to publish Carlyle's *Life of Friedrich Schiller* (1825) and Samuel Taylor Coleridge's *Aids to Reflection* (1825) before their financial situation was such that the partnership was dissolved in 1825. Hussey was declared bankrupt in 1829. Taylor kept his publishing business going by producing textbooks, and managed to publish Clare's third book *The Shepherd's Calendar with Village Stories* in 1827.

Blasphemous Libels • 55 Fleet Street

An increasing demand in the early 1800s for parliamentary reform led to a corresponding growth in parody. William Hone, bookseller and publisher at 55 Fleet Street, was indicted for publishing blasphemous libels in the form of political parodies of the catechism, litany and creed in May 1817. Here is a sample:

> *Our Lord who art in the Treasury, whatsoever be thy name, thy power be prolonged, thy will be done throughout the empire, as it is in each session. Give us our usual sops, and forgive us our occasional absences on divisions; as we promise not to forgive those that divide against thee. Turn us not out of our places; but keep us in the House of Commons, the land of Pensions and Plenty; and deliver us from the people. Amen.*

Unable to afford the £1,000 bail, Hone prepared his own case and was tried on 18, 19 and 20 December 1818 for each case. Among the judges was Lord Ellenborough, who had previously imprisoned James Leigh Hunt and his brother John for two years for effectively describing the Prince Regent in the 22 March 1812 issue of *The Examiner* as a liar, gambler, libertine and disgrace. However, the jury was in no mood to follow his lead and Hone was acquitted three times. Since then, parodies and political squibs have been immune from prosecution. Hone, with cartoonist George Cruikshank, continued to publish parodies against the Government and pressed the cause of free speech. Their satire *The Political House That Jack Built* (1819) sold almost 100,000 copies. The work satirized the Peterloo Massacre – the violent suppression of a pro-reform meeting in St Peter's Fields, Manchester, in 1819. Eleven people were killed and 400 injured before the meeting had even begun, and the event became known as the Peterloo Massacre in allusion to the Battle of Waterloo, which had taken place four years previously.

After attending Hazlitt's talks on 'English Comic Writers' at the Crown and Anchor in the Strand, Hone published Hazlitt's most important political work *Political Essays* (1819), in which he noted that the admiration of power turns many writers into 'intellectual pimps and hirelings of the press'.

The Thunderer

Founded as the *Daily Universal Register* on 1 January 1785 by coal merchant John Walter, the newspaper became known as *The Times* on 1 January 1788. When John Walter II took over in 1803 he introduced logotype to allow whole words rather than individual letters to be pre-set. He dispensed with government handouts and developed his own news gathering organisation, based on correspondents and editors for specific areas of information, drawing on the Lamb-Coleridge circle of writers and lawyers.

Hazlitt, Lamb and Thomas Barnes wrote for several newspapers. Hazlitt wrote theatre and art criticism for *The Times, Morning Chronicle* and *The Examiner*. He elevated the art of criticism to a higher level and remains one of the greatest exponents of the essay in the whole of English literature.

The Royal Courts of Justice on the Strand

The Times supported the government until 1819 and was a strong opponent of radicals who wanted universal suffrage. After the Peterloo Massacre, however, Hazlitt wrote of the paper's owner:

> *Mr Walter's hair stands on end, and he is in a perfect cold-sweat at the sacrifices and dangers he has been exposed to in making head against the abuses of power. He gives one desperate instance. He ventured to*

*condemn "the Manchester Massacre" – a measure that only one man
in three kingdoms was forward to applaud. Yet with public opinion at his
back, with popular clamour, with the indignant scorn of all "the honest
and independent part of the community" directed against this illegal,
unmanly, and indecent outrage, the Editor looks back with horror at the
dangers that beset him.*

Barnes became editor of *The Times* in 1817 and acquired full editorial control two
years later. He remained the paper's editor until his death in 1841, and during his time
in charge became a more committed supporter of parliamentary reform. He called
for the people to 'petition, ay, thunder for reform', giving the paper its nickname 'The
Thunderer'. In 1832 Sir Robert Peel stated that *The Times* had been the principal and
most powerful advocate of reform. After the 1832 Reform Act was passed (extending
suffrage to £10 householders and £50 tenant farmers, and reorganising constituency
representation), *The Times* called it the 'greatest event in modern history'. Under
Barnes's editorship circulation grew from 7,000 copies in the 1820s to 20,000 copies
in the 1830s. In 1846 a new machine that printed 6,000 sheets of 8 pages per hour
was introduced and circulation rose to 30,000 copies.

Dickens and Thackeray

More than eight hundred periodicals appeared in London, mostly from The Strand
and Fleet Street, during the 1840s. Out of this profusion of journalism and literary
endeavour two writers rose to prominence. Both were linked with the veteran satirical
illustrator George Cruikshank and thus with the Regency satirical pamphleteers and
comic illustrators. Both wrote monthly serialisations of new sketches and stories for
periodicals. They were Charles Dickens and William Makepeace Thackeray.

Charles Dickens had begun writing short stories for the *Monthly Magazine* (based
in Johnson Court, off Fleet Street) and political journalism for the *Morning Chronicle* in
1833. He worked hard to avoid running into debt and wrote for as many journals as
he could. Dickens was part of the liberal reforming movement, and used illlustrations
by his friend Cruikshank in *Sketches by Boz* (1836) and *Oliver Twist* (1837). Dickens
was also a friend of liberal lawyer Thomas Noon Talfourd from the Lamb-Coleridge
circle. Talfourd had become a Sergeant at the Bar, playwright and Liberal M.P.

William Makepeace Thackeray – a gentleman by birth and education, who
had been forced to earn his living as a hack writer after losing his money in an
investment – collaborated on Cruikshank's *Comic Almanacks* of 1839 and 1840.
Both Thackeray and Dickens worked in and around Fleet Street for several publishing
companies and periodicals. Their novels are littered with references to Fleet Street,
the Temple and Inns of Court. Thackeray began working for the *Constitutional*

(and Public Ledger), a Whig Reformist newspaper, based at 162 Fleet Street, in September 1836. The newspaper failed to prosper against stiff competition. Thackeray wrote essays, journalism and instalments of novels for periodicals such as *Fraser's Magazine, Morning Chronicle, New Monthly Magazine* and *The Times*. His work first attracted attention when he wrote about English snobbery for *Punch*. These sketches reappeared in 1848 as *The Book of Snobs*.

Punch • 99 Fleet Street

Founded in June 1841 at the Punch Tavern by Mark Lemon and other journalists as a reforming magazine that would combine humour with political comment, *Punch* was printed and illustrated by Joseph Last in Fleet Street and edited by Lemon. Initially *Punch* sold about 6,000 copies a week. However, when Lemon and his friends sold the magazine to Bradbury & Evans, circulation began to increase as they reduced the political comment in favour of the satirical content. They employed a team of young journalists and engravers, including Lemon as editor, Douglas Jerrold, Gilbert à Becket, Henry Mayhew, Thackeray and Thomas Hood, who contributed an attack on sweat labour in the poem, 'The Song of the Shirt', in 1843. By 1850 *Punch* was selling 50,000 copies per issue.

Punch established the tradition of weekly dinners, held at different venues in the Strand, Fleet Street and Bouverie Street, to develop new material. This suited Thackeray perfectly. The serialisation of *Vanity Fair: Pen and Pencil Sketches of English Society – 'A Novel without a Hero'* in 1848 was an instant success. Set a generation earlier, *Vanity Fair* is full of contemporary allusions and jokes. The amorality and bohemianism of the novel's 'heroine', Becky Sharp, perfectly offset the book's satire of greed and corruption. Becky 'I think I could be a good woman if I had five thousand a year' Sharp continues to captivate audiences as the 1988 and 2002 television versions of *Vanity Fair* testify.

Although Thackeray never sold in the tens of thousands like Dickens, *Vanity Fair* established his reputation as a major novelist and he became a literary celebrity. Charlotte Brontë, who dedicated the second edition of *Jane Eyre* to him, met Thackeray in London in 1849 and wrote of the harassed writer chasing society ladies. He in turn described holding her hand as if he held a butterfly.

In 1851 Thackeray lectured on the 'English Humorists' at Willis's Rooms in St James's. Dictating to amanuenses in hotels during reading tours and writing in clubs on his return to London, he incorporated his version of the coffee house scene, featuring Joseph Addison, Richard Steele and Alexander Pope, in *The History of Henry Esmond* (1852). From 1860 to 1862 Thackeray edited *Cornhill Magazine*. By this time he was burned out; the sheer grind of deadlines and reading tours had taken its physical toll and he died at the age of 52.

Dickens, haunted by his father's imprisonment for debt and his childhood labour experiences, became a freelance reporter. Adept at shorthand, he joined the *Morning Chronicle*, reporting parliamentary debates. He wrote quickly for cheap serial publication and instantly found a growing audience by faithfully recreating the roar and rattle of local streets and characters. As Blackwood's *Edinburgh Magazine* put it in 1858:

> *Dickens led the Muse out into the street, or the muse led him; she took her course up Fleet Street, drove through the borough and turned into the courtyard of a miserable old inn; there she found Sam Weller cleaning boots. Many an elegant novelist, while the travelling carriage stopped to change horses, had glanced at some such figure and noted an accidental oddity of manner and speech. Charles Dickens, loitered up the yard, entered into conversation, got into the very heart of the man, chose him for his hero and presented him before the world at large. The world at large received him with open arms.*

Chapman & Hall serialized *The Posthumous Papers of the Pickwick Club, Edited by Boz*. The first number appeared in green wrappers, with 32 pages of print and four engravings by Robert Seymour, in an edition of 400 copies. By the end of the series they were appearing in editions of 40,000 copies.

From David Copperfield taking Peggotty to a waxwork on Fleet Street; to Tom Pinch of Pump Court, in *Martin Chuzzlewit*, imagining lost documents decaying in forgotten corners of Temple cellars; to Jerry Cruncher, the occasional porter and messenger of Tellson's Bank, in *A Tale of Two Cities*, supplementing his wages by digging up recently buried bodies and selling them to doctors, Dickens vividly evoked both time and place. His extensive descriptions of characters and keen sense of speech patterns enabled a wide readership to locate and absorb his tragicomic narratives.

Dickens's attempt to found and edit a daily newspaper, the *Daily News* in 1846, lasted only seventeen days. In the 1850s he edited *Household Words*, a weekly magazine combining entertainment with social purpose, and from 1859 he edited *All the Year Round*. Spurred on by Thackeray's success, Dickens's work in *Bleak House* (1852–53), *Hard Times* (1854) and *Little Dorrit* (1855–57) took on stronger social concerns and a broader social sweep.

THE TIPPLING STREET – FLEET STREET'S WATERING HOLES
The Golden Truth • 145 Fleet Street
Ye Olde Cheshire Cheese tavern in Wine Office Court is one of London's oldest pubs. Rebuilt in 1667 after the Fire of London, it still has the original small rooms with fireplaces, black timber-panelled ceiling and walls, tables and benches.

Entered at No. 145 Fleet Street, Ye Olde Cheshire Cheese has been a gathering place for several generational waves of writers and journalists, from Alexander Pope and William Congreve in the early 18th century, to Dr Samuel Johnson and Oliver Goldsmith in the latter half of the same century, then Dickens, Thackeray and Conan Doyle in the 19th century. Dr Johnson is commemorated by a plaque near his favourite seat in the right-hand corner of the ground floor. A copy of Sir Joshua Reynolds's portrait of the sturdy lexicographer used to be hung next to the inscription. In *The Forsyte Saga*, the early 20th-century writer John Galsworthy mentions the 80lb pies once served here.

The Cheshire Cheese in Wine Office Court

The Rhymers' Club, started as a mutually supportive literary circle by W.B. Yeats, Ernest Rhys and Thomas Rolleston in January 1890, was concerned with the development of a national Irish literature. Members met upstairs at the Cheshire Cheese to drink, read aloud and discuss their work. Most members, although not all, were either Irish or had Celtic connections. They were mostly bohemian, into hashish, drink and *belles de nuit*; some were homosexual and counted Oscar Wilde as their patron. Early members included John Todhunter, the formidably well-read Lionel Johnson, Ernest Dowson, Arthur Symons, Richard Le Gallienne and John Davidson.

Yeats was studying William Blake, the Cabbala, Swedenborg and Boehme at the time. The group regularly reviewed for periodicals such as the *Star*, the *Pall Mall Gazette*, the *Speaker*, the *Daily Chronicle* and the *Bookman*. Symons, who was already a published poet, introduced the poetry of Verlaine and Mallarmé. The first *Book of the Rhymers Club* appeared in February 1892 and included Yeats's 'Innisfree' and Symons's 'The Man Who Dreamed of Faeryland'. A second *Book of the Rhymers Club* appeared in 1894. Le Gallienne went on to write an account of the era, *The Romantic 90's*, Symons later wrote a definitive book on the Symbolist movement, *The Symbolist Movement in Literature* (1899). This was read by many of the emerging poets of the modernist movement. Le Gallienne and Symons were contributors to Aubrey Beardsley's *Yellow Book (see p190)*.

Davidson wrote two *Fleet Street Eclogues*, in 1893 and 1896, shortly before committing suicide. His 'Ballade' evoked the Cheshire Cheese thus:

> *Beneath this board Burke's, Goldsmith's knees*
> *Were often thrust – so runs the tale –*
> *'Twas here the Doctor took his ease*

> *And wielded speech that like a flail*
> *Threshed out the golden truth. All hail,*
> *Great souls! that met on nights like these*
> *Till morning made the candles pale,*
> *And revellers left the 'Cheshire Cheese.'*

At the Cheshire Cheese's period costume dinners G.K. Chesterton would dress up as Dr Johnson. Dylan Thomas ate and drank at the restaurant with American G.I.s, including his future biographer, Constantine FitzGibbon. In 1943 Thomas pretended to be an English professor from Wales and FitzGibbon a Dr Johnson specialist from Harvard, meeting to discuss the great man, in order to get plied with drinks.

Truth Itself Doth Flow in Wine • 1 Fleet Street

The site of the Devil Tavern, where Ben Jonson's Apollo club met, is at No. 2 (formerly No. 1) Fleet Street. Child's, the bankers, bought the site in 1787.

Jonson's verse 'Over the Door at the Entrance into the Apollo' was painted on a panel still preserved in the dining room at the building. The verse was printed in the *Jonson Folio* (1692) and reprinted in the *Dryden Miscellany Poems* (1716).

> *Welcome all, who lead or follow,*
> *To the Oracle of Apollo.*
> *Here he speaks out of his Pottle,*
> *Or the Tripos, his Tower Bottle:*
> *All his Answers are Divine,*
> *Truth itself doth flow in Wine.*

The *Leges Conviviales* – twenty-four house rules for hospitality, based on parts of Horace and Martial – were 'Engraven in Marble over the Chimny, in the APOLLO of the Old Devil Tavern at Temple-Bar'. Emblazoned with the words 'LET THE FIRE BE ALWAYS BURNING', these rules included: 'Let no musician in who has not been summoned. Let our private mysteries be celebrated with laughter, dances, choruses, songs, jokes all the festivity of the Graces. All jokes must be without gall. No flat poems must be recited. Let no one be compelled to write verses. There must be no clamour of argument'.

A later group of writers, including William Browne, George Wither, Michael Drayton and Christopher Brooke, met here from 1610 to 1614, contributing to the revival in Spenserian poetry and political debate among the young lawyers who attended the meetings. They saw themselves as part of the emerging opposition to the Court. Wither was imprisoned for his moral and political satire and popular success *Abuses, Stript and Whipt* (1613), a veiled attack on corruption and abuse by courtiers. He believed that it was a Protestant poet's duty to speak out in times of political crisis. His lengthy satire *Wither's Motto* (1621) had printers vying with each other to publish pirate versions and sold more than 25,000 copies.

Later patrons included Pepys, John Evelyn, Swift, Steele, Addison and Dr Johnson. Dryden deposited £50 at the bank next door to the Devil Tavern in 1679 as a reward for information about the assailants who beat him up in Rose Alley *(see p87)*. Actor-playwright Colley Cibber used to rehearse his court odes to music at the tavern – behaviour that Pope derided in his poem *The Dunciad*.

The Cock Tavern • 190 Fleet Street

The site of the original Cock Tavern is at No. 190 Fleet Street. In April 1667 Pepys took Mrs Pierce and the actress and singer Mrs Knapp to dine at the Cock. He eventually spent the night with Mrs Knapp, 'the most excellent, mad-humoured thing', and repented by taking his own wife for a meal at the Cock on another night.

In 1842 Tennyson dined at the Cock, writing 'Will Waterproof's Lyrical Monologue':

> *O plump head-waiter at the Cock,*
> *To which I most resort,*
> *How goes time? Tis five o'clock.*
> *Go fetch a pint of port.*

Virginia Woolf in *Orlando* (1928) has Nicholas Greene meet Orlando at the Cock and relate the story of a drunken night at the tavern with Christopher Marlowe and Shakespeare. The pub that welcomed Dr Johnson, Dickens and Thackeray was demolished in 1887 and rebuilt across the road at No. 22 as Ye Old Cock Tavern. It was here that T.S. Eliot, the art critic Herbert Read and Harold Munro, the proprietor of the Poetry Bookshop in Bloomsbury *(see p143)*, met in the 1920s to plan the launch of *Criterion* magazine.

The Rainbow Tavern • 15 Fleet Street

The Rainbow Tavern used to be at No. 15 Fleet Street. It was originally opened as a coffee house – the second in London after Pasqua Rosee's Head *(see p67)* – by James Farr in 1657 and subsequently became a tavern, famous for its stout. Mentioned by Dickens in *Sketches by Boz*, it also features regularly in Old Bailey records as the scene of various crimes.

The novelist Arnold Bennett lunched here on 13 July 1897 and thought it a type of City restaurant that was passing away. Obsequious waiters served conservative lawyers and men of importance. The dark rooms were sombrely furnished in mahogany and ladies were not permitted into the downstairs dining room labelled the 'coffee room'.

No. 17 Gough Square , former home of Dr Johnson

Between the Presses

St Dunstan-in-the West, Fleet Street was where William Tyndale preached in 1523. His translation of the New Testament from the Greek formed the basis of the *King James Bible*. Poet, writer of masques and musician Thomas Campion, who wrote *A Book of Ayres to be Sung to the Lute, Orpherian and Bass Viol* (1601), was buried here in 1620. John Donne became rector in 1624. His friend, Izaak Walton ran an ironmonger's in Fleet Street and lived in Chancery Lane in the 1610s and 1620s. His manual and meditation on angling, *The Compleat Angler*, one of the most reprinted books in English letters, was first printed by the church's press in 1653. Walton also wrote *The Life of Dr John Donne* (1640), *The Life of Richard Hooker* (1665) and *The Life of George Herbert* (1670). St Dunstan's church clock, mentioned in Goldsmith's *Vicar of Wakefield* (1766), was the first in London to mark minutes.

House of Words • 17 Gough Square

Dr Samuel Johnson earned a living as a journalist and critic – famously remarking 'No man but a blockhead ever wrote, except for money' – while working on plays, poetry, biography and studiously compiling the first ever English dictionary. Today his aphorisms and his shambling, obsessive, melancholic character are perhaps better known than his writing.

In his *Life of Johnson* (1791) Boswell records many of the great scholar's aphorisms and anecdotes, including Johnson's celebrated refutation of Bishop Berkeley's theory of the non-existence of matter by kicking a stone and saying, 'I refute it thus,' and his remark 'We proceed, because we have begun; we complete our design, that the labour may not be in vain.'

Johnson is possibly best seen as a writer and scholar who helped consolidate the achievements of the English imagination. From 1748 to 1758 Johnson lived in the large brick house at 17 Gough Square, where he welcomed a miscellany of guests and acolytes, including Goldsmith, Garrick, Reynolds, Burke, Lord Orrery and, of course, James Boswell. Here he produced *The Rambler* twice weekly in 1750, and compiled the bulk of the first *Dictionary of the English Language*.

Johnson had estimated the *Dictionary* would take him three years to complete. In fact, it took him nine years, working with six (mainly Scottish) assistants who laboured in the attic, standing at their writing desks to complete the manuscript of 2,300 pages. The *Dictionary* was finally published in April 1775.

In 1758 Johnson moved to 1 Inner Temple Lane where, over the following two years he produced *The Idler* – in the first issue of which he wrote 'Every man is, or hopes to be, an idler.' From 1776 until his death in 1784 Johnson lived at 8 Bolt Court. His Gough Square address is now home to a museum that contains much of interest, including a first edition of the *Dictionary* and his 'gout' chair from the Cock Tavern.

El Vino • 47 Fleet Street

El Vino's wine bar has been famous as a watering hole for generations of writers, journalists and lawyers. G.K. Chesteron drank and wrote at El Vino's and once had to be taken home the worse for wear at the end of the day by Hilaire Belloc. Evelyn Waugh, author of the classic Fleet Street novel *Scoop* (1938), with its scoop within a scoop and comedy of mistaken identity, used to drink there, as did his son, Auberon Waugh, who wrote a number of novels early in his career but was more celebrated as a journalist and contrarian via his regular columns in *Private Eye* and 'Way of the World' in *The Daily Telegraph* (a column now under the stewardship of Craig Brown).

The bar always had a strict dress code and used to refuse to serve ladies until the Sex Discrimination Act was enforced. In 1962, Ned Sherrin recruited Keith Waterhouse, Willis Hall, Michael Frayn and Christopher Booker at El Vino's to contribute to the pilot episodes of the groundbreaking satirical television programme *That Was The Week That Was*.

Michael Frayn later wrote *Towards the End of Morning* (1967), a novel about a Fleet Street gentleman-journalist thrust into a discussion of race relations on television. The enormously prolific Keith Waterhouse, latterly most famous for the play *Jeffrey Bernard is Unwell*, began his long Fleet Street career with the *Daily Mirror* in 1951. He wrote the novel *Billy Liar* (1959), and with Willis Hall collaborated on the screenplay for the film of the book in 1963 and its television series in 1977.

El Vino's also provided the inspiration for Pomeroy's, purveyor of 'Château Thames Embankment' to Rumpole in John Mortimer's long-running series of novels and television plays *Rumpole of the Bailey*.

THE CITY

WITH A HISTORY STRETCHING BACK to the major Roman settlement of Londinium, the City is the historical core of London. It is the place where the Court, religious leaders and London's merchants have competed for power, and where writers have fought for freedom of thought and expression. In literary terms, the City's star was at its brightest from the late 16th century to the late 17th century: a period that began with the plays of Shakespeare and Ben Jonson and the poetry of John Donne and Sir Walter Ralegh, and concluded with the age of the great diarist Samuel Pepys.

London had been a trading and mercantile centre since the Middle Ages, and by the 16th century was developing into one of the world's greatest financial centres. Trade was not only in commodities, however, but also in ideas – particularly the ideas expressed in classical tales and philosophy. Classical writing fed the minds of London's thinkers and debators, and much was translated and reworked by the greatest writers of the age.

The City had great economic and cultural strength, but also a rival to its power in the shape of the Palace of Westminster, the seat of Court and government. This division between legislative and economic power has become a defining characteristic of London, and the City has always been keen to maintain its independence from Westminster. A vital part of that opposition to government (whenever it was seen as unjust), was provided by writers. They gathered to discuss ideas in the coffee shops of Cornhill and Threadneedle Street and in taverns such as the Mermaid on Friday Street and the Boar's Head in Eastcheap. They presented their work through the publishers and bookshops of St Paul's Churchyard and Paternoster Row, and they had their plays performed on stage. In the late 16th and early 17th centuries the theatre was emerging as an important cultural form. As Thomas Dekker observed in *The Gull's Horn-Booke* (a satirical guide to playhouse etiquette), 'the theatre is your Poets' Royal Exchange', and Elizabethan and Jacobean theatre provided that vital platform for ideas and expression that stirred the hearts and minds of Londoners.

Playwrights and poets frequently paid a high price for dissent, however, and the prisons of the Fleet, Newgate and The Tower of London were all too familiar to writers such as Marlowe, Ralegh, Donne, Jonson and Defoe.

The City

Key

1. Playhouse Yard
2. Farringdon Street
3. St Paul's Cathedral
4. Paternoster Row
5. Old Bailey
6. Viaduct Tavern
7. Smithfield Market
8. Cloth Fair
9. Bread Street
10. Royal Exchange Building
11. St Mary Woolnoth
12. Jamaica Wine House
13. Eastcheap
14. St Magnus the Martyr
15. London Bridge
16. St Olave's
17. Tower of London

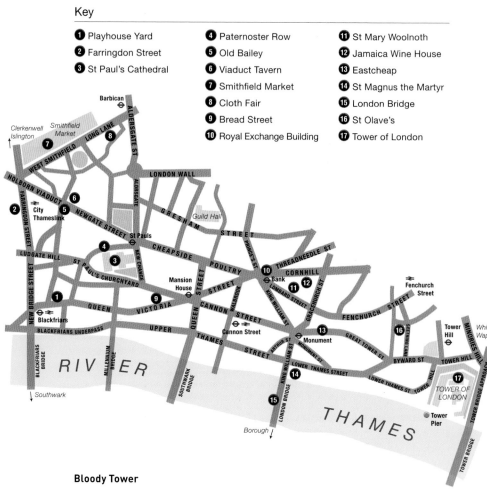

Bloody Tower

Following William the Conqueror's victory at the Battle of Hastings in 1066, the Tower of London was constructed, in 1078, to inspire awe in London's citizenry and to act as William's royal palace. It subsequently served as a fortress, observatory, public records office, Royal Mint and infamous jail. Within the walled confines of the Tower of London are several towers, in fact, including the White Tower (the Keep of the fortress), the Bell Tower, Devereux Tower, the Garden Tower (more commonly known as the Bloody Tower) and Beauchamp Tower; each has had its share of prisoners.

Thomas More was imprisoned by Henry VIII in Beauchamp Tower for refusing to take the oath of the Act of Succession *(see p15)*. While jailed here he wrote *A Dialogue of Comfort Against Tribulation* before being beheaded on Tower Hill in 1535.

Poet and statesman Thomas Wyatt was first imprisoned in the Fleet for fighting in 1534, before being held in the Tower in 1536 for his affair with Anne Boleyn and again in 1539 when accused of verbal treason and immorality. He was released at the request of Queen Catherine Howard. Wyatt studied Petrarch and introduced the terza rima and ottava rima verse structures into English poetry. His first translation was of Plutarch's *Quyete of Mynde* and he later translated sixteen sonnets of Petrarch.

By imitating Petrarch's play of opposites and contrasts, Wyatt developed his own distinctive and haunted voice. His poems are forthright, colloquial and physical, arising out of sexual passion. His famous sonnet for Anne Boleyn, 'Whoso list to hunt, I know where is an hind', is modelled on Petrarch's 'Rime 190'. The image of the spring or river that runs through English poetry starts with Wyatt.

In the reign of Mary Tudor, Anne Askew was tortured in the Tower for refusing to accept the Catholic sacrament. Part of the Catherine Parr Protestant reform circle, she recorded her experiences in *The First Examinacyon of the Worthy Servant of God Mistress Anne Askewe* (1546) and *The Lattre Examinacyon* (1547). These works are part diary, part spiritual biography and part testimonial. She was moved to Newgate, released, then put on the rack again at the Tower. Yet she never wavered from her faith. Here she wrote and sang ballads, translated the Psalms, as Wyatt had done, and never incriminated Protestant women at Court.

Devereux Tower commemorates Robert Devereux, Earl of Essex *(see pp27–28)*, who was imprisoned in the Tower in 1601 prior to his execution. Essex's poetic efforts, however, are not memorable.

The Salt Tower, built in 1235, was used to imprison Jesuits, especially during Elizabeth's reign. Among them were Edmund Campion and John Gerard, who wrote an account of his imprisonment and escaped from the roof of the Cradle Tower.

The Queen's Tower, built in 1530 as the Lieutenant's Lodgings, held Anne Boleyn on charges of adultery in 1536, Guy Fawkes for attempting to blow up the Palace of Westminster in 1605, and essayist and statesman Francis Bacon on charges of bribery in 1621. Ralegh was held in the Brick Tower in 1592 for seducing Elizabeth Throckmorton, one of the Queen's maids-of-honour. He married Elizabeth and lodged with his cousin the Master of Ordnance at the Brick Tower. Here he wrote poems, including 'Cynthia, the Lady of the Sea'.

From 1604 to 1616 Ralegh lived with his wife and servants in rooms on the second floor of the Bloody Tower. Their second son, Carew, was born in the Tower in 1605. Ralegh wrote poetry as well as *History of the World*, *Instructions to His Son* and *War with Spain*. He was appointed tutor to Queen Anne's son, Prince Henry, who

St Paul's and the Tower of London

became the patron of Ralegh's friend, the playwright George Chapman. The patronage ended in 1612, however, when Henry died of typhoid after swimming in the Thames.

King James's need for finance led to Ralegh being released in order to find the gold that was rumoured to be hidden along the banks of the Orinoco river in South America. But in 1618 Ralegh was back in the Tower, accused of abusing the king's confidence. His earlier reprieve from execution was rescinded and he was finally beheaded on 29 October 1618. His wife carried his head in a bag back to Sherborne Castle, Dorset, where it was displayed so that friends and servants could pay their respects.

Samuel Pepys was briefly imprisoned in the Beauchamp Tower on the trumped-up charge of Piracy, Popery and Treachery in May and June 1679. While inside he was visited by friends, including the City merchant James Houblon and diarist John Evelyn, with whom he dined on venison. Bail of £25,000 was eventually granted and Pepys was released from the Tower, later to be acquitted.

Other writers imprisoned in the Tower include Thomas Malory, Thomas Norton, co-author of *Gorboduc* (who wrote long tracts to Walsingham justifying the use of torture on suspected traitors during his time in the Bloody Tower), the poet-king James I of Scotland and John Wilkes, the 18th-century politician and pamphleteer. Cell location records are patchy and the most reliable evidence is found in carvings on the walls.

The Tower is used as a setting in Shakespeare's *Henry VI Part I* (1590) and *Henry VI Part III* (1591), Christopher Marlowe's *Edward II* (1594) and much later in Walter Scott's *Peveril of the Peak* (1823).

St Paul's Cathedral

St Paul's contains memorials to a number of writers, including John Donne, Samuel Johnson, painter and essayist Sir Joshua Reynolds, William Blake, historian of London and founder of the Society of Authors Walter Besant, the cartoonist and essayist Max Beerbohm and poet Walter de la Mare. Christopher Wren, who rebuilt the church after the Great Fire destroyed old St Paul's in 1666, has a relatively modest tomb in the crypt. However, the epitaph reads: 'Lector si monumentum requiris circumspice (Reader, if you seek his monument look around you)'.

John Donne was Dean of St Paul's from 1621 until his death in 1631. Born in Bread Street the son of a Catholic ironmonger, Donne embarked upon a tortuous journey to become an Anglican priest and poet. Educated at Oxford, he refused to take the Oath of Supremacy (recognizing the monarch as head of the Church in England) and left without a degree. He entered Lincoln's Inn and joined a group of hard-drinking young lawyer-writers and their theatrical friends, spending his inheritance on women, books and the theatre. He then joined the Earl of Essex's naval expedition against Spain and started writing poetry. In 1598 Donne became private secretary to Sir Thomas Egerton, later Lord Ellesmere, and secretly married his niece, Anne More. He was promptly dismissed from his post and thrown into Fleet Prison. Without Court patronage after his release, he made a meagre living as a lawyer. His *Satires and Songs and Sonnets* were published in manuscript form and built up a loyal readership based on a coterie of friends that included Ralegh, Jonson, Lady Magdalen Herbert (George Herbert's mother), and Lucy, Countess of Bedford.

In 1607 King James advised him to enter the Church if he wanted any preferment. Donne had to decide whether the Anglican or Roman Church was the true faith; he finally joined the Anglican Church in 1615. Renowned as a spellbinding preacher, he continued to write poetry and produced the *Holy Sonnets* in 1618.

Jonson wrote about the irregularity of Donne's poems, yet was in awe of their daring. In the *Holy Sonnets*, Donne's staccato lines mingle the sacred and profane, allowing the spiritual dimension a human face and universality:

> *Spit in my face ye Jews, and pierce my side,*
> *Buffet, and scoff, scourge, and crucify me,*
> *For I have sinned, and sinned, and only he,*
> *Who could do no iniquity, hath died:*

The *Holy Sonnets* contain a great sense of sinfulness and spirituality based on fear. In Holy Sonnet 19, 'Oh, to vex me', the narrator's spiritual devotion fluctuates like Donne's affection for past mistresses. Donne remained faithful to his wit and lust for life, even though becoming Dean of St Paul's.

St Paul's Churchyard

St Paul's Churchyard is the site of the original St Paul's school, where both Milton (in the 1620s) and Pepys (in the 1640s) were educated. In 1884 the school was relocated to Hammersmith and is now in Barnes. The Churchyard became a centre for bookshops, taverns and coffee houses.

Joseph Johnson, a radical bookseller and publisher, held weekly dinner parties above his shop at 72 St Paul's Churchyard in the early 1790s. His guests included his engravers, William Blake and Henry Fuseli, and writers such as Mary Wollstonecraft, William Godwin and Thomas Paine. A liberal Dissenter, Johnson published Wollstonecraft's *A Vindication of the Rights of Women*, 1792 *(see pp275–6)* and the *Analytical Review* (from 1788 to 1799), which pressed for republican reform.

Paternoster Row

Paternoster Row, to the north of the cathedral, and Paternoster Square to the west formed a major publishing centre until their destruction during the Blitz. They have subsequently re-emerged as streets between high-rise offices. In the 18th century, James Boswell and Thomas Chatterton frequented the Chapter Coffee House in Paternoster Row. Chatterton, while starving, wrote to his mother in Bristol that he knew all the geniuses at the Chapter Coffee House. Charlotte and Anne Brontë stayed at the coffee house when they visited London in July 1848 to meet their publishers. According to Mrs Gaskell's *Life of Charlotte Brontë* (1857), the narrow flagged street, with posts at each end to stop carriages, had a gloomy atmosphere. Dismayed by the crowded streets – so at odds with their rural upbringing – the sisters rested in the old tavern building, with its low ceilings, away from the roar of the city. They were coaxed out on occasion,

Playhouse Yard, site of early London theatrical life

though, to see Rossini's *Barber of Seville* be performed at Covent Garden, to inspect the paintings at the National Gallery, and to dine with their publisher at Cornhill. When they had seen enough of the city, they left for Haworth laden with books.

Blackfriars Theatre • Playhouse Yard

Blackfriars, named after a Dominican monastery established in 1275, is situated southeast of Fleet Street between Ludgate Hill and the Thames. After Henry VIII dissolved the monastery in 1538 the estate was sold off. The area retained its 'liberty' outside City of London jurisdiction until 1608, however. Blackfriars also served as a parliamentary meeting place.

In 1596 theatre owner James Burbage opened a playhouse in a part of the monastery. His son Richard, principal actor with the Chamberlain's Men, inherited the theatre in 1597 and introduced the work of the actor-playwrights William Shakespeare and Ben Jonson, as well as their contemporaries Thomas Marston and George Chapman. Shakespeare's *The Merry Wives of Windsor* (1600) and *Othello* (1604), Jonson's *The Poetaster* (1601) and *The Alchemist* (1609), Marston's *The Malcontent* (1602) and *The Dutch Courtesan* (1605) were among the most celebrated plays produced here. Shakespeare bought the gatehouse to the monastery, in Ireland Yard, with William Johnson of the Mermaid Tavern, in 1613.

Playwrights needed to protect themselves from misinterpretation and possible imprisonment for upsetting one authority or another. Shakespeare rewrote *King Lear* in 1609–10 for its winter performance at Blackfriars to appease the censor. As Ben Jonson wrote in his Prologue to *The Poetaster*:

> ... 'tis a dangerous age
> Wherein, who writes, had need present his Scenes
> Forty-fold proof against the conjuring means
> Of base detractor and Illiterate apes.

The Poetaster, written for the Court audience that came to Blackfriars, distinguishes between 'those dissolutes' who write for common hire and hard-working poets, such as Horace, whose writing has a more serious and elevated purpose. Jonson denigrates his contemporaries through thinly concealed portraits of Thomas Dekker as Demetrius and Marston as Crispinus. Dekker and Marston wrote an immediate riposte, *Satiromastix* (1601), attacking Horace as a diligent but inferior poet.

Dekker wrote at least fifty plays, many in collaboration with others, and was the most active playwright of his time. A heavy drinker and womaniser, in and out of prison for debt, he had an eye for odd characters rather in the manner of Dickens. His *The Shoemaker's Holiday* (1599) vividly portrays tradesmen, apprentices, aldermen, courtiers, their wives, daughters and lovers in their daily lives in shops and taverns. The play was performed on New Year's Day for Queen Elizabeth and went into six published editions by 1657. He wrote *The Honest Whore* (1604) with John Webster and *The Roaring Girle* (1611) with Thomas Middleton as well as pamphlets depicting London's social life and a set of ironical instructions on how to conduct oneself in playhouses and taverns, *The Gull's Horn-Booke* (1609).

The playhouse was the first to introduce actresses (from France), under the patronage of Queen Henrietta Maria, in 1629. They were greeted by a storm of hisses and cited by William Prynne in *Histriomastix* (1632), his diatribe against theatre, masques and dancing.

The Boar's Head Tavern

The Boar's Head Tavern in Eastcheap was a medieval gathering place for writers, and used as a setting in Shakespeare's *Henry IV Part 1* (1598). The original tavern, destroyed in the Great Fire, was rebuilt and became a tourist attraction. By the 18th century a Shakespeare club was meeting to re-enact scenes from his plays.

Washington Irving, the American biographer and essayist, wrote in his *Sketch Book of Geoffrey Crayon* (1820) about his pilgrimage in 1819 to find the tavern.

The Mermaid Tavern

To the east of St Paul's Cathedral, on the southwest junction between Cannon Street and Bread Street, lies the site of the Mermaid Tavern; it originally had entrances on Friday Street and Bread Street. This was the meeting place of the Friday Street Club – also known as the Mermaid Club – founded by Ralegh in 1603. Members included John Donne, Ben Jonson, Christopher Brooke, Shakespeare (who became a business partner of the owner of the Mermaid, William Johnson), Francis Beaumont and John Fletcher. Inigo Jones and Francis Bacon were known to attend, as well as Michael Drayton, George Chapman, John Marston and Thomas Dekker.

Ralegh, Donne and Jonson were the poetic instigators. The Mermaid was a safe house, where they could exchange manuscripts and discuss potential patrons and information about the Court. Ralegh was the inheritor of the Sidney-Spenser circle following Essex's execution for rebellion in 1601 *(see p51)*. His tutor, mathematician and astronomer Thomas Herriot, was in regular contact with John Dee – by then warden of a Manchester college, having fallen out of favour at Court following the deaths of Leicester and Sidney and having come under suspicion following accusations of 'angel-conjuring'.

Corner of Bread Street – site of the Mermaid Tavern

These were times in which writers could rapidly fall out of favour and be imprisoned on the whim of Court or government. No writer exemplifies this better than Ralegh, whose spectacular Court career, which saw him lead Elizabeth's funeral cortege, ended with confinement in the Tower and finally execution. Ralegh had won and lost fortunes, all the while keeping abreast of literary and scientific advances. His poem 'The Lie' described the Court as a place that 'glows and shines like rotting wood'. His friend, playwright and wit Christopher Marlowe, had been murdered in suspicious circumstances in 1593 *(see p316)*. Others, such as Robert Greene, George Peele and Thomas Nashe, had died impoverished when cut off from patronage.

Shakespeare and Jonson solved the problem of patronage by working for the theatre. By acting and writing (and investing in property), they made a living. Both had prodigious memories, the result in part of a grammar school education, and in part because of their work as actors. Living nearby, they found the Mermaid a convenient meeting place to read and memorise scripts. The development of memory was vital when books were banned and a wide range of source material was required.

After Ralegh's imprisonment, Donne kept a low profile and slowly withdrew from the club. Jonson, joined by Inigo Jones, became the club leader, and set the tone by introducing translations of Horace, Ovid and Virgil. Michael Drayton – who had been the first to publish his imitations of Horace's *Odes* in *Poems Lyric and Pastoral* (1606) – was Jonson's main rival. Like Jonson, he was also using classical sources in his satires, such as *The Owle* (1604), but had fallen out of Court favour by accusing it of corruption. Jonson's poem 'Inviting a Friend to Supper', written about 1607, evokes the enjoyment of friendship and liberty in an atmosphere without malice, faction, or government spies: 'And we will have no Pooly, or Parrot by'.

Jonson was regularly at Court, having to defend his plays in order to keep his freedom. Having escaped hanging for murder by claiming to be a Catholic and after being briefly imprisoned again for sedition, Jonson adeptly began to write Court masques from 1605. His wit and erudition ensured his pre-eminence as Court poet and enabled the Mermaid gatherings to continue without arrests. The atmosphere of the Mermaid is illustrated in Francis Beaumont's 'Letter to Ben Jonson':

What things have we seen
Done at the Mermaid! heard words that have been
So nimble and so full of subtle flame,
As if that everyone from whence they came
Had meant to put his whole wit in a jest,
And had resolved to live a fool the rest
Of his dull life ...

Souls of Poets Dead and Gone • 76 Cheapside

John Keats subsequently commemorated the Mermaid club in his poem 'Lines on the Mermaid Tavern' (1820). Composed towards the end of 1818 after an evening spent at the Mermaid and copied in his letter to the poet J.H. Reynolds on 3 February, 'Lines on the Mermaid Tavern' refers to Jonson's 'Inviting a Friend to Supper' in the lines 'Have ye tippled drink more fine / Than mine host's Canary wine?' and ends with the refrain:

> Souls of poets dead and gone,
> What Elysium have ye known,
> Happy field or mossy cavern,
> Choicer than the Mermaid Tavern?

Keats lived at 76 Cheapside while working as a dresser at Guy's Hospital between 1816 and 1817. While there, he wrote 'Ode on a Grecian Urn' *(see also p145)*, before moving to Hampstead *(see p282)*. Michael Drayton's *Endymion and Phoebe* (1595), an erotic treatment of mythological narratives, was one of the sources for Keats's *Endymion* (1818), which he began in 1816 while based in Cheapside.

An Exchange of Virtue and Vice • Cheapside

The City gave rise to several satirical sex comedies – including John Marston's *Dutch Courtesan* (1603), Thomas Middleton and Thomas Dekker's *Honest Whore Part 1* (1604) and Middleton's *A Chaste Maid in Cheapside* (1611) – that were concerned with money, desire, marriage and ways of finding appropriate partners. They saw the City as an expanding market of exchange for goods and services.

A Chaste Maid in Cheapside, for example, has a merchant, Allwit, sell his wife's sexual favours to Walter Whorehound in exchange for a comfortable lifestyle; then the Yellowhammers marry their son to the 'Welsh Gentlewoman' (Whorehound's former whore) to gain wealth and status. The play's title is intended ironically, of course, as Cheapside was renowned for rogue merchants and prostitutes.

Dekker and Middleton were adept at using their local knowledge in their plays. They wrote *The Roaring Girle, or Moll Cut-purse* (1611), based on Mary Frith, a City character known as Moll Cutpurse, who dressed as a man with pipe and sword. Having realised that power in the City lay with men, Moll dressed as one and became a notorious street robber.

Fifty Sons of Phoebus • Fleet Prison, Farringdon Street

> Few sons of Phoebus in the courts we meet;
> But fifty sons of Phoebus in the Fleet
>   Prologue to *The Rivals*, Sheridan

Built in 1197, the Fleet Prison was damaged and rebuilt several times – following the Peasants' Revolt (1381), the Great Fire (1666) and the Gordon Riots (1780).

It was situated off Farringdon Street between Fleet Lane and Ludgate Hill, the site now occupied by Caronne House. Jonson and other actors were imprisoned here for their part in the production of Thomas Nashe's *The Isle of Dogs* (1597). This satirical comedy was sufficiently seditious for the Privy Council to close the Rose Theatre and imprison the author. It is thought that Jonson wrote the play with Nashe. However, the play is lost and there is little evidence about its contents. Nashe, who wrote *Pierce Penilesse*, 1592 (in which the narrator, fed up with being broke, asks the Devil to be his patron), seemingly ran away to escape prison.

In 1601 poet John Donne was imprisoned in the Fleet when he secretly married 17-year-old Anne More. His poet friends Christopher and Samuel Brooke, who helped organise the wedding, were imprisoned along with him.

George Chapman, who completed Christopher Marlowe's *Hero and Leander* (1598) and translated Homer's *The Iliad* (1611) and *The Odyssey* (1616), was first imprisoned in 1599 for debt and later with Dekker and Marston in 1605 for writing *Eastward Hoe!* Jonson, a co-author, may have voluntarily joined them in order to gain an earlier release through his Court patrons. Chapman was imprisoned yet again for upsetting the French ambassador with his play *The Conspiracy and Tragedy of Charles, Duke of Normandy* (1608). Some have considered Chapman to be the 'rival poet' of Shakespeare. He was much admired by Keats, who wrote the sonnet 'On First Looking into Chapman's Homer' in 1817. Most of the Romantics, with the exception of Byron, read Chapman's *Homer* in preference to Pope's.

Thomas Dekker spent almost three years in the Fleet for debt. His vast output was crammed into a life of drinking, smoking and casual sex. Chapman and Dekker both died in poverty.

Aphra Behn was imprisoned in the Fleet for debt when the government did not pay for her spy work in Antwerp in 1672. Actor-manager Thomas Killigrew probably helped her pay off her debts, and the experience inspired her to write prolifically to avoid any further financial troubles *(see pp92–3)*.

William Wycherley, who had great success with comedies such as *The Country Wife* (1675) and *The Plain Dealer* (1676), married the widowed Countess of Drogheda in 1680, against the wishes of Charles II. She died shortly afterwards and, being unable to gain access to her estate and out of favour at Court, Wycherley found himself committed to the Fleet by his creditors. Something of a libertine, he had written the couplet from 'Love in a Wood' (1671):

> *The end of Marriage, now is liberty,*
> *And two are bound – to set each other free.*

He was finally released in 1688 by James II.

A Little World of Woe

> *A Prison is a grave to bury men alive ... it is a microcosmos, a little world of woe, it is a map of misery ...*
> *It is a place that hath more diseases predominant in it than the Pest-house in the Plague time, and it stinks more than the Lord Mayers dogge-house, or Paris garden in August ...*

Essays and characters of a prison and prisoners by Geffray Mynshull (1618) Between 1671 and 1750 the Fleet doubled its capacity from 150 to 300 cells. John Cleland spent his time completing the risqué *Fanny Hill*, 1737 *(see p200)* and managed to write his way out of debt. Mainly used for debtors, the Fleet was a profit-making enterprise, with a taproom, coffee house and a begging wall; the Warden charged prisoners rent. The prison is featured in Hogarth's *The Rake's Progress* and Dickens's *The Pickwick Papers* (1837). Dickens incessantly returns to the Fleet and other prisons as a means of investigating psychological horrors. It was finally demolished in 1846.

Lud Heat • Ludgate

Ludgate derives its name from the 1st-century BC warrior King Lud. Lud inspired London novelist Iain Sinclair, whose collection of poems *Lud Heat* (1975) explores the contemporary city and the historical and mythological patterns that lie beneath its surface. Nicholas Hawksmoor's churches – centres of power built to a mathematical plan on ley lines in a London ravaged by fire and plague – are seen as sites of mystery and energy in this pioneering work that effectively kick-started the psycho-geographical movement. Subsequently, Peter Ackroyd wrote the mystery novel *Hawksmoor* (1985) and Andrew Sinclair wrote *King Lud* (1988).

London Coffee House • 42 Farringdon Street

The London Coffee House occupied this site from 1731 to 1868. Benjamin Franklin held a fortnightly supper club here between 1764 and1772, and James Boswell and various dissenters and polemicists, including James Burgh, regularly attended. The London Coffee House was also where Arthur Clennam sheltered from the rain in Dickens's *Little Dorrit* (1857).

Reviled Jail • Newgate Street

The Old Bailey, the Central Criminal Court, stands on the site of Newgate Prison. Henry I built the prison in 1188, and it became London's most reviled jail. Sir Thomas Malory wrote most of *Le Morte D'Arthur*, published by Caxton (1485), in Newgate and the

Tower between 1452 and 1470. *Le Morte D'Arthur* was the last medieval work of the Arthurian legend, drawing upon earlier versions and inspiring Tennyson's 'Idylls of the king'. No stranger to jail, Malory also spent time in Southwark's Marshalsea prison.

Ben Jonson was imprisoned in Newgate for killing fellow actor Gabriel Spencer in a duel at Shoreditch in 1598. He converted to Catholicism to claim benefit of the clergy and gain release. Christopher Marlowe, remanded to Newgate in 1589 while awaiting sentence for murder, was also acquitted. In Newgate he learned about coining and mixing of metals from a fellow prisoner, and used the knowledge in his play *Doctor Faustus* (1590).

Daniel Defoe was imprisoned in Cornhill pillory and Newgate prison from May to November 1703 for ridiculing the Tories in the seditious work *The Shortest Way With The Dissenters*, a notorious pamphlet that ironically demanded the total and savage suppression of dissent. He drew on his Newgate experience for the prison scenes in *Moll Flanders* (1722) – Moll is born in the prison.

During the Gordon Riots of June 1780, rioters released 300 prisoners and set fire to the building. The poet George Crabbe, lodging near the Royal Exchange, witnessed the riots, as did a young William Blake *(see p104)*.

William Cobbett, imprisoned between 1810 and 1812 for writing about flogging in the army, was able to continue publishing his radical journal *The Political Register* while in Newgate. The prison is a setting in John Gay's *The Beggar's Opera* and a potent psychological symbol throughout Dickens's work.

Statue of King Lud standing in ill-repair in the side porch of St Dunstan-in-the-West, Fleet Street

On 6 July 1840 François Courvoisier, a servant who had slit his master's throat, was publicly hanged at Newgate Prison. Both Charles Dickens and William Thackeray witnessed the hanging, and wrote of their revulsion. Dickens wrote about it several years later in *The Daily News*:

> *From the moment of my arrival ... to the time when I saw the body with its dangling head, being carried on a wooden bier into the gaol ... I did not see one token in all the immense crowd ... of any one emotion*

suitable to the occasion. No sorrow, no salutary terror, no abhorrence, no seriousness; nothing but ribaldry, debauchery, levity, drunkenness, and flaunting vice in fifty other shapes.

Thackeray's 'Going to See a Man Hanged' appeared soon after the event, in the July 1840 issue of *Frazer's* magazine:

There were, with me, some gentlemen of education and distinction in imaginative pursuits, who had, as I had, a particular detestation of that murderer; not only for the cruel deed he had done, but for his slow and subtle treachery, and for his wicked defence.

In his defence Courvoisier had claimed that he had been driven to commit his crime by an evil book – namely, *Jack Sheppard, A Romance* (1839) by William Harrison Ainsworth, which tells the story of highwayman Jack Sheppard who was hanged at Tyburn in 1724. This marks one of the first exchanges in the long-running dispute as to whether art can inspire criminality.

As to public execution, Thackeray's conclusion is similar to that of Dickens:

And yet, if any one among us could have saved the man (we said so, afterwards, with one accord), he would have done it. It was so loathsome, pitiful, and vile a sight, that the law appeared to be as bad as he, or worse; being very much the stronger, and shedding around it a far more dismal contagion.

Oscar Wilde was held at Newgate after being found guilty of gross indecency at the Central Criminal Court in 1895, shortly before the prison was demolished in 1902.

Viaduct
Tavern

The Viaduct Tavern • 126 Newgate Street

Dating from 1869 and opened by Queen Victoria, this pub has a cellar in the old cells of Newgate prison that can be viewed by appointment. It was here that Jake Donaghue and friends began their pub crawl in their quest to find the philosopher Hugo Belfounder in Iris Murdoch's first novel, *Under The Net* (1954).

I've Read a Lot of Pornographic and Obscene Books • Old Bailey

D.H. Lawrence's sexually explicit novel *Lady Chatterley's Lover* was published in Italy in 1928 and in Paris in 1929, but was banned in Britain for 30 years. It was finally published, unexpurgated, by Penguin Books in 1960 and immediately charged under the Obscene Publications Act 1959. The six-day trial at the Old Bailey began on 27 October and gripped the nation. The defence produced 35 witnesses, including bishops and leading literary figures such as Dame Rebecca West, E.M. Forster and Richard Hoggart. Norman St John-Stevas M.P. memorably stated in the witness box, 'I've read a lot of pornographic and obscene books … and *Lady Chatterley's Lover* is not one of them'.

The defining words of the trial were uttered by prosecuting counsel Mr Griffith-Jones, who enquired of the jury: 'Would you approve of your young sons, young daughters – because girls can read as well as boys – reading this book? Is it a book you would have lying around in your own house? Is it a book you would even wish your wife or your servants to read?'

These were questions that belonged to an earlier age. The jury acquitted, and it must have seemed like the beginning of a new era. As Philip Larkin famously put it in 'Annus Mirabilis' (1974):

> *Sexual intercourse began*
> *in nineteen sixty-three*
> *(Which was rather late for me) –*
> *Between the end of the Chatterley ban*
> *And the Beatles' first LP.*

Lady Chatterley's Lover became an immediate bestseller: 200,000 copies were sold on the first day of publication alone. Within a year it had sold two million copies.

Obscenity was back centre stage at the Old Bailey in 1971 with 'The Schoolkids issue' (issue 28) of *Oz*, the underground magazine. After a lengthy trial, Richard Neville, Jim Anderson and Felix Dennis were found guilty of conspiracy to corrupt minors and faced severe sentences – including deportation back to Australia in the case of Anderson and Neville. However, the judgement was overturned on appeal. Felix Dennis went on to build a magazine publishing empire and become a poet.

John Mortimer, creator of *Rumpole of the Bailey* and the powerful autobiographical work *A Voyage Round My Father* (1971), acted for the defendants and recalled the *Oz* trial as the 'longest and funniest' in which he had been involved.

> We called the most extraordinary witnesses. We called George Melly. He gave his evidence about oral sex. And I said, 'Is oral sex all right?' and he said, 'Yes. When I was in the navy we called it, "yodelling in the canyon," by the way.' And the judge said, 'For those of us who haven't had a classical education, what do you mean by cunnilinctus?' as though it was a sort of cough mixture.

Inconstant Love • Smithfield

Isabella Whitney, the first Englishwoman to publish poetry, was born and lived in Smithfield. She started writing after losing her job, and produced *Copy of a letter, largely written in meeter, by a Yonge Gentilwoman to her unconstant lover* (1567) and *A sweet Nosegay* (1573). The form of her work is loosely modelled on Ovid's *Heroides*, which comprised verse epistles written between lovers – a model later adopted by Aphra Behn. Whitney's voice is jocular, teasing and sceptical, far removed from the Petrarchan courtly love poets.

At the end of her second book, in the poem entitled 'Wyll and Testament', she appoints London her executor and makes various bequests to the city and its inhabitants. To Ludgate debtor's prison she initially leaves nothing, but then changes her mind and leaves the prison a legacy of bankrupts.

Parliament of Monsters • Bartholomew Fair

To the west of St Bartholomew's Hospital and southeast of West Smithfield roundabout is the site of Bartholomew's Fair. This medieval cloth fair was held annually from 1133 to 1855. Formerly lasting a fortnight, it was restricted to four days every August from 1691 and reduced to three in 1708. The event was made famous by Ben Jonson's play *Bartholomew Fair* (1614). This comedy follows the fortunes of several characters, some drunk, who are duped at the Fair, and satirises religious and legal justice.

The Fair was an occasion for great theatricality, with puppet shows and street performers, and was free of social distinctions. For some it was too much. John Bunyan, author of the Christian allegory *The Pilgrim's Progress* (1678), collapsed and died on 31 August 1688 at the corner of Snow Hill and Cock Lane.

By the 18th century the fair had become a spectacular national and international event featuring sideshows, prize-fighters, musicians, wire walkers, acrobats, Punch and Judy shows and exhibitions of freaks and wild animals. It was marked by gambling and drinking by people of all classes and occupations. One of its ballads ran:

Betjeman's local, The Hand & Shears

> *Bellfounders, fellmongers*
> *Pumpmakers, glassmakers, chamberlains and matmakers*
> *Collarmakers, needlemakers, buttonmakers, fiddlemakers*
> *Fletchers and bowyers, drawers and sawyers*
> *Room for company, well may they fair.*
>
> *Cutpurses and cheaters, and bawdy house door keepers*
> *Punks, ay, and panders, and cashier'd commanders*
> *Room for company, ill may they fair.*

Charles Lamb gave Dorothy and William Wordsworth a guided tour of Bartholomew Fair on their return from France in August 1802. This experience fed into Wordsworth's reflective, philosophical poem *The Prelude* (1805), where his nightmarish account of the fair in Book VII acts as a metaphor for the city as a whole. Wordsworth contrasts the Lake District with the noise of the fair:

> *Upon some showman's platform. What a shock*
> *For eyes and ears! what anarchy and din,*
> *Barbarian and infernal, – a phantasma,*
> *Monstrous in colour, motion, shape, sight, sound!*

He saw the freak shows as the City's unnatural body.

> *All freaks of nature, all Promethean thoughts*
> *Of man, his dullness, madness and their feats.*
> *All jumbled up together, to compose*
> *A Parliament of Monsters, Tents and Booths*

For Wordsworth the City represented artifice, commerce, empire and a loss of individual identity, all epitomised by Bartholomew Fair, where 'thousands upon thousands' live in 'blank confusion', inhabiting the same 'perpetual whirl'.

Betjeman's City • 43 Cloth Fair

John Betjeman had his London base here from August 1954 until 1972. He viewed the City as a village of about 400 people who kept secrets. He fought to guard its heritage. Here everything that he wanted could be reached on foot. He enjoyed the bells of St Bartholomew the Great, which he attended on Sunday, meat from Smithfield 'with its cheerful Chaucerian characters', fish from Billingsgate and beer from the Hand & Shears on Middle Street. While living at Cloth Fair, Betjeman wrote for *The Spectator*, made programmes for BBC Radio and Television, wrote poems and articles about conservation, and was visited by his lovers, including Lady Elizabeth Cavendish.

Crime Against Literature • 17 Cornhill

T.S. Eliot worked for the Colonial and Foreign Department at Lloyd's Bank, No. 17 Cornhill from 1917, causing Ezra Pound to write that 'it was a crime against literature to let him (Eliot) waste eight hours per diem in that bank.' Eliot claimed that he needed the routine to write poetry and produced 'The Love Song of J. Alfred Prufrock' (1917) and *The Waste Land* (1922) while employed at the bank. He made notes in his office and found inspiration from the area and its buildings. In 1920 he moved to Lloyd's head office at 71 Lombard Street, returned to Cornhill in 1923, and finally left for publishers Faber & Gwyer (later Faber & Faber), in Russell Square in 1925.

Both T.S. Eliot's *The Waste Land* and Peter Ackroyd's *Hawksmoor* mention St Mary Woolnoth of the Nativity in Lombard Street, the church Hawksmoor rebuilt in 1717. When editing *The Waste Land*, Pound suggested removing the reference to the church. However, Eliot clearly liked the 'dead sound' of its clock and retained the lines.

Meeting of Opposites • 32 Cornhill

A carved panel on the street door at No. 32 features a relief of Charlotte Brontë's meeting with William Makepeace Thackeray at the shop, when she defended herself 'like a great Turk at a heathen'. Formerly No. 65, these were the offices and bookshop

of Smith & Elder, the Brontës' publishers, which
Charlotte and Anne visited briefly in 1848.

Babel • Threadneedle Street and Cornhill

The Royal Exchange at Threadneedle Street
operated from 1565 to 1939 for city merchants to
meet and talk business. It was founded by Thomas
Gresham, who had a shop at the sign of the
Grasshopper in Lombard Street. When walking in
the Exchange, early 17th-century playwright Thomas
Dekker noted how 'a man is put in mind of Babel,
there is such confusion of languages'.

London's first coffee house, Pasqua Rosee's
Head, opened in St Michael's Alley, off Cornhill
(where the Jamaica Wine House now stands) in
1652. The area soon filled with coffee houses and
Charles II tried to ban them on the grounds that
they provided a meeting place for the disaffected
to spread scandalous stories about the King, Court
and government. His efforts failed and the coffee
house movement of free discussion grew rapidly: in
the early 18th century there were 26 coffee houses
between Cornhill and Threadneedle Street alone.

The church that Pepys regularly attended and
where he and his wife were buried, St Olave's on
the corner of Seething Lane and Hart Street

And So to Bed • Seething Lane

In 1660 Samuel Pepys was appointed Clerk of the
Acts to the Navy Board, and on 17 July took up lodgings in the Navy Office at Seething
Lane. On 1 January that same year, Pepys began his *Diary*, recording his burgeoning
professional and social successes. The practice of keeping diaries had become
increasingly popular since Elizabethan times. These were generally daily accounts of
personal events, confessional diaries, or memoirs of affairs of state. Pepys's *Diary*
combines all three in an unprecedented way, providing a unique insight into the
private man and the public events of the period.

Pepys was ideally placed to witness at close hand the Restoration of the monarchy.
He moved in Court circles and was deeply involved in the City's commercial and
social life. His observations on his own health are as detailed as his comments on the
state of the Navy – and the contented reflection on the state of his finances. The eye
for detail that made him a successful administrator, in the *Diary* helps to bring every
incident to life, from the streets emptied by the Plague to the poor pigeons 'loath

to leave their houses' in the Great Fire. Along the way, we are introduced to such characters as his rival, John Creed, who 'is too wise to be made a friend of and acts all by interest and policy' and Gosnell, his wife's maid, who manages to become an actress for the Duke's Company despite the fact that, in Pepys's opinion, she can't sing.

Pepys's worldly success and position gave him many opportunities to indulge his sexual appetite, all of which he confides to his journal using a mixture of anglicised Latin, French and Spanish to conceal the matter from prying eyes. No maid in the Pepys household was safe from his advances, and in October 1668 he was caught in flagrante with their maid Deb Willets:

> ... and after supper, to have my head combed by Deb, which occasioned the greatest sorrow to me that ever I knew in this world; for my wife, coming up suddenly, did find me imbracing the girl con my hand sub su coats; and endeed, I was with my main in her cunny. I was at a wonderful loss upon it, and the girl also ...

After several mighty rages and silences, 'my wife full of trouble in her looks', the Pepyses were eventually reconciled – though Deb, needless to say, lost her job. Pepys's vigour and appetite for life, which makes the *Diary* such compulsive reading, remained with him throughout his life, surviving his failing eyesight which caused him finally to give up writing his journal on 31 May 1669. He died on 26 May 1703, and on 4 June was buried at St Olave's. In 1884 Pepys's monument was erected in St Olave's, and in 1983 a statue of Pepys was erected in Seething Lane.

Unreal City • London Bridge

Eliot's *The Waste Land* (1922) is full of London references and locations. It shows the city, its people, their culture, faith and relationships in a juxtaposition of broken images. The reader is taken on a journey through 1920s London, an 'unreal city' that Eliot compares to Dante's *Inferno*, where the streets flow with the living dead:

> Under the brown fog of a winter dawn,
> A crowd flowed over London Bridge, so many
> I had not thought death had undone so many.
> Sighs, short and infrequent, were exhaled,
> And each man fixed his eyes before his feet.
> Flowed up the hill and down King William Street
> To where Saint Mary Woolnoth kept the hours
> With a dead sound on the final stroke of nine.

This seminal work finely interweaves themes of death, spiritual emptiness and potential regeneration. Lines from other literary works, different languages and modes of speech, high art and low culture, fleeting observations and conversations are combined in a radically new way. The poem contrasts the modern river, freighted with refuse and sweating 'oil and tar', with the river scene in Spenser's *Prothalamion*, and Elizabeth and Leicester 'beating oars'.

Ba-Room! • London Bridge

Invalided out of the French army after being wounded at Ypres in the First World War, Louis-Ferdinand Céline was assigned to the French passport office in London. In 1915 he married Suzanne Nebout, a Frenchwoman working as a barmaid in London, but left in 1916 to work for a French lumber company in Cameroon. His novels *Guignol's Band* (1943, English translation 1954) and *London Bridge* (*Le pont du Londres*), also called *Guignol's Band II* (1964 and 1988, English translation 1995), are clearly informed by this period in London.

Telegraphed in nervy fragments of exclamatory prose, the narrative traces the blackly comic misadventures of the anti-hero 'Ferdinand' and takes the reader on a phantasmagoric journey through a London underworld populated by pimps, prostitutes, crooks, con-men, arsonists and vagabonds drawn from the four corners of Europe and pursued by the stolid Inspector Matthew of Scotland Yard. From the din of an air attack on the battlefields of France, 'enough to shatter sky and earth!' (with which *Guignol's Band* begins), to a final manic crossing of (the old) London Bridge, buffeted by high winds in which 'the great current roars under the arches way down below, swelling, furrowing, frothing…' the writing evokes a shell-shocked and splintered world of nihilistic violence, paranoia, rage, desire and dementia. Big Ben striking the hour echoes the bursts of shellfire on the western front – '… right then Ba-room! Ba-room! Big Ben strikes six … the boom bouncing through the fog … what an echo! it shook the air…', sending Ferdinand's friend lurching, rattling 'his whole body, every last inch of his bag of bones …'

Céline trained and worked as a doctor, but gained success and a measure of notoriety with his first and best known novel, *Journey To The End of the Night* (*Voyage au bout de la nuit*, 1932). In 1937 he attracted further notoriety as the author of the virulently anti-semitic *Bagatelle pour un massacre* (1937). Accused of collaboration in 1944, Céline fled to Germany and then to Denmark in 1945. He was tried in absentia in France, declared a national disgrace and condemned to a year's imprisonment. However, in 1951 he was pardoned and returned to France.

SOUTHWARK & WATERLOO

SOUTHWARK LIES JUST SOUTH OF LONDON BRIDGE. Its name derives from 'south work' (or southern defence) and historical Southwark equates approximately to the area now called Borough. Traditionally, this was the last staging post for travellers heading to the City, and a starting point for those journeying south to Surrey, Kent and beyond. Borough High Street, Southwark's main thoroughfare, was thus lined with inns. Indeed, in 1600 dramatist Thomas Dekker observed that the high street was 'a continual ale house with not a shop to be seen'.

In Elizabethan times Southwark was London's prime spot for entertainment. Outside the walls of the City, it enjoyed a greater degree of liberty, and here players, prostitutes and pickpockets mingled with city dwellers in search of a good time. Theatres, including the Rose, the Globe and the Swan, brought to Southwark writers and actors such as Jonson, Marlowe and Shakespeare. These theatres jostled for space with venues for other popular entertainments and pastimes, such as bull-baiting, prize-fighting and gambling.

The area had a notorious reputation for riots and disorder and, by the 17th century, Southwark had seven prisons, including the Clink, which gave its name to other such institutions. However, it is Marshalsea prison that has the greatest number of literary associations. Thomas Malory, Ben Jonson and Walter Ralegh were among those locked up there, and

Charles Dickens's father was imprisoned for non-payment of his debts at the relocated Marshalsea in 1824. The jail made a strong impression on Dickens, and features in two of his novels, *David Copperfield* and *Little Dorrit*.

The great Elizabethan theatres were pulled down by Puritans in the Civil War (1642–46), and when theatres began to flourish again, following the Restoration of the Monarchy in 1660, the centre of theatrical life moved to Covent Garden.

In the late 20th century, the area resumed its theatrical connections to a lesser degree a little further west of Borough on the South Bank and at Waterloo. Here, you'll find The Old Vic, a former music hall and first home of the National Theatre; the purpose-built Royal National Theatre, designed by Denis Lasdun; and The Young Vic, which provides a space for the development of young actors and directors.

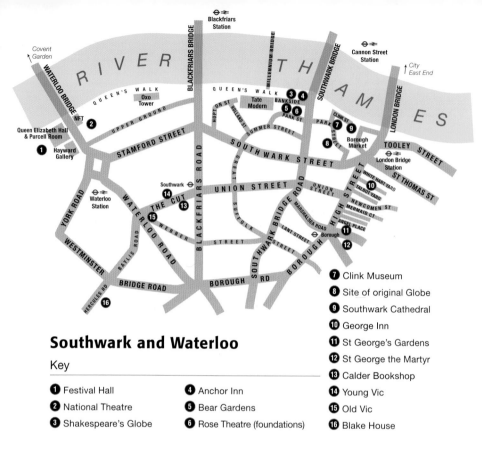

Southwark and Waterloo

Key

1 Festival Hall

2 National Theatre

3 Shakespeare's Globe

4 Anchor Inn

5 Bear Gardens

6 Rose Theatre (foundations)

7 Clink Museum

8 Site of original Globe

9 Southwark Cathedral

10 George Inn

11 St George's Gardens

12 St George the Martyr

13 Calder Bookshop

14 Young Vic

15 Old Vic

16 Blake House

Pilgrims Were They Alle • The Tabard Inn

Tabard House, which became the Tabard Inn, at Talbot Yard on what is now Borough High Street, was built in 1307. It was from here that Chaucer's pilgrims began their pilgrimage to Thomas à Becket's shrine at Canterbury Cathedral in *The Canterbury Tales* (1380s–90s, printed 1483):

> Bifil that in that seson on a day,
> In Southwerk at the Tabard as I lay
> Redy to wenden on my pilgrimage
> To Caunterbury with ful devout corage,
> At nyght was come into hostelrye
> Wel nyne and twenty in a compaignye,
> Of sundry folk, by aventure yfalle
> In felaweship, and pilgrims were they alle,
> That toward Caunterbury wolden ryde.

The pilgrimage was a favourite pastime of the devout. Every year, when the rains of April had laid the dust of March to the root, the desire to go on a pilgrimage gripped people from all walks of life. Chaucer seems to have originally intended that each of some thirty pilgrims should tell two tales on the way to Canterbury and two on the way back. He did not complete this ambitious plan, but the pilgrims whose tales are included nevertheless cover a wide range of 14th-century society, from the Knight, Squire, Man of Law, Merchant, through to the Monk, Wife of Bath, Miller and Parson. Each is sharply individual; together they offer a social portrait of a nation.

The Tabard offered spacious rooms and stables, good food and strong wine. The Innkeeper, Henry Bailley, was M.P. for Southwark in the 1380s. In his introduction to the Tales, Chaucer describes the Innkeeper as:

> *A seemly man our hoste was with-alle*
> *For to han been a marshall in an halle;*
> *A large man he was with eyen stepe,*
> *A fairer burgeys is ther noon in Chepe;*
> *Bold of his speche, and wys, and well y-taught,*
> *And of manhood him lakkede right naught.*
> *Eke thereto he was right a merry man.*

The Miller blames any muddled words he may use on 'the ale of Southwerk'. The Inn was reconstructed in 1628, but burnt to the ground in 1676. A new Tabard emerged, built to the old plan, but was demolished in 1875. A plaque was erected on the site of the Tabard in July 2002 with Monty Python star and medievalist Terry Jones and Southwark and Bermondsey M.P. Simon Hughes in attendance.

The George Inn • 77 Borough High Street

The George is London's only remaining galleried inn. Its known history can be traced to the mid-16th century, but the present building dates from 1676, when the inn had to be rebuilt (in identical form) following a fire.

Built around three sides of a courtyard (only the south side remains today), The George was frequently used as a place for plays to be performed in the 16th and 17th centuries, its galleries providing excellent vantage points from which to view the action in the yard below. It is very likely that Shakespeare acted in plays at The George, performances often taking place on the back of a cart, which was used as an impromptu stage. In more recent times there have been performances of Shakespeare's plays in the inn's courtyard.

Dickens, who used to drink in The George's Coffee Room, uses it in *Little Dorrit* (1857) as the place where Edward Dorrit writes his begging letter to Mr Clenman.

The Jack Cade Rebellion • White Hart Inn

In 1450 Jack Cade made use of the White Hart Inn for his headquarters during what became known as the Jack Cade Rebellion (an uprising of mostly Kentish peasants against conditions of forced labour and high taxation imposed by King Henry VI). Shakespeare made dramatic use of this event in *Henry VI Part II*. Situated in White Hart Yard, the inn survived until 1889. It is also where Dickens has Sam Weller meet Mr Pickwick in *The Pickwick Papers* (1837).

Let Not Our Wine Be Mixt • The Bear Inn

The Bear Inn was situated at the foot of London Bridge and was one of the oldest inns in Southwark. It had a large enough garden to offer archery as a pastime for its customers. In the 17th century it was a favourite meeting place of the wits and poets who enjoyed gaming and drinking. These included Sir John Suckling, who wrote 'The Wine-drinkers to the Water-drinkers' at the Bear. His poems, plays and prose were collected in *Fragmenta Aurea* (1646). When Pepys visited Southwark Fair in 1668 he used the Bear as his base, leaving behind £40 in the safe keeping of his waterman. Frances Stuart, a Court beauty and royal mistress, arranged her liaisons with lovers at the Bear so that, if necessary, they could quickly leave for Kent. The Inn survived until 1761.

Southwark Fair

Talbot Yard, formerly home to Chaucer's Tabard Inn

Southwark Fair, which occupied much of Borough High Street and surrounding side streets and inn yards, was held every September from 1462 to 1762. Like Bartholomew Fair in the City *(see p64)*, it was famous for its performers and puppet shows. Pepys and John Evelyn record their visits in their diaries. Hogarth painted *The Fair* (or *The Humours of the Fair*; now in a private collection) in 1733.

Love Me little, Love Me Long • The Rose

The first theatre in the area, The Rose, was situated in Rose Alley, Park Street. It was built and managed in 1587 by Philip Henslowe, whose diary, now held at Dulwich College, is a valuable source of information on Elizabethan theatre. Henslowe recorded payments to Ben Jonson, Thomas Middleton, George Chapman, Thomas Dekker, John Marston and Michael Drayton. He also had interests in the Swan and Newington Butts theatres and owned inns, lodging houses and brothels along

Bankside. In 1592 he married the daughter of the leading actor of the Admiral's Men, Edward Alleyn, the later founder of Dulwich College *(see p318)*.

Henslowe built the Fortune Theatre for the Admiral's Men north of the Thames in 1600 when the Rose began to lose audiences to the Globe. In 1604 Henslowe and Alleyn bought the patent as Master of the Royal Games of Bears, Bull and Mastiff Dogs and presented bull and bear baiting near the Swan Theatre, in the Paris Garden. Henslowe's theatres provided employment for many playwrights. Younger dramatists served apprenticeships by working on new themes or plots, with older playwrights as mentors. Their plays belonged to the acting company which would then sell them to touring and other companies. Alleyn took the lead roles in Christopher Marlowe's *Tamburlaine the Great* (1587), *The Jew of Malta* (1588) and *The History of Doctor Faustus* (1589). These plays created historic and heroic drama and made a name for both author and actor.

Tamburlaine, the story of an Oriental Napoleon, was written in blank verse employing ten syllable lines. Marlowe focused on a protagonist and illuminated his complex motivations. His poetic and musical language, full of classical references, captivated audiences and inspired Shakespeare, who acted at the Rose when he first arrived in London. Competing for precedence, Shakespeare pushed his central characters to further extremes and extended the range and emotional intensity of his plays through sub-plots and new kinds of action.

After Marlowe was killed in a Deptford pub in 1593 *(see p316)*, Dekker and Chapman became the leading dramatists for The Rose.

Corruption, Sedition and Spectacle • The Swan

The Swan Theatre, some 500 yards from the Rose, sited west of Hopton Street, was the largest of the Elizabethan theatres. Francis Langley, the inspector of wool and cloth, who owned brothels and was a fence for stolen goods, built the Swan in 1595 as an investment. Shakespeare acted at the Swan in 1596 after he moved from Bishopsgate to live in the Paris Garden.

The Swan was the venue for Thomas Nashe's seditious play *The Isle of Dogs* (1597), which saw Jonson imprisoned for his part in the production *(see p59)* and the temporary closure of all London's theatres. Sadly the play has not survived. Lady Elizabeth's Men performed Thomas Middleton's *A Chaste Maid in Cheapside (see p58)* here in 1613.

All The World's A Stage • The Globe

Richard and Cuthbert Burbage built the Globe Theatre on a site south of Park Street using timbers from the first Blackfriars Theatre in 1598. Its sign was Hercules carrying the world on his shoulders with a quotation from Petronius, 'Totus mundus agit histrionem' ('the whole world is a playhouse'), carved in Latin over the front. From Hester Thrale's observation and earlier sources we know that the theatre was hexagonal on the outside and circular on the inside. Shakespeare altered the Petronius quote in *As You Like It* (1599) to 'All the world's a stage'.

The first recorded performances at the original Globe theatre were of Shakespeare's *Julius Caesar*, *Henry V* and *As You Like It* in summer 1599. The theatre opened with *Julius Caesar* on 12 June, the date of the old summer solstice, after astrological advice had been taken. Shakespeare was a shareholder in the company as a result of his earlier success as an actor-playwright. His work developed in competition with other dramatists. For example, *Twelfth Night* (1601) can be read as his riposte to Jonson's criticism of romantic comedy in *Every Man Out of His Humour* (1600). *Twelfth Night* combines social satire and bittersweet melancholy in a battle of the sexes involving lost twins, mistaken identity and cross-dressing. Both plays were performed at the Globe.

Shakespeare responded to the movement away from historical drama, led by Jonson, Marston, Chapman and later Middleton and Dekker, by employing mythological, magical, historical and literary sources that he reworked into new drama. His sources for *King Lear* (1605) certainly included the old anonymous play *King Leir*, in which he may have acted in the 1590s, and Spenser's *Faerie Queene* (for the part of Cordelia). Others sources are thought to have included Sidney's *Arcadia* (for the sub-plot of Gloucester and his sons), the *Mirror for Magistrates*, a popular verse anthology of the tragic downfall of famous people, Samuel Harsnett's 1603 publication *Declarations of Egregious Popish Impostures* (for documentary evidence of psychological disturbance, the storm scene and the language of pain), and Erasmus's *Praise of Folly* (for the Fool's deconstruction of power).

Shakespeare may also have derived some unusual vocabulary, such as 'compeer', 'disnatured', 'goatish', 'handy-dandy', 'sectary' and 'sumpter', from John Florio's translation of Montaigne's *Essays* (1603).

He removed all the Christian references from the old *King Leir* and gave it a pagan setting, replacing humble submission to the divine will with rage against the dying of the light, and changing the original happy ending into a painfully tragic one. Astrologers were prophesying doom for the autumn of 1605 and by writing about the dismemberment of Britain and the collapse of a king, Shakespeare caught the mood of the time. By assimilating all kinds of material and absorbing contradictory points of view (both religious and secular), he also ensured that the play had no single perspective and would therefore be open to many interpretations. In this way his play, performed before and immediately after the Gunpowder Plot of 1605, did not offend the monarch or Privy Council and Shakespeare remained free to continue writing. *King Lear* contains some of the most powerful verse in the English language:

Lear: Come, let's away to prison;
We two alone will sing like birds I' the cage.
When thou dost ask me blessing, I'll kneel down,
And ask of thee forgiveness; so we'll live,
And pray, and sing, and tell old tales, and laugh
At gilded butterflies, and hear poor rogues
Talk of court news, and we'll talk with them too,
Who loses, and who wins; who's in, who's out;

In 1604 the Chamberlain's Men – who played every summer season at the Globe and in winter retreated to the covered Blackfriars Theatre *(see p54)* – received the royal warrant and became the King's Men. The company repeated their repertoire so that the new monarch, James I, could see their famous dramas. The plays that followed at the Globe, such as *King Lear*, *Antony & Cleopatra* (1606) and *Macbeth* (1606), have been interpreted as Shakespeare's responses to the new monarch and contemporaneous events.

The Globe was destroyed by fire during a performance of Fletcher and Shakespeare's *Henry VIII* in June 1613. Thereafter, Shakespeare returned to Stratford. The theatre was rebuilt by King James I, and Francis Beaumont and John Fletcher became its leading dramatists. Thomas Dekker, George Chapman and Thomas Middleton – as prolific as Shakespeare yet quite different in focus – also had work performed at the Globe. Their work, especially Dekker's, is notable for its vivid portrayal of contemporary City life, and sympathetic insight into the plight of the poor.

The Globe survived until 1644, when the Puritans demolished it. A succession of buildings replaced the theatre, the last being a brewery. When this closed, only a plaque placed by the Shakespeare Reading Society remained. American actor-director Sam Wanamaker came across this in 1949 and led the campaign to rebuild the Globe. The original foundations were excavated in 1989 and the restored Globe, with the only thatched roof allowed to be built in London since the Great Fire of 1666, was constructed close by, opening at New Globe Walk, Bankside in 1996 with a production of *Two Gentlemen of Verona*.

The site of the original Globe is marked by a plaque and its stage partly delineated in the cobbled driveway of a small housing development on Park Street.

A Very Rude and Nasty Pleasure • The Hope

Situated at the Bear Garden, Park Street, The Hope Theatre was opened by Philip Henslowe in 1614 after the original Globe burnt down. Lady Elizabeth's Men first performed Jonson's *Bartholomew Fair* at the Hope in October 1614. The theatre was demolished in 1656, though the site was later used for dog fighting and bear baiting, which Samuel Pepys attended here in 1666 and 1670. On the first of these occasions he reports seeing 'some good sport of the bull's tossing of the dogs', but concludes, somewhat paradoxically (as was his wont), that 'it is a very rude and nasty pleasure'.

A Most Horrid Malicious Flame • The Anchor Inn and Brewery

The Anchor is thought to be the site of the 'small ale house on Bankside' from which Samuel Pepys watched the Great Fire on 2 September 1666. He had watched the fire spread from a boat on the water at first, but singed by 'fire-drops' his party retreated to the southern bank, where they 'stayed till it was dark almost, and saw the fire grow; and, as it grew darker, appeared more and more, and in corners and upon steeples, and between churches and houses, as far as we could see up the hill of the City, in a most horrid, malicious, bloody flame'.

The Inn itself was rebuilt after fires in 1750 and 1876. The Anchor Brewery was owned by the Thrale family, and Henry and Hester Thrale's literary club met here from 1764. Hester had married Henry against her inclinations and once commented that Henry only married her because the other ladies to whom he proposed refused to live in the Borough. Hester was not allowed to run the household, so she threw herself into organising literary meetings, parties and dinners.

Anchor Inn Bankside Members of the club included Dr Johnson and Boswell, and among their wider artistic and literary circle were Sir Joshua Reynolds, actor-writer David Garrick, society hostess Elizabeth Montagu *(see p170)* and Henry's oldest friend, barrister, journalist and actor-playwright Arthur Murphy. Murphy wrote biographies of Johnson, Henry Fielding and David Garrick, and edited the *Gray's Inn Journal* from 1752 to 1754. Johnson wrote a Latin 'Ode to Hester Thrale' and Sir Joshua Reynolds painted Hester and her eldest daughter, Queeney, in 1781.

Hester herself wrote prose and verse, including *Anecdotes of the Late Samuel Johnson* (1786). In 1942, Clarendon Press published *Thraliana*, the contents of four notebooks in which Hester wrote diary entries, poems, anecdotes and observations in the period 1776 to 1809.

After Henry's death, Hester married Gabriel Piozzi, an Italian musician, in 1784; Johnson was outraged and wrote a letter of protest that ended their friendship. Hester then started a new circle of artist friends, which included the actress Sarah Siddons, and published *Letters To and From the Late Samuel Johnson* in 1788, which continued her distinct presentation of Johnson and intensified her running feud with Johnson's main biographer, James Boswell.

Thought Hath No Prison • Marshalea

The Marshalsea Prison, second in importance to the Tower of London as a national prison, was originally on a site close to Mermaid Court, Borough High Street from about 1300. The prison developed from being a jail for pirates, smugglers and maritime criminals into one for debtors and dissenters.

Thomas Malory, author of *Le Morte D'Arthur* (printed by Caxton in 1485), was imprisoned and escaped from the Marshalsea in the 1450s. Nicholas Udall, Headmaster of Eton College and author of one of the first English comedies, *Ralph Roister Doister* (1541), served a short sentence here for sodomy. Court poet and adventurer Walter Ralegh was briefly held in 1580 for fighting at Court and Spenserian poet Christopher Brooke, who belonged to the Mermaid and Devil Tavern literary clubs, was incarcerated for helping his friend John Donne marry Anne More in 1609 without her father's permission.

Another regular at the Devil Tavern, poet George Wither, was imprisoned for his satire *Abuses Stript and Whipt* (1613), an enormously popular work in the tradition of *Piers Plowman*, in which he attacked corruption in government and Court circles. He wrote one of his most famous poems, 'The Shepherd's Hunting', while in the Marshalsea. In it he attacked the 'hunting of foxes, wolves and beasts of prey', which further attracted the ire of the Court. Having been released in around 1614, Wither worked on another satirical poem, 'Motto' (1621). It sold several thousand copies in official and pirate editions, and led to a second spell behind bars. During the Civil War, Wither initially sided with the royalists, but changed sides and raised a troop of horsemen for Parliament. It was a bold but untimely gambit, and at the Restoration Wither was returned once again to the Marshalsea.

Marshalsea 1811–42

> *'Anyone can go in,' replied the old man,*
> *'but it is not every one who can go out.'*
> *Little Dorrit*, Charles Dickens

By 1811 the old Marshalsea prison had been replaced by a new building at Angel Place, close to St George's Church. It was here that Charles Dickens's father served a sentence for debt between February and May 1824. Dickens was put into lodgings and forced to work in a boot-blacking factory. This experience inspired the writing of *David Copperfield* (1850), and later *Little Dorrit* (1857), whose eponymous heroine was born in the prison. St George the Martyr Church, Borough High Street at Long Lane, is known as 'Little Dorrit's Church'. This is where (in the book) she was christened and married. A church window commemorates her.

The Tomb of John Gower, Southwark Cathedral

Southwark Cathedral

The Cathedra and Collegiate Church of St Saviour and St Mary Overie (to give Southwark Cathedral its full name) has been a cathedral only since 1905, when the Anglican Diocese of Southwark was formed. However, the building dates from the 13th century when it was a priory church. It contains the tomb of one of England's first poets, John Gower *(see p9)*, and there are also memorial windows to Chaucer, John Bunyan, Shakespeare and Dr Johnson.

Shakespeare, who probably attended services here, is commemorated with a reclining alabaster effigy and a stained-glass window depicting scenes from his plays. Next to the statue is a tablet dedicated to actor Sam Wanamaker, founder of the new Globe Theatre. Shakespeare's younger brother, Edmund, was buried here in December 1607, as was the dramatist John Fletcher. Fletcher collaborated with Shakespeare to write *Henry VIII* (1613) *The Two Noble Kinsmen* (1612) and *The History of Cardenio* (1612). The two writers probably first met at the Mermaid Tavern *(see p56)*, where they would also have made the acquaintance of Francis Beaumont. Together, Beaumont and Fletcher wrote the comedy *The Knight of the Burning Pestle* (1607). They collaborated on subsequent works, including *The Maid's Tragedy* (1610), a tale of murder and betrayal, and *A King and No King* (1611), a black comedy involving mistaken identities and incest. Beaumont and Fletcher, who was buried in the church in 1640, were more popular than Shakespeare with Restoration audiences.

Hard as a Pearl, and the Grit that Lies Inside It • Lant Street

In the 19th century, Southwark was a place of industry and trade, the area's warehouses and factories standing tall above dark roads and alleys that lay inland from the river. One such road was Lant Street, where Dickens lodged as a boy while his father resided nearby in Marshalsea prison.

Sarah Waters recreates something of that Dickensian world in her historical novel *Fingersmith* (2002). Lant Street of the 1860s provides the location of Mr Ibbs's locksmith's shop through which stolen goods, or 'poke', are brought in through the front door and leave via the dark passage at the back, having been altered beyond recognition in the kitchen. This is the domain of Mrs Sucksby, the baby farmer whose patient, dark heart is at the centre of the web of treachery within which the orphan Susan Trinder is unwittingly caught: 'there was not much that was brought to our house that was not moved out of it again, rather sharpish. There was only one thing, in fact, that had come and got stuck – one thing that had somehow withstood the tremendous pull of that passage of poke – one thing that Mr Ibbs and Mrs Sucksby seemed never to think to put a price to … I mean of course, Me.'

Monstrous City, Endless Night • 178 Stamford Street

In March 1874 the French poet Rimbaud came to London for a third time *(see pp123 & 263)*, on this occasion accompanied not by Verlaine, who was in prison (reading the copy of *Une Saison en Enfer* that Rimbaud had sent him), but by the young French poet Germain Nouveau.

The pair stayed at No. 178 Stamford Street (now demolished) – possibly in the basement if these lines from *Illuminations* are any guide: 'At an enormous distance above my subterranean living-room the houses take root, the mists assemble. The mud is red or black. Monstrous city, endless night!'

They also travelled on the world's first underground railway, alluded to in the title and imagery of the prose poem 'Metropolitain': 'fleeing in a straight line, with the sheets of fog spread out in hideous layers in the sky that curves backwards and falls away, formed of the most forbidding black smoke that the Ocean in mourning can produce.'

South Bank Centre

The National Theatre moved here in 1976, producing, under the successive direction of Sir Peter Hall, Sir Richard Eyre and Trevor Nunn, a mixture of world drama, musicals and new writing by, among many others, David Hare, Alan Bennett and Tom Stoppard.

As well as a performance space, the neighbouring Royal Festival Hall is also home to the National Poetry Library, a resource centre and venue for poetry readings. Between the National Theatre and the Royal Festival Hall, second-hand book traders set up stalls under the arch of Waterloo Bridge. It's a good place to search for London-based reference works and fiction, as well as old prints.

The National Theatre

Old Vic • The Cut

Eternity's a terrible thought. I mean, where's it all going to end?
Rosencrantz and Guildenstern Are Dead, Tom Stoppard

The Old Vic Theatre, at the Cut and Waterloo Road, opened in 1818 as the Royal Coburg; by the 1920s it had become London's leading Shakespearean theatre, and in 1929 John Gielgud became Artistic Director. In 1963, under Laurence Olivier, it became the first home of the National Theatre.

Rosencrantz and Guildenstern Are Dead by Tom Stoppard was given its first professional production here on 11 April 1967. The play places the two courtiers from *Hamlet* at the centre of a drama in which they appear as bewildered witnesses and victims. Beneath the verbal wit and Shakespearean parody there is a sense of man's solitude and lack of control over his own destiny. The play was an overnight success and catapulted Stoppard to fame. His subsequent plays include *Jumpers* (1972), *Travesties* (1974), *Every Good Boy Deserves Favour* (1977), *Hapgood* (1988) and *Arcadia* (1993). Stoppard has also written numerous screenplays, including an adaptation of *Rosencrantz* for the screen; in 1999 (with co-author Marc Norman), he won the Best Screenplay Oscar for *Shakespeare in Love* (1998).

John Calder Bookshop

You must go on, I can't go on. I'll go on
John Calder Bookshop & Bookshop Theatre, 51 The Cut

Born in 1927, John Calder began publishing in 1953 and is the English publisher of Samuel Beckett and other modernist writers and dramatists. He published, with Marion Boyars, most of Beckett's fiction, including the Trilogy (*Molloy, Malone Dies, The Unnamable*, 1951–53) and remained a close friend of Beckett until the latter's death in Paris in 1989.

In 1960 Calder was responsible for introducing the Nouveau Roman to Britain by organising a national reading tour for Marguerite Duras, Nathalie Sarraute and Alain Robbe-Grillet. Calder and Boyars also published Henry Miller's landmark novel *Tropic of Cancer* (1963) and novels by William Burroughs, including *The Naked Lunch* and *The Soft Machine*. The room at the back of the shop is used for literary events.

Songs of Experience • 13 Hercules Buildings (Now Blake House), Hercules Road

In the autumn of 1790 Catherine and William Blake moved from Soho to the three-storey house that stood on this site. This gave Blake greater space for his work and, at the time, an uninterrupted view to the river.

The following years were the most creative of Blake's life. Here he worked to perfect his method of relief etching, or illuminated printing, in which he aimed to combine 'the Painter and the Poet' in the manner of earlier illuminated manuscripts. The resulting works, which he wrote, designed, etched, printed and coloured during the ten years he lived in Lambeth, included *The Marriage of Heaven and Hell* (1790), *Visions of the Daughters of Albion* (1793) and the combined *Songs of Innocence and Experience* (1794).

Hercules Road and Blake House, the red brick building on the left

The poems in *Songs of Experience* are a striking indictment of the loss of childhood innocence. They concern childhood oppression, as in 'Nurses Song' and 'The Chimney Sweeper'; the slave trade, in 'The Little Black Boy'; moral oppression, as in 'The Garden of Love' and 'A Little Girl Lost'; social injustice, in 'London'; and child prostitution in 'The Little Vagabond'.

At this time he also wrote and printed the series of 'prophetic books', including *America: A Prophecy* (1793), *The Book of Urizen* (1794), and *The Book of Los* (1795). In these works he combined poetry, exhortation and the language of the visionary in dramatising the struggle between freedom – of the soul and of the imagination – and the constraints of industrialisation and organised religion.

In 1795, having created a stock of illuminated books (very few of which he managed to sell) Blake turned his attentions to the somewhat less arduous task of illustration and printmaking. He produced a series of large colour-print drawings, such as 'Nebuchadnezzar', and 'The Night of Enitharmon's Joy', as well as illustrations for volumes of Edward Young's *Night Thoughts*, and Thomas Gray's *Poems*.

In 1800 the wealthy poet and patron William Hayley persuaded the Blakes to move to Felpham in Sussex. Hercules Buildings, where the Blakes had lived, was demolished in 1920 and replaced by Blake House, part of the William Blake Estate.

After three years in Felpham, Blake returned to London, to a house in South Molton Street *(see p187)*.

COVENT GARDEN

COVENT GARDEN BEGAN LIFE as Westminster Abbey's 13th-century walled garden – the Convent Garden. The land was granted to the Duke of Somerset by Henry VIII after the dissolution of the monasteries and was acquired by John Russell, 1st Earl of Bedford, in 1552. The Russell family developed the fruit, flower and vegetable market and hired Inigo Jones to design the Palladian piazza and build houses 'fit for gentlemen and men of ability' in 1631.

The growth of the market from the 1670s made it less attractive as a residential location and the area became fashionable as a centre for theatre, opera, lodging houses, brothels and coffee houses. London's first coffee house – Pasqua Rosee's Head in the City *(see p67)* – was opened in 1652. An instant success, it was copied throughout the city.

Coffee houses became a central part of London's social life, and between the late 17th century and the late 18th century they served as the cultural stage for wits such as John Dryden, Alexander Pope, Jonathan Swift, David Garrick and Richard Brinsley Sheridan to hold court, pontificating, discussing, arguing and gossiping about the politics, opinions and literature of the day. Coffee houses came alive in the evening and stayed open until the early hours. Most functioned as reading rooms and included the cost of newspapers and periodicals in their charge for admission.

At the same time that the coffee houses blossomed, Covent Garden also became the epicentre of London's theatrical life. Prior to the Civil War, Southwark had been the home of London's theatres, but under the Puritanical regime that accompanied Cromwell's leadership of the country, the performance of plays was banned and theatres torn down.

After the Restoration in 1660, drama was legitimised again, and the first new productions took place in Covent Garden, first using the courts of Lincoln's Inn and then in purpose-buillt theatres in and around Drury Lane. The area's dramatic tradition continues to the present day, and there are currently around twenty-three theatres in the vicinity.

The western border of Covent Garden was known for its bookshops. While the plethora of bookshops along Charing Cross Road has ebbed in recent years, a resolute group hangs on, both on Charing Cross Road itself and on Cecil Court.

Covent Garden

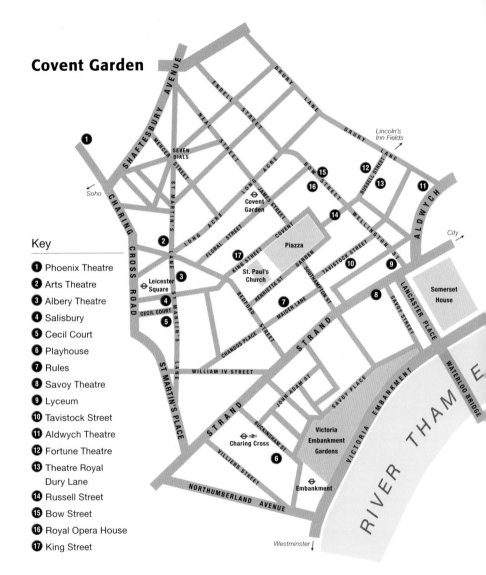

Key

1. Phoenix Theatre
2. Arts Theatre
3. Albery Theatre
4. Salisbury
5. Cecil Court
6. Playhouse
7. Rules
8. Savoy Theatre
9. Lyceum
10. Tavistock Street
11. Aldwych Theatre
12. Fortune Theatre
13. Theatre Royal Dury Lane
14. Russell Street
15. Bow Street
16. Royal Opera House
17. King Street

COFFEE HOUSES

Lying snug at Will's • 20 Russell Street [cat 3 subhead]

William Unwin's, known as Will's, at 20 Russell Street, became the meeting place of dramatist John Dryden and his circle from 1671 to 1701. Songs, epigrams and satires circulated from table to table. The wits (as they became known) judged plays, discussed sonnets and ruminated on the merits of blank verse – that was the big question in 1668: to rhyme or not to rhyme.

Among Will's literary coterie were playwrights William Wycherley, William Congreve, Thomas Otway, Samuel Butler and Aphra Behn (one of the first female dramatists of the era), as well as the diarist Samuel Pepys. Dryden was the centre of attention, however, and had a reserved seat. He wrote exclusively for Thomas Killigrew's King's Company at the Theatre Royal Drury Lane and was published by Jacob Tonson. His verse found a ready market, especially his political satire *Absalom and Achitophel* (1681), and he was kept busy by an eager publisher. He edited *Tonson's Miscellanies* from 1684 until his death in 1700. The *Miscellanies* continued to be published until 1709 and featured work by Alexander Pope and Jonathan Swift.

Multiple affairs, disguise, duelling, brawling and violent acts of revenge were commonplace. Aphra Behn's bisexual lover, the lawyer John Hoyle, was murdered in a brawl in May 1692 following an amorous scandal. And on the night of 18 December 1679, as he left Will's to walk back to his home in Gerrard Street *(see p102)*, Dryden was mugged by a masked gang outside the Lamb and Flag tavern in Rose Alley (now 33 Rose Street). His attackers were paid by John Wilmot, the Earl of Rochester, who had surmised (wrongly) that Dryden was behind the anonymous 'Essay on Satire' in which Rochester and his French mistress, the Duchess of Portsmouth, were ridiculed. In fact it had been written by the Earl of Mulgrave, who later paid for Dryden's monument at Westminster Abbey *(see p11)*.

A beautiful woman named Moira was an additional attraction at Will's – until, that is, she found a different haunt. As John Gay (creator of *The Beggar's Opera*) wrote to William Congreve in 1715:

> *There is a grand revolution at Will's. Moira has quitted for a coffee house in the City; and Titcomb is restored, to the great joy of Cromwell, who was at a great loss for a person to converse with upon the Fathers and church history.*

The literary credentials of Will's were attested by Jonathan Swift, who in *On Poetry: A Rhapsody*, urged young poets to publish a poem and then go to Will's to 'lie snug and hear what the Critiks say.'

Button's

After Dryden's death the wits, led by essayist Joseph Addison, decamped for Button's at No.10 Russell Street. Addison and his cohort Richard Steele promoted Button's through their periodical *The Guardian* and erected a letter-box at the coffee house in which contributions for the journal could be left.

Alexander Pope, John Gay and Swift were regulars at Button's, and became frequent contributors to *The Guardian*. The distribution of periodicals throughout the coffee houses helped to create a forum for literature and the arts.

Tom's, at 17 Russell Street, was frequented more by aristocrats and the theatrical profession, led by actors Charles Macklin and David Garrick. In 1714 seven hundred aristocrats and gentry subscribed at a guinea a head for the building of a card room, which was completed in 1718.

In a letter of 1726 (later collected in *A Foreign View of England in the Reigns of George I and George II*), César de Saussure wrote that some coffee houses were the resort of learned scholars and wits but that others were 'temples of Venus where you are waited on by amiable and dangerous nymphs.' In short, several coffee houses were fronts for brothels.

Bedford

From the 1730s the Bedford Coffee House attracted a strong following from theatregoers and was the meeting place for actors and dramatists. It is mentioned in Tobias Smollett's first novel *The Adventures of Roderick Random* (1748) as a central meeting place. By the 1750s, the Bedford, at 10–11 Great Piazza, had become the new 'emporium of wit, seat of criticism and standard of taste.' Frequented by Henry and John Fielding, William Hogarth, Charles Churchill, Oliver Goldsmith, David Garrick and Laurence Sterne, the Bedford would, no doubt, have echoed with jokes and discussion of literature.

Henry Fielding (who edited the *Covent Garden Journal*), playwright Oliver Goldsmith and painter William Hogarth were members of a gaming club that met in the Bedford's parlour. In 1744 Fielding received a report that the great number of brothels and taverns in Covent Garden was the cause of increased robberies. The gin craze was at its height. One

The Lamb & Flag, Rose Street

tavern in Bow Street advertised that 'here you may get drunk for a penny, dead drunk for twopence and get straw for nothing.' Fielding organised freelance 'thief-takers', who became known as the Bow Street Runners in 1754. This organisation was succeeded by Robert Peel's police force that subsequently evolved to become the Metropolitan Police.

Charles Churchill was another prominent member of the Bedford circle. He was a satirist, critical of Smollett, Dr Johnson and Hogarth, and wrote 'Night' (1761) in praise of drinking and talking late into the night at coffee houses. He also wrote 'The Rosciad' (1761), a poetic criticism of contemporary actors, contrasting the old artificial and new emotional acting styles. Garrick was one of the very few actors he praised. For Churchill the theatre was a public space open to all, and the rightful place for criticism.

The stage I choose – a subject fair and free,
'Tis yours - 'tis mine – 'tis public property
All common exhibitions be,
For praise or censure to the common eye.

Laurence Sterne regularly visited London after publication of the first two volumes of *The Life and Times of Tristram Shandy* in 1760, enthusiastically embracing coffee-house life at the Bedford, where the opportunities for drinking and womanising were significantly greater than at his Yorkshire vicarage.

Sterne died in his London home at No. 41 Old Bond Street *(see p186)* aged 54, just a month after celebrating the publication of *A Sentimental Journey through France and Italy*, his account of European travels he had made in 1765 in an effort to defeat the tuberculosis that plagued his later years.

Tristram Shandy, Sterne's bawdy and innovative masterpiece, completed in 1767, thoroughly defied convention by employing a seemingly chaotic structure of partial character sketches, blank pages, transposed chapters and digressions based on the association of ideas. It enlarged the scope of the novel from the recording of external incidents to the depiction of internal impressions, thoughts and feelings. Its delight in the disorder of things has inspired writers such as Richard Brinsley Sheridan, James Joyce, Samuel Beckett and B.S. Johnson.

Richard Brinsley Sheridan held court with his friends at the Piazza from 1775. It served as a meeting place for members of the Beefsteak Club, Literary Club and the hangers-on of the Devonshire House circle of Georgiana, Duchess of Devonshire, an influential hostess and important figure in the Whig party. Later, in the 1830s, it became the home of the Shakespeare Club, whose members included Charles Dickens, actor William Charles Macready and historian John Forster. The club met every Saturday evening to discuss the state of London's periodicals and literary standards. The Bedford survived until 1858.

Cock Tavern • Bow Street

In June 1663 three Court poets, Sir Charles Sedley, Sir Thomas Ogle and Sir Charles Sackville, later Lord Brockhurst, caused a riot by stripping naked and blaspheming from the balcony of the Cock Tavern. Fined, imprisoned for a week and bound over to the keep the peace for three years, they nevertheless continued to get drunk at Oxford Kate's. In 1668 Pepys records them running naked through Covent Garden, fighting and getting locked up for the night. Sedley's verse commemorated his all-night drinking and wenching:

Café Valerie, No 8
Russell Street

Yet we will have store of good Wenches,
Though we venture fluxing for't,
Upon Couches, Chairs, and Benches,
To out-do them at the Sport.

Boswell Meets Johnson • 8 Russell Street

During his first stay in London (1762–63), James Boswell visited Thomas Davies's bookshop several times. On Christmas Day he met the author and publisher Robert Dodsley and poet Oliver Goldsmith. Drinking tea with Davies on 16 May 1763, he fulfilled one of his early ambitions when …

about seven came in the great Mr Samuel Johnson, whom I have so long wished to see. Mr Davies introduced me to him. As I knew his mortal antipathy at the Scotch, I cried to Davies, "Don't tell where I come from." However, he said, "From Scotland." "Mr Johnson," said I, "indeed I come from Scotland, but I cannot help it." "Sir," replied he, "that, I find, is what a very great many of your country-men cannot help." Mr Johnson is a man of a most dreadful appearance. He is a very big man, is troubled with sore eyes, the palsy, and the king's evil. He is very slovenly in his dress and speaks with a most uncouth voice. Yet his great knowledge and strength of expression command vast respect and render him very excellent company … I shall mark what I remember of his conversation.

So begins one of the greatest friendships in English literature between the young Scot, Boswell, and Samuel Johnson, 30 years his senior and eminent author of the acclaimed *Dictionary* (1755).

Russell Street's cafés today

Leaving London later that year, Boswell toured Europe, meeting Voltaire, Rousseau and, through him, the Corsican rebel Pasquale Paoli. On returning, Boswell published his *Account of Corsica* (1768), a combination of diary and description, which made his name: 'I had got upon a rock in Corsica and jumped into the middle of life'.

Boswell fitfully attempted to develop a legal career at the Scottish bar, but took every opportunity to return to London and the stimulating company of Johnson and other members of The Club, such as Burke, Garrick, Reynolds and Goldsmith, all the while filling his notebooks with material for his planned biography of Johnson.

In 1773 Boswell persuaded the elderly, and supposedly anti-Scottish, Johnson to join him on a tour of Scotland. This formed the basis of Johnson's *Journey to the Western Islands of Scotland* (1774) and Boswell's *Journal of a Tour to the Hebrides* (1785). Boswell used his account as a trial run for the techniques he would later employ in the *Life of Samuel Johnson* (1791), in which the subject is vividly portrayed scene by scene, in great detail, with word-for-word recording of conversations and a high degree of frankness.

Not all readers, however, were prepared for such forthrightness. The first edition of the *Tour* was quickly followed by a second, in which certain passages were excised, but too late to prevent Boswell from gaining a reputation for indiscretion – a charge that would be levelled by some at his *Life*.

Sunday Night. No Hope of Me! • 10, later 43 King Street

Samuel Taylor Coleridge lodged here at Hudson's Hotel in November 1801, seeing William Godwin, Charles Lamb and Humphrey Davy, and again in October and November 1810, having been rejected by Wordsworth as 'an absolute nuisance'. He took to wandering the streets and sitting up late into the night smoking opium and writing the poem 'The Visionary Hope'. His friend, John Morgan, rescued him and took him to his home *(see p250)*.

Confessions of an Opium Eater

Thomas De Quincey lived at 4 York Place (which later became 36 Tavistock Street) in 1821–22. Here he wrote *Confessions of an English Opium-Eater*. This study of opium addiction and its psychological effects was first published in *London Magazine* in September 1821. It traces how childhood and youthful experiences – such as those on the streets of Soho *(see p105)* – are transformed, under the influence of opium, into symbolic dreams. De Quincey's fascination with opium, German philosophy and psychological criticism stemmed from his involvement with Coleridge and his circle during the previous decade.

Lincoln's Inn

Oldest of the four Inns of Court, with its *Black Books* (the records of the inn) dating from 1422, Lincoln's Inn lies south of High Holborn, north of the Temple and west of Chancery Lane, its green square and old buildings having a collegiate atmosphere.

Sir Thomas More, who joined the Inn in 1496, becoming a bencher and inn governor, lived most of his professional life in the medieval hall, the oldest building in the area. The membership also included writers such as Horace Walpole, Charles Kingsley, Wilkie Collins and John Galsworthy. Poet John Donne, who had been the preacher here from 1616 to 1622, dedicated the chapel in 1623.

Behind Lincoln's Inn Fields lies the 'Old Curiosity Shop', at No. 13 Portsmouth Street, a legacy from the Dickens novel of that name. The wonderful Sir John Soane's Museum is located at No. 13 Lincoln's Inn Fields and contains the original paintings of Hogarth's *The Rake's Progress* and *The Election*.

Lincoln's Inn also has an important association with the rebirth of theatre in Restoration London, resulting in what has come to be known as …

THEATRELAND

After the Restoration in 1660, theatre returned to London when Charles II licensed two theatres: the King's Company and The Duke's Company, the latter named in honour of his brother (James II). The King's Company was under Killigrew, first at Vere's Tennis Court in Lincoln's Inn and from 1663 at Bridges Street, Drury Lane. The Duke's Company, under Sir William D'Avenant, opened in Portugal Street, Lincoln's Inn Fields. D'Avenant, who was not averse to referring to himself as Shakespeare's son, died in 1668 and the company was handed over to actors Henry Harris and Thomas Betterton (who gives his name to Betterton Street, home of the Poetry Café – www.poetrysociety.org.uk). The King's and Duke's companies merged in 1682.

The wits, poets and fashionable socialites enjoyed the theatre as a social event – a place to see and be seen. During this period, the theatre was a rowdy place of entertainment and the audiences were a good social mix, though divided by the structure of the theatre, from the pit, through the galleries to the boxes. Aristocrats and other privileged members of the audience would sit in seats on the stage, as they had done in Elizabethan times. Pepys was an avid theatregoer, and his *Diary* relates much about life in the theatre. At the theatre, he could join the King's mistress, Lady Castlemaine, and other Court ladies, and his *Diary* records a performance of *Macbeth* played before the king and Court. He was not a fan of Shakespeare, however, much preferring Ben Jonson and the later Restoration comedies.

After the puritanical regime of the Commonwealth, the Restoration was a period of great liberty and creativity, providing opportunities for women to make their theatrical mark. The first English actress of the period appeared on stage on 8 December 1660, playing Desdemona in the King's Company's production of *Othello*. Pepys saw actresses for the first time on 3 January 1661 in a play called *Beggars Bush* and thought the performance 'very well done'.

Women dramatists, such as Margaret Cavendish and Aphra Behn, had their plays performed too. The most successful was Behn, a poet who had been a spy in Antwerp during the Dutch War. Imprisoned for debt, she became a prolific writer. Her second stage play, *The Amorous Prince* (1671) a tragic sex comedy, was a great success.

The Restoration playwrights pioneered a sexual and moral revolution through their comedies. George Etherege, William Wycherley, William Congreve, Aphra Behn and others continually attacked arranged and inappropriate marriages and advocated sexual freedom. In Congreve's *The Way of the World*, for example, witty lovers reach their own marital agreement based on their knowledge of the ways of a world dominated by fops, fools and intrigue. And in Behn's *The Forc'd Marriage* (1669) the focus is on, and sympathy with, those who love against parental wishes and outside their own social class. Her *Feign'd Courtisans* (1679), dedicated to actress Nell Gwyn, celebrated the transgressive lives of actresses.

Gwyn, illiterate but intelligent, used her wit and charm to rise from being an orange seller at Drury Lane to become one of the most popular comic actresses and singers of her time – as well as the King's mistress. When an Oxford mob mistook her coach for the Duchess of Portsmouth Louise de Kéroualle (Charles's unpopular French Catholic mistress), Nell famously called out, 'Pray, good people, be civil; I am the *Protestant* whore.' Nell Gwyn is remembered by two Covent Garden pubs – The Nell of Old Drury (29 Catherine Street) and the Nell Gwynne Tavern in Bull in Court, between the Strand and Maiden Lane.

After 1700 sentimental comedy and Italian operas replaced Restoration comedy. Jonathan Swift was keen to discredit this soft-edged entertainment and encouraged John Gay to write a riposte to Italian opera. The result, *The Beggar's Opera* (1728), with its popular tunes, witty text and political, social and cultural satire, was a new theatrical genre. It proved an unparalleled success, and ran for sixty consecutive performances (a record for its day).

The Beggar's Opera used contemporary low-life characters, such as a highwayman, thieves, prostitutes and corrupt managers, but placed them in 'high-life' situations. Gay also shocked his audience by taking an erotic or sleazy contemporary tune and giving it sweet lyrics. The sequel, *Polly* (1729), was banned by the Lord Chamberlain, Horace Walpole (the office of Lord Chamberlain assessed all plays for public suitability up until the 1960s). However, the play sold well on its publication. Gay went on to write the librettos for two of Handel's operas before his death in 1732.

The Cockpit and Phoenix Theatres • Drury Lane
The first theatre in Drury Lane, near the site of the Theatre Royal, was the Cockpit, originally a venue for cockfighting from 1609 and converted into an indoor playhouse in 1616. It was destroyed by Puritan rioters in 1617 and rebuilt in 1618 and renamed the Phoenix. The Queen's Servants Company played here, performing Marlowe's *The Jew of Malta*, Heywood's *Woman Killed With Kindness*, Rowley, Dekker and Ford's *The Witch of Edmonton*, Webster's *White Devil* and Massinger's *New Ways To Pay Old Debts*. In 1642 an act of parliament led to the closure of all theatres, but when the act was rescinded in 1660 the theatre reopened and reverted to its original name, The Cockpit. Here on 11 October 1660 Pepys saw the *Merchant [Moor] of Venice* performed.

Theatre Royal Drury Lane

This is Covent Garden's oldest surviving theatre. The first theatre on this site was established just off Drury Lane, on Bridges Street, in 1663. It was home to the King's Company, who had moved here from Lincoln's Inn. The Bridges Street theatre revived plays by Ben Jonson, and Beaumont and Fletcher, and commissioned new work by Dryden, Otway and Lee, and the comedies of Wycherley, Congreve and architect-playwright John Vanbrugh.

The theatre was destroyed by fire in 1672 and rebuilt by Wren with an enlarged capacity, reopening as the Theatre Royal in 1674. Its first big success was Wycherley's *The Country Wife* (1675), which contrasts town ladies (the Fidgets and Squeamishes), to whom outward form is all, and the country wife, simple and forthright. The play is shot through with double-entendres and duplicity, and may owe something to activities in the playwright's own life. Wycherley was overly fond of Will's coffee house and the Cock Tavern *(see above)*, much to the chagrin of his wife – as too his affair with Lady Castlemaigne. The play was tremendously popular and elevated Wycherley into Court circles. However, when his wife, the Countess of Drogheda, died, Wycherley fell into debt and spent seven years in Fleet Prison.

Theatre Royal Drury Lane

From 1747 to 1777 the theatre's company was run successfully by actor David Garrick. He raised the status of actors by moving the audience off stage and established an extensive repertoire based on the works of Shakespeare. With his exaggerated facial expressions and bodily movements, Garrick excelled in low and high comedy and tragedy. By contrast, his contemporary Charles Macklin pioneered the movement from declarative to naturalistic acting. His revolutionary portrayal of Shylock in *The Merchant of Venice* showed him as a tragic rather than comic character, prompting Pope to write 'This is the Jew / That Shakespeare drew'. Notable actresses in this period included Hannah Pritchard, Peg Woffington (Garrick's lover) and Kitty Clive (the lover of Horace Walpole).

Richard Brinsley Sheridan, whose comedy *The Rivals* had enjoyed enormous success at Covent Garden in 1775, took over as owner-manager from Garrick in 1776. Sheridan presented his play *The School for Scandal* on 8 May 1777. Georgiana, Duchess of Devonshire (who partly inspired the Lady Teazle character), and the

Devonshire House circle of Whig politicians, fashionable ladies, libertines and wits arrived en masse for the opening night, ensuring the play received great publicity. Sheridan wrote one more farce, *The Critic or A Tragedy Rehearsed* (1779) before entering politics *(see p17)*. *The Critic* revealed the inner workings of the theatrical business, hilariously confusing the real and the illusory. At the height of his powers, Sheridan was an irrepressible figure, held in rhapsodic regard by Byron and Hazlitt, both leading critics in their day. The growing popularity, and cultural and political importance of the theatre gave playwrights and actors increased importance. Ultimately, Sheridan became part of the society he had formerly satirised, all too often drinking and womanising rather than writing.

Sheridan was in the House of Commons on the evening of 24 February 1809 when news came that the Theatre Royal was on fire. The blaze was enormous, illuminating the river and Westminster and by midnight was said to have been visible as far away as Fulham. Sheridan calmly nursed a drink as he watched the spectacle of his financial ruin. Questioned regarding his composure in the face of disaster, he replied 'A man may surely be allowed to take a glass of wine by his own fireside.'

Funds to finance the rebuilding of the theatre, with increased capacity and soft seating, were raised by Samuel Whitbread and Lord Byron. Byron wrote the 'Address' for the theatre's reopening on 10 October 1812 in honour of his friend Sheridan:

> *Far be that hour that vainly asks in turn*
> *Such verse for him as crown'd his o'er Garrick's urn.*

The growing popularity and cultural importance of the theatre gave its actors increased status and celebrity. For Hazlitt, Sarah Siddons was 'tragedy personified'. Gainsborough and Reynolds both painted Siddons, Reynolds portraying her as *The Tragic Muse*.

In the late 19th century, pantomime and music hall artist Dan Leno (featured in Peter Ackroyd's novel set in 1880, *Dan Leno and the Limehouse Golem*, 1994) was a popular performer at the theatre until he was up-staged by Henry Irving and Ellen Terry's popularity at the Lyceum Theatre.

During the Second World War it was the home of the Entertainments National Service Association (ENSA). Among the actor-writers involved with ENSA were David Gascoyne, Joyce Grenfell and Spike Milligan. In recent years it has staged American musical comedies such as *Mame* (1969) and *Miss Saigon* (1989).

Beef and Liberty • Theatre Royal Covent Garden and the Beefsteak Club

Actor-manager John Rich's success with *The Beggar's Opera (see above)* provided the capital to buy the first Theatre Royal Covent Garden (now the Royal Opera House), in Bow Street. It opened on 7 December 1732, under the patent of the

Duke's Company, with Congreve's *The Way of the World*. It was here in 1735 that John Rich founded the 'sublime society of the Beef Steaks', a club of prominent actors, managers, writers and others that met weekly at the theatre to drink red wine and eat beefsteak. Members included Hogarth, Dr Johnson, Thomas Sheridan, Garrick and the beautiful and mesmeric actress Peg Woffington – for many years the only female member of the Beefsteak Club. Woffington's attachment to Garrick was the most publicised of her numerous affairs. From 1742 to 1744 she and Garrick shared a house with actor Charles Macklin and his wife at No. 6 Bow Street.

With its motto of 'Beef and Liberty', the club continued meeting despite fires at Covent Garden in 1808 and 1858, moving to the Bedford coffee house during the years 1830–38, and to actor Henry Irving's home (15a Grafton Street) in the 1890s. Its members included Oscar Wilde, Bram Stoker, Whistler and the Prince of Wales.

The Theatre Royal Covent Garden pioneered the use of limelight, a new calcium light that revolutionised stage lighting; it was introduced here in 1837. The theatre burned down once again on 3 March 1856, and this time was rebuilt in a Romanesque style by E.M. Barry, son of the House of Commons' architect Charles Barry. The theatre reopened as the Royal Opera House Covent Garden on 15 May 1858. At the end of the 20th century the Opera House underwent a major refurbishment, overseen by the architect Jeremy Dixon.

Albery Theatre • St Martin's Lane

The Albery Theatre (renamed after impresario Sir Bronson Albery in 1973) began as the New Theatre in 1903. It was here that John Gielgud's *Hamlet* ran for 155 nights in 1934. During the 1940s it was home to the Old Vic and Sadler's Wells companies, which had been bombed out of their homes. Ralph Richardson made his name playing the title roles in *Peer Gynt* (1944) and *Uncle Vanya* (1946).

The theatre has produced a wide variety of works from Somerset Maugham's *The Constant Wife*, through A.A. Milne, Noel Coward, George Bernard Shaw, Dylan Thomas, T. S. Eliot and Tennessee Williams to Willy Russell's musical *Blood Brothers* (1989). Between 1960 and 1967 there were more than 2000 performances of Lionel Bart's musical *Oliver!* at the Albery.

Lyceum Theatre • 71 Wellington Street

When Jane Austen stayed at the flat above her brother's bank at No. 10 Henrietta Street in the summer of 1813 and in March 1814 she regularly attended both the Lyceum and Drury Lane theatres. Henry Irving made his name in *Hamlet* at the Lyceum in the 1870s. In 1878 he took control of the theatre, with Ellen Terry as his leading lady, and drama critic and novelist Bram Stoker as manager. They produced Shakespeare's plays to capacity audiences and critical acclaim. Subsequently the

Lyceum became a music hall and, latterly, a rock concert venue. Most notably, Bob Marley and The Wailers released 'Live at the Lyceum', recorded at the venue on 18 July 1975. The Lyceum has recently been refurbished for staging popular musicals.

Savoy Theatre
Built by Richard D'Oyly Carte for the performance of Gilbert and Sullivan operettas, the Savoy was the first theatre in the country to use electric lighting. *Iolanthe* (1882), *Princess Ida* (1884) and *The Mikado* (1885) are among their works that premiered here. The theatre was redesigned in 1929, creating a wonderful Art Deco interior. Several plays by Shaw were performed in the new theatre, including *The Devil's Disciple*. The theatre now mixes drama and opera. The nearby Queen's Chapel of the Savoy has a D'Oyly Carte memorial window.

Aldwych Theatre
Built in 1905 for actor-manager-dramatist, Seymour Hicks, the Aldwych presented Anton Chekhov's *The Cherry Orchard* (1904) to a largely confused audience, many of whom walked out, in 1909. The Royal Shakespeare Company successfully revived the play in 1961 and 1989 with Dame Judi Dench starring. Between the wars the theatre was known largely for the 'Aldwych farces', such as Ben Travers' *A Cuckoo in the Nest* (1925) and *Rookery Nook* (1926). In 1949 it staged the London premiere of Tennessee Williams's *A Streetcar Named Desire* (1947) with Vivien Leigh as an acclaimed Blanche Dubois.

Fortune Theatre
Standing on the site of the Albion Tavern, a literary haunt of the 19th century, the small Fortune Theatre was built after the First World War. The ground-breaking revue *Beyond the Fringe*, written and performed by Alan Bennett, Jonathan Miller, Peter Cook and Dudley Moore, made its London debut here on 10 May 1961.

Playhouse
Under the arches of Charing Cross Station, the Playhouse is now principally associated with the radio shows that were recorded here in the 1950s, including *Hancock's Half Hour* and *The Goon Show*. In its early life, however, it staged premieres of George Bernard Shaw's *Arms and the Man* (1894) and two plays by Somerset Maugham, *A Man of Honour* (1903) and *Home and Beauty* (1919).

Fortune Theatre

The Phoenix Theatre, Charing Cross Road

The Phoenix opened in 1930, premiering Noël Coward's *Private Lives*. In a cast that included Coward was the young Laurence Olivier. The theatre has witnessed several significant premieres since, including Terence Rattigan's *The Browning Version* in 1948 and Tom Stoppard's *Night and Day* in 1978, as well as the first British stagings of Arthur Miller's *Death of a Salesman* (1949) and Stephen Sondheim's *Into the Woods* (1990). A musical adaptation of *The Canterbury Tales* proved surprisingly successful in 1968 and ran for 2,000 performances.

Arts Theatre

Built in 1927, the Arts Theatre had its creative heyday in the 1950s and early 60s. Peter Hall directed the English-language premiere of Beckett's *Waiting for Godot* here in 1955. It was Hall's invention to characterise the protagonists, Estragon and Vladimir, as vagabonds rather than clowns – a feature that has stuck ever since. Five years later, in 1960, the theatre also saw the premiere of Pinter's *The Caretaker*.

CLUBS, RESTAURANTS AND BOOKSHOPS

The Garrick Club Affair • 35 King Street

The original site of the Garrick Club was at No. 35 King Street, the location of the famous argument between William Makepeace Thackeray and Charles Dickens over a letter written by Thackeray on 14 June 1858 to journalist Edmund Yates. Yates had come to Dickens's defence, with a few lines in a weekly magazine, after damaging rumours had escalated in the club about Dickens's marital difficulties and liaison with Ellen Ternan *(see p123)*. The dispute went on for weeks with the older, aristocratic members broadly for Thackeray, who was close to Catherine Dickens, and the younger, more bohemian members, for Dickens and Yates. Yates was eventually forced to resign and Dickens did not speak to Thackeray until the final year of Thackeray's life. As an act of reconciliation, the two authors shook hands at the Athenaeum Club in May 1863; Thackeray died on Christmas eve of the same year.

Rules Restaurant • 35 Maiden Lane

Rules has rooms named after Charles Dickens, Graham Greene and Sir John Betjeman, all of whom had extensive contact with London's oldest restaurant. Actors, who are celebrated in the Green Room, and writers such as Dickens, Thackeray, John Galsworthy and H.G. Wells, have been regulars at Rules. Graham Greene celebrated his birthdays here and featured the restaurant in *The End of The Affair* (1951). John Betjeman described the ground floor as a 'unique and irreplaceable interior'. Rosamund Lehmann, Evelyn Waugh, John Le Carré and Penelope Lively have featured the restaurant in their novels.

The Salisbury • 90 St Martin's Lane

This Victorian pub with Art-Nouveau decoration is a haunt of actors and filmmakers. Novelist H.E. Bates met Graham Greene here for lunch in 1933. Dylan Thomas started drinking here in August 1940 and used it to meet his acting friends, away from the maelstrom of Soho and Fitzrovia. He brought his New York lover Pearl here in September 1950. Laurence Olivier and Vivien Leigh visited in 1949 and Gered Mankowitz famously photographed singer Marianne Faithfull at The Salisbury in 1964.

Bookshops • Charing Cross Road and Cecil Court

Charing Cross Road, once practically lined with bookshops, still hosts the mighty Foyle's at 113–119 Charing Cross Road. Women's bookshop Sister Moon is now a concession within Foyles, as is Ray's Jazz Shop. Blackwell's, at 100 Charing Cross Road, is more or less opposite. Any Amount of Books, at No. 56, remains one of the best second-hand bookshops, but 84 Charing Cross Road – an address made famous by Helene Hanff's story of a literary friendship using the address as its title – is no longer a bookshop. Al Hoda at No. 76–78 Charing Cross Road specialises in Islamic books.

Many rare and antiquarian bookshops can be found in nearby Cecil Court. In Hanif Kureishi's *Buddha of Suburbia*,1990 *(see p329)* Haroon Amir buys books on 'Buddhism, Sufism, Confucianism and Zen' in Cecil Court, and Christopher Petit's *Robinson* (1993) features Cecil Court bookshops.

Charing Cross Road bookshops

SOHO

AS DEFINED BY THE GREAT DRINKER and chronicler Jeffrey Bernard, Soho proper 'was and is enclosed by Oxford Street, Charing Cross Road, Shaftesbury Avenue and Berwick Street Market'. However, the flow of ideas and Soho characters spill across these boundaries, as far west as Broadwick Street and south of Shaftesbury Avenue into what is now Chinatown. Here Joshua Reynolds founded 'The Club' in 1764, and the giants of the Enlightenment would gather on Monday evenings in a pub room at No. 9 Gerrard Street.

'So ho' was originally a cry used in rabbit hunting (the equivalent of 'tally ho' in fox hunting). It first appears as the name of this part of London in the 1630s, when the area was still mainly pastureland and used for hunting. By this time a number of houses had been built here, despite the law passed by Elizabeth I in 1582 forbidding the construction of dwellings within three miles of the City. This was intended to ensure sufficient local food supply and act as a kind of 'cordon sanitaire' against the spread of plague.

In the 1660s Charles II made a grant of land here to his bastard son, James Scott, Duke of Monmouth, who built a mansion, Monmouth House, just south of what is now Soho Square (the house was demolished in 1773). Monmouth used 'So Ho!' as his rallying cry at the Battle of Sedgemoor in 1685 in his abortive attempt to seize the crown from his uncle, the Catholic James II. Routed in the battle and captured as he tried to flee, Monmouth was beheaded on Tower Hill on July 15, 1685.

By around 1700 Soho's cosmopolitan character had begun to be established, with Greeks escaping from the Ottoman controlled Balkans and Huguenots escaping persecution in France.

William Blake was born and spent much of his life in Soho. Other poets came here to find a place of refuge: Shelley after being sent down from Oxford in 1811; Verlaine and Rimbaud in 1872, following the collapse of the Paris Commune. At this time Soho was a hotbed of plotting and intrigue following the arrival of many Communards who had fled after the fall of the Paris Commune.

In the 20th century Soho remained a sanctuary for writers, artists, bohemians, café-philosophers and refugees of all persuasion – whether fleeing tyranny or convention. For some, the intoxicating allure of the place proved the graveyard of their careers. Many others, from Joseph Conrad in *The Secret Agent* to Alan Hollinghurst in *The Swimming Pool Library*, have drawn on the unique characteristics of Soho in their writing.

Soho

Key

1 Gerrard Street
2 Golden Lion
3 The French House
4 Old Compton Street
5 Groucho Club

6 Blake House
7 Poland Street
8 Quo Vadis
9 The Colony Room
10 Frith Street

11 Pillars of Hercules
12 Coach & Horses
13 Kettner's
14 Bar Italia

Dryden's Abode • 43 Gerrard Street

John Dryden, habitué of the coffee shops in neighbouring Covent Garden *(see pp86–9)*, lived in Gerrard Street from 1687 until his death in 1700. Here he wrote 'A Song for St Cecilia's Day' (1687) and 'Alexander's Feast, An Ode in Honour of St Cecilia's Day' (1697), written to be set to music for the 22 November celebrations. In his epistle 'To My Dear Friend, Mr Congreve', printed in the first edition of Congreve's *The Double Dealer* (1694), he defends the young playwright, whose play had been a partial flop, and refers to his own loss of Court positions after the Glorious Revolution in 1689.

43 Club

In the mid-1920s Joseph Conrad and J.B. Priestley were members of the 43 Club (also known as Merrick's) at Dryden's old address, No. 43 Gerrard Street. It became a fashionable jazz nightclub, attracting literati, aristocracy and gangsters until Ma Merrick, the proprietor, lost her licence due to the club's rowdiness.

A Very Clubbable Man • 9 Gerrard Street

A plaque at No. 9 marks the site of the Turk's Head Tavern, where members of The Club met once a week for conversation. The Club was the idea of painter Sir Joshua Reynolds, and he proposed it in part to lift the spirits of his friend Dr Samuel Johnson, by providing him with 'an unlimited opportunity of talking'. The founder members in 1764 included Johnson, the renowned Whig intellectual and orator Edmund Burke, and playwright Oliver Goldsmith. In 1773 Johnson proposed James Boswell (later his biographer) as a member, and that same year the celebrated actor David Garrick was also admitted. Many of the leading intellectuals, politicians and writers of the day became members, including the Whig politician Charles James Fox, the political economist Adam Smith and playwright Richard Brinsley Sheridan.

As it became known that Boswell was keeping a detailed journal, concern grew amongst members that private conversations might be made public. Garrick went so far as to suggest that Boswell be searched and his notebook confiscated – an idea Boswell scorned in his journal: 'Nonsense. As if I had book and wrote in company and could not carry in my head'. After the death of Garrick in 1779, The Club became known as 'The Literary Club'.

Site of Mont Blanc Restaurant • 16 Gerrard Street

In the early 20th century the Mont Blanc was one of very few foreign restaurants in Britain, and became a favourite meeting place for pre-First World War literary circles that included Joseph Conrad, Ford Madox Ford, John Masefield, John Galsworthy and poet Edward Thomas. In 1900 G.K. Chesterton and Hilaire Belloc met for the first time at the Mont Blanc. The two became lifelong friends and together founded *The New Witness*, a weekly political newspaper (dubbed 'the Chesterbelloc' by George Bernard Shaw) in which the two Catholic thinkers propounded 'distributism', a medievalist, anti-capitalist and anti-Fabian socialist philosophy.

Sour Sweet • Gerrard Street

Chinese restaurants and grocery shops now occupy most of Gerrard Street, as since the 1950s it has been the main thoroughfare of London's Chinatown. In Timothy Mo's novel *Sour Sweet* (1982), it is referred to simply as 'Chinese Street'. The novel provides a fascinating insight into the largely hidden world of Chinese immigrants; of those who have been in Britain 'long enough to have lost their place in the society from which they had emigrated but not long enough to feel comfortable in the new'; and of the controlled yet casual violence of the Triad gangs.

The title 'Sour Sweet' also alludes to the taming of Chinese food for the Western palette, hilariously illustrated when the waiter, Chen, confuses orders, taking 'lurid orange sweet-and-sour pork with pineapple chunks to outraged Chinese customers and white, bloody chicken and yellow duck's feet to appalled Westerners.'

Heaven and Hell • 28 Broadwick Street

William Blake was born at 28 Broad Street (now Broadwick Street, site of 'Blake House' tower block) into the chaotic mixture of opulence and destitution that was Soho in the mid-18th century. Blake displayed a wild impetuosity and outspokenness from an early age – so much so that it was decided not to send him to school. Between lessons from his mother, he spent much of his time exploring London, sketching street scenes, composing verse and, like his older brother, occasionally experiencing visions *(see p320)*. At the age of ten Blake took lessons in drawing and copying text at Henry Pars' Academy near Beaufort Buildings in the Strand, and at 14 became an apprentice engraver. He later spent an unhappy year as a student at The Royal Academy, before leaving in 1779 to make his own way as a writer, painter and engraver.

Although he was not politically active in any organised sense, the political turmoil of the period did not pass Blake by and in 1780 he witnessed, all too closely, one of the most violent disorders in London's history. While out walking in Holborn one day, he found himself caught up in the Gordon Riots (the protests against Parliament's decision to remove civil restrictions from Catholics). Blake 'encountered the advancing wave of triumphant blackguardism, and was forced (for from such a great surging mob there is no disentanglement) to go along in the very front rank, and witness the storm and burning of the fortress-like prison, and release of its three hundred inmates'.

Blake married Catherine Boucher, a market gardener's daughter, in 1782, and they lived for the next two years at No. 23 Green Street, Leicester Fields (now Leicester Square). They moved back to Broad Street shortly after the death of Blake's father in 1784, setting up a printing and engraving business at No. 27 Broad Street (next door to his mother and brother). Having moved once again (round the corner to No. 28 Poland Street), Blake was devastated by another death in 1787 – that of his younger brother Robert, to whom he had been devoted. This emotional distress unleashed new creativity, with Blake later ascribing the breakthrough to a vision of Robert whose form 'revealed the wished-for secret … the technical mode by which could be produced a fac-simile of song and design.' He would become a poet-painter-engraver, combining words and images in a unified expression. The way forward to works such as *The Marriage of Heaven and Hell* (c.1790) and *Songs of Innocence and*

Experience (1794) had been found. In 1790, William and Catherine Blake left Soho and moved to the Hercules Buildings in Lambeth *(see p83)*.

Ye are Many – They are Few • 15 Poland Street

Percy Bysshe Shelley lived here briefly in 1811, sharing the house with his friend Thomas Jefferson Hogg. They had both just been expelled from Oxford for failing to deny authorship of the pamphlet 'The Necessity of Atheism', the first of many radical pamphlets Shelley wrote. While living in Poland Street Shelley met and then eloped to Scotland with Harriet Westbrook, the 16-year-old daughter of a retired merchant and Grosvenor Square coffee house keeper. This caused consternation to both families and prompted extended travels around the country by the pair. Back in London in March 1814 they remarried in church so as to legitimise their Scottish union and provide legal protection for the daughter Ianthe, born the previous June.

The relationship, however, did not last, and while encouraging Hogg's feelings towards Harriet, Shelley met and fell in love with another 16-year-old, Mary Godwin *(see p138)*. In July 1814 Shelley and Mary eloped to Switzerland, taking along Mary's step-sister Jane 'Claire' Clairmont. Mary was soon expecting – and so was Harriet. Harriet and Shelley's second child, named Charles, was born on 30 November, but Shelley did not return to Harriet. Harriet was never reconciled to the failure of their marriage, and in the early winter of 1816 drowned herself in the Serpentine. The following year Harriet's parents obtained a decree from the Lord Chancellor stating that Shelley was unfit to have custody of his children.

Mary's child, a daughter, was born on 22 February 1815 but lived only a few days. They had another child, named William, in 1816, and not long after the birth the couple returned to Geneva – again with Claire Clairmont (who became Lord Byron's mistress). Here they met up with Byron and his entourage, visiting each other daily and regularly sailing on the lake. The famous ghost story competition, for which Mary wrote *Frankenstein*, took place in June of that year *(see p234)*.

Oh, That I Had the Wings of a Dove

At the beginning of *Confessions of an English Opium-Eater* (1821, 1850–59), Thomas De Quincey recalls how, after running away from Manchester Grammar School in 1802 and wandering through parts of the country, he ended up penniless in Soho, gaining lodgings at 38 Greek Street, owned by a Mr Brunell, solicitor, who slept elsewhere to evade the bailiffs. De Quincey believed himself alone, apart from noisy rats, but discovered there was another lodger, a 10-year-old girl who 'amidst the real fleshly ills of cold and, I fear, hunger, the forsaken child had found leisure to suffer still more (it appeared) from the self-created one of ghosts. I promised her protection against all ghosts whatsoever, but alas! I could offer her no other assistance. We lay upon the floor, with a bundle of cursed law papers for a pillow, but with no other covering than a sort of large horseman's cloak; afterwards, however, we discovered in a garret an old sofa-cover, a small piece of rug, and some fragments of other articles, which added a little to our warmth'.

De Quincey spent his days walking or sheltering in doorways in Soho and Oxford Street. Here he met Ann, a prostitute, who one night saved his life when he had collapsed with hunger on the steps of a house in Golden Square. To his extreme anguish, he later missed an arranged rendezvous with Ann and never found her again, though he 'looked into many, many myriads of female faces' in a restless search.

De Quincey's detailed account of his early Soho years not only provides the background and circumstances which led to his laudanum addiction but also introduces the images and experiences that, many years later, came back to haunt him in his dreams. The 'Preliminary Confessions' end with a powerful and lyrical reflection on the anguish of homelessness and loss:

> 'So then, Oxford Street, stony-hearted step-mother! thou that listenest to the sighs of orphans and drinkest the tears of children, at length I was dismissed from thee; the time was come at last that I no more should pace in anguish thy never-ending terraces, no more should dream and wake in captivity to the pangs of hunger. Successors too many, to myself and Ann, have doubtless since then trodden in our footsteps, inheritors of our calamities; other orphans than Ann have sighed; tears have been shed by other children; and thou, Oxford Street, hast since doubtless echoed to the groans of innumerable hearts. ... Meantime, I am again in London, and again I pace the terraces of Oxford Street by night; and oftentimes, when I am oppressed by anxieties that demand all my philosophy and the comfort of thy presence to support, ... I look up the streets that run northwards from Oxford Street, upon moon-light nights, and recollect my youthful ejaculation of anguish; ... and if I could allow myself to descend again to the impotent wishes of childhood, I should again say to myself, as I look to the North, "Oh, that I had the wings of a dove — " and with how just a confidence in thy good and gracious nature might I add the other half of my early ejaculation — "And THAT way I would fly for comfort!"'

De Quincey bought his first packet of opium in 1804 from a chemist's shop at 173 Oxford Street (now the site of Marks & Spencer's) to alleviate his facial neuralgia – until then, he had resorted to plunging his face in cold water, which served little purpose. Twelve years later, in 1816, he was taking 320 grains a day of this 'dread agent of unimaginable pleasure and pain.'

A Happy Life • 6 Frith Street

Here the essayist and literary critic William Hazlitt wrote *The Sick Chamber*, dying not long afterwards on 18 September 1830. His last whispered words were 'Well, I've had a happy life' – a far more positive assessment than suggested in 'My First Acquaintance with Poets' (April 1827):

> *'My soul has indeed remained in its original bondage, dark, obscure, with longing infinite and unsatisfied; my heart, shut up in the prison-house of this rude clay, has never found, nor will it ever find, a heart to speak to;'*

In this essay Hazlitt describes his life-changing meeting with Samuel Taylor Coleridge, whose magnetic personality inspires him to believe he can write:

> *'I was at that time dumb, inarticulate, helpless, like a worm by the way-side, crushed, bleeding lifeless; but now, bursting from the deadly bands that bound them ... my ideas float on winged words, and as they expand their plumes, catch the golden light of other years.'*

For his part, in a letter in 1803, Coleridge described the 25-year-old Hazlitt as 'a thinking, observant, original man of great power as a Painter of Character Portraits ... but he is jealous, gloomy, and of an irritable Pride – and addicted to women, as objects of sexual indulgence ... yet he says more than any man I ever Knew ... He sends well-headed and well-feathered Thoughts straight forwards to the mark with a Twang of the Bow-string.'

Hazlitt had arrived in London in 1793 to attend the New Unitarian College in Hackney, where he absorbed Enlightenment philosophy and radical politics. Losing the desire to enter the ministry, he left the college in 1797 with the aim of becoming a painter. He met Charles Lamb, who introduced him to Coleridge, Wordsworth, Robert Southey, Leigh Hunt, Benjamin Haydon, William Godwin, Shelley, Mary Shelley, Lord Byron and other London literary figures.

Hazlitt went on to become one of England's greatest prose stylists, a parliamentary reporter, drama critic, radical journalist – and one of Coleridge's most penetrating critics. His major works include *Liber Amoris* (1823), in which he recounts the doomed, middle-aged infatuation with his landlord's daughter that led to the break-up of his first marriage, *The Spirit of The Age* (1825) and the four-volume *Life of Napoleon* (1828–30).

A commemorative stone to Hazlitt can be seen in the churchyard of St Annes, Wardour Street, which was rebuilt in 1990–91 (all but the tower having been destroyed when the church received a direct hit in World War II). A plaque commemorating Dorothy L. Sayers, creator of aristocratic sleuth Lord Peter Wimsey, can also be found here. In 1763 Henry and Hester Thrale *(see p78)*, friends of Dr Johnson, were married at St Anne's. Number 6 Frith Street is now a small, boutique hotel named Hazlitt's; from this hotel Bill Bryson began his travels around Britain, which he turned into the bestseller *Notes from a Small Island* (1995).

Leaders, Artists and Bums • 67 Frith Street

The poet and critic T.E. Hulme held weekly Tuesday evening meetings here, at the home of his mistress Dolly Kibblewhite, throughout 1913 and somewhat less frequently in 1914 and 1915. Modelled on the Mermaid Tavern gatherings *(see

p56)*, Hulme favoured intellectual discussion over drunkenness. Attendees included Ezra Pound, Ford Madox Ford, Rupert Brooke, Aldous Huxley, poet Hilda Doolittle (H.D.), Wyndham Lewis, and sculptors Jacob Epstein and Henri Gaudier-Brzeska. Hulme invited speakers on French *vers libre*, German aesthetics, new art theories and personalities. Nevinson recalled: 'There were journalists, writers, poets, painters, politicians of all sorts, from Conservatives to New Age Socialists, Fabians, Irish yaps, American bums and Labour leaders', the whole gaggle of 'oddities and notables' held in check by the 'genially aggressive' personality of the host.

Hulme's nascent friendship with Wyndham Lewis ended in a furious altercation over Kate Lechmere, Lewis's partner in the Rebel Arts Centre *(see p144)*. Lewis marched over to the Frith Street house to confront Hulme and a brawl ensued. Lewis was dragged down the stairs and out into the garden in the centre of Soho Square. The fight ended when Hulme hung Lewis upside down by his trouser turn-ups on the iron railings surrounding the garden.

Bar Italia Hulme and Kate Lechmere subsequently had a passionate affair.

When war broke out Hulme enlisted within the first few months and wrote Lechmere a series of erotic love letters from the trenches in France. On 28 September 1917, just after his 34th birthday, Hulme was killed in action, suffering a direct hit from a large shell that literally blew him to pieces.

Bar Italia • 23 Frith Street

A favourite meeting place of Soho regulars, this authentic Italian café was used as a location in the film version of *Absolute Beginners*, Colin MacInnes's 1959 exploration of 1950s Notting Hill and Soho. Hugo Williams' poem 'Bar Italia' (from *Billy's Rain*, 1999) tells the story of the end of a liaison. The opening lines are:

> *How beautiful it would be to wait for you again*
> *in the usual place,*
> *not looking at the door,*
> *keeping a lookout in the long mirror*

The Moka • 29 Frith Street

Opened in 1953 by Italian actress Gina Lollobrigida, the Moka was the first Soho café with its own genuine espresso machine. Connoisseur of coffee-bar life Quentin Crisp described the shifting clientele as 'bookies and burglars, actresses and artisans, poets and prostitutes'. American novelist William Burroughs subjected the Moka to weeks of 'para-psychic bombardment' after being provoked by what he claimed was discourteous service and a poisoned cheesecake. His continual use of taped 'playback' (playing, just outside the Moka, ambient recordings made inside the café and outside in the street) in August 1972 led to altercations with the owners – and their abandonment of the premises in October of the same year.

Material World • 28 Dean Street

In May 1850 Karl Marx and his large family were thrown out of their flat in Chelsea for failing to pay the rent. After six miserable months staying with a Jewish lace dealer at 64 Dean Street (now demolished), the Marxes found a more permanent home at No. 28, above what is now Quo Vadis restaurant. Marx lived here in two small rooms on the top floor with his wife Jenny, their many children, and maid Helene 'Lenchen' Demuth. Their meagre circumstances provided little in the way of an 'accumulation of commodities'. A visitor reported:

> *'There is not one piece of good, solid furniture in the entire flat. Everything is broken, tattered and torn, finger-thick dust everywhere, and everything in the greatest disorder ... When you enter the Marx flat your sight is dimmed by tobacco and coal smoke so that you grope around at first as if you were in a cave, until your eyes get used to these fumes and, as in a fog, you gradually notice a few objects.'*

The situation was not improved when Marx got first Jenny and then Lenchen pregnant.

Jenny agreed to keep the matter of Lenchen's pregnancy hushed up, and Lenchen's child was fostered soon after birth. Marx and Jenny's child, who they named Franziska, died in the back room at 28 Dean Street little more than a year after her birth. A French neighbour lent them £2 for the burial.

'A week ago I reached the pleasant point where I am unable to go out for want of the coats I have in pawn, and can no longer eat meat for want of credit,' wrote Marx to Engels in February 1852. Their impecunious state could have been alleviated to a degree had Marx not sought to maintain a veneer of respectability – his background was solidly middle-class, and Jenny was the daughter of a Baron. Precedence was given to employing a private secretary, piano lessons for the girls and annual holidays as opposed to more mundane matters such as paying the butcher or grocer.

Marx supplemented handouts from Engels and other friends with occasional freelance work for the *New York Tribune*, but spent most of his days in the British Library Reading Room *(see p146)*. In 1856 Jenny Marx received two small inheritances and the family were able to move to a small house at 9 Grafton Terrace, Kentish Town.

During their years in Soho three of the Marxes' children died. However the youngest, Eleanor, born in 1855, survived and went on to help Marx finish *Capital* and herself became a prominent Socialist campaigner. In 1898 she swallowed prussic acid as part of a suicide pact with her unfaithful lover Edward Aveling. He had provided the poison – but never intended to keep his side of the agreement.

Marx died aged 65 on 14 March 1883 at No. 41 Maitland Park Road in the Chalk Farm area, without leaving a will; his estate was valued at £250. There were eleven mourners at his funeral on the 17th, when he was buried in unconsecrated ground in the Eastern section of Highgate Cemetery. On the first anniversary of his death some 3,000 supporters, including William Morris, gathered to pay their respects. Every year the Marx Memorial Library *(see p157)* holds a ceremony by the grave.

Anything Goes • The Gargoyle Club, 69 Dean Street

Founded in 1925 by David Tennant and his wife Hermione Baddeley, The Gargoyle Club was a chic nightclub where members could act with abandon – and often did. Henri Matisse designed the ballroom's interior with murals and lithographs and a twenty-thousand-piece mosaic of mirrored red tiles. The club provided a meeting place for the rich and well-connected and the 'deserving' artistic poor, and unified a generation of bohemian writers and artists. By day it was a sober luncheon club patronised by politicians, literati and nobility. At night it became a cosmopolitan theatre where exceptional minds and unconventional spirits mingled.

The 'Gargoyle Set' of the 1920s and 30s included socialites such as Nancy Cunard, Iris Tree and Marie Beerbohm; aesthetes and dandies such as Brian Howard (inspiration for Waugh's Anthony Blanche character in *Brideshead Revisited*, 1945);

writers including Anthony Powell, Cyril Connolly and Stephen Spender; and painter Augustus John, who once wrote: 'I drink in order to become more myself.'

During the Second World War the party dimmed, but was revived with a more raffish set that created what Dan Farson describes in *The Gilded Gutter Life of Francis Bacon* (1993) as 'an upper-class bedlam, where the difference between the drunks and the lunatics was imperceptible.' The membership in 1949 was practically a 'Who's who' of the leading writers and artists of the day, including George Orwell, Graham Greene, John Betjeman, Olivia Manning, poets George Barker, Humphrey Jennings and Dylan Thomas (who commented 'I drink to correct the imbalance between the disorder outside and the order within'), Michael Wishart, Anne Dunn, Sonia Brownell, Lucian Freud, Roland Penrose, Lee Miller, A.J. Ayer, Bertrand Russell – and the spies Guy Burgess and Donald Maclean.

The French House

Tennant sold the Gargoyle in 1952 and it gradually lost aristocratic support; by the late 50s it was presenting strippers. In 1978 the dance floor once again found a certain glamour as the club night hosted by Steve Strange and Rusty Egan spawned the New Romantic movement, with regular characters such as Boy George and Marilyn and bands including Spandau Ballet and Depeche Mode. A year later, the Comedy Store opened here (later moving to Oxendon Street), bringing acclaim to, among others, Alexei Sayle, Rik Mayall and Adrian Edmonson.

The French House • 49 Dean Street

Victor Berlemont, the first Frenchman to hold a publican's licence in London, opened The York Minster (affectionately called and much later renamed The French House) in April 1914. He had worked in the kitchens of Escoffier and rapidly established a reputation for excellent cuisine, especially among French stars visiting or performing in the West End – the walls are lined with signed photographs of famous diners of the era, including Maurice Chevalier and the boxer Georges Carpentier. Augustus John and Max Beerbohm drank absinthe together here, and Edith Piaf sang.

During the Second World War, the pub became a rendezvous for General De Gaulle and the Free French movement. De Gaulle reputedly wrote his famous declaration 'À Tous les Français' here, rejecting the collaborationist Vichy government. A copy hangs behind the bar. Whisky could be obtained only under the counter, with a request for *'vin blanc écossaise'*. After the war Victor retired and his son Gaston (who had been born in the pub) took over. In the post-war atmosphere of austerity, Gaston made 'the

French' an oasis of civilised and sybarite cheer. For the young Jeffrey Bernard, fresh out of public school, it was love at first sight: a pub with 'a genuine feel of Parisian café society', offering a heady mix of writers, artists, tradesmen, a sprinkling of prostitutes, the odd villain, and characters such as Madame Valerie (of Patisserie Valerie on Old Compton Street) who 'held court and poured great quantities of Guinness into her gigantic body'.

Shortly before his American tour of October 1953 Dylan Thomas lost the original hand-written manuscript of *Under Milk Wood* (1952); it was eventually found beneath one of the bench seats at the French. Here also the blind poet John Heath-Stubbs met the deaf poet David Wright; together they conceived and edited *The Faber Book of Twentieth Century Verse* (1953).

Caroline Blackwood, who wrote for *Picture Post* and later became a novelist, was one of several muses to the writers and artists living in and around Dean Street in the early 1950s. She had married Lucian Freud in December 1953, and was being pursued by, among others, Cyril Connolly. Their marriage produced several paintings by Freud, none more haunting than *Hotel Bedroom* (1954), painted shortly after their wedding, and depicting the couple with a chilling separateness.

Another regular was Gerald Hamilton, on whom Christopher Isherwood modelled Mr Norris in *Mr Norris Changes Trains* (1935). Before the war Hamilton had sold forged passports to German Jews, and then informed on them to Nazi guards at the border. He had escaped wartime conscription by fleeing to Ireland dressed as a nun.

Gaston retired aged 75 on Bastille Day 1989. Francis Bacon and other regulars protested outside the pub when there were rumours of a sale to the porn baron Paul Raymond. In the event, the pub was left to two journalists who had been regulars. Under their stewardship the restaurant upstairs has reopened and the pub has been officially re-named the French House.

Philip O'Connor and the Underbelly of Dean Street

Beneath the surface of successful Soho bohemianism many writers and artists have struggled for success. Surrealist poet Philip O'Connor lived in a Dean Street basement cellar with his mother in 1923–24 and returned there in 1936, having published his first poems. He lived in low-rent accommodation in Fitzrovia and Chelsea throughout the 1940s, drinking at the Swiss Tavern, Old Compton Street, editing *Seven* magazine in 1941 and surviving from hand to mouth.

O'Connor's breakthrough did not come until Faber & Faber published his uplifting *Memoirs of Public Baby* in 1958. He subsequently wrote radio plays, worked for the BBC, was a regular at Peter Cook's Establishment Club, and wrote *Vagrancy* (1963). In 1967 he made a short film with Quentin Crisp, and later became involved with Allen Ginsberg, William Burroughs, Ed Dorn and other Beat writers. He published *Selected Poems* (1968) and *Arias of Water* (1981).

Dean Street

Sohoitis • Caves de France, 39 Dean Street

The Caves (always pronounced 'calves') was, according to Daniel Farson, 'true bohemia', which in its long, ground-floor bar hosted 'a rich assortment of eccentrics and veteran drinkers, young and old and mostly poor' such as the disreputable ex-*Vogue* photographer John Deakin (when he was barred from The Colony Room, two doors down), and the artist Nina Hamnett, 'still jaunty' but a wreck of the woman she had once been, trading on her past as the toast of the Left Bank in Paris ('Modigliani said I had the best tits in Europe') to scrounge drinks and eventually leave for the night with a sailor or two on her arm. Other regulars included 'the two Roberts' *(see p228)*, Julian Maclaren-Ross and drifters, drinkers and fading artists of every kind. In her novel *The Old Man and Me* (1964) Elaine Dundy, Kenneth Tynan's first wife, describes the Caves as 'a sort of coal-hole in the heart of Soho that is open every afternoon, a dead-ended subterranean tunnel … in an atmosphere almost solid with failure'.

The Caves became the last resting place of those who had fallen under the spell of Soho, suffering from Sohoitis, as defined by *Poetry London* editor Tambimuttu – 'It's a dangerous place … if you get Sohoitis … you will stay there always day and night and get no work done ever.'

Soho Dandy

Writer Julian Maclaren-Ross, the inspiration for Anthony Powell's tragicomic character X Trapnel in *Books Do Furnish a Room* (1971), established himself as a conspicuous figure in wartime Soho, always dressed immaculately and dispensing literary gossip as he waved his cigarette holder. From August 1942 to May 1943 he wrote documentaries for Strand Films at 1 Golden Square, working with Dylan Thomas, Australian novelist Philip Lindsay, and Iris Tree's son, the scriptwriter Ivan Moffat. Moffat later adapted Lawrence Durrell's *Justine* and Scott Fitzgerald's *Tender is the Night* for Hollywood, and had a long-term affair with Caroline Blackwood.

During this period Maclaren-Ross wrote short stories based on his army experiences; these were published in *Penguin New Writing*, *Horizon* and *Lilliput* magazines. He drank with Dylan Thomas, Ruthven Todd, John Davenport, Tambimuttu and many others in a daily round that would start in the early afternoon at the Horseshoe Club (in the basement at 21 Wardour Street), proceed to the Swiss Tavern at 53 Old Compton Street, the Wheatsheaf in Fitzrovia, before ending up at the Gargoyle Club in Dean Street after the pubs had closed.

Though his writing was greatly admired by Evelyn Waugh, John Betjeman and Olivia Manning among others, financial success eluded him, and Maclaren-Ross lapsed into alcoholism and drug dependency. He died of a heart attack in 1964, finally worn down by his self-destructive lifestyle. He left behind, unfinished, *Memoirs of the Forties*, posthumous publication of which in 1965 belatedly secured his literary reputation. His novel *Of Love and Hunger* (1946) is a Penguin Modern Classic and a *Selected Stories* was brought out in 2004.

'You *are* home, cunty' – The Colony Room • 41 Dean Street

At the top of a flight of 'shabby and disgraceful stairs' in 'a smallish room with a faded air and threadbare carpet' Muriel Belcher created The Colony Room, an afternoon drinking club whose most famous and generous customer was painter Francis Bacon.

Bacon was introduced to the Colony shortly after it opened in 1949 and was immediately adopted by Muriel, who for a time gave him ten pounds a week to 'bring in the people you like'. Asked years later by Daniel Farson why he went to Muriel's, Bacon replied: 'Because it's a place where you can lose your inhibitions. It's different from anywhere else. After all, that's what we all want, isn't it? A place to go where one feels free and easy.'

Muriel liked artists, but had no interest in art, which was just fine with Bacon and the other artists labelled by R.B. Kitaj 'the School of London' – Bacon, Freud, Minton, Michael Andrews and Frank Auerbach – who had no desire to talk about art and made Muriel's their second home, so much so that they were also referred to as 'Muriel's boys'. Other regulars included Henrietta Moraes (Bacon's favourite model), Dan Farson, Caroline Blackwood, Isabel Lambert (later Rawsthorne), Jeffrey and Bruce Bernard, and John Deakin. Led by Bacon, who relished and insisted upon the role of host, it became the custom to spend the afternoon at the Colony and then go on to the Gargoyle, having first started the day with lunch at Wheeler's. This famous seafood restaurant, which used to stand on Old Compton Street, was owned in the 1950s by

Bernard Walsh. Walsh allowed Bacon to run up huge tabs until the sale of a painting or a gambling win would enable him to settle the bill – at which point Walsh would send over a bottle of champagne, and the cycle would start over again.

At the Colony Room, Muriel presided over her domain from a stool at the corner of the bar. 'Chin tilted upwards, cigarette in raised hand, she gave an impression of haughtiness, an eagle surveying the carrion of her membership.' She referred to all her customers as 'she', 'miss' or 'clara', or with epithets such as 'cunty' or 'sweetie'. Bacon was known as 'daughter'. Loyal and welcoming to those she liked, she could be vicious to those she didn't. Daniel Farson recalls the time he introduced her to John Braine. Unimpressed, she announced 'I can see there's plenty of room at her top!' and, opening the door, dispatched him with the cry 'on your way, Lottie.' She also refused to serve Dennis Potter and Barry Humphries.

Though a regular, Colin MacInnes described Muriel's (thinly disguised as Mabel's) unfavourably in a March 1957 essay in *Encounter* magazine: 'Of course the spell of the drinking club is partly morbid. To sit in Mabel's place with the curtains drawn at 4 pm on a sunny afternoon, sipping expensive poison and gossiping one's life away, has the futile fascination of forbidden fruit: the heady intoxication of a bogus Baudelairean romantic evil.'

The green doorway to The Colony Room

The Groucho Club • 45 Dean Street

Named after the Groucho Marx quip about refusing to join any club that would have him as a member, The Groucho was founded in 1985 by the publishers Carmen Callil, Liz Calder and other friends who wanted an alternative to the male-only clubs of Pall Mall. It quickly became a favourite hangout of London's media gliterati. Salman Rushdie made his second public appearance here in December 1990 after being forced into hiding by the fatwa issued by Ayatollah Khomeini. In the 90s The Groucho became the first club to stock absinthe again, and it has remained a place where members can behave very badly – although in 2000 the management finally tired of over-frequent displays of artist Damien Hirst's penis and banned him.

Another Round at the Pillars • The Pillars of Hercules, 7 Greek Street

The Pillars was featured in Charles Dickens's *A Tale of Two Cities* (1859), and the street to the pub's side is named after the novel's Dr Manette. A possibly apocryphal story has Wilfred Meynell, editor of the Catholic literary monthly *Merry England*, coming to the aid of the poet and opium addict Francis Thompson who had passed out in the doorway of the pub in 1888. Whatever the truth of this particular incident, Meynell was the first to publish Thompson's poetry, and became a lifelong friend and benefactor to him.

Born into a devoutly Catholic middle-class family, Thompson had studied first for a career in the priesthood, and then medicine, before turning to writing. Perhaps unwisely, his mother had given him a copy of De Quincey's *Confessions of an English Opium-Eater* for his 18th birthday and this prompted an interest in the drug. Ten years later Thompson was a homeless match-seller wandering Soho and the West End in De Quincey's drug-induced footsteps, submitting his poems to Wilfred and Alice Meynell care of a post office or chemist's shop. Thompson's poetry gives expression to the realization of God as a presence in the world, and in his most famous poem, the autobiographical 'Hound of Heaven', he speaks of a God who pursues the most wayward soul. He had a vision of Christ:

> *walking on the water*
> *Not of Gennesareth, but Thames*

In the 1970s the Pillars became the 'outer office and club room' of the literary magazine *The New Review* (based next door at No. 11), as the title of a volume of testimonials produced in memory of the Review's editor suggests: *Another Round at the Pillars: Essays, Poems, & Reflections on Ian Hamilton.*

A poet and biographer of Robert Lowell, Ian Hamilton had previously edited the short-lived *Tomorrow Magazine* and *The Review*, one of the most successful poetry magazines of the 1960s. With *The New Review*, Hamilton's reputation as a literary force gained further weight. He published many significant new writers including Ian McEwan, Martin Amis, Jim Crace, James Fenton and Tom Paulin. Craig Raine became the books editor and Julian Barnes a contributing editor.

The New Review group's prominence drew occasional accusations in the press of a 'literary mafia'. However, in the unfriendly economic climate of the early 1980s and the withdrawal of Arts Council funds, escaping the creditors took up more and more of the editor's time – eventually forcing the closure of the magazine. Ian Hamilton went on to write a biography of J.D. Salinger although, because the famous recluse refused to meet him or allow access to any fresh information, the book was eventually called *In Search of J.D. Salinger* (1988), necessarily focusing on the hunt as much as the prey.

David Archer's Bookshop • 35 Greek Street

In the 1950s and 60s, way before Channel 4 gave us *Black Books*, David Archer perfectly exemplified the potential commercial pitfalls of the book lover becoming bookseller – he often couldn't bear to part with the stock. At the back of the shop he had a small café where writer friends such as George Barker, W.S. Graham, Colin Wilson, Christopher Logue and Colin MacInnes would regularly gather. As lunchtime approached, the convivial group often found it hard to resist the siren call of the Coach and Horses pub and Archer would close the shop door behind him – with the contents of the till jingling in his pocket.

The Establishment Club • 18 Greek Street

Comic writer Peter Cook founded the Establishment Club with Nicholas Luard at 18 Greek Street, and moved his satirical magazine, *Private Eye*, into offices at 22 Greek Street, in October 1961. The Establishment showcased the talents of Cambridge Footlights' graduates and other young satirists and comedians, including Alan Bennett, Dudley Moore, John Bird, Eleanor Bron and John Fortune. The club presented American iconoclast Lenny Bruce, and Australian writer and performer Barry Humphries (most famous in his alter ego Dame Edna Everage) made his debut at the Establishment Club. However, when Cook and the cast of *Beyond The Fringe (see also p97)* went to perform in New York the club could not sustain their absence and was forced to close in September 1962.

Kettner's • 29 Romilly Street

Oscar Wilde frequently dined at Kettner's (on the corner of Romilly Street and Greek Street), a restaurant founded by Napoleon III's chef Auguste Kettner in 1867, entertaining 'renters' in the private upstairs rooms, as was disastrously revealed under cross-examination in the ill-advised action for libel he launched against the Marquess of Queensberry. Edward VII and Lillie Langtry also enjoyed discreet liaisons upstairs at Kettner's. The restaurant stills stands, maintaining a fair degree of grandeur too, though it is now owned by the Pizza Express chain.

Jeff Bin In? • Coach and Horses, 29 Greek Street

One of London's best-known pubs, the Coach and Horses was made famous by Michael Heath's cartoons and the weekly dispatches of one of its most dedicated regulars, Jeffrey Bernard. Bernard's 'Low Life' column ran in *The Spectator* from 1978 to 1997. Memorably described by one commentator as a suicide note in weekly instalments, 'Low Life' chronicled in sharp, witty prose the vicissitudes of life as seen from the bottom of a large vodka (or three).

In 1989 Keith Waterhouse created a play from the columns entitled *Jeffrey Bernard is Unwell* – the device used by *The Spectator* when, from time to time, their columnist failed to connect with his typewriter. The action takes place entirely in the Coach and Horses. Bernard could never be accused of letting work get in the way of the next drink, despite being warned in 1965 that he would drop dead if he touched another drop (he was a diabetic). In the introduction to *Reach for the Ground: The Downhill Struggle of Jeffrey Bernard* (2002) he wrote, 'The immediate success of the play was heady stuff for me and although it didn't accelerate my drinking, my intake was a steady two years of celebration. First night after first night.'

Jeff's brother Bruce also remained a Soho regular. A highly regarded picture editor of magazines (including *The Sunday Times Magazine* from 1972 to 1980) and books on art and photography, his last work was *Century* (2000) a magisterial history of the 20th century in photographs. Lucian Freud painted his portrait in 1992.

The Coach and Horses' dining room upstairs provides the venue for the fortnightly lunches held by *Private Eye* magazine, based nearby in Carlisle Street.

Coach & Horses

A Kind of Inferno • Old Compton Street

Sex has always been an intrinsic part of Soho, a fact reflected in many writers' work. In Joseph Conrad's *The Secret Agent* (1907) Soho is the location for Mr Verloc's dirty bookshop, in the back of which the anarchists plot their futile and tragic attempt to blow up the Greenwich Observatory. In Graham Greene's *The Human Factor* (1978) 'the names against the flat bells – Lulu, Mimi and the like – were all that indicated the afternoon and evening activities of Old Compton Street.' Greene wrote from experience; in the 1950s he would leave his St James's flat by the back door to evade any prying eyes when on his way to Soho. In Colin MacInnes's *Absolute Beginners* (1958) Soho is a place where 'all the things they say happen, do: I mean vice of every kink.'

Philip Larkin complained in a letter to the historian Robert Conquest that the permissive society 'never permitted me anything, as far as I can recall'. He was nevertheless, as publication of his letters in 1992 revealed, an avid reader of porn. In the same letter he noted that clubs in Newport Court, a small alleyway off Charing Cross Road, had branched into 'Dominant females and Fladge'.

Gerald Kersh's novel *Night and The City* (1938) is set in the nether world of Soho strip clubs and clip joints. The central character, Henry Fabian, a blackmailer and pimp, is 'familiar with every rat-hole in West One and West Central' and sees London as 'a kind of Inferno – a series of concentric areas with Piccadilly Circus as the ultimate centre.'

The 1957 Wolfenden Report and subsequent 1959 Street Offences Act drove prostitutes off the streets, but in place of prostitution the 1960s and 70s saw a huge growth in the number of sex shops in Soho, and a rising tide of associated gangland crime and police corruption. This era is explored in Jake Arnott's series of novels beginning with *The Long Firm* (1999) and followed by *He Kills Coppers* (2001) and *Truecrime* (2003). In the novels Arnott interweaves real and imagined characters, and some, like Lord Teddy Thursby, psychotic Soho club boss Harry Starks and moll Ruby Ryder, inhabit both the real and imagined world at once. The character of Thursby, for example – corrupt politician, homosexual socialite and right-wing newspaper pundit – was surely inspired by Lord Boothby, who notoriously had a close friendship with the Krays. The homosexuality of many characters in *The Long Firm* allows an evocation of gay Soho, a constant and now increasingly visible part of Soho's make up.

The poets Arthur Rimbaud and Paul Verlaine stayed for a short time at 5 Old Compton Street before finding more long-term lodgings in Howland Street *(see p123)*. They arrived shortly after the fall of the Paris Commune in 1872, having come to the attention of spies of the French government as much for their relationship as for their political allegiances. They occasionally attended the Cercle d'Études Sociales, a refugee club that met above the Hibernia Store pub at 6–7 Old Compton Street.

The Golden Lion, at 51 Dean Street, was one of Soho's earliest gay pubs. It was known as such in the 1920s and was frequented by Noël Coward. In the 1970s and 80s it gained a much darker connection, however: the mass murderer Dennis Nilsen used to pick up his victims here.

In *The Naked Civil Servant*, Quentin Crisp recalls his early years as a male prostitute in 1930s Soho as a dangerous occupation of dismal exchanges in dark doorways, interspersed 'day after uneventful day, night after loveless night' with drinking tea 'combing each other's hair and trying on each other's lipsticks' in The Black Cat café on Old Compton Street.

Will Beckwith, the privileged and promiscuous central character in Alan Hollinghurst's debut novel *The Swimming Pool Library* (1988) inhabits a changed world – but nevertheless one in which the past still exerts a very palpable influence, and over which hangs an uncertain future. In 'the last summer of its kind there was ever to be' Will enjoys casual, anonymous sex in the 'Brutus Cinema', located in 'the basement of one of those Soho houses which, above ground-floor level, maintain their beautiful Caroline fenestration, and seemed a kind of emblem of gay life (the piano nobile elegant above the squalid, jolly sous-sol) in the far-off spring of 1983.'

FITZROVIA

THIS SMALL ENCLAVE, bordered by Soho to the south and Bloomsbury to the east, comprises Rathbone Place, Charlotte Street, Fitzroy Street and the surrounding area north of Oxford Street and west of Tottenham Court Road. The name derives from the fame of the Fitzroy Tavern, which became a meeting place for writers, artists, musicians, actors, music-hall artistes and wayward souls in the 1920s. For a brief but exciting period, from the 1920s to the 1950s, Fitzrovia was at the centre of literary and artistic creativity and debate in the capital.

From the late 19th century successive waves of French, German, Swiss and Italian immigrants – mostly radicals looking for a fresh start – settled here and contributed to the campaigns for the right to vote, to free education and for the rights of women. They also opened shops and restaurants specialising in their own cuisines, adding to the large number of coffee houses and inns in the area. The Henry Saas art school at No. 6 Charlotte Street and the nearby Slade School of Art in Bloomsbury meant that the area was attractive to artists, art students and artists' models.

Cultural difference gave Fitzrovia its fascination and allure, and the immigrant-led business community quickly realised that they could cultivate the custom of London's bohemian avant-garde. The Austrian chef Rudolf Stulik made the Restaurant de la Tour Eiffel fashionable by encouraging Wyndham Lewis, Nancy Cunard and their literary and artistic cohorts to become regulars.

Polish-born Judah Kleinfield converted a German tavern called The Hundred Marks into The Fitzroy Tavern and drew a clientele of musicians and artists. The Fitzroy and the Eiffel became the dual epicentres of Fitzrovia's bohemian life from the late 1920s to the late 1930s, attracting writers such as Aldous Huxley, Evelyn Waugh, George Orwell and, most famously perhaps, Dylan Thomas.

By the mid-1930s, however, Orwell was drinking more regularly at The Wheatsheaf, and this soon became a rallying point for aspiring writers and artists, though other pubs, such as the Marquis of Granby and the Duke of York also featured as hubs of intellectual discussion, debate and literary sparring. The pubs of Fitzrovia, as well as such restaurants as L'Etoile and Bertorelli's, remained popular with London writers through the war years and into the 1950s, but by then such haunts were also attracting a 'tourist' crowd, and Fitzrovia's star was in decline.

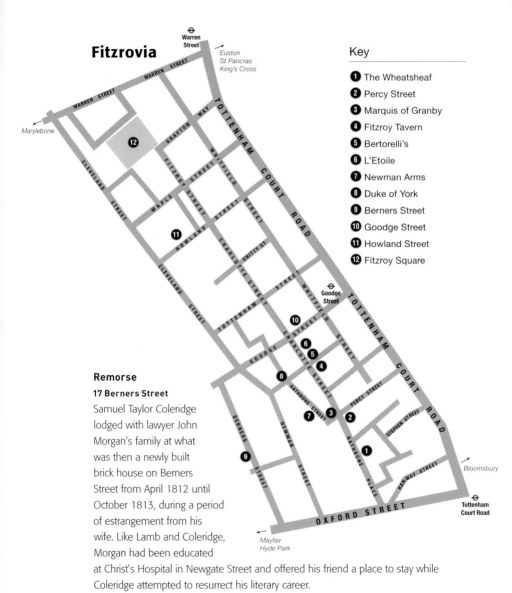

Fitzrovia

⊖ Warren Street

→ Euston
St Pancras
King's Cross

← Marylebone

← Mayfair
Hyde Park

→ Bloomsbury

⊖ Goodge Street

⊖ Tottenham Court Road

Key

1. The Wheatsheaf
2. Percy Street
3. Marquis of Granby
4. Fitzroy Tavern
5. Bertorelli's
6. L'Etoile
7. Newman Arms
8. Duke of York
9. Berners Street
10. Goodge Street
11. Howland Street
12. Fitzroy Square

Remorse

17 Berners Street

Samuel Taylor Coleridge lodged with lawyer John Morgan's family at what was then a newly built brick house on Berners Street from April 1812 until October 1813, during a period of estrangement from his wife. Like Lamb and Coleridge, Morgan had been educated at Christ's Hospital in Newgate Street and offered his friend a place to stay while Coleridge attempted to resurrect his literary career.

Coleridge's relationship with Wordsworth was in crisis, mostly as a result of the former's opium dependency. Henry Crabb Robinson and Charles Lamb managed to arrange a reconciliation of sorts, but the hitherto intimacy of the two writers was never restored. While at Berners Street Coleridge revised his verse play *Remorse* (1813) for performances at the Theatre Royal, Drury Lane.

Ellen Ternan • 31 Berners Street

Frances Eleanor Ternan and her daughters lived here from July 1858 to March 1859. They all began their early careers as actresses. Fanny, later Trollope, wrote novels, including *Mabel's Progress* (1867). Ellen Lawless Ternan met Charles Dickens, who fell in love with her in April 1857 when they were acting in a charity production of *The Frozen Deep* (1857), co-written by Dickens and Wilkie Collins. Although he separated from his wife Catherine in 1858, Dickens managed to keep his relationship with Ellen secret. Ellen remained Dickens's mistress until his death in 1870. Theirs was a platonic relationship for some years and it may have inspired the relationship between Pip and Estella in *Great Expectations* (1860).

In his essay 'The White Woman', Dickens recalled seeing a simpering madwoman, dressed entirely in white, in Berners Street. This was one of the many sources for the Miss Havisham character in *Great Expectations*.

Angel in the House • 14 Percy Street

Coventry Patmore, a poet and associate of the Pre-Raphaelite Brotherhood, lived here in 1863–64 after the death of his first wife, Emily, to whom he had written the poems collectively called *The Angel in the House* (1854–63) in praise of married love. Immensely popular with the Victorian public, its mixture of sentimentality and the mundane details of middle-class life were mocked by Swinburne, Gosse and others. Patmore travelled to Rome, where he met his second wife, Marianne, and converted to Catholicism. Both factors contributed to a subsequent decline in his popularity.

A Season in Hell • 34 Howland Street

Stepping off the train at Charing Cross Station on 10 September 1872, on their first visit to London, the French poets Rimbaud and Verlaine were immediately delighted and astonished by the clamour, mayhem and filth of the capital. Verlaine wrote: 'Such noise and chaos. Such magnificent and terrible abandon. It's like stepping into the future.' It proved the perfect inspiration for the 'atrocities' (as Rimbaud described them) of *Une Saison en Enfer*, 1873. In fact Rimbaud spent more of his life in London than in Paris. Compared with London, Paris was left looking like a 'pretty, provincial town.'

The fugitives arrived in London in flight from Verlaine's in-laws (outraged by his abandonment of his wife and young son) and, to a lesser extent, from the French police. They found rooms in Howland Street, in part of a Georgian terrace that had fallen into disrepair. By the time Rimbaud and Verlaine arrived, No. 34 was a warren of small, grimy furnished rooms. The 'mud of the street' and the 'recent ghosts moving through the thick, eternal coal-smoke' that Rimbaud sees from his window in 'Ville' (published in *Illuminations*, 1874) are probably inspired by the view from the building, which was pulled down in 1938 to make way for the BT (formerly Post Office) Tower.

Rimbaud and Verlaine threw themselves into a routine of writing, drinking and sightseeing - interspersed with occasional work writing French business letters for American newspapers. They divided their time between Soho, their Fitzrovia lodgings and The British Museum. With its free heating, light, pens and ink, and a moderately priced restaurant, the museum's Reading Room *(see p146)* rapidly became a second home which they shared with Marx and Swinburne among others.

Verlaine describes himself at this time as 'entirely given over to poetry', and many of the poems that make up *Romances Sans Paroles* (1874) – including the lines 'There is weeping in my heart / Like the rain falling on the city' – were written during this period. Rimbaud sketched the first drafts of *Une Saison en Enfer* in the Soho pubs.

After briefly returning separately to France, the pair returned to London in May 1873 and found new lodgings at No. 8 Great College Street *(see p263)*.

George Bernard Shaw • 29 Fitzroy Square

Irish playwright and critic George Bernard Shaw lived here from 1887 to 1898, when he moved from 36 Osnaburgh Street with his mother; he had previously lived at 37 Fitzroy Street in the early 1880s. During his time at Fitzroy Square he was music and drama critic for the *Pall Mall Gazette*, *Saturday Review* and other journals; writer of political and economic tracts for the Fabian Society in which he advocated gradual social reform; and the author of several unsuccessful novels. He began to make his name as a dramatist with an attack on slum landlords, *Widowers' Houses* (1892), written in collaboration with William Archer, his friend and neighbour at No. 27. A series of witty plays – *Mrs Warren's Profession* (1893), banned as it concerned prostitution, *Arms and the Man* (1894), *Candida* (1894) and *The Devil's Disciple* (1897) consolidated his career. Shaw campaigned for a theatre of ideas comparable to that of Ibsen and Strindberg in Scandinavia and was a member of St Pancras Council, which he claimed was 'cheerfully corrupt'. In June 1898 he married fellow-Fabian Charlotte Payne-Townshend. The couple eventually moved to 10 Adelphi Terrace, off the Strand, where they lived for the next 28 years.

Bloomsbury Salon • 29 Fitzroy Square

Adrian and Virginia Stephen (later Woolf) moved into the same house on Fitzroy Square in 1907, while their sister Vanessa, who was married to Clive Bell, occupied the family house at No. 46 Gordon Square in Bloomsbury *(see p141)*. They revived the 'Thursday evenings' started by Thoby Stephen, and by the end of 1907 had begun regular Friday evening literary readings, the choice of authors ranging from Restoration dramatists and Shakespeare to Swinburne and Ibsen. Lytton Strachey proposed to Virginia while she was living here, but the engagement was broken off to the relief of both parties. In 1911 Virginia and Adrian moved back to the bosom of Bloomsbury *(see p142)*.

No. 29 Fitzroy Square, formerly the home of first George Bernard Shaw and then Virginia Woolf

The Poet's Club • Restaurant de la Tour Eiffel, 1 Percy Street

When The Poet's Club was established in 1908, it first met above Rumpelmeyer's at No. 10 St James Street. Poet T.E. Hulme was the secretary and driving force behind the club, and in 1909 he moved it to Percy Street. Hulme established the rules, allowing the readings of 'original compositions in verse' and twenty-minute papers 'on a subject connected with poetry', followed by five-minute reaction speeches after dinner.

Hulme's concern for a more intimate and simple poetry was shattered by Ezra Pound's reading of 'Sestina: Altaforte' in April 1909. Pound roared his poem in a voice loud enough to rattle the cutlery.

> *I have no life save when the swords clash.*
> *But ah! when I see the standards gold, vair, purple,*
> > *opposing*
> *And the broad field beneath them turn crimson,*
> *Then howl I my heart nigh mad with rejoicing.*

A screen was hastily brought out to protect the restaurant's other customers. The Poet's Club, though, published both Hulme and Pound in *The Book of the Poet's Club* (1909). Pound later founded the Imagist school with F.S. Flint *(see p209)*.

No. 1 Percy Street, former home of the Eiffel Tower

Stulik's Eiffel Tower

In 1910 Rudolf Stulik, an Austrian Jew, acquired the existing restaurant business at No. 1 Percy Street and set about cultivating a clientele of artists and aristocrats. Living almost opposite at No. 4 Percy Street was Percy Wyndham Lewis – writer, painter and leader of The Vorticist movement; he was among the first to adopt The Eiffel.

The main restaurant was a simply decorated, L-shaped room, dominated by a huge brass urn filled with hydrangeas and ferns. There were eight or nine tables, each with a white tablecloth and red lampshade. Upstairs was a small hotel. Lewis decorated one room in his own fashion – the Vorticist room – while the other private room was more Edwardian in style, full of mahogany and pots of aspidistras. After closing time, Stulik's favoured clients were allowed in by the hotel entrance to spend the last part of the evening drinking. In this way, the Eiffel Tower became a club for the artists and their friends, and in July 1914 Lewis launched his magazine *Blast* at the Eiffel, with Ezra Pound in attendance. The magazine gave added impetus for rival artists to visit Stulik's, despite the fact that it was more expensive than other restaurants in the neighbourhood. Artists such as David Bomberg, Mark Gertler, Winifred Gill and Nina Hamnett – employed at the time at the Omega Workshop – made the Eiffel their second home. Augustus John and Jacob Epstein soon became regulars, together with their models and students from the Slade.

Stulik's offered the ideal location, with a plentiful supply of drink, credit and walls to hang paintings. Lewis's *Blast*, Epstein's radical sculptures, Stravinsky's challenging music, the Ballets Russes and jazz from America played by black musicians all contributed to a heady, intoxicating mix, where fashionable society mixed with bohemian artists. The erosion of social and sexual conformity, hastened in part by the First World War, allowed Stulik's to flourish. It become a venue for the 'new woman', who dared to wear short hair and trousers, smoke cigarettes, get drunk in public, and readily offer views on art and life.

Most striking among the Eiffel's female clientele were Nancy Cunard and Iris Tree. The daughter of the actor-manager Sir Herbert Beerbohm Tree, Iris at that time was a student at The Slade and rented a studio in Fitzroy Street. Nancy was the only child of an American society hostess and an English baronet. A renowned hell-raiser and iconoclast, as well as a tireless campaigner for the rights of African Americans, Nancy stayed at the Eiffel whenever she visited London. 'The comfort was nil, the room cheap, the convenience considerable … Food, drink and hours perfect.' Marie Beerbohm, Sybil Hart-Davies and Lady Diana Cooper joined them in bringing society friends to the Eiffel in its 1920s heyday. In the words of Nancy Cunard again, it became their 'carnal-spiritual home' (*To the Eiffel Tower Restaurant*, 1923).

Michael Arlen, Aldous Huxley, Seymour Leslie, Anthony Powell and Evelyn Waugh all frequented the Eiffel, putting it and some of the regulars in their novels. *Arlen's Piracy* (1922) has a thinly disguised 'Mont Angel' as the restaurant. Leslie's *The Silent Queen* (1927) has 'The Big Wheel' as the restaurant and sketches of Stulik and the interior of the restaurant by Nina Hamnett. In 1922 Aldous Huxley became infatuated with Nancy Cunard, and she provided the basis for characters in *Antic Hay* (1923) and *Point Counter Point* (1928). Anthony Powell's affair with Nina Hamnett brought him into contact with a wider bohemian world that fuelled several characters in *A Dance To The Music Of Time (see pp180 & 197)*. And Evelyn Waugh used the Eiffel as a model for Lottie Crump's hotel in *Vile Bodies* (1930).

Dylan Thomas and Caitlin Macnamara consummated their relationship while staying for a week at the Eiffel in April 1936. They left the bill to be picked up by Augustus John.

Omega Workshop • 33 Fitzroy Square

Art critic and painter Roger Fry, organiser of the 1910 and 1912 Post-Impressionist exhibitions at the Grafton Galleries, ran the Omega Workshop here from May 1913 until 1919. His aim was to provide employment and a living wage for young artists, and to apply Post-Impressionist principles to interior design. Duncan Grant and Vanessa Bell were the other artistic directors of Omega, while David Bomberg, Winifred Gill, Mark Gertler, Nina Hamnett, Paul Nash, William Roberts, and Wyndham Lewis were all associated with Omega for varying periods. Lewis did not remain a member for long and left over an argument with Fry concerning a commission to decorate a room for the Ideal Home Exhibition in October 1913. In addition to Fry's Bloomsbury friends, such as Virginia Woolf and Lytton Strachey, there was a steady stream of literary and artistic visitors, including George Bernard Shaw, W. B. Yeats, H.G. Wells, Arnold Bennett and Augustus John. In Evelyn Waugh's *Brideshead Revisited* (1945), Charles Ryder buys a screen at Omega's closing-down sale in 1919.

The Fitzroy Tavern • 16 Charlotte Street

Situated at the corner of Charlotte Street and Windmill Street, The Fitzroy Tavern – from which the term Fitzrovia derives – became London's most famous literary pub from the mid-1920s to the 1950s. Judah 'Papa' Kleinfeld, a naturalised Polish Jew, became the landlord of the pub in March 1919. Although re-named The Fitzroy Tavern, the pub was soon referred to as 'Kleinfeld's' by its saloon bar clientele of writers, poets, sculptors, composers, showgirls, music hall artistes, criminals, rebels, students, drifters and those on the run – from the police or from their pasts. The pub benefitted from the proximity of bohemian haunts, such as the Eiffel Tower restaurant and Bertorelli's *(see p132)*, ensuring that there was never a shortage of writers and artists looking for a quick drink before eating. Bertorelli's had no alcohol licence, in fact, and so its proprietor, David Bertorelli, sent his waitresses, trays in hand, over to the Fitzroy to collect orders for drinks and liqueurs.

One of Kleinfeld's first additions to the pub in the early 1920s was an electric pianola that could be played by hand or automatically. The composer Constant Lambert, who lived in Percy Street, regularly entertained the assembled crowd. The Irish composer E.J. Moeran also used the instrument to try out his compositions. Philip Heseltine, better known as 'Peter Warlock,' the composer and editor of music journal *The Sackbut*, became a regular and was generally to be found at a table with two or three young women carrying portfolios and scrolls. Cecil Gray, Michael Birkbeck, Dennis Arnold, Frederick Bontoft and many other composers also went to Kleinfeld's to enjoy the liberal atmosphere and stimulating intellectual discussion.

Kleinfeld was a model host, allowing his customers to behave pretty much as they wished. He happily tolerated unconventional dress and sexuality. Among the earliest artists to discover Kleinfeld's were Augustus John, Nina Hamnett, Vorticist painter Christopher Nevinson and Jacob Epstein, who would typically arrive accompanied by a beautiful model, such as Betty May. Poets Roy Campbell and Tommy Earp, freshly down from Oxford, found Kleinfeld's through John and Hamnett, and where they went, others followed.

Many British artists and writers of the 1910s and 1920s had been to Paris to absorb the new ideas in art and literature, and now sought opportunities to recreate a similar creative ambience in London. Kleinfeld's offered the ideal place to meet, talk, find work or outlets for publication and to keep up with the latest news. It was also, for a short time, quieter than the alternatives. As its reputation grew, it attracted a wide circle of young writers. Regulars included Malcolm Lowry, Roy Campbell, Tommy Earp, Lawrence Durrell and George Barker, and later Norman Cameron, Edwin Muir, Rayner Heppenstall, George Orwell, Ruthven Todd and Dylan Thomas.

Soho and Fitzrovia held a powerful magnetic pull for intelligent young men and women who were unable, financially, to go to university. Instead, they found an open university in the art galleries, museums, theatres and concert halls, the bookshops of Charing Cross Road, David Archer's bookshop in Soho and Meg's Café in Parton Street, as well as the shops and restaurants of the foreign communities that gave neighbourhoods such as Fitzrovia their distinct taste and smell.

In the 1950s the Fitzroy became a popular, although not exclusively, gay bar, extending Kleinfeld's original permissiveness and attracting leading politicians, writers, entertainers, broadcasters, comedians, sailors and washed-out bohemians. Kleinfeld's daughter Annie and her husband, Charlie Allchild, maintained the pub's liberal tradition, but by the 50s its fame was drawing more tourists than artists.

The Wheatsheaf • 25 Rathbone Place

By the mid-1930s the old bohemian haunts were changing hands and the poets and writers who were to become known as the 'Fitzrovians' moved down the road to The Wheatsheaf pub at 25 Rathbone Place. The move, led by Orwell in 1934, involved no great distance, being scarcely a hundred yards, but it had significance for this new generation of writers. And indeed the young contributors and editors of little magazines – such as *New Verse*, *Twentieth Century Verse*, *Purpose* and *Contemporary Poetry and Prose* – who made up the group were briefly known as the Wheatsheaf Writers.

The Wheatsheaf was smaller and quieter than the Fitzroy, and was also conveniently situated next to a pawnbrokers. It had a long, narrow bar panelled in dark wood and sold Younger's Scotch Ale – one of the stronger ales at the time, at 6d a pint. The pub also boasted two pretty barmaids, Betty and Sadie, and Jacob Epstein's model Betty May (known as Tiger Woman) as additional attractions. To mix with a demi-monde of car dealers, bookmakers, pimps and tarts was both economically and politically attractive to the Wheatsheaf writers, and it quickly became the place to talk, argue, fight, write and join the latest literary and political movements.

Surrealism at the Wheatsheaf

In the mid-1930s, some of London's intellectuals were picking up on ideas originating from the Surrealist movement in Paris. Many of these intellectuals were habitués of The Wheatsheaf. David Gascoyne, who in 1935 published *A Short Survey of Surrealism*, would criss-cross London during this time, visiting Roland Penrose in Hampstead and Antonia White, Charles Madge and Kathleen Raine in Chelsea. The Wheatsheaf provided a useful stopping-off point, and Gasgoyne, in turn, provided an energetic link between various intellectual groupings and the Wheatsheaf writers.

Wheatsheaf regulars Rayner Heppenstall, Humphrey Jennings, Roger Roughton and Blake scholar Ruthven Todd were all keen to explore Surrealist ideas, and in June 1936 Roger Roughton produced the Surrealism issue of *Contemporary Poetry and Prose*. The issue featured the leaders of the movement on the Continent, such as Breton, Buñuel, Dalí, Éluard, Jarry, Mesens and Péret, as well as the American poet E.E. Cummings, British filmmaker Humphrey Jennings and Dylan Thomas.

In 1936 Herbert Read and Roland Penrose presented the International Surrealist Exhibition at Burlington Place. Jennings and Ruthven Todd were on the organizing committee. Many Wheatsheaf regulars participated or visited the event, and Dylan Thomas handed out cups of boiled string, enquiring politely, 'Weak or strong?'

Political and Cultural Cross-fertilisation

The Fitzrovians occupied a fringe position, geographically and culturally. What they shared was a willingness to explore, to seek out what was new and to be experimental. In addition to the influx of modern French poetry – which Rayner Heppenstall, Humphrey Jennings, Roger Roughton and Ruthven Todd had all been busily translating in the 1930s – there was a steady flow of American modernist poetry exerting an influence, including the work of Ezra Pound, William Carlos Williams, Marianne Moore, E.E. Cummings, Hart Crane and Allen Tate. There was also an interest, most noticeably from Geoffrey Grigson, David Gascoyne and Kathleen Raine, in the English visionary tradition of Blake, Thomas Traherne and Samuel Palmer.

Many of the Wheatsheaf writers of 1934–36 produced first-rate work, including David Gascoyne, Dylan Thomas, Len Lye, Nigel Henderson and George Barker. But the flow of ideas also led to developments outside the traditional cultural sphere of art and literature. The Mass-Observation Project, founded in 1937 by Humphrey Jennings, Madge and Tom Harrisson, was a scheme that recruited observers, including poets and novelist, to collect data about everyday life and popular culture. It impacted on the development of English sociology as well as on documentary filmmaking and TV and radio broadcasting. And Jennings's wartime documentaries, such as *London Can Take It* (1940), *Listen to Britain* (1942) and *A Diary for Timothy* (1945), represent a milestone in British filmmaking.

The Girl from the Fiction Department • 18 Percy Street

Sonia Brownell moved here, into rooms above the White Tower restaurant, in August 1940. With the characteristic boldness that captivated all the men she met, she remained here throughout the Blitz, taking on an increasingly central role at *Horizon* magazine *(see p151)*. She first met George Orwell in 1940, and by the time they met again, in 1945, he was recently widowed, lonely, and struggling with incipient tuberculosis and the care of his adopted son. Sonia helped with babysitting and the two became close. However, like all the other women Orwell asked at the time, she declined his offer of marriage. Instead, that summer she left for Paris where she fell in love with the philosopher Maurice Merleau-Ponty. Orwell retired to the island of Jura to write *Nineteen Eighty-Four* (1949), in which he recreated Sonia as Julia, 'the girl from the Fiction Department', whose uncompromising fearlessness enthrals Winston, the novel's hero: 'She still expected something from life … she did not understand that there is no such thing as happiness, that the only victory lay in the far future, long after you were dead.' The room where Winston and Julia meet to make love is based on Sonia's room in Percy Street.

By the time the book was published, Orwell's condition had severely deteriorated, and Sonia's love affair with Merleau-Ponty had ended. Sonia married Orwell at his bedside in University College Hospital, Gower Street on 13 October 1949. Plans were made to move to Switzerland in the hope of stabilising his condition, but Orwell died of a lung haemorrhage on 21 January 1950, days before they were due to leave.

As his literary executor, it was one of Sonia Orwell's great achievements that, with the assistance of archivist and editor Ian Angus, Orwell's numerous letters, essays and journalism were systematically collected and published.

The Marquis of Granby • Corner of Rathbone Street and Percy Street
The boundary between Holborn and Marylebone ran down the middle of Charlotte Street and the two boroughs had different licencing restrictions. So, whereas The Fitzroy Tavern and The Wheatsheaf closed at 10.30 pm, the Marquis of Granby and the Duke of York were open until 11pm, resulting in a regular dash to these pubs after 10 pm.

The Marquis of Granby was both rougher and dirtier than the Wheatsheaf, but was quiet enough at lunchtimes for Desmond Hawkins and Dylan Thomas to use as a meeting place, in the summer of 1935, to write *Murder of the King's Canary*, a satire on the contemporary literary scene. In September of the same year, T.S. Eliot dropped in for a glass of 'its indifferent sherry' to celebrate the new issue of *Purpose*, with the magazine's literary editor, Desmond Hawkins, and contributors George Barker, John Pudney, Randall Swingler and Dylan Thomas. Whenever Barker or Thomas came to London they would go to the Marquis of Granby to write and discuss work in progress. By 1936 Barker had begun to arrange meetings in quieter pubs. Thomas, though, would return for the thrill of entertaining. An image of the witty exuberance of Thomas, represented in the poem as Gwilym, is shown in Louis MacNeice's 'Autumn Sequel':

> *Gwilym begins: with the first pint a tall*
> *Story froths over, demons from the hills*
> *Concacchinate in the toilet, a silver ball*
>
> *Jumps up and down in his beer till laughter spills*
> *Us out to another bar followed by frogs*
> *And auks and porpentines and armadills.*
>
> *For Gwilym is a poet; analogues*
> *And double meanings crawl behind his ears*
> *And his brown eyes were scooped out of the bogs,*
>
> *A jester and a bard. Archaic fears*
> *Dog him with handcuffs but this rogue's too quick,*
> *They grab and he turns a cartwheel and disappears.*

At Dylan Thomas's funeral an inebriated MacNeice is reported to have thrown his sandwiches on the coffin in the belief that they were a bunch of daffodils.

The Duke of York • 47 Rathbone Street

During the 1940s the Duke of York was considered too violent for all but the hardest Fitzrovians, such as Roy Campbell, Julian Maclaren-Ross, Louis MacNeice, and W.R. Rodgers. Anthony Burgess recalled a 1943 visit in the first volume of his autobiography *Little Wilson and Big God* (1987), involving Pirelli's gang, who entered the pub and ordered several pints of beer. When they poured them on the floor, Burgess's wife, Lynne, protested that it was a waste. Pirelli ordered the landlord, Major Alf Klein, to pour more pints and Lynne to drink them. She drank three straight pints and was instantly offered Pirelli's personal protection from the O'Flaherty and Maltese mobs.

L'Étoile Restaurant • 30 Charlotte Street

L'Étoile Restaurant, darkly lit and romantic, with celebrity photographs on its walls, was a favourite haunt of the young T.S. Eliot. Wyndham Lewis and Ezra Pound celebrated here after the launch of *Blast* magazine. Lewis used the restaurant for liaisons in the 1920s and 30s. Nina Hamnett brought the young Anthony Powell here during their affair. In *A Buyer's Market* (1952), Nick Jenkins describes Charlotte Street as retaining 'a certain unprincipled integrity of character'.

Bertorelli's Restaurant • 19 Charlotte Street

Established by four Italian brothers in 1912, Bertorelli's was frequented by Cyril Connolly, Anthony Powell and other 1940s writers. In the 50s, novelist Philip Toynbee established the Wednesday Club in honour of Richard Hannay's Thursday Club in John Buchan's *The Three Hostages* (1924); Buchan had lived at nearby 76 Portland Place from 1913 to1919 and been a customer here. Toynbee's dining club attracted many writers, including T.S. Eliot and Rex Warner.

After the success of *Lucky Jim* (1954) and *That Uncertain Feeling* (1955), Anthony Powell, literary editor of *Punch*, invited Kingsley Amis here for lunch in November 1957. Amis became a weekly visitor in the 1960s after moving to London from Swansea. These lunches became mildly notorious as Amis became more right wing in his political sympathies, and attracted diners such as poet and historian Robert Conquest, novelist John Braine and others sympathetic to his views.

Newman Arms and Newman Passage • 23 Rathbone Street

On circumstantial rather than textual evidence, The Newman Arms is generally accepted as the model for Orwell's pub scenes in *Keep The Aspidistra Flying* (1936) – the episode in which Comstock and Ravelston argue about socialism – and

Nineteen Eighty-Four (1949), where Winston unsuccessfully tries to find out about life before the revolution from a prole. The Newman exclusively served beer and was renowned as a working-class pub with its upstairs pie room. Julian Maclaren-Ross in *Memoirs of the Forties* (1965) recalls that Newman Passage to the left of the pub was known locally as Jekyll and Hyde Alley and was where 'one sometimes guided girls in order to become better acquainted'. Film-director and writer Christopher Petit acclaimed Newman Passage, with its 'partly roofed, narrow alley-way with a hidden dog-leg, out of sight at either end' as the secret heart of Fitzrovia in his 1993 story *Newman Passage, or J. Maclaren-Ross and the case of the Vanishing Writers*. Petit also identified the passage as the alleyway used in a famous film scene, where a murder victim is led before being taken inside and killed in Michael Powell's psychological thriller *Peeping Tom* (1959).

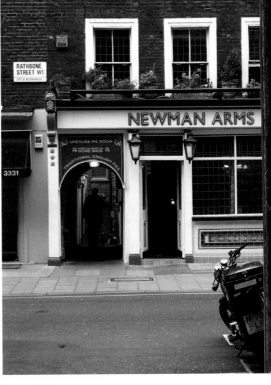

Newman Arms

The Tiger's Lair • 27 Goodge Street

This address is the headquarters of Quartet publishing house, presided over by Naim Atallah from his penthouse office at the top of the building, where, according to Jennie Erdal in her memoir *Ghosting* (2004), behind his large leather-topped desk, hangs a huge tiger skin, complete with head.

Adopting a similar approach to staffing as Cyril Connolly some 40 years earlier at *Horizon*, Atallah employed only stunning, sophisticated young women. Among the slender girls of means who began their careers at Quartet, all of whom Atallah apparently addressed as 'Beloved', was Nigella Lawson.

In her memoir Erdal provides a meditation on the process and skills of ghost-writing, and describes the 'uneasy alliance', the 'unusual relationship, part symbiotic, part parasitic' that underlies it. The identity of her erstwhile employer is lightly veiled under the name Tiger.

BLOOMSBURY & KING'S CROSS

BOUNDED BY TOTTENHAM COURT ROAD, Euston Road, Gray's Inn Road and High Holborn, Bloomsbury is named after William de Blemund who in 1201 built a manor house on land just to the south of what is now Bloomsbury Square. Bloomsbury is often regarded as the intellectual heart of the capital and is home to the British Museum and University College. The area is most immediately associated with the 'Bloomsbury Group' of writers, artists and intellectuals who lived here in the early 20th century, when the address was far from fashionable.

The seeds of the Bloomsbury Group can be traced back to the mid-19th century, when the area attracted the Pre-Raphaelites and their friends who began holding literary salons. This tradition was taken up and extended by Lady Ottoline Morrell's salon, as well as Harold Monro and the circle of writers connected with the Poetry Bookshop. Wyndham Lewis and the short-lived Rebel Arts Centre, and Ezra Pound, H.D. and others connected with *The Egoist* magazine also contributed to Bloomsbury's evolving cultural scene.

During the Second World War, *Horizon* literary magazine, based at Lansdowne Terrace in Bloomsbury and edited by Cyril Connolly, came to prominence. Running throughout the 1940s, *Horizon* published George Orwell, Evelyn Waugh, Angus Wilson, Stephen Spender, W.H. Auden and Geoffrey Grigson among others.

T.S. Eliot remained a constant presence in Bloomsbury through the war years. Fortunately he was away from his Russell Square office when a flying bomb hit, though the event is alluded to in *The Four Quartets* (1943). Like many writers Eliot contributed to the war effort with intelligence work for the Ministry of Information (based at Senate House on Malet Street) and the BBC, as well as carrying out fire duty on the rooftop of Faber & Faber's offices.

George Orwell also found occasional work at the Ministry of Information, (Britain's answer to Goebbels' Ministry of Propaganda), and it provided one of the sources for the Ministry of Truth in his novel *Nineteen Eighty-Four* (1949). At the time publishers had to submit manuscripts to the Ministry of Information, whose role it was to 'advise' on the suitability or otherwise of publishing material.

Bloomsbury & King's Cross

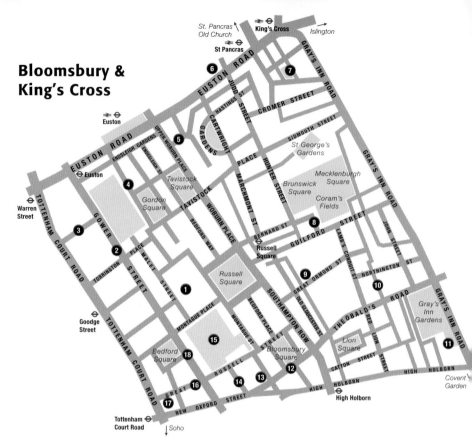

Key

1. Senate House
2. Gower Street
3. University Street
4. Gordon Street
5. Woburn Walk
6. British Library
7. Argyle Square
8. Landsdowne Terrace
9. Great Ormond Street
10. Great James Street
11. Gray's Inn
12. Bloomsbury Way
13. St George's Bloomsbury
14. Museum Street
15. British Museum
16. Great Russell Street
17. YMCA
18. Bloomsbury Street

Comedy of Errors • Gray's Inn

Gray's Inn, on the Bloomsbury/Holborn border, is one of the four Inns of Court and dates from the 14th century as a centre for the practice and study of law.

Shakespeare's *Comedy of Errors* was first performed at Gray's Inn Hall on 28 December 1594. Francis Bacon, historian, statesman and author of *Novum Organum* (1620), a Latin treatise on scientific method, occupied chambers at Gray's Inn from 1576 until his death in 1626.

Jerusalem's Pillars • St Pancras Old Church

William Blake's famous quatrain from *Jerusalem* (1804–20) maps a landscape, pointing to St Pancras Old Church as the New Jerusalem:

> *The Fields from Islington to Marybone*
> *To Primrose Hill and Saint John's Wood*
> *Were builded over pillars of gold*
> *And there Jerusalem's pillars stood*

Central to Blake's vision is the altar at St Pancras Old Church, one of the first churches in Britain, built no later than 312 AD, on the site of a Roman encampment. St Pancras, patron saint of truth, children and dancing, was a boy-Martyr who resisted the Roman Empire until it killed him.

> *Here Little-ones ran on the fields,*
> *The Lamb of God among them seen,*
> *And fair Jerusalem his Bride*
> *Among the little meadows green.*

The architect and collector Sir John Soane is buried here in a vault of his own design. Mary Wollstonecraft and William Godwin were married and were buried here. In 1865 their coffins were removed by Sir Percy Shelley to lie with his mother, Mary Shelley, at St Peter's in Bournemouth, in advance of the removal of hundreds of coffins to make way for the Midland Railway cutting.

The young Thomas Hardy, who at the time was working as an apprentice to Mr Arthur Blomfield, an architect based in Covent Garden, supervised the disinterment and removal of coffins. The removed tombstones were placed around an ash tree, generally known as the 'Hardy Tree', which over the years has grown in among the stones. At this time Hardy became an avid reader of Shelley's *Queen Mab (see below)*, and his work here probably inspired his poem 'In The Cemetery', about graves that have been moved to make way for a drain.

Some years before Hardy's involvement, Old St Pancras Churchyard is featured in Charles Dickens's *Tale of Two Cities* (1859) as the churchyard in which Roger Cly was buried and where Jerry Cruncher was known to 'fish' (19th-century slang for tomb robbery and body snatching).

Coleridge, Yeats and Rimbaud were all fascinated by the church, and more recently Aidan Andrew Dun wrote his epic and visionary poem *Vale Royal* (1995) with St Pancras Old Church at its centre. *Vale Royal* chronicles the area's history and summons the spirits of former habitués such as Blake and Chatterton.

The Hardy Tree
at St Pancras
Old Church

During June 1814 the married Percy Bysshe Shelley secretly courted Mary Godwin, the daughter of Mary Wollstonecraft. Together with Mary's stepsister Jane 'Claire' Clairmont, the pair would meet by her mother's grave at Old St Pancras Churchyard. The Godwins ran a bookshop nearby at Skinner Street, High Holborn. Shelley gave Mary a copy of *Queen Mab* (1813) and wrote a number of poems for her, including 'To Mary Wollstonecraft Godwin':

> Upon my heart thy accents sweet
> Of peace and pity fell like dew
> On flowers half-dead; – thy lips did meet
> Mine tremblingly; thy dark eyes threw
> Their soft persuasion on my brain,
> Charming away its dream of pain.

A year later Shelley abandoned his wife, leaving England for Switzerland with both Mary and Claire *(see p105)*.

The Good Son • 12 Argyle Square

In June 1874 French poet Arthur Rimbaud took a room at the small hotel opposite King's Cross Station to await the arrival of his mother and sister. He had been sharing rooms in Stamford Street *(see p81)* with the poet Germaine Nouveau, who had returned to Paris. Over the following week the 'diabolical beauty' (as Verlaine had called Rimbaud) was the perfect host, taking his mother and little Vitalie on sightseeing tours and shopping trips. 'Arthur is so very kind' Vitalie wrote in her journal of one particularly hot day. 'I was longing to treat myself to an ice, and Arthur anticipated my desire.'

Sketches by Boz • 147 Gower Street

Charles Dickens lived here from Christmas 1823 until February 1824 when his father was imprisoned in the Marshalsea for debt. He used St George's, the Hawksmoor church between Museum Street and Bury Place, as a setting in *Sketches by Boz*.

From March 1837 until December 1839, Dickens lived at No. 48 Doughty Street, now the Dickens House and Museum. The house was within walking distance of the Saffron Hill slums and criminal underworld. Here he finished *The Pickwick Papers*, wrote *Oliver Twist*, wrote most of *Nicholas Nickleby* (1839) and started *Barnaby Rudge* (1841). Dickens's sister Mary died at the house in May 1837.

At the beginning of *Bleak House* (1853), Dickens famously describes the scene on Holborn Hill (now High Holborn), close to the Inns of Court, thus:

> *Implacable November weather. As much mud in the streets, as if the waters had but newly retired from the face of the earth, and it would not be wonderful to meet a Megalosaurus, forty feet long or so, waddling like an elephantine lizard up Holborn Hill.*

The Brotherhood • 17 Red Lion Square

The Pre-Raphaelite painter and poet Dante Gabriel Rossetti rented three rooms on the ground floor during 1851 with fellow painter Walter Deverell. The landlord stipulated that lady models should be 'kept under some gentlemanly restraint' to avoid succumbing to their charms. It was here that Rossetti's future wife, Elizabeth Siddall, first sat for him. Later, when his friends William Morris and Edward Burne-Jones needed accommodation, he recommended these rooms. They lived here from 1856 to 59, developing their medievalist style furniture. While here Morris developed his ideas on art and design, stipulating that an object should be both beautiful and useful.

When Morris married Jane Burden they moved to 41 Great Ormond Street, but returned to Bloomsbury in 1865, where they lived at 25 Queen Square until 1871. Here he wrote *The Earthly Paradise* (1868–70), which established him as a popular poet. He also ran a decorating shop on the ground floor of 26 Queen Square. His wife Jane had an affair with Rossetti at this time.

Lady Ottoline Morrell • 44 Bedford Square

Lady Ottoline Morrell ran a regular Thursday evening literary salon here from 1908 and throughout the years of the First World War. These were attended by many of the foremost writers of the day, such as Lytton Strachey, Virginia Woolf, T.S. Eliot,

D.H. Lawrence (who was accepted as the sole representative of the common man), Aldous Huxley, Bertrand Russell and W.B. Yeats. Tall and striking, Morrell is unmistakably present as Lady Hermione in Lawrence's *Women In Love* (1920), Mrs Wimbrush in Huxley's *Crome Yellow* (1921) and Mrs Aldwinkle in *Those Barren Leaves* (1925) by the same author. All these portraits caused considerable offence.

She continued to entertain writers and artists at her country home at Garsington Manor, Oxfordshire from 1915 to 1927. Between 1924 and 1935 she lived at 10 Gower Street; Graham Greene used the address as the house of Lady Caroline Bury in *It's A Battlefield* (1934).

Tears Before Bedtime • Bedford Square

William Plomer wrote 'The Plane Trees of Bedford Square', which were never loftier or leafier than 'one afternoon / warm in the last world-peace before / the First World War.'

The future poet laureate Robert Bridges lived at No. 52 Bedford Square with his mother from 1877 to 1881. Bridges worked as a young doctor in the casualty department at St Bartholomew's Hospital. Among his visitors was the Jesuit poet Gerard Manley Hopkins who was assistant priest at the Farm Street church, Mayfair. In 1918 Bridges was responsible for the publishing of Hopkins' collected work.

Cyril Connolly, who wrote *The Unquiet Grave* (1944), lived at No. 49 Bedford Square from May 1942 until July 1945 with his mistress Lys Lubbock, whom he had charmed away from her husband to work at his magazine *Horizon*. In May 1944 they entertained Ernest Hemingway, who was working in London as a war correspondent.

Bedford
Square

Connolly let the upstairs rooms to his friend Peter Quennell, who was working at Senate House for the Ministry of Information and, in 1943, became editor of *Cornhill* magazine. Rather unwisely, Quennell introduced Connolly to his lover of the time, Barbara Skelton – who in 1950 became Connolly's second wife.

Skelton includes an account of this period of her life in the first book in her memoirs, *Tears Before Bedtime* (1987).

Bloomsberries • 46 Gordon Square

The Bloomsbury Group was founded here at the home of the Stephen family, on 16 February 1905 when Thoby Stephen started his Thursday evening art discussions. When Thoby died of typhoid in November 1906, his sister Vanessa, who subsequently married Clive Bell, continued the meetings at the house. In 1908 they ran a Play Reading Society. Adrian and Virginia Stephen (later Woolf) also held meetings at No. 29 Fitzroy Square *(see p124)*.

The group included the painters Clive and Vanessa Bell, Duncan Grant, who became Vanessa's lover, critic Roger Fry, the writer and biographer Lytton Strachey, his sister Marjorie, novelist E.M. Forster and the economist John Maynard Keynes (who lived at the house from 1916).

Their association was based on friendship and a conscious revolt against the artistic, social and sexual restrictions of Victorian society. They were inspired by the teachings of Cambridge philosopher G.E. Moore – an elated Lytton Strachey proclaimed that Moore's *Principia Ethica* (1903) marked the birth of the 'Age of Reason' – and members of the group played a key role in the development of modernist art and literature in England.

Nevertheless, the group has never been short of critics, many finding the members precious, immoral or elitist – or indeed all three. D.H. Lawrence broke with them, reviling 'this horror of little swarming selves', while Wyndham Lewis condemned them as 'elitist, corrupt and talentless'; he satirized them mercilessly in his novel *Apes of God* (1930). The poet Rupert Brooke described them as treacherous and wicked, while Osbert Sitwell used terms such as 'how simply too extraordinary' to ridicule their manner.

Lytton Strachey • 51 Gordon Square

Lytton Strachey, author of the landmark collection of biographical essays *Eminent Victorians* (1918), lived here from 1919 to 1924. An advocate of tolerance in personal relations, he lived in a *ménage à trois* with Dora Carrington and Ralph Partridge from 1916. He also wrote *Queen Victoria* (1921), an irreverent biography debunking Victorian myths, and *Elizabeth and Essex: A Tragic History* (1928), a Freudian reading of the relationship between Elizabeth I and the Earl of Essex.

Virginia and Leonard • 38 Brunswick Square

Virginia Stephen moved here in November 1911, sharing the house and living expenses with her brother Adrian, Maynard Keynes, and Duncan Grant. Another Cambridge friend, Leonard Woolf, joined them in December. Soon Virginia and Leonard were writing in the morning, having lunch together and spending the afternoons sitting in Bloomsbury Square; they were married in May 1912. Shortly afterwards Virginia had a nervous breakdown, and the couple moved to Richmond for Virginia's recuperation *(see p259)*. She drew on her experiences of mental illness to write the interior monologue of the shell-shocked soldier, Septimus Warren Smith, in her novel *Mrs Dalloway* (1925).

In October 1914 Duncan Grant left Brunswick Square to return to Vanessa Bell's home at 46 Gordon Square. No. 38 Brunswick Square, and No. 29, where E.M. Forster lived after he published *A Passage To India* (1922–4), were destroyed in the Blitz.

The Hogarth Press • 52 Tavistock Square

Virginia and Leonard Woolf moved here from Richmond in March 1924, bringing with them the Hogarth Press, which they set up in the downstairs rooms. While living here Virginia wrote the principal works in her oeuvre – *Mrs Dalloway* (1925), *To the Lighthouse* (1927), *Orlando* (1928), *A Room of One's Own* (1929), and *The Waves* (1931) – in which she further developed and extended the use of the interior monologue and 'stream of consciousness' in the modern novel. Her essay 'Mr Bennett and Mrs Brown' (1923) attacked the realism of Arnold Bennett's fiction and advocated a more fluid, internal approach to characterisation.

The policy of the Hogarth Press was to publish new and experimental work. Literary editor John Lehmann became their assistant in 1931, returning as part owner in 1938. They published T.S. Eliot, Virginia Woolf, Katherine Mansfield, translations of Chekhov, Dostoevsky, Freud, Rilke and Tolstoy, and pamphlets on psychoanalysis, politics, aesthetics and disarmament.

In the crisis atmosphere of August 1939 the Woolfs moved the Hogarth Press and their possessions into 37 Mecklenburgh Square, as Tavistock Square was to be pulled down and redeveloped. Here Virginia finished her biography of Roger Fry. From October they lived at Monk's House, Rodmell, near Lewes, travelling up to London once a week, sometimes staying a few days. This went on until 10 September 1940 when Mecklenburgh Square was bombed and they could not reach the severely damaged house. Just over a month later, on 16 October 1940, the house at Tavistock Square was also bombed. The site is now occupied by the Tavistock Hotel.

At Monk's House, Elizabeth Bowen, Vita Sackville-West and Dr Octavia Wilberforce visited them in February 1941. Despite the more restful environment Virginia's health deteriorated. She never fully escaped the shadow of mental illness and eventually took her own life, by drowning in the river Ouse on 28 March 1941. The Hogarth Press became part of Chatto & Windus in 1947.

A Room with a View • Kingsley Hotel, Bloomsbury Way

E.M. Forster lodged here from 1902 to 1904 and wrote parts of his 'Italian' novels, *Where Angels Fear To Tread* (1905) and *A Room With A View* (1908).

At Cambridge in the late 1890s Forster had come under the influence of G.E. Moore and joined the Apostles, an exclusive intellectual society with a membership that included many of the leading figures of what would later become the Bloomsbury Group – Maynard Keynes, Lytton Strachey, Bertrand Russell and Leonard Woolf. After travelling to Italy and Greece with his mother, he moved to Bloomsbury and began writing fiction for the *Independent Review*. Quickly established, he went on to write *Howards End* (1910) and *A Passage to India* (1922–24).

The Other Bloomsbury • Harold Monro and The Poetry Bookshop

Harold Monro established the Poetry Bookshop at 35 Devonshire Street (now Boswell Street) to encourage the sale of poetry and to promote poetry readings. The Bookshop provided a literary meeting place for bohemians and others unable to gain access to the more aristocratic salons. While on his travels in Europe, Robert Frost stumbled into the bookshop on the day it opened – 8 January 1913. Here he came into contact for the first time with the poetry of Ezra Pound, Edward Thomas and T.E. Hulme.

Monro founded the *Poetry Review* (1911) and published Edward Marsh's five anthologies of *Georgian Poetry* (1912–22), which included work by James Elroy Flecker, Rupert Brooke, Walter de la Mare and W.H. Davies. In 1916 the bookshop moved to 38 Great Russell Street from which address Monro traded until 1932.

Among the poets most closely associated with the Poetry Bookshop were Charlotte Mew, the American poet H.D. (Hilda Doolittle) and Richard Aldington. The Poetry Bookshop published Aldington's first book *Images 1910–15*, in 1915. Alida Monro – homosexual, as was her husband – arranged the publication of Mew's books *The Farmer's Bride* (1916) and *The Rambling Sailor* (1929).

Charlotte Mew • 9 Gordon Street

Charlotte Mew lived here in modest circumstances with her mother and sister, Anne. Her style and approach owed much to the decadence of Wilde and Yeats, and her first published story appeared in Beardsley's *Yellow Book*. Mew's restrained poems are dominated by an emotional recognition of the physical world. They lament the passing of beauty, passion, people and life, and are pervaded by a troubled sensuality. Emotionally engaged, she had great presence (despite being less than five foot tall) and esteemed the human voice and poetry in performance. Alida Monro's account of

143

their first encounter at a Poetry Bookshop reading in November 1915 describes the tiny figure of Mew stalking into the room in a tweed coat and pork pie hat, wielding an umbrella as if it were a weapon against the world.

W.H. Davies, Poet and Super-Tramp • 14 Great Russell Street

The poet W.H. Davies, who lived much of his life as a tramp, was persuaded to move here by publisher and editor Harold Monro, after the two had met at Monro's Poetry Bookshop. Davies lived here from 1916 until 1922. He had previously crossed America (losing a leg while trying to jump boxcars in the process) and travelled widely in Britain, writing poems in response to the natural world. His book *The Soul's Destroyer and Other Poems* (1905) came to the attention of George Bernard Shaw and led to his gradual return to conventional society. His most famous work is *The Autobiography of a Super-Tramp* (1908).

The Rebel Arts Centre • 38 Great Ormond Street

Kate Lechmere, business partner and former lover of Percy Wyndham Lewis, rented the first floor of No. 38 Great Ormond Street for the Rebel Arts Centre in March 1914, while she occupied the top floor flat. Lewis set up the Rebel Arts Centre as a base from which to oppose Roger Fry's Omega Workshop *(see p127)*, and – as he saw it – the elitist Bloomsbury Group. He held exhibitions and talks here, and published *Blast* magazine. Lewis, Lechmere, Christopher Nevinson, Edward Wadsworth, David Bomberg and Henri Gaudier-Brzeska helped decorate the rooms with murals and other paintings. The Futurist Filippo Marinetti, Ezra Pound and Ford Hueffer (later Ford Madox Ford) gave lectures, while Arthur Symons, T.E. Hulme and Richard Aldington were generally supportive of the venture.

The Rebel Arts Centre was short-lived, however, and plagued by emotional and artistic (Modernist versus Futurist) infighting. By July 1914, Lechmere had withdrawn her financial support and Lewis moved to Percy Street, Fitzrovia *(see p126)*.

The Egoist • Oakley House, Bloomsbury Street

H.D. (Hilda Doolittle) had followed her friend Ezra Pound from America to London, where he introduced her to Richard Aldington in 1911. Aldington and H.D. married in 1913, but Aldington was far from faithful and the two eventually parted in 1927. Both worked as literary editors for Harriet Shaw Weaver's Imagist magazine, *The Egoist*, which was based at Oakley House. Aldington was literary editor from 1914 until he went to fight in the First World War in 1916. He was succeeded in the post by H.D. who reviewed only the work of Marianne Moore, Amy Lowell and Charlotte Mew in a conscious effort to promote the writing of modernist women. H.D. was succeeded by T.S. Eliot in 1917.

Bid me To Live • 44 Mecklenburgh Square
Recovering from a miscarriage, H.D. had shared a flat in this house with Aldington's mistress, Dorothy Yorke. In November 1917 she lent her room to D.H. Lawrence and his (German) wife Frieda – the couple had had to leave Cornwall in haste on suspicion of being spies.

Lawrence corrected the proofs of *Women in Love* here, and began to write *Aaron's Rod* (1922). The characters Julia and Robert Cunningham, a 'half-bohemian' American writer married to 'a stoutish young Englishman in khaki', are inspired by H.D. and Aldington. H.D.'s book *Bid Me To Live: A Madrigal* (1960) is a fictional account of her life at this period in which the married protagonists are in a private war of the sexes. The character of the charismatic Federico is inspired by Lawrence.

Stone Lies Solid • The British Museum
The British Museum was established by Act of Parliament in 1753 and first housed in a 17th-century mansion, Montagu House, which stood on the site of today's building. The doors were first opened to the public on 15th January 1759; entry was free and directed to be given to 'all studious and curious Persons'.

Percy Bysshe Shelley was inspired to write 'Ozymandias' (1818) in response to the Egyptian treasures, including the Rosetta Stone and a massive sculpture of Ramses II, that had been added to the collection in 1802. Expressing his scepticism and hatred of tyranny, the poem was published in Leigh Hunt's *Examiner* before Shelley left England:

> *I met a traveller from an antique land*
> *Who said: Two vast and trunkless legs of stone*
> *Stand in the desert ... Near them, on the sand,*
> *Half sunk, a shattered visage lies, whose frown,*
> *And wrinkled lip, and sneer of cold command,*
> *Tell its sculptor well those passions read*
> *Which yet survive, stamped on these life less things,*
> *The hand that mocked them, and the heart that fed:*
> *And on the pedestal these words appear:*
> *'My name is Ozymandias, king of kings:*
> *Look on my works, ye Mighty, and despair!'*
> *Nothing beside remains. Round the decay*
> *Of that colossal wreck, boundless and bare*
> *The lone and level sands stretch far away.*

Keats wrote 'On Seeing the Elgin Marbles' (1817) and 'Ode on a Grecian Urn' (1820) in response to the Museum's antiquities. The Elgin Marbles had been acquired the year before, in 1816; he visited regularly with his friend, the painter Benjamin Haydon, and would sit for an hour or more rapt in reverie before the sculptures.

The present quadrangular building dates from the mid-1850s. The need for larger premises had been growing, and King George IV's donation of his father's library (The King's Library) in 1823 had provided the spur for action. The building was designed by Sir Robert Smirke, and the first phase largely completed by 1852.

Lawrence Binyon worked in the Department of Prints and Drawings at the British Museum for forty years. His lines from 'For the Fallen' are carved on the entrance wall to the museum as a memorial to the museum staff who died in the First World War. In *Jacob's Room* (1922), Virginia Woolf wrote 'Stone lies solid over the British Museum, as bone lies cool over the visions and heat of the brain'. The novel evokes life and death in the First World War through indirect narration and poetic impressionism.

The Reading Room at the British Museum

The Reading Room • The British Museum

Books and manuscripts formed an important part of the British Museum's foundation collection, and a reading room had been provided for the use of scholars from the beginning. Construction of the round Reading Room, located in the central courtyard, began in 1854. This was designed by Sir Robert Smirke's brother, Sydney.

For a short period at the time of its opening in May 1857, access to the Reading Room was available to all, but soon after admission was by pass only. For 150 years scholars and revolutionaries, writers and poets, students and eccentrics have laboured at the long tables fanning out from the room's hub under the brilliant gold, blue and cream domed ceiling.

In 1873 readers included Marx, Swinburne, Verlaine and Rimbaud. The 18-year-old Rimbaud obtained a reader's ticket on 25 March 1873, confirming that he was 'not under twenty-one years of age'. Back in London in 1874, this time with the even younger poet Germain Nouveau, Rimbaud returned to the library on 4 April to renew his ticket. Signing the register, they each gave themselves an extra Christian name: Jean Nicolas 'Joseph' Arthur Rimbaud and 'Marie' Bernard Germain Nouveau.

In 1902 Gertrude Stein stayed at 20 Bloomsbury Square with her brother Leo and spent her time at the British Library reading Trollope's novels.

At this time Lenin was also a regular reader at the library. He first obtained a ticket in 1902, using the pseudonym 'Jacob Richter' (adopted to elude the Tsarist police). Over the following nine years he returned to the library as frequently as his visits to London allowed, occupying by preference (according to folklore) seat L13.

Well acquainted with many of the major libraries of Europe and Russia, Lenin considered The British Library had no equal, commenting in 1907:

> It is a remarkable institution, especially that exceptional reference section. Ask them any question, and in the very shortest space of time they'll tell you where to look to find the material that interests you ... Let me tell you, there is no better library than the British Museum. Here there are fewer gaps in the collections than in any other library.

Angus Wilson worked at the museum's Department of Printed Books and lived at 3/11 on the top floor of Endsleigh Court in Tavistock Square in 1939. He reworked his experiences of packing and transporting treasures during the 'phoney war' into his novel *The Old Men at the Zoo*, 1961 *(see p268)*. After the War he became Deputy Superintendant of the Reading Room, leaving in 1955 to become a full-time writer.

Wilson's knowledge of those working at the museum went into his *Anglo-Saxon Attitudes* (1956), a novel concerned with an archaeological forgery. Sonia Orwell, who helped Wilson get his first stories published when she worked for *Horizon* magazine, inspired a minor character, Elvira Portway. She was not amused to find herself characterised as the hair-twirling, intellectually lightweight Elvira.

Today, although the Reading Room remains a working library open to scholars and researchers, the British Library has moved to a new home, adjacent to St Pancras.

Landmark Collection • The British Library at St Pancras
Famously denounced by Prince Charles as looking like an 'academy for secret policemen', the new British Library opened in 1998 and has turned out to be much loved by readers and visitors. The controversial project – the largest public building constructed in the UK in the 20th century – took 20 years to complete. It offers on-site space for more than 1,200 readers and incorporates some 300 kilometres of underground shelving in basements that extend to a depth of nearly 25 metres.

Outstanding works in the collection include the world's earliest printed book, *The Diamond Sutra* (868), a unique papyrus of Aristotle, Magna Carta, the Lindisfarne Gospels, *Beowulf*, a Gutenberg Bible, manuscripts of Jane Austen, James Joyce and the Beatles, and the first edition of *The Times* newspaper.

Wild Dionysus • 3 Great James Street

Algernon Charles Swinburne, who had been at Balliol College with Rossetti, lived here in 1872–75 and again in 1877–79. His *Poems and Ballads* (1866) caused a scandal on publication, as it had revealed Swinburne's interest in schoolboys. The book was hastily withdrawn by the publishers. Around this time heavy drinking and other excesses undermined his health, and in July 1868 Swinburne suffered a seizure in the British Library Reading Room. His later collection, *Poems and Ballads: Second Series* (1878) was more subdued, containing the poem 'A Forsaken Garden'.

Swinburne's poetry shows an interest in sexual experimentation and sado-masochism, an interest he shared with a circle of friends that included Monkton Milnes and Richard Burton, translator of *The Kama Sutra* (1883) and *The Perfumed Garden* (1886). When solicitor and minor novelist Theodore Watts-Dunton, who lived at No 15, first called on his near neighbour, he found Swinburne stark naked performing a Dionysian dance; the enraged poet chased him down the road. However, Watts-Dunton was not put off and they became friends, moving to Putney together in 1879. Watts-Dunton wrote for the *Athenaeum* magazine from 1876 to 1902 and championed the Pre-Raphaelite movement.

Peter Pan sculpture at Great Ormond Street Hospital

A Man in the Zoo • 16 Great James Street

This was the home of novelist and critic David Garnett, a member of the Bloomsbury Group, who ran the Nonesuch Press and wrote the biography *Pocahontas: or The Nonpareil of Virginia* (1933) here. His reputation was established by *Lady into Fox* (1922), an enigmatic fable about a young wife transformed into a vixen, and the equally quirky *A Man in the Zoo* (1924), about a thwarted lover who donates himself as a specimen of *homo sapiens* at a zoo. His second wife was Angelica, daughter of Vanessa Bell.

Murder Must Advertise • 24 Great James Street

Dorothy L. Sayers created her best-known character, Lord Peter Wimsey, while living at No. 44 Mecklenburgh Square in 1918. She lived on Great James Street between 1921 and 1941, working as an advertising copywriter in Holborn until the success of her detective novels gave her financial independence. Among her best works are *Murder Must Advertise* (1933) and *The Nine Tailors* (1934). Her character Harriet Vane, Wimsey's fiancée, was given the address 100 Doughty Street.

Great Ormond Street Hospital for Sick Children

The present-day hospital stands close to the site of London's Foundling Hospital, established in 1747 by Thomas Coram. Robert Bridges was appointed assistant physician at the hospital in 1878, and his poem 'On a Dead Child' recalls some of the tragedies he witnessed while working here.

In 1929 J.M. Barrie donated all the royalties and performing rights of *Peter Pan* (1904) – which is set in Bloomsbury – to the Great Ormond Street hospital. The children's hospital has a Barrie Wing and Peter Pan ward, and a sculpture of Barrie's famous character outside the hospital's entrance.

W.B. Yeats • 5 Woburn Walk

In February 1896 W.B. Yeats moved into rooms at 18 Woburn Buildings, later No. 5 Woburn Walk, with his mistress, the novelist Olivia Shakespear, with whom he shared an interest in the occult. His rooms were furnished with a settee, leather armchair, a chest containing his manuscripts, astrological papers and tarot cards, a bookcase with editions of William Blake and William Morris, and on the walls works by Blake, Aubrey Beardsley and Dante Gabriel Rossetti.

Here he wrote such collections as *The Wind Among The Reeds* (1899) and *The Green Helmet and Other Poems* (1910). At this time Yeats was engaged in a quest to produce a national Irish literature that would help to heal the deep divisions within Irish society. Nationalist themes and his unrequited love for the beautiful Irish revolutionary Maud Gonne underpin his work in the 1890s and early 1900s. Subsequently, his work broadened its scope and began to move away from Irish politics. A *Collected Works* was published in 1908.

Yeats belonged to many literary clubs and societies, such as the London Irish Literary Club *(see p191)* and the Literary Theatre Club. He gradually gained acceptance into established literary society, but maintained his links with literary and artistic bohemianism through regular Monday evening gatherings throughout his time in Bloomsbury. Among his guests were old friends, such as Arthur Symons from the Rhymers Club *(see p43)*, Augustus John and, from 1909, Ezra Pound, who cemented his place in Yeats's circle by marrying Olivia Shakespear's daughter, Dorothy, in 1915. Pound inspired Yeats to write more succinctly with precise and concrete imagery. His influence can be seen in the *Responsibilities: Poems and a Play* (1914) and *The Wild Swans at Coole* (1919).

Yeats left Woburn Buildings for Dublin in June 1918, having married Georgie Hyde Lees, twenty-four years his junior, on 20 October 1917.

The Plough

Plough Tavern • Museum Street

With its proximity to the British Museum and the many bookshops that once occupied Bloomsbury, the Plough Tavern was where Dylan Thomas ended up on his first visit to London in August 1933. Here he met the poet George Reavey, who in turn introduced him to the delights of Fitzrovia. Thomas believed that drinking was part of a poet's image – if not vocation – and would certainly have relished his first meetings with writers (and notable drinkers) such as John Davenport, Ruthven Todd and Rayner Heppenstall, all of whom became lasting friends.

Ulysses Bookshop, just down the road at No. 40 Museum Street, is one of London's best second-hand literary bookshops.

Ministry of Truth • Senate House

Senate House, London University's administrative centre on Malet Street, was the basis for Orwell's Ministry of Truth in *Nineteen Eighty-Four* (1949). During the Second World War the building had housed the Ministry Of Information, responsible, among other functions, for the censorship of information – a role Orwell viewed with some suspicion. Indeed the ministry, worried about offending the Russian allies, advised against the publication of *Animal Farm*, and Jonathan Cape, the publisher, returned the manuscript to Orwell in June 1944. However, Orwell found another publisher, Victor Gollancz, who ignored the advice and the novel appeared in 1945. He used his *Tribune* magazine column to write:

> *When you see what has happened to the arts in the totalitarian countries, and when you see the same thing happening here in a more veiled way through the Ministry of Information and the BBC and the film companies – organisations which not only buy up promising young writers and geld them to work like cab horses, but manage to rob literary creation of its individual character and turn it into a sort of conveyor-belt process – the prospects are not encouraging.*

The ministry suffered from the contradiction of having to propagandise and promote news of Britain's war successes as well as censoring any information that might be of use to the enemy or damaging to the war effort. The failure to resolve this situation was not lost on the writers employed there. Graham Greene's *Ministry of Fear* (1943) owes much to his period of employment here.

In *Put Out More Flags* (1942), his novel about the 'phoney war' of the late 1930s, Evelyn Waugh puts the absurdities of the ministry to work with a billeting officer taking bribes from householders wishing to avoid awful child evacuees. Orwell, Dylan Thomas, Laurie Lee and others worked on films made for the Ministry of Information.

Cyril Connolly and Horizon • 2 Lansdowne Terrace

Horizon, Cyril Connolly's low-priced and high-minded literary monthly, was based here for ten years from October 1939. During this time *Horizon* became established as one of London's leading literary magazines – along with John Lehmann's *New Writing* and Tambimuttu's more occasional *Poetry London* – and Connolly made his name as an outstanding editor and critic.

Determined to contribute to a vibrant literary culture during wartime, the charismatic Connolly set out on this new venture with gusto. As an old Etonian he had the social contacts to fill the literary void left by the closing of such magazines as Grigson's *New Verse*, Eliot's *Criterion* and Squire's *London Mercury*. He persuaded the arts patron Peter Watson to become the publisher and underwrite the expenses, and poet Stephen Spender to loan his rooms at Lansdowne Terrace. Watson was art editor and Spender assistant literary editor until he was called up in 1941.

To replace Spender, Connolly appointed Sonia Brownell (later, Orwell). She had approached Connolly and Spender two years earlier and gained a commission to produce an outline for a 'Young Painters Number' of the magazine. She was well placed to provide this as she had sat as a model for many of the painters of the Euston Road School, who had named her 'The Euston Road Venus'. The 'Young Painters' issue never materialised, although an article along similar lines was published in May 1941. Despite this setback Sonia continued to help out at *Horizon*, along with a team of (mostly unpaid) bright and pretty women, such as Lys Lubbock, that the tubby Connolly managed to attract.

The magazine continued publishing despite the destruction of the Blitz all around Bloomsbury. In Connolly's phrase, it was a time 'when literature seemed to follow life like a barge on a quiet canal towed by a madman on a motor-cycle.' Connolly came to rely heavily upon Sonia's literary judgement and editorial flair.

Horizon became famous for its bold and fresh approach to literature and criticism, and included among its contributors Auden, Orwell, Dylan Thomas, Waugh, Elizabeth Bowen, Augustus John, Julian Maclaren-Ross, Laurie Lee, Arthur Koestler, Antonia

White and Angus Wilson. The magazine also reproduced works by the most significant artists of the time, such as Henry Moore, Graham Sutherland, Lucian Freud, Paul Nash, Barbara Hepworth, Ben Nicolson and John Piper.

In June 1948 Connolly and his publishing partner Peter Watson moved the *Horizon* office from Lansdowne Terrace to 53 Bedford Square. To try to cheer the team, Watson commissioned a chandelier from Alberto Giacometti and his brother Diego, and hung Picassos (from his private collection) on the walls. Evelyn Waugh visited, and wrote to Nancy Mitford, 'I saw the inside of the *Horizon* office, full of horrible pictures collected by Watson … and Miss Brownell working away with a dictionary translating some rot from the French.'

By this time, however, Connolly was beginning to lose interest in the magazine and when the lease expired in December 1949 *Horizon* ceased publication.

Faber & Faber • 25 Russell Square

T.S. Eliot, who lived at 28 Bedford Place in 1914 and rented lodgings at Gordon Square in 1915, worked for nearly forty years as poetry editor for publishers Faber & Faber. From 1925 to 1965 Faber & Faber set the benchmark in poetry publishing, with a list that included W.H. Auden, George Barker, Eliot himself, Louis MacNeice, Ezra Pound and Stephen Spender. And towards the end of his career at Fabers, Eliot helped establish Ted Hughes and Thom Gunn.

Persuaded to settle in England by Pound, Eliot married Vivien Haigh-Wood in June 1915. His first collection, *Poems* (1919), was hand printed by the Woolfs at the Hogarth Press and struck a new and allusive note in poetry. In the mid-1930s Eliot sought to revive poetic drama. *Murder in the Cathedral* (1935), based on St Thomas à Becket's martyrdom, drew on Greek tragedy, Christian liturgy and biblical imagery. A chorus of townswomen opens and closes the drama and comments on the action. These speeches contain some of Eliot's most haunting verse.

During the Blitz, Eliot slept in the office and carried out fire-watching duty. His experiences went into the Little Gidding section of *The Four Quartets* (1943).

In September 1941 Roy Campbell and Dylan Thomas, scrounging for beer money, went to Harold Nicolson at the BBC. He lectured them on the evils of drink and gave them one pound. When Cecil Day-Lewis at the Ministry of Information, Malet Street, refused them, they plucked up courage to visit Eliot at his office. To their surprise, he treated them lavishly and kept them in beer money for days.

The Corinthian Club • YMCA, Great Russell Street

The YMCA in Great Russell Street provides the inspiration for The Corinthian Club in Alan Hollinghurst's *The Swimming-Pool Library* (1988), containing in its basement a gym and swimming pool – 'a gloomy and functional underworld full of life, purpose and sexuality'. Just a short walk away in Russell Square, the Russell Hotel ('Queensberry Hotel' in the book), with its huge Edwardian façade and 'convulsed top stages … executed in a sickly mixture of orange brick and dully shining beige faience', provides one of the other main loci of the book.

Celia Naked • High Holborn

Walking along this busy, rather nondescript thoroughfare lying at the south-eastern border of Bloomsbury and generally choked with traffic and fumes can be transformed by thinking of Adrian Mitchell's poem about his wife, 'Celia, Celia'. This poem has been voted one of the nation's favourite love poems and was the first poem in English to be displayed on the Paris Metro:

> *When I am sad and weary*
> *When I think all hope has gone*
> *When I walk along High Holborn*
> *I think of you with nothing on.*

The Great Russell Street YMCA

Saturday • University Street

This road is the scene of the critical collision between neurosurgeon Henry Perowne's Mercedes and a BMW in *Saturday* (2005) by Ian McEwan. The sweep of the book is a single Saturday – that of 15 February 2003 – the day of the march against the then imminent war in Iraq, one of the largest protests in London's history.

Here, between an empty Tottenham Court Road, closed off for the march, and Gower Street, with thousands of people 'packed in a single dense column … walking in silence to the funereal beat of marching drums', Henry Perowne squares up for possible confrontation. As the three occupants of the BMW approach, he prepares to play his part in a ritual in which 'despite the varied and casual dress code, there are rules as elaborate as the politesse of the Versailles court.'

CLERKENWELL & ISLINGTON

SITUATED BETWEEN THE CITY and Islington, Clerkenwell grew around the religious institutions of The Convent of St Mary and The Priory of the Knights of St John, both established c.1140. Accounts suggest that clerks performed mystery plays – enactments of the miracles performed by saints – here around the Clerk's Well, which gave the area its name, in the late 12th century. The well was situated in what is now Farringdon Lane, and rediscovered during an archaeological dig in 1924.

On 13 June 1381, during the Peasants' Revolt, St John's Priory was raided and burned as the Prior, Sir Robert Hales, was the government's chief tax collector. During the revolt, many rebels camped on Clerkenwell Green. Some days later, King Richard II met them at Clerkenwell Fields after their leader, Wat Tyler, had been killed by the Mayor of London. This marked the end of the revolt.

Historically, Clerkenwell has been a place of refuge also. Those made homeless by the Great Fire of 1666 came here, and later the Huguenots – protestants fleeing persecution in 18th century France – settled here.

From the late 16th century the area has also had a significant population of printers, writers and booksellers. The medieval St John's Gate, formerly home to the offices of the Master of Revels, was a centre for writers such as Samuel Johnson in the early 18th century. The Clerkenwell of the late 19th century, densely populated and with an ingrained reputation for poverty and dissent, was memorably chronicled by George Gissing in works such as *New Grub Street*.

Clerkenwell's radical tradition continued into the 20th century with *Iskra* (*The Spark*) edited by Vladimir Lenin at 37a Clerkenwell Green in 1902–03.

To the north of Clerkenwell, Islington was originally renowned for its dairy farms and spring water. It was popular as a retreat from the City, a place for country walks, bathing and hunting. It also became known for its theatres and tea gardens. When Pepys visited, he drank at the (original) King's Head Tavern on Upper Street.

The Angel, at the centre of Islington, takes its name from the Angel Inn, which stood on the High Street. There Tom Paine wrote parts of the *Rights of Man* (1790).

Many writers have been attracted to the area, from Charles and Mary Lamb seeking a semi-rural retreat to Joe Orton looking for cheap digs in the decidedly more urban Islington of the 1960s.

Clerkenwell and Islington

Key

1. Bunhill Fields
2. Milton Street
3. St John's Gate
4. Clerkenwell Green
5. Farringdon Lane
6. Granville Square
7. Myddelton Square
8. Claremont Square
9. Oakley Crescent
10. Noel Road
11. Duncan Terrace
12. Canonbury Crescent
13. Canonbury Tower
14. Canonbury Place
15. Canonbury Park South

Oliver Twist's Clerkenwell

When Charles Dickens wrote *Oliver Twist* (1839) while living in Doughty Street, Bloomsbury, he drew on the social conditions of Clerkenwell. Saffron Hill is the setting for Fagin's den of thieves and No 54 Hatton Garden is where Mr Fang is in charge of the Metropolitan Police Office. Fagin's gang of pickpockets robs Mr Brownlow outside a Clerkenwell Green shop as Oliver looks on in horror.

Riceyman Steps • Granville Square

The steps of Arnold Bennett's novel *Riceyman Steps* (1926) are the 21 steps leading from Gwynne Place, a tiny passage on the eastern side of King's Cross Road, to Granville Square. Bennett mockingly refers to the 'great metropolitan industrial district of Clerkenwell' in the novel, which concerns events that occur in a second-hand bookshop. Bennett refers to the building of the Metropolitan Railway, the first Underground line in 1863, which helped remove some of the area's worst slums.

The Clerk's Well • 14 Farringdon Lane

In Peter Ackroyd's *The House of Dr Dee* (1993), Matthew Palmer lives at No. 14–16 Farringdon Lane, supposedly the house of Dr John Dee, the Elizabethan astrologer and magician. The remains of the Clerk's Well can just be seen through the façade of the office building that now stands at this address, and a plaque details the well's history.

Revolt • Clerkenwell Green

Clerkenwell Green has been the site of political demonstrations since rebels involved in the 1381 Peasants' Revolt destroyed the St John Priory. In 1816 Henry 'Orator' Hunt spoke in favour of universal suffrage outside Merlin's Cave Tavern, north of the Green. William Cobbett, who wrote *Rural Rides* (1830), spoke here in February 1826 against the Corn Laws that had been introduced in 1815.

In 1842 public meetings were banned from the Green by Robert Peel's Tory government as a result of demonstrations by the Chartists. However, the Chartists continued meeting weekly south of the river at Lunt's coffee house in Camberwell.

In November 1887 Annie Besant, William Morris and George Bernard Shaw addressed a large crowd at Clerkenwell Green in support of the right to assembly, and led the subsequent march to Trafalgar Square to protest about unemployment. This meeting led to a riot – known as the Bloody Sunday riot – which caused fear and panic in the West End.

Marx Memorial Library

37a Clerkenwell Green

In 1872 philosopher John Stuart Mill founded the London Patriotic Club, open to men and women, at this address. When the club closed in 1893, the poet and designer William Morris based his Twentieth Century Press at the premises, producing *Justice*, a weekly journal that campaigned for social democracy.

Marx Memorial Library, Clerkenwell Green

**Clerkenwell
Green**

In 1902 Vladimir Lenin edited the communist journal *Iskra* from the building (his desk and the printing press still survives). The Marx Memorial Library was opened here in 1933 as a response to the pyres of books in Nazi Germany. The museum, which houses a large collection of socialist publications, was saved from demolition in the 1960s after a campaign in which the poet John Betjeman played a part.

Master of the Revels • St John's Gate

Built in 1504, St John's Gate was originally part of the Priory of St John, until Henry VIII closed down the monasteries in the 1530s. The Gatehouse was used as the offices of the Master of the Revels, whose duties included theatre censorship. Every play acted during the Tudor and Stuart period was supposed to pass through this office. Given the extent of political and religious censorship, disputes over passages in some plays would have seen many celebrated playwrights, such as Shakespeare and Ben Jonson, called to account here.

Offices in the gatehouse became used as a coffee house, established by Richard Hogarth, father of artist, William Hogarth, in the 1720s. A little later, in 1737, Dr Johnson had an office in the gatehouse, when he wrote for *The Gentleman's Magazine,* founded by Edward Cave. Johnson devised a way of getting round the ban on parliamentary reporting by pretending his reports were from 'Lilliput'. He continued to write for Cave after leaving his employment, contributing editorials, poems, biographies and parliamentary debates.

Grub Street

Traditionally associated with hack writing, Grub Street – renamed Milton Street after a local property owner in the 1830s – was a medieval City street. Originally a seat of fletchers, bowyers and bow-string makers, it became the home of printers and a diverse range of writers, such as John Foxe, author of the *Book of Martyrs* (1563), and John Taylor, 'the water poet' (so-called because he earned his living as a Thames waterman). Taylor refers, in 1630, to 'the Quintesence of Grubstreet, well distil'd Through Cripplegate in a contagious Map'.

By the 18th century there was a *Grub Street Journal*, an anonymous literary weekly, with which Pope and other wits were involved. In 'The Dunciad' (1728) Pope wrote about Grub Street writers 'While pensive poets painful vigil keep / Sleepless themselves, to give their readers sleep'. According to Dr Johnson's *Dictionary* (1755), Grub Street was 'much inhabited by writers of small histories, dictionaries, and temporary poems, whence any mean production is called grubstreet'.

In the 1960s much of Milton Street was demolished to make way for the Barbican.

Outcast London • New Grub Street

George Gissing's best-known work, *New Grub Street* (1891), concerns writers trying to establish themselves in the 1880s and shows the impact of poverty on artistic endeavour. As a struggling, desperately poor writer in the 1880s, Gissing described living in London as:

> *very much like holding yourself, after a shipwreck, first by one floating spar and then another; you are too much taken up with the effort of saving yourself to raise your head and look if anyone else is struggling inthe waves, and if you do come into contact with anyone else, ten to one it is only to fight and struggle for a piece of floating wood.*

Most of Gissing's novels are set in Clerkenwell at a time when the clock and watch industry and certain forms of printing, book-binding and paper and box manufacture were in serious decline and 'house-knackers' were exploiting the fag-end of leases by dividing houses into tenement rooms to garner increased profit. In *The Nether World* (1889), the novel's hero goes from an angry radical journalist to a misanthropic and cynical rent collector.

The misery of overcrowded housing was compounded by high rents, estimated to be more than half their income for 45% of the Clerkenwell poor in the mid-1880s. The revelations of the horrors of 'outcast London' in Gissing, and such works as Andrew Mearns's *The Bitter Cry of Outcast London* (1883), coupled with the riots of

February and November 1887 which saw large numbers of downtrodden Londoners gathering at Trafalgar Square, led to a change in middle-class attitudes to poverty – if only due to the perceived threats to property and order.

Another aspect of Gissing's *The Nether World* is the depiction of the second-hand book trade on Farringdon Road – where the Saturday morning book market attracted dealers, runners and collectors. Under a local by-law, the right to sell on Farringdon Road passed from father to son. Iain Sinclair, John Baxter and others have written accounts of the market and such colourful dealers as Martin Stone and Driff Field.

John Milton • Bunhill Row

In 1663 poet John Milton married his third wife, Elizabeth Minshull, and moved to No. 125 Bunhill Row, where he lived, apart from a visit to Chalfont St Giles to avoid the plague in 1665, for the rest of his life. Here he composed *Paradise Lost* (1667), *History of Britain* (1670) and *Paradise Regained* (1671). A prominent Puritan, Milton had articulated civil and religious rights under the Commonwealth, including the right to depose and punish tyrants and defence of press freedom. He was briefly imprisoned after the Restoration. Blind since 1651, he dictated his epic poems.

Paradise Lost was originally published in ten books, subsequently being rearranged into twelve for the second edition of 1674, which included a strong defence of his use of blank verse. Book I states the theme of the Fall of Man through disobedience, and Milton's aim to 'justifie the wayes of God to men'. Satan is thrown out of Heaven and wakes on a burning lake in Hell to find himself surrounded by stunned followers. Milton drew on Anglo-Saxon sources, particularly the Creation poem 'Genesis B', for the fall of the angels into darkness and Satan's subsequent soliloquy:

> *All is not lost; th' unconquerable Will,*
> *And study of revenge, immortal hate*
> *And courage never to submit or yield*

Milton's powerful portrait of Satan impressed Dryden, Pope, Blake, Byron, Keats, and Shelley, who saw Satan as a rebel against the tyranny of Heaven. Milton was buried in St Giles Cripplegate.

Tombstone Blues • Bunhill Fields

Bunhill Fields, originally 'Bone Hill Fields', bounded by City Road to the east and Bunhill Row to the west, was opened as a burial ground for plague victims in the 1660s. As the land was never consecrated it became a Dissenters' cemetery from 1657 until 1855. Since 1867 it has been used as a green space – a quiet oasis on the edge of the City, with a fence enclosing the crowded tombstones of the disused cemetery.

Bunyan's Tomb, Bunhill Fields

Among those buried here are William Blake, John Bunyan, Daniel Defoe, George Fox, founder of the Quaker movement, and Susanna Wesley, mother of John Wesley, the founder of Methodism. Wesley's Chapel and House are at No. 49 City Road, just opposite Bunhill Fields. As Defoe was escaping creditors and in hiding when he died in 1731, his tombstone was marked 'Mr Dubow'. An obelisk was later erected by his grave. This was stolen, but later found in Southampton in the 1930s. It now resides in the public library in Stoke Newington, where he lived for part of his life *(see p275)*.

ISLINGTON
Charles and Mary Lamb • Colebrook Cottage, 64 Duncan Terrace
Islington's main street market, at Chapel Street, was built in 1787. Essayist Charles Lamb moved to No. 45 in July 1797 to be near his sister, Mary, who was in Hoxton House, the Hackney asylum, for stabbing her paralysed mother to death. When Mary was released in April 1799 they moved to No. 36, where they lived until July 1800. Samuel Taylor Coleridge gave the Lambs great support during this period and was a regular visitor. He encouraged Lamb to write and publish his own verse and Lamb, in turn, honed his critical skills in correspondence with his friend. During this period the Lambs widened their literary circle, meeting, among others, Thomas Manning, William Godwin and George Dyer.

Lamb's response to Wordsworth and Coleridge's *Lyrical Ballads* was to declare his passionate involvement with London and its people as a source of poetry. For him, poetry was the image of human nature:

Colebrook Cottage, Duncan Terrace

*LONDON, whose dirtiest drab-frequented alley,
and her lowest bowing Tradesman, I would not
exchange for Skiddaw, Helvellyin, James, Walter,
and the Parson in the bargain ...
All the streets and pavements are pure gold, I
warrant you. At least I know an ALCHYMY that turns
her mud into that metal – a mind that loves to be
at home in CROWDS.*

The Lambs returned to Islington in August 1823,
moving into Colebrooke Cottage, where they lived
until September 1827. Their new home was a
white house with six large rooms and a spacious
garden with, as Lamb wrote to a friend, 'a vine (I
assure you), pears, strawberries, parsnips, leek,
carrots, cabbages, to delight the heart of old
Alcinous.' Mary Shelley, visiting shortly after their move, wrote to Leigh Hunt, 'I cannot
say much for the beauty or rurality of the spot but they are pleased.' Short sighted,
George Dyer famously fell in the New River, which flowed past the front door, and had
to be rescued. This incident was recalled in one of the *Essays of Elia* (1823).

In May 1833 the Lambs moved to Bay Cottage in Church Street, Edmonton. On
22 December 1834 Charles slipped and fell over, grazing his face in Edmonton High
Street. He contracted erysipelas, an acute skin disease, and was dead within a week.
He was buried in the nearby churchyard, later joined by Mary, who died in 1847, aged
83. Charles Lamb's presence in Islington lives on with an Elia Mews and Elia Street.

Lunching – the Albanian way • 3 Oakley Crescent

The Albanian writer and scholar Faik Bey Konitza lived here in 1903–04, before
moving to Chingford. Here he continued to edit and publish, under the pseudonym
Thrank Spirobeg, the dual language (French/Albanian) periodical *Albania* that he had
founded in Brussels in 1897. He contributed bitingly sarcastic articles on what he saw
as the cultural backwardness and naivety of his compatriots.

Albania helped spread awareness of Albanian culture across Europe, and was
highly influential in the development and refinement of Southern Albanian prose,
which in turn formed the basis of the modern Albanian literary language (gjuha
letrare). In the words of the French poet Guillaume Apollinaire, Konitza 'turned a rough
idiom of sailors' inns into a beautiful, rich and supple language.'

Apollinaire published a memoir of Konitza in the Mercure de France on 1 May
1912, which begins 'Of the people I have met and whom I remember with the

greatest pleasure, Faik Bey Konitza is one of the most unusual.' He recalls that:

> *'we would have lunch the Albanian way, which is to say, endlessly … The lunches were so long that I could not visit a single museum in London, as we would always arrive when the doors closed'.*

Apollinaire also remarks that the attention with which Konitza edited his articles:

> *'meant that the journal always came out very late. In 1904, only the issues for 1902 appeared; in 1907, the issues for 1904 came out at regular intervals. The French journal* L'Occident *is the only one which could compete with* Albania *in that respect.'*

The Old House, Canonbury Place

Diary of a Nobody
The Old House, 5 Canonbury Place

Weedon Grossmith, co-author with his brother George, of *The Diary of a Nobody* (1892), originally serialised in *Punch* magazine, lived here from 1891 to 1899.

The diary of the fictitious Charles Pooter covers fifteen months of his life in the early 1890s, and reveals his social anxieties in exact, cumulative and hilarious detail. Immensely popular, it presages later comic 'diaries' such as Sue Townsend's *The Secret Diary of Adrian Mole* (1984) and its sequels.

Diary of a Somebody
Flat 4, 25 Noel Road

Joe Orton and his partner, Kenneth Halliwell, lived here from 1959 until Halliwell killed Orton with a hammer on 9 August 1967 and then committed suicide by taking an overdose of sleeping tablets. He left a note: 'If you read his diary all will be explained. K.H. P.S. Especially the latter part.'

Orton and Halliwell had written unpublished collaborative novels, *The Boy Hairdresser* and *Lord Cucumber*, posthumously published in 1999, and were enthusiastically involved in absurdist pranks such as Orton's correspondence as 'Edna Welthorpe (Mrs)' with the Ritz Hotel manager over the loss of a handbag.

Between 1959 and March 1962 Orton and Halliwell systematically stole books from Islington Library on the Holloway Road, defaced them by adding fake blurbs, then returned them to the library to witness the reaction. They were eventually arrested and charged with stealing and defacing 72 library books, including the removal of 1,653 plates – used for making collages at their flat. For these crimes and misdemeanours, both men were sent to prison for six months.

After his release, Orton began writing the plays that made his name. *Entertaining Mr Sloane* (1964) and *Loot* (1967) were huge successes, establishing Orton's name and making him a symbol of the 'Swinging Sixties'; *What the Butler Saw* (1969) was produced posthumously to similar acclaim. Encouraged by actor Kenneth Williams, who starred in *Loot*, Orton kept a diary, entitled 'The Diary of a Somebody', in which he recorded his conquests in graphic detail, in particular his sexual expeditions to the public lavatories on the Holloway Road.

Noel Road

Subsequent interest in their lives and work has remained high, with regular revivals of the plays, and publication of a biography *Prick Up Your Ears* (1978) by John Lahr. This was filmed in 1987 by Stephen Frears, with a screenplay by Alan Bennett.

Canonbury Tower

Canonbury Tower is one of the oldest buildings in the area, dating from about 1509. In 1535 Thomas Cromwell lived here and organised the dissolution of the monasteries for Henry VIII from this address. In 1539, presumably as a mark of his gratitude, Henry gave Canonbury Manor to Cromwell. However, a year later Cromwell was executed on trumped up charges of treason.

From 1616 to 1625 Canonbury Tower was the home of Elizabethan philosopher and essayist Sir Francis Bacon. The poet Oliver Goldsmith lived here in 1762–64, and wrote his breakthrough poem 'The Traveller' (1764) while at the tower. Washington Irving, the American journalist and humorist who wrote a biography of Goldsmith and adapted German folk tales such as 'Rip Van Winkle' and 'The Legend of Sleepy Hollow', also lived here for a time.

Between 1953 and 2003 the Tower Theatre Company (founded in 1932 as the Tavistock Repertory Company) was based here. For many centuries Canonbury Tower has had connections with Freemasonry, and the building is now home to the Canonbury Masonic Research Centre.

Evelyn Waugh • 17a Canonbury Square

Evelyn Waugh lived here from 1928, having just completed his first novel, *Decline and Fall* (1928), and married Evelyn Gardner. He left in 1930 claiming that he was tired of explaining why he chose to live in a down-at-heel district – a description of the area that's hard to imagine today. He later rented the flat to Nancy Mitford.

Marmalade and Strong Tea
27B Canonbury Square

George Orwell moved here in 1944 precisely because of its shabbiness. He stayed in Canonbury Square until he moved to Jura in 1947 to complete *Nineteen Eighty-Four*. His wife Eileen O'Shaugnessy died in 1945, shortly before the instant success of *Animal Farm* brought Orwell fame.

He enjoyed entertaining at the flat and relished English cuisine – particularly kippers, scones, marmalade and strong tea. With adopted son Richard, he cut a somewhat austere figure, tall and gaunt; described by Violet Powell as 'like St Christopher with the Christ child'. In constant search of a new wife, Orwell made a pass at most women who came within his orbit, including Anne Popham, who lived in the flat below, and Sonia Brownell who

Canonbury Square

helped with babysitting. Anne Popham later married Vanessa Bell's son, Quentin. Sonia eventually married Orwell at his bedside in University College Hospital *(see pp130–31)*.

Resurrection • 52 Canonbury Park South

Poet Louis MacNeice lived here from November 1947 to December 1950 when he was working and writing for the BBC. While here he published *Holes in the Sky* (1948). The collection begins with the ballad-like 'The Streets of Laredo' concerning the Blitz and the continual rebuilding of London:

At which there arose from a wound in the asphalt,
His big wig a-smoulder, Sir Christopher Wren
Saying: 'Let them make hay of the streets of Laredo;
When your ground-rents expire I will build them again.'

Then twangling their bibles with wrath in their nostrils
From Bonehill Fields came Bunyan and Blake:
'Laredo the golden is fallen, is fallen;
Your flame shall not quench nor your thirst shall not slake.'

Oh Fuck All This Lying • 34 Claremont Square

In April 1961 the novelist B.S. Johnson moved to the ground-floor flat here. Deeply influenced by writers such as Sterne, Joyce and Beckett, he was dedicated to technical innovation and experimentation in the novel form.

After the relatively conventional *Travelling People* (1963), his first novel, Johnson wrote *Albert Angelo* (1964), in which the fragmentary and episodic narrative concerning Albert, a frustrated architect who lives (as B.S. Johnson did at the time) in a rented room on an early Victorian square not far from the Angel, is interrupted by an authorial outburst, 'an almighty aposiopesis' in which Johnson revolts against the requirement of a novel to tell a story:

> *– I'm trying to say something not tell a story telling stories is telling lies*
> *and I want to tell the truth about me about my experience about my truth*
> *to reality about sitting here writing looking out across Clarement Square*
> *trying to say something about the writing and nothing being an answer to*
> *the loneliness to the lack of loving ...*

Bleak and exuberant by turns, *Albert Angelo* is a book in which Johnson plays with the physical form of the novel. It was produced with a hole in page 149; this is later claimed to represent the knife-cut that killed Christopher Marlowe, and is also presented as a chance to read the future and past through the present. The country at large proved not entirely ready for such innovation: many booksellers returned the novel, believing they had been supplied with damaged copies.

Johnson tested the commitment of his publishers and printers (and public) still further with *The Unfortunates* (1969) in which the 27 sections of the 'book' are packaged, unbound, in a box, to be read in any order the reader may wish. The format was intended as a physical, tangible metaphor for the randomness and chaos of life. Subsequent works included *House Mother Normal* (1971) and *Christie Malry's Own Double-Entry* (1973), into which the author intrudes to converse directly with the hero.

Claremont Square

Johnson saw himself as one of a small group of writers – in which he included Alan Burns, Alan Brownjohn, Ann Quinn, Eva Figes and Rayner Heppenstall – attempting to push the novel away from illusion, and away from the conventions of plot, narrative and characterisation. An approach that was unfashionable then and, arguably, even more so today.

The title of one of Johnson's last prose pieces is 'Everyone Knows Somebody Who's Dead', in which he wrote that 'an uncomfortable number of my contemporaries are dying before … their times, simply jacking it all in.' The most recent had been Ann Quinn, who drowned herself in the sea off Brighton Beach. Bryan Johnson committed suicide in his home at 9 Myddelton Square on the night of 12/13 November 1973.

MARYLEBONE

THE SMALL NEIGHBOURHOOD OF MARYLEBONE derives its name from 'St Mary at the bourne' – that is, St Mary's church by the (now underground) Tyburn stream. The area lies north of Oxford Street between the Edgware Road to the west and Portland Place to the east, and stretches as far north as Regent's Park. The church of St Mary's once had a pleasure garden nearby on what is now Marylebone High Street. The garden was visited by Samuel Pepys and the actress Mrs Elizabeth Knipp on 7 May 1668, Pepys determining that 'a pretty place it is; and here we ate and drank and stayed till 9 at night'.

The church in Marylebone was also some distance from the City and used by couples wishing to marry in a hurry. Richard Brinsley Sheridan married the singer Eliza Linley here on 13 April 1773. He had eloped with Eliza, having previously fought two duels with his rival Captain Matthews to win her hand.

The area began to develop from a village with open fields and a royal park to the north (now Regent's Park) in the second half of the 18th century. Before then, Henry VII had used the park for hunting; it was enclosed by James I.

By the early 19th century Marylebone had become part of London and was laid out by the Montagu family, who owned the land, as a fashionable residential area. It became a neighbourhood of elegant mansions, crescents and squares – notably Cavendish, Bryanston and Montagu. Successful 19th-century writers, such as Charles Dickens, Wilkie Collins, George Eliot and Anthony Trollope, came to live

here. Lord's Cricket Ground, the home of the Marylebone Cricket Club from 1787, was developed on what is now Dorset Square before moving to Marylebone Bank, Regent's Park in 1811 and then to St John's Wood (its present home) in 1814. The library at Lord's possesses a fine collection of cricket literature.

Since 1932 one of the area's best-known landmarks has been the BBC Studios at Broadcasting House in Portland Place. This brought a great many writers, actors and musicians, who found employment at the corporation and, in their spare time, frequented the nearby pubs and clubs – The George (otherwise known as the Gluepot), The Stag's Head and the Marie Lloyd (M.L.) Club.

Marylebone also contains one of London's best-known fictional addresses: 221B Baker Street, the abode – should you need reminding – of Sherlock Holmes and his trusty friend and deductive interlocutor Dr John H. Watson.

Marylebone

Key

1 Portman Square
2 Upper Berkeley Street
3 Montagu Street
4 Lisson Grove
5 Blandford Square
6 Clarence Terrace
7 Glentworth Street
8 St Marylebone Parish Church
9 No. 50 Wimpole St
10 Broadcasting House
11 The George
12 Duchess Street
13 Stag's Head

Elizabeth Montagu and the Blue Stocking Club • 22 Portman Square

After the death of her husband in 1775, essayist and society hostess Elizabeth Montagu decided to build herself a new home. To the designs of James 'Athenian' Stuart, the house was finished in 1781, complete with one room decorated entirely with birds' feathers. The Blue Stocking Club met here, as a more formal grouping than Elizabeth's previous salons in Mayfair, where attendees had included Samuel Johnson, David Garrick and Georgiana, Duchess of Devonshire. The club's name alludes to 'blue stockings' as a term for ordinary clothes, implying that her club was more interested in fine minds than fine attire. Membership consisted principally of women from the upper-middle class who scorned frivolous accomplishments in favour of literary and intellectual discussion and philanthropic activities. They supported and promoted women writers, most notably Fanny Burney. Playwright Hannah More, actress Sarah Siddons, poet Elizabeth Carter, Frances Boscawen, Elizabeth Vesey, Anna Seward and Fanny Burney herself were among the many members who met here.

L.E.L. • 28 Upper Berkeley Street

Letitia Elizabeth Landon, who wrote under the initials L.E.L., lived here from 1837 until June 1838. Supporting herself as a writer from the age of 18, she contributed to periodicals, such as *Literary Gazette*, and literary annuals. A prolific novelist and poet, she overcame scandal-mongering to become a respected writer. She finished her best novel, *Ethel Churchill* (1837), here at Upper Berkeley Street. Rumours caused her to end her relationship with the writer William Maginn and her engagement to Dickens's friend and biographer John Forster.

In June 1838 Letitia married George Maclean, Governor of Gold Coast Castle; she was given away by Edward Bulwer-Lytton. The couple left for West Africa, where she became lonely and isolated. She died in mysterious circumstances from an overdose of prussic acid on 15 October 1838.

The Immortal Dinner • 22 (later 116) Lisson Grove

In his *Autobiography* (1847) the artist Benjamin Haydon recalled the literary dinner he held here at his home in late December 1817:

> *On 28 December, the immortal dinner came off in my painting room, with Jerusalem towering up behind us as background. Wordsworth was in fine cue, and we had a glorious set-to – on Homer, Shakespeare, Milton and Virgil. [Charles] Lamb got exceedingly merry and exquisitely witty; and his fun in the midst of Wordsworth's solemn intonations of oratory was like the sarcasm and wit of the fool in the intervals of Lear's passion.*

In a famous exchange at the dinner, Wordsworth asked Keats what he had been doing; Haydon interposed, stating that Keats had just finished an exquisite ode to Pan (from *Endymion*) and begged him to recite it. Keats walked up and down the room half chanting his poem, making Haydon think that he had heard a young Apollo. Wordsworth dismissively replied that it was 'a very pretty piece of paganism'.

Haydon unveiled his half-finished painting *Christ's Entry Into Jerusalem* (1820), which depicted Christ on a donkey blessing a crowd, and included portraits of Hazlitt, Keats, his star pupil William Bewick, Wordsworth, Isaac Newton and Voltaire.

Notable absentees from both dinner and painting were Leigh Hunt, William Hazlitt and Shelley. Shelley's atheism would have been too much for Haydon to bear over dinner, while Hunt and his wife, lodging in the same street, had failed to return tableware they had borrowed from Haydon. Hazlitt's crime was having failed to support the painter's attacks on the Royal Academy.

The success of *Christ's Entry Into Jerusalem* (currently held in a private collection) brought disaster to Haydon, as creditors soon called for their money. He was never able to put his life on a secure financial footing and was imprisoned several times for debt. He eventually committed suicide, leaving behind his *Autobiography* and *Journals* (eventually published in 1960) which contain valuable information on the contemporary literary scene. He was buried at St Mary's New Churchyard, Paddington Green, the funeral attended by a large crowd of mourners.

Sonnet Competition • 13 Lisson Grove (North)

Leigh Hunt lived here from September 1817 until August 1818, editing *The Examiner*, in which he published large parts of Shelley's Spencerian social and moral epic *Laon and Cythna*. This was later revised, to avoid prosecution, and published as *The Revolt of Islam* (1818). Here on 14 February 1818 Hunt, Keats and Shelley held a sonnet-writing competition on the subject of the river Nile. They gave each other fifteen minutes to complete the task, and Hunt won. Keats's 'To the Nile' was not published until 1838. Shelley's 'To the Nile' was found among Hunt's papers and published in 1876. Hunt's sonnet begins:

> *It flows through old hush'd Egypt and its sands*
> *Like some grave mighty thought threading a dream;*
> *And times and things, as in that vision, seem*
> *Keeping along it their eternal stands ...*

Love Letters • 50 Wimpole Street

Elizabeth Barrett lived at No. 74, later No. 99, Gloucester Place from 1835 to 1838 and then at No. 50 Wimpole Street until September 1846. The eldest daughter of a tyrannical businessman whose wealth was derived from Jamaican plantations, Elizabeth Barrett studied classics and wrote poetry. Seriously ill after breaking a blood vessel, and heartbroken from the death of her eldest brother, she became a recluse, rarely leaving her room. Her third volume of poetry, *Poems* (1844), established her as a leading poet and she was considered a possible future poet laureate.

Through a distant cousin, John Kenyon, she met other writers such as Wordsworth and Mary Mitford, and the painter Benjamin Haydon. The poet Robert Browning, the son of a Camberwell clerk, had fallen in love with Elizabeth through her poetry, and in January 1846 wrote to her declaring 'I love your verses with all my heart, dear Miss Barrett … and I love you too.' After exchanging several hundred letters, Elizabeth finally agreed to meet Browning, whose poetry she admired, in May.

Although initially angered by his marriage proposal, her spirits and health gradually improved, and they continued to exchange letters. Browning reduced her morphine dependency and eventually she was able to stroll in Regent's Park and post her own letters. They secretly married in St Marylebone Church on 12 September 1846 *(see p176)* and eloped to Casa Guidi in Florence. They returned briefly to London in 1850 to publish their poetry, living at No. 26 Devonshire Street, and again in 1852, living at No. 58 Welbeck Street. Elizabeth's *Sonnets from the Portuguese* (1850), dedicated to Browning, contains her most famous sonnet:

No. 50 Wimpole Street

> *How do I love thee? Let me count the ways.*
> *I love thee to the depth and breadth and height*
> *My soul can reach, when feeling out of sight*
> *For the ends of Being and ideal Grace.*
>
> *I love thee to the level of everyday's*
> *Most quiet need, by sun and candlelight.*
> *I love thee freely, as men strive for Right;*
> *I love thee purely, as they turn from Praise.*
>
> *I love thee with the passion put to use*
> *In my old griefs, and with my childhood's faith.*
> *I love thee with a love I seemed to lose*
> *With my lost saints, – I love thee with the breath,*
> *Smiles, tears, of all my life! – and, if God choose,*
> *I shall but love thee better after death.*

The Brownings lived at 13 Dorset Street in 1855–56 and entertained Tennyson, Thackeray, Ruskin, Holman Hunt, and Pre-Raphaelite painters Ford Madox Brown and Rossetti, who sketched both poets. Elizabeth published *Casa Guidi Windows* (1851) about the Italian *Risorgimento* (reunification) and *Aurora Leigh* (1856), an epic verse novel. She died in Browning's arms in 1861. The Brownings' romance was sentimentally portrayed in Rudolph Besier's play *The Barretts of Wimpole Street* (1930).

After Elizabeth • 19 Warwick Crescent

After Elizabeth's death, Browning and their son, Pen, lived with Arabel, Elizabeth's sister, at Delamere Terrace, Paddington. In June 1862 they moved to Warwick Crescent, close to the Grand Union Canal (the canal basin now known as Little Venice used to be called Browning's Pool in honour of the poet). Here, Browning supervised publication of Elizabeth's *Last Poems* (1862) and *The Greek Christian Poets and English Poets* (1863). He became editor of *Cornhill Magazine*, succeeding Thackeray, and resumed literary life.

However, the grief he continued to feel at the loss of Elizabeth is expressed in *Dramatis Personae* (1864). This collection was his first popular success, and was followed by the epic *The Ring and the Book* (1868), which became a bestseller, encouraging publication of his six-volume *Poetical Works* that same year. Thereafter he wrote abundantly and published another collected works in 1888–89.

The Science of Deduction • 221B Baker Street

The address of fiction's most famous 'consulting detective' Sherlock Homes and Dr Watson, 221B Baker Street afforded 'a couple of comfortable bed-rooms and a single large airy sitting-room, cheerfully furnished, and illuminated by two broad windows.'

There is no actual 221B on Baker Street. However, in Conan Doyle's 'The Empty House' story (1903), Holmes and Watson wait in a deserted Baker Street building, Camden House, opposite their rooms at 221B, to apprehend a villain. Camden House was then a prep school at No. 13 York Place, later No. 118 Baker Street, and survives.

The Woman in White • 17 Hanover Terrace

Wilkie Collins, who achieved great success as a writer of intricately plotted stories of mystery, suspense and crime, lived most of his life in Marylebone. He was born at 11 New Cavendish Street, the eldest son of portrait painter William Collins. After his father's death in 1847, which he made the subject of his first book, the family moved to Hanover Terrace, on the western fringes of Regent's Park.

Dickens admired Collins's second novel, *Basil* (1852), and employed him as a writer for *Household Words*. They became close friends, collaborated on Christmas issues and were involved in theatrical productions. They acted together in Edward Bulwer-Lytton's comedy *Not So Bad As We Seem* (1851) and co-wrote plays. In 1856 Collins became a permanent staff writer at *Household Words*, contributing stories and articles.

In 1859 Dickens founded the weekly periodical *All the Year Round*, and serialised Collins's fifth novel, *The Woman in White* (1860). Crowds would gather outside the offices in Wellington Street on publishing day to buy the next instalment. The novel went into seven editions in 1860, was parodied in *Punch*, and even had cloaks, bonnets and perfumes named after it.

Lady Rosina Bulwer-Lytton, estranged wife of Edward, was rumoured to be the model for *The Woman in White*. She had been put into an asylum by her husband and wrote *Cheveley, or the Man of Honour* (1839) about his brutal treatment of her. Collins's subsequent novels *No Name* (1862) and *Armadale* (1866) also featured portrayals of attractive and transgressive women. *Armadale* is a complex novel of mistaken identity and secret relationships. Collins took copious amounts of opium to offset pain from rheumatic gout and made use of the effects in the plot of *The Moonstone* (1868), one of the first English detective stories and a key inspiration for Anthony Trollope and Conan Doyle.

In September 1867, Wilkie Collins moved to No. 90 Gloucester Place (later No. 65) with his companion Caroline Graves – also an inspiration for *The Woman in White* – and her daughter, Harriet. They never married. By 1868 Collins had installed the much younger Martha Rudd (as Mrs William Dawson) at No. 33 Bolsover Street, within walking distance of Gloucester Place. They also never married but maintained their relationship until his death.

Caroline married Joseph Clow in October 1868 at St Marylebone Parish Church, but in April 1871 returned to Gloucester Place to live with Collins. From February 1888 until Collins's death in September 1889 they lived at No. 82 Wimpole Street. Collins's later work included *Man and Wife* (1870), in which he attacked marriage laws; *The Law and The Lady* (1875), featuring a female detective; and an anti-vivisection novel, *Heart and Science* (1883).

Mind At The End Of Its Tether • 13 Hanover Terrace

Novelist, journalist and historian H.G. Wells lived here throughout the Second World War. One of the most influential voices of his time, he wrote his last works here – *You Can't Be Too Careful* (1942) and *Mind At The End Of Its Tether* (1945), which offered a pessimistic view of humanity.

All Tomorrow's Parties • 25 Sussex Place

Cyril Connolly, poet and editor of *Horizon* magazine, lived here, in one of John Nash's terraced houses that encircle Regent's Park, from June 1945 until November 1951. Sussex Place was the scene of dazzling weekly literary parties organized by Connolly's partner Lys Lubbock throughout 1948 and into 1949. In March 1948 there was a party for W.H. Auden, briefly visiting from America, attended by John Betjeman, Elizabeth Bowen, Lucian Freud and Louis MacNeice. In December 1948 some seventy guests celebrated the award of the Nobel Prize for Literature to T. S. Eliot; they were treated to Eliot singing 'Under the Bamboo Tree' from *Sweeney Agonistes* (1932).

After the war, Connolly struggled to motivate himself. He was unable to complete commissioned books or write novels and lost direction. Sonia Brownell and Lys

Lubbock effectively ran *Horizon* in its last years. When Lys left in May 1949, having finally tired of Connolly's various affairs, the parties came to an abrupt end. In the summer of 1950 Barbara Shelton, direct descendant of Richard Brinsley Sheridan, moved in and married Connolly in October 1950.

The gardens and exterior of St Marylebone Parish Church

Ceremony, Secrets – and Torment
St Marylebone Parish Church

On 12 September 1846 Elizabeth Barrett secretly married Robert Browning here. After the ceremony, Elizabeth returned home with her maid and waited a week before she was able to elope to Italy. There is a Browning room and memorial window at the church.

Charles Dickens, who lived at No. 1 Devonshire Terrace (now Ferguson House), Marylebone Road from 1839 to 51, occasionally worshipped at this church and baptised his second son, Walter, here. The description of a baptism in *Dombey and Son* (1848) is based on the experience. Some of Dickens's wealthier characters live in Marylebone, including Mr Dombey near Bryanston Square and Mr Podsnap from *Our Mutual Friend* (1864–65) near Portman Square.

The church clock was a torment for Edwin Reardon in George Gissing's *New Grub Street* (1891) and for Bob the barman in Patrick Hamilton's *Twenty Thousand Streets Under the Sky* (1935) while he waited to meet Jenny Maple outside the Green Man public house, opposite the church.

To the southeast is the garden of the former St Mary's Church, where Lord Byron was baptised in 1788.

George Eliot • 16 Blandford Square

After the publication of *Mill on the Floss* (1860), George Eliot took a three-year lease on a property in Blandford Square with her partner, George Henry Lewes. Eliot's friend, the radical Barbara Leigh Smith Bodichon, inherited No. 5 Blandford Square in the same year and she supported Eliot for a time. While at No. 16 Blandford Square, Eliot wrote parts of *Silas Marner* (1861), before travelling to Florence to research her next novel, *Romola* (1863). In November 1863 Eliot and Lewes moved to the Priory,

No. 21 North Bank, Regent's Park. Almost a decade later, Eliot achieved great financial success when George Smith, owner of *Cornhill Magazine*, paid the huge sum of £7,000 for serialisation rights to *Romola* in 1872.

On Grub Street • 7K Cornwall Residences, Marylebone Road

George Gissing lived alone here from September 1884 until 1890, surviving by tutoring and writing. A number of his novels about London's poor were written here, including *Demos* (1886), *Thyrza* (1887), *The Nether World* (1889) and *New Grub Street* (1891), and the locale of Marylebone and Regent's Park features in his work. The workhouse, located between Luxborough Street and Marylebone Road, was a significant source of inspiration. Works such as *New Grub Street* and *The Nether World* are, however, most closely associated with Clerkenwell *(see p159)*.

Death Cancels All Engagements • 48 Upper Berkeley Street

Critic, essayist and caricaturist Max Beerbohm lived here from 1890 to 1910. Here he completed *The Works of Max Beerbohm* (1896), delineating the foibles of writers, artists and politicians, *The Happy Hypocrite* (1897), *More* (1899), *Yet Again* (1909) and his only novel, *Zuleika Dobson* (1911), before moving to Italy. *Zuleika Dobson* is a satire about Oxford in the 1890s and includes many wonderful lines – such as 'Death cancels all engagements'.

As an associate of Wilde, Beardsley, the Rhymers Club and the New English Art Club, Beerbohm was able to observe and comment upon the avant garde of this period, and his caricatures of poets were published in *The Poet's Corner* (1904). From 1898 to 1910 he was drama critic of the *Saturday Review*.

Work Ethic • 39 Montagu Street

Novelist Anthony Trollope lived here from 1871 to 1880, during which time he wrote some of the Palliser novels and his *Autobiography* (1883). He maintained a daily routine of rising at 5.30 am and writing 250 words every quarter of an hour in a little back room behind the dining room on the ground floor.

Trollope began working for the Post Office as a junior clerk in 1834 and steadily rose in the organisation. He was responsible for the introduction of the pillar-box for letters, and between 1841 and 1859 he travelled extensively around the world on Post Office business. Following the success of the Barsetshire series of novels he left the Post Office (in 1867) to write full-time. Working to his daily routine he produced forty-seven novels, travel books, biographies and short stories. By 1879 he had earned £70,000 from writing, which he thought 'comfortable but not splendid'.

Trollope wrote that an author needed to live with his characters to establish an intimacy that can be conveyed to the reader. They should be with him 'as he lies down to sleep, and as he wakes from dreams.' He established the form of the novel sequence in English literature – where characters appear in more than one novel in a series.

John Forster, Dickens's friend and biographer, lived at 46 Montagu Place in the 1850s and Ian Fleming, creator of James Bond, lived at 5 Montagu Place in 1946–47.

Ezra Pound • 8 Duchess Street

American poet Ezra Pound first lodged here in 1906, returning in August 1908 after deciding to settle in London. He read and dined in the upstairs 'artists room' at Pagani's Restaurant, No. 42 Great Portland Street. Unable to pay his rent in Duchess Street, he moved to No. 48 Langham Street, next to the Yorkshire Grey pub at No. 46 Langham Street, while awaiting money from his father.

He had been attracted to London by the poetry of Rossetti, Swinburne, and Yeats – whom he considered the greatest living poet. He was soon spending his afternoons with Ford Hueffer (later Ford Madox Ford) in Kensington *(see p209)* and walking to the home of Yeats at Woburn Buildings, Bloomsbury *(see p149)*, in the evenings. From October 1908 he had permanent admission to the British Museum Reading Room and was able to pursue his studies of Dante, Villon and the Provençal troubadours.

Pound quickly immersed himself in literary London. On 22 April 1909 he read 'Ballad of the Goodly Fere', published by *English Review*, at the Eiffel Tower Restaurant for T.E. Hulme's Poet's Club *(see p125)*, and by 1910 was at the hub of London's avant-garde artistic community.

Pound was sufficiently happy with Miss Withey's lodgings at 8 Duchess Street to recommend them to his former fiancée, Hilda Doolittle (H.D.), who stayed there in the autumn/winter of 1911. H.D. joined Pound in promoting Imagist poetry and signed her work 'H.D. Imagiste'.

0 0 0 0 That Shakespeherian Rag • 9 Clarence Gate Gardens, Glentworth Street

T.S. Eliot and his first wife Vivien Haigh-Wood moved here in 1920, and this is where Eliot wrote *The Waste Land*, 1922 *(see p68)*. The couple had married only two months after meeting at Oxford in 1915, and first set up home at 18 Crawford Mansions in Crawford Street, not far from Baker Street. Vivien was a vivacious bohemian dilettante as well as an accomplished dancer, and at Crawford Mansions the couple would roll up the carpet and dance the fox trot to music on a gramophone; Eliot once cancelled a meeting with Wyndham Lewis rather than miss accompanying Vivien to a dance studio. Vivien also took ballet lessons, which were paid for by Bertrand Russell – with whom she had an affair.

It was Russell who provided the Eliots entrée to the Bloomsbury Group, and this eventually led to the publication of Eliot's *Poems* (1919) by the Hogarth Press *(see p142)*. Eliot published *The Waste Land* in the first issue of his magazine *Criterion*, which he and Vivien would edit together in the evenings after he returned from his job at Lloyds Bank. Vivien wrote short stories, criticism and poems that were published in 1924–25 under pen names. Her poem 'Necesse est Perstate?' (1925) satirised the Bloomsbury crowd:

> And there was an end (for a session)
> Of the eternal Aldous Huxley
> Elizabeth Bibesco – Clive Bell –
> Unceasing clamour of inanities.

The offending author was unmasked and prevailed upon to cease – and, indeed, Vivien published no more poems.

Both Eliot and Vivien suffered from nervous and physical ailments. Vivien's persistent ill health was exacerbated by an increasing drug dependency, and she entered a downward spiral. By 1925 the marriage was in trouble, with Eliot seeking a more ordered life in place of the passionate *imbroglio* of the early years with Vivien. He adopted a personal style somewhere between City Gent and Sherlock Holmes.

Following a period when Eliot lived in Burleigh Mansions at No. 20 Charing Cross Road, the couple moved back to Clarence Gardens in 1928, this time to No. 98. In fairly quick succession they moved to No. 177 and then to No. 68, where the marriage went into its last stages in 1930. In September 1935 a classified ad. appeared in *The Times*, placed by Vivien: 'Will T.S. Eliot please return to his home 68 Clarence Gate Gardens, which he abandoned September 17 1932.'

Elizabeth Bowen • 2 Clarence Terrace

Anglo-Irish writer Elizabeth Bowen lived close to Regent's Park at No. 2 Clarence Terrace from 1935 to 1952, and there she wrote *The House of Paris* (1935) and her celebrated London novels. Born into the 'Protestant ascendancy', with its unsettled and dwindling future, Bowen was privately educated in Kent and married a civil servant, Alan Cameron, in 1923.

She was an outsider perfectly at home within the English literary intelligentsia and upper-middle-class society. *The Heat of the Day* (1949) and *The Demon Lover and Other Short Stories* (1945) are among the best writing on wartime London. She wrote for the *Tatler* as well as *Horizon* and *Penguin New Writing*. Her best-known work, *The Death of the Heart* (1938), is a story of betrayed innocence set in 1930s London that explores the limits of female identity. It exposes the cruelty that lies beneath the surface of conventional society and subverts the coming of age novel, refusing the traditional ending of marriage or death. The novel begins with a description of Regent's Park in the frozen depths of winter:

That morning's ice, no more than a brittle film, had cracked and was now
floating in segments. These tapped together or, parting, left channels
of dark water, down which swans in slow indignation swam. The islands
stood in frozen woody brown dusk: it was now between three and four
in the afternoon. A sort of breath from the clay, from the city outside the
park, condensing, made the air unclear; through this, the trees round the
lake soared frigidly up.

In her private life, Elizabeth Bowen had many female and male admirers and lovers. Poet May Sarton recorded her brief romantic encounter and long friendship with Bowen in *A World of Light* (1977).

The Dance Begins • 1 Chester Gate
Novelist Anthony Powell lived here from 1937 until 1953, during which time he wrote the first two volumes of his twelve-volume satire on English political and cultural life, *A Dance to the Music of Time* (1951–75).

The title comes from Nicolas Poussin's painting *Et in Arcadia Ego* (1655). In Chapter two of *A Question of Upbringing* (1951), the narrator, Nick Jenkins, while watching a garden fire, reflects on the painting:

The image of Time brought thoughts of mortality: of human beings,
facing outward like the Seasons, moving hand in hand in intricate
measure, stepping slowly, methodically sometimes a trifle awkwardly, in
evolutions that take recognizable shape: or breaking into seemingly
meaningless gyrations, while partners disappear only to reappear again,
once more giving pattern to the spectacle: unable to control the melody,
unable, perhaps, to control the steps of the dance.

The Gluepot • The George, 55 Great Portland Street
The pubs and drinking clubs of Great Portland Street became an important post-war meeting place for the most successful Fitzrovian and Marylebone-based writers, poets and composers. In the 1930s Sir Thomas Beecham named The George Inn, at the corner of Mortimer Street and Great Portland Street, the Gluepot, as so many musicians got stuck there. Fitzrovians such as Philip Heseltine, Constant Lambert, Cecil Gray and E.J. Moeran had gravitated to The George after the Fitzroy and the Wheatsheaf *(see pp127 & 129)* became too popular in the mid-1930s.

During and immediately after the Second World War, The George was a meeting place for young composers, such as Elizabeth Lutyens, William Walton, Alan

The George, dubbed 'The Gluepot' by Thomas Beecham in the 1930s

Rawsthorne, Humphrey Searle, Alan Bush, Denis Aplvor and Elizabeth Maconchy. Bush, Professor of Composition at the Royal Academy of Music 1931–75, drank with Rawsthorne, the Marxist poet and librettist Randall Swingler and campaigning journalist James Cameron. Maconchy, Aplvor and Rawsthorne wrote choral settings to poems by Dylan Thomas and Louis MacNeice.

After the war, many Fitzrovians found work at the BBC through friends who had worked for the corporation or Ministry of Information throughout the conflict. By 1946 Rayner Heppenstall, Roy Campbell, John Arlott and other BBC radio producers were all regulars at The George, along with commissioned writers and poets such as George Orwell, Dylan Thomas, Louis MacNeice and Michael Ayrton, establishing a pattern that would continue into the 1960s. Richard Burton, Henry Moore and Margot Fonteyn also drank at The George.

A Floating Population

Joan and Michael Ayrton lived at No. 4 All Souls Place, adjacent to Broadcasting House, and let rooms to Constant Lambert and John Arlott. Lambert, musical director of the Sadler's Wells company, was having an affair with ballerina Margot Fonteyn, while his wife, Isabel, was conducting her own affairs, between her painting and design work. Frederick Ashton, co-director (with Ninette de Valois) of the Sadler's Wells company, engaged artists he met at The George, such as Michael Ayrton, Johnny Minton *(see p224)* and Isabel Lambert, to create set designs. Rayner Heppenstall, in *The Intellectual Part* (1963), described his drinking companions as 'a floating population of outside writers, musicians, actors, war heroes, distinguished foreigners and gardening experts, who added colour and diversity to mid-days and early evenings during which it was agreeably easy to drink oneself silly on weak beer, day after day and from one quarter's end to another.'

Visionary Landscapes

The underlying theme for the poets, artists and composers of The George – such as MacNeice, Heppenstall, Ayrton and Grigson – was a concern for forgotten places and the English visionary tradition that extended from Blake, via the Romantic imagery of Samuel Palmer, to the modernist landscape paintings of Paul Nash.

Nash's influence can be seen in *Clausentum* (1946), a book consisting of John Arlott's sonnets and Michael Ayrton's lithographs. It suggested that there was solace and wisdom in the neglected corners of the land that Blake called Albion, and that these corners held the key to rebuilding a shattered and still vulnerable country. Alan Bush's *English Suite for String Orchestra* (1946) best captures the mood of the bohemian quest for spiritual reconstruction.

Coming to Blows

It was at The George that poets Roy Campbell and Louis MacNeice famously came to blows in May 1946. Both men were prodigious drinkers and displaced outsiders for whom poetry and the pub provided a sense of belonging. However Campbell, who had fought for Franco during the Spanish Civil War, had caused great controversy by satirising what he dubbed the 'MacSpaunday' poets – an amalgam of MacNeice, Stephen Spender, Auden and Cecil Day-Lewis – in *Talking Bronco* (1946). He implied that the MacSpaunday poets were cowards who lacked commitment, and who had run away from actual physical conflict in the war.

Campbell gave MacNeice a black eye, while MacNeice inflicted a bloody nose on his opponent. This was enough to satisfy Campbell regarding MacNeice's bravery. He bought him a drink, and thereafter became a staunch defender of his poetry. Instead, he went after Stephen Spender *(see p243)* and Geoffrey Grigson for publishing, in his opinion, some of the worst poetry of the 1930s.

Stag's Head • 24 Hallam Street

Rayner Heppenstall led the move to the more intimate Stag's Head, followed by Orwell, C.P. Snow, Rose Macaulay, Laurie Lee and Muriel Spark. Dylan Thomas and Elizabeth Lutyens drank there too, but they tended to be more promiscuous in their choice of pubs. In *Portrait Of The Artist As A Professional Man* (1969) Heppenstall recalls seeing W.H.Auden and Theodore Roethke at the Stag's Head, together with MacNeice, Robert Graves and Lawrence Durrell.

The M.L.

For some The M.L. (Marie Lloyd) – a small out-of-hours private drinking club, near Broadcasting House in Portland Place – became a bohemian refuge where they went to drink and conduct their non-work-related affairs. In some ways the M.L. Club was a precursor to Muriel Belcher's Colony Room *(see p114)*, and both Heppenstall and Lambert made the switch from the M.L. in Marylebone to The Colony Room in Soho in 1948. However, the M.L. remained a popular afternoon drinking place, until the early 1960s, for BBC poets and producers such as Louis MacNeice, who would often read drafts of new poems to friends there.

The Stag's Head

G. HEYWOOD HILL LTD.

MAYFAIR & ST JAMES'S

LOCATED WITHIN THE BORDERS of Park Lane, Piccadilly, Oxford Street and Regent Street, Mayfair is named after the May Fair, held annually until the 1730s on a site close to what is now Shepherd Market. In its earliest days the area was notorious for its proximity to Tyburn, which from the 12th century until 1783 was London's principal execution site; it was situated near to present-day Marble Arch. Mayfair grew in size significantly following the Great Fire in the City in 1666, when those who could afford to relocated further west.

Since the late 18th century Mayfair has been a centre of wealth and power, with a concentration of peers, politicians, bankers, princes and playboys. The world of Mayfair, its grand houses and the intricate web of relationships between money, influence and sex, has been portrayed in many novels, most notably Thackeray's *Vanity Fair* (1847), Oscar Wilde's *The Picture of Dorian Gray* (1891) and Evelyn Waugh's *A Handful of Dust* (1934).

In the late 19th century the Café Royal on Regent Street was the locus of affluent literary gatherings. Oscar Wilde and George Bernard Shaw regularly dined there, and it became the haunt of later writers, including D.H. Lawrence, Katherine Mansfield and Evelyn Waugh.

St James's, south of Piccadilly, between Mayfair and Westminster, is named after St James the Less, the dedicatee of a leper hospital, on the site of which Henry VIII built St James's Palace in 1532–36. Henry created the manor of St James as a royal playground. This was handed down to Charles II, who appointed trustees, including Henry Jermyn (after whom Jermyn Street is named), to develop the area further for the benefit of courtiers and their friends. By the end of the 17th century St James's had become a highly fashionable locale.

Numerous coffee shops lining St James's Street and Pall Mall provided a rich source of gossip and intrigue for Joseph Addison and Richard Steele (founders of *Tatler* and *The Spectator*) regarding those vying for attention at Court or in the corridors of power on the other side of St James's Park in the Palace of Westminster.

St James's Palace remains an official and ceremonial royal residence, and the Royal Court is still formally based here.

Mayfair and St James's

Key

1. Speaker's Corner
2. Culross Street
3. Mount Street
4. Brook Street
5. South Molton Street
6. Hanover Square
7. Savile Row
8. Heddon Street
9. Vigo Street
10. Café Royal
11. Criterion
12. The Albany
13. Hatchard's
14. Old Bond Street
15. Albermarle Street
16. Bolton Street
17. Shepherd Market
18. Chesterfield Street
19. Curzon Street
20. St James's Street
21. Duke Street St James's
22. London Library

Life and Opinions • 41 Old Bond Street

Novelist Laurence Sterne lived here from 1767 until his death in March 1768. Here he published the ninth and last volume of *The Life and Opinions of Tristram Shandy* (1759–67) and *A Sentimental Journey through France and Italy* (1767). His body, sold by grave robbers, was recognised at an anatomy lecture in Cambridge and returned to its grave near Hyde Park Place. In 1969 his remains were lawfully dug up and buried in Coxwold, Yorkshire.

Jerusalem • 17 South Molton Street

William Blake lived here from October 1803 until spring 1820. Here he wrote and etched *Milton* (1804–1808), *Jerusalem: The Emanation of the Giant Albion* (1804–20) and revised and extended *Vala* (1797–1804) into the more sexually explicit *The Four Zoas*, rediscovered in 1889. Revised against a backdrop of war and bread riots, *The Four Zoas* offers a vision of renewal and restoration through a complex and private visionary system. With a succession of poor harvests, the Luddite protests of 1812 and 1813, and the intensification of the reform movement, Blake found himself more engrossed in *Jerusalem*. He saw the task of Jerusalem 'To open the Eternal Worlds, to open the immortal Eyes / Of Man inwards into the Worlds of Thought: into Eternity.' An eternity he saw in the streets of London:

> *In Felpham I heard and saw Visions of Albion.*
> *I write in South Molton Street what I both see and hear*
> *In regions of Humanity, in London's opening streets.*

Blake saw London as 'a Human awful wonder of God!' and called for London and Albion to awake, evoking the wandering dead souls of Oxford Street from Hyde Park to Tyburn (the bones of victims hanged at Tyburn had been dug up in 1811 during the construction of Regent Street).

Jerusalem takes the form of journeys made by Los (Blake) through the darkness that is mythic London and Britain. Los essentially walks the boundaries of the city that Blake sees as 'blind & age-bent begging thro the Streets / Of Babylon, led by a child', coming to sit and listen to 'Jerusalems voice':

> *My Streets are my Ideas of Imagination.*
> *Awake Albion, awake! And let us awake up together.*

The Royal Institute • 21 Albemarle Street

Here in 1808 Samuel Taylor Coleridge gave a series of lectures on 'The Principles of Poetry' in the Great Lecture Room at the invitation of the scientist Humphry Davy. Nerves and ill health beset Coleridge at the first lectures; De Quincey, who was in the audience, was unimpressed. However, Coleridge regained his composure and went on to excel as a public speaker, eventually giving twice-weekly two-hour long extemporising talks before large and demanding audiences. He illustrated poetic processes, delineating the Romantic theory of Imagination, and effectively dramatised his own creative struggles. His most famous lecture, on 3 May, was essentially one long digression, calling for the state to educate poor children. He also attacked the method of learning by rote, with its elaborate system of punishment and rewards, which he had experienced at Christ's Hospital. As a public speaker renowned by his contemporaries, Coleridge would not be equalled until Dickens began his mesmerising readings half a century later.

Siege of Corinth • 13 Piccadilly Terrace

Lord Byron moved into No. 13 Piccadilly Terrace on 29 March 1815, having previously lived at The Albany *(see over)* and, before that, at No. 8 St James's Street *(see p200)*. When he moved into Piccadilly Terrace, he did so with his pregnant wife Annabella Milbanke. However, Byron was also involved in the management of Drury Lane theatre, which led to an affair with actress Susan Boyce.

While at Piccadilly Terrace Byron published *Hebrew Melodies* (1815), with musical score by Isaac Nathan, *Siege of Corinth* (1815) and *Parisina* (1815), as well as poems in Leigh Hunt's *The Examiner*. He was a regular at Samuel Rogers' literary breakfasts, at No. 22 St James's Place, along with writers such as Sheridan and Coleridge. He encouraged Coleridge to publish his poetry, and met with his publisher, John Murray, to enable this to happen. Byron finally convinced Coleridge to publish *Christabel and Other Poems*, and to give a reading of 'Kubla Khan' at No. 13 Piccadilly Terrace.

In January of the same year, Byron's wife left him and began proceedings for a separation, citing his incest with his half-sister, Augusta Leigh. Claire Clairmont, the half-sister of Shelley's mistress Mary Godwin, promptly seized the opportunity to declare her love for Byron, and to ask for his help as an aspiring novelist and actress. Shortly afterwards she accompanied Shelley and Mary when they eloped to Geneva *(see p105)*. Byron, finding himself socially ostracised on account of his scandalous affairs, followed them on 25 April 1816.

Debt and Death • 14 Savile Row

Playwright Richard Brinsley Sheridan lived at No. 10 Hertford Street in the 1790s and here in Savile Row from 1813 until his death on 7 July 1816.

Following his arrest for debt in May 1814 and again in August 1815 after losing his parliamentary seat, both new friends and old rallied round. Byron, for whom Sheridan was a literary and political hero, became a regular visitor from March 1814, eager to learn more about the political upheavals of the previous decades. Together with banker and poet Samuel Rogers, Byron arranged for John Murray to publish an edition of Sheridan's plays and poems in May 1816, two months before his death.

Hatchards Bookshop • 187 Piccadilly

The evangelical Tory John Hatchard opened his first bookshop in June 1797 at No. 173 Piccadilly, between Mayfair and St James's. His early customers included scholars and evangelists such as playwright Hannah More. By 1801 he had moved to No. 187

and attracted custom from Tory politicians and residents of the Albany, such as Lord Byron, allowing the shop to act as an unofficial gentleman's literary club.

Oscar Wilde's wife, Constance, had a brief affair with the manager, Arthur Humphreys, in the 1890s, and in 1917 budding playwright Noël Coward tried to fill a suitcase (stolen from Fortnum & Mason's) with books from Hatchards, but was challenged by an assistant; he was allowed to leave without prosecution.

Bachelor's Chambers • The Albany, Piccadilly

This large town house, built in 1774, was converted into gentleman's bachelor chambers in 1802. House rules demanded that gentlemen had no connection with trade and did not keep a musical instrument or wife.

Many writers have stayed at the Albany, including Lord Byron (who lived at No. 2 in 1814), Gothic novelist Matthew 'Monk' Lewis (author of *The Monk*, 1796), Edward Bulwer Lytton, Arnold Bennett, J.B. Priestley, Compton Mackenzie, Aldous Huxley, Terence Rattigan, Patrick Hamilton and Graham Greene.

John Murray • 50 Albemarle Street

The publishing house of John Murray has occupied these premises since 1812. John Murray II, son of the founder, published Byron, Jane Austen, Coleridge, Robert Southey, Leigh Hunt and George Crabbe. He became close friends with Byron – who was his most successful author with *Childe Harold's Pilgrimage* (1812–18) and *Don Juan* (1819–24). When the first part of the epic satire *Don Juan* appeared in 1819, Albemarle Street was filled with booksellers' agents demanding copies; Byron's celebrity and popularity as a radical poet extended across Europe. Murray held regular literary meetings in his drawing room, and here Byron met novelist Sir Walter Scott in 1815.

After Byron's death in 1824, Murray obtained his memoirs. Worried that they might damage Byron's popularity, he burned them in his fireplace.

Since 2000 the publishing house has been part of the Hodder Headline group.

Brown's Hotel • 23 Albemarle Street

Founded in 1837 at No. 23 Dover Street by James Brown, Lord Byron's valet, Brown's is London's oldest operating deluxe hotel and now occupies eleven townhouses with a frontage on Albermarle Street. It became popular with visiting American writers, including Henry James, Mark Twain and Edith Wharton, who depicted the hotel in several of her novels.

In 1876 Alexander Graham Bell made Britain's first successful telephone call from Brown's. Rudyard Kipling had his wedding breakfast here in 1892 and was a frequent visitor until his death in January 1936. Part of the suite that Kipling regularly occupied is now offered as 'The Kipling Suite' following a £19 million pound refurbishment by

189

Rocco Forte Hotels in 2005. He completed *The Jungle Book* (1894) here. The creator of Winnie the Pooh, A.A. Milne, held annual parties here until February 1954.

Agatha Christie used the hotel as her London base and in her Miss Marple novel *At Bertram's Hotel* (1965); Miss Marple found the hotel, renowned for its afternoon tea, an oasis of old-fashioned calm.

The plot for his novel *Misery* (1987) came to American horror writer Stephen King on a Concorde flight from New York to London, where he was staying at Brown's. That night, unable to sleep and not wishing to disturb his wife, he asked the receptionist for a quiet place to work and was directed to a beautiful cherry wood desk on the second floor landing. Sixteen pages of longhand and several cups of tea later, he went to thank the receptionist and discovered that Kipling had suffered a fatal brain haemorrhage at the same desk. Spooked, King checked out of the hotel the next day.

My Works are My Life • 19 Curzon Street

Novelist and Prime Minister Benjamin Disraeli *(see also p17)*, the man who bestowed upon Queen Victoria the title of Empress of India and who declared 'My works are my life', lived here from 1876 until his death in 1881. He was able to buy the house after receiving a £10,000 advance for *Endymion* (1880), his last completed novel. His novels were intended as portraits of prominent men and women of his time and, although popular, were not highly regarded critically.

Excellent Lodgings • 3 Bolton Street

American-born novelist Henry James lived here from winter 1877 until 1885. He followed a strict regime of writing during the morning and early afternoon, followed by dining out at one of the clubs in Pall Mall, frequently the Athenaeum. While here he wrote *The Europeans* (1878), *Daisy Miller* (1879), *Washington Square* (1881) and *The Portrait of a Lady* (1881), which became his most successful early novel and was concerned with the impact of European life on various types of American character. He wrote to his parents in Boston that he had 'excellent lodgings in this excellent quarter'.

James got to know London by walking its streets. His observations went into *The Suburbs of London* (1877) and *London* (1888). He later lived in Kensington *(see p208)*.

The Yellow Book • 8 Vigo Street

The Bodley Head publishing house – established by John Lane and Charles Elkin Matthews, who ran a bookshop on the ground floor – began here in 1887. From 1894 until 1897 they published *The Yellow Book*, a fashionably bohemian publication edited by the American writer Henry Harland and artist Aubrey Beardsley.

Among the contributors to *The Yellow Book* were Henry James, Max Beerbohm, Arnold Bennett, Edmund Gosse, Walter Sickert, Ernest Dowson, Richard Le Gallienne and other members of the Rhymer's Club *(see p43)*. The controversy surrounding Beerbohm's essay 'A Defence of Cosmetics' in the first issue of 1894 did not subside until 1900. Further controversy occurred when Oscar Wilde was charged for indecency in 1895 and was seen to be carrying a yellow book. Mistaking this for *The Yellow Book*, with its decadent images, a mob arrived at Vigo Street and smashed windows.

The Bodley Head published Wilde, J.A. Symons, Le Gallienne, John Davidson and other members of the Rhymer's Club, and was at the forefront of literary ferment in the 1890s. They later published Ezra Pound's *Personae* (1909).

In 1935, Lane's distant cousin, Allen Lane, began the Penguin book series, pioneering the paperback revolution in publishing. The first ten titles, which sold for sixpence each, included fiction by Agatha Christie, Ernest Hemingway and Dorothy L. Sayers.

London Irish Literary Society
20 Hanover Square

The Irish Literary Society, established in December 1891 by D.J. O'Donoghue and W.B Yeats, with T.W. Rolleston, who became the club secretary, John Todhunter and members of the Rhymer's Club *(see p43)*, held its first meeting here in April 1892 when Yeats toasted Ireland's intellectual life.

No. 20 Hanover Square

The club published the quarterly *Irish Home Reading Magazine* and, despite frequent rifts, attracted large audiences for its lectures and recitals. Yeats was a club stalwart, regularly introducing new writers to the society and giving talks from the 1890s through to the 1930s. T.E. Hulme and Ezra Pound, who attended events, also held meetings of their Poet's Club *(see p125)* here in 1909.

Of Human Bondage • 6 Chesterfield Street

Novelist, playwright and short-story writer W. Somerset Maugham lived here from 1911 to 1919. Maugham first achieved fame as a playwright with *Lady Frederick* (1907), a comedy of marriage and money, and had four drawing-room dramas running in the West End by 1908. Although married to Syrie Wellcome, with whom he had a daughter, he spent more time with his secretary and companion Gerald Haxton.

At Chesterfield Street he wrote further plays and his epic semi-autobiographical novel *Of Human Bondage* (1915), which charts the progress of Philip Carey, an orphan looking for life, love and adventure, and the tortured, masochistic affair that nearly ruins him. Maugham also wrote *The Moon and Sixpence* (1919) about banker Charles Strickland, a Gauguinesque figure, who leaves his dull lifestyle behind in order to go off and paint in Tahiti and neglect his domestic duties.

Food, Art, Sex • Café Royal

Opened by French gambler Daniel Nicolas Thévenon in 1865, this heavily gilded and ornate venue followed the style of a grand Parisian café and was a favourite with members of the Aesthetic Movement.

In the 1890s Oscar Wilde would lunch here at exactly one o'clock most days with other regulars, including Lord Alfred Douglas (Bosie, Wilde's lover), Aubrey Beardsley,

George Bernard Shaw, Max Beerbohm, William Rothenstein and J.M. Whistler.

John Betjeman – a regular in the 1930s and 40s, along with Stephen Spender, Cyril Connolly and Dylan Thomas (who was banned for a time in 1935) – re-imagines the 1890s in his poem 'On Seeing an Old Poet in the Café Royal' (1940), in which the unnamed protagonist asks for Oscar and Bosie.

In the early 20th century the Café Royal became a central meeting place for members of various, and variously competing, literary and artistic circles. Regular diners included Augustus John, Walter Sickert, Auguste Rodin, Toulouse-Lautrec, Wyndham Lewis, Jacob Epstein, Nina Hamnett, Nancy Cunard, Iris Tree, D.H. Lawrence, Evelyn Waugh and John Buchan – this is where Richard Hannay dines in the opening of *The Thirty Nine Steps* (1915).

T.E. Hulme, a man renowned for his carnal appetites, once famously claimed a pressing engagement and left friends in the middle of dinner. He returned 20 minutes later, complaining that the steel staircase by the emergency exit in Piccadilly Station was 'the most uncomfortable place in which

Doorway at the Café Royal he had ever copulated'. Enid Bagnold, author of *National Velvet* (1935), remained on the premises when she lost her virginity to the sexually voracious Frank Harris, former editor of *Vanity Fair* magazine: 'He told me sex is the gateway to life, so I went through the gateway in an upper room of the Café Royal'.

In *Women in Love* (1920), D. H. Lawrence used the Café Royal as the basis for the Pompadour Café to which Gudrun always returns, despite hating the place:

> ... *She loathed its atmosphere of petty vice and petty jealousy and petty art. Yet she always called in again, when she was in town. It was as if she had to return to this small, slow, central whirlpool of disintegration and dissolution: just give it a look.*

The ensuing incident in which Gudrun rescues one of Birkin's letters is most likely based on Katherine Mansfield's action in the Café Royal in 1916 when a copy of Lawrence's verse collection *Amores* was being read out loud and ridiculed as it was passed around at a table of several supposed friends: she went to the table, seized the copy of *Amores* and marched out of the café.

Lawrence's fiction was often informed by elements of biography – which tended to further inflame an already tempestuous life. On recognising herself in the character of Lady Hermione (in *Women in Love*), Lady Ottoline Morrell threatened to sue for libel. It marked the end of another friendship; their intense correspondence stopped and they made no contact for ten years.

One friendship that lasted was with Samuel Solomonovich Kotaliansky or 'Kot' as he became known. A Ukrainian Jewish law student who had come to London on a scholarship in 1911 and stayed, Kot supported himself with translation work – an occupation made especially precarious given his shaky command of English. Lawrence helped him out on a translation of some Ivan Bunin stories from Russian for the American magazine *The Dial*. The characters Libidnikov in *Women in Love* and Ben Cooley in *Kangaroo* (1923) are partly based on Kot.

In 1928 Kot took delivery of three dozen copies of the first, banned edition of *Lady Chatterley's Lover* at his house on Acacia Avenue in St John's Wood. Lawrence oversaw distribution of the book himself, taking orders and dealing with customers long distance from his room at the Grand Hotel at Chexbres-sur-Vevey in the Swiss Alps, where he had gone for his health.

In *Keep the Aspidistra Flying* (1936) George Orwell drew on an embarrassing incident of his own in the Café Royal – in which he insisted on picking up the bill when he and the much wealthier Richard Rees, *The Adelphi* editor, had dined together – in his depiction of Gordon Comstock at the Café Imperial.

Cave of the Golden Calf • 9 Heddon Street
Founded by Madame Frida Strindberg, second wife of the Norwegian playwright, this avant-garde nightclub, which included a cabaret theatre, attracted pre-War London's literati for eighteen months from 1912.

Dramatic Vorticist decorations by Wyndham Lewis, Spencer Gore and Jacob Epstein provided a suitably vibrant backdrop for the bohemian mix of writers, artists, journalists, debutantes and guardsmen dancing and drinking the night away. Membership was five guineas, reduced to one guinea for fifty supporters representing the arts. These included Ezra Pound, Dorothy Shakespear, Ford Madox Ford, Wyndham Lewis, H.D. (Hilda Doolittle), Nina Hamnett and Katherine Mansfield. The club presented new music from Schoenberg to ragtime, short plays, new art exhibits and champagne tango nights. It served as a model for the Gargoyle Club *(see p110)*.

Standing and Waiting • Swan & Edgar's, 1 Piccadilly

The pavement in front of Swan & Edgar's (now a Virgin store) at Piccadilly Circus has a long history as a pick-up point for male and female prostitutes. It is where Phillip, 'overwhelmed with horror', finds Mildred, after he had broken off their relationship in Somerset Maugham's autobiographical novel *Of Human Bondage* (1915).

This is also where Nigel Slater breaks off his deliciously evocative autobiography *Toast, The Story of a Boy's Hunger* (2003). The book ends with the young Slater, newly arrived in London and homeless, on his way with a crisply starched white jacket over his arm bearing the proud legend 'Savoy Grill' to stand outside Swan & Edgar's, following advice from an old lag at the hotel on the best way to find a bed for the night.

Alroy Kear • 90 Piccadilly

Novelist Hugh Walpole divided his time between No. 90 Piccadilly and Cumberland from 1930 to 1941. During this time he completed his historical sequence of novels set in Cumberland, the *Herries Chronicle*, consisting of *Rogue Herries* (1930), *Judith Paris* (1931), *The Fortress* (1932) and *Vanessa* (1933).

It was while in Piccadilly that Walpole first read a proof copy of W. Somerset Maugham's *Cakes and Ale* (1930), with its character Alroy Kear, the hypocritical literary careerist. Walpole recognised himself in the portrait of the barely literate novelist and was not amused. Maugham was getting revenge on Walpole for having taken one of his lovers many years previously. Walpole in turn portrayed Maugham as the arrogant pessimist in *John Cornelius* (1937). Aspects of Maugham can also be seen in the homosexual novelist in Noël Coward's *Point Valaine* (1935) and Kenneth Marchal Toomey in Anthony Burgess's *Earthly Powers* (1980).

Gilded Youth • The Criterion

The original ornate period décor (dating to 1870) of the Criterion dining room – complete with gold mosaic and Arabic murals – was revealed once again as part of a complete refurbishment in the late 1980s. At the beginning of the first Sherlock Holmes story, *A Study in Scarlet* (1887), Dr Watson, recently invalided out of the

Afghan war, has 'gravitated to London, that great cesspool into which all the loungers and idlers of the Empire are irresistibly drained' and is leading, as he puts it, 'a comfortless, meaningless existence, and spending such money as I had, considerably more freely than I ought.' Standing at the Criterion's bar one day, he is spotted by Stamford, his former hospital dresser. On hearing that Watson is looking for lodgings, Stamford responds that he knows another man who is 'trying to solve the problem as to whether it is possible to get comfortable rooms at a reasonable price' – namely, a Mr Sherlock Holmes, who is looking for someone to share a suite of rooms he has found in Baker Street.

'… oh my ! / I wish you'd seen the rag we had in the Grill Room at the Cri.' The last line of the chorus in John Betjeman's 'Varsity Students' Rag' (1932) depicts

No. 3 Culross Street

the Criterion as the kind of place you could expect to find the rowdier type of well-connected student – the type satirised a few years earlier by Evelyn Waugh through the character Vaine-Trumpington in *Decline and Fall* (1928).

Savile Club • 69 Brook Street

The Savile Club, founded in 1868 as the Eclectic Club and renamed in 1871 when it moved to Savile Row, moved to its Brook Street address in 1927. The club has always had a strong literary tradition, and past members have included Robert Louis Stevenson, Thomas Hardy, Henry James, Max Beerbohm, W.B. Yeats, H.G. Wells, Lytton Strachey and Cecil Day-Lewis. In Evelyn Waugh's Mayfair novel *A Handful of Dust* (1934), the Greville, famed for its 'tradition of garrulity', is based on the Savile Club.

Artist, writer and broadcaster Michael Ayrton was a lifelong member, having been introduced to the club as a teenager. Ayrton produced paintings, sculptures, poetry, short stories and novels, such as *The Maze Maker* (1967) and *The Midas Consequence* (1974). His work was concerned with flight, myths, mirrors and mazes, and drew upon a wide range of references. Ayrton would typically occupy the bar, testing out ideas in conversation with other members.

Mount Zion • 3 Culross Street

John Betjeman shared rooms with Randolph Churchill here in the house of his publisher, Edward James, from 1931 to 33, while working for *The Architectural Review* and pursuing Penelope Chetwode, whom he married in 1933.

James had published Betjeman's first book, *Mount Zion* (1931), but became increasingly irritated by the boxes of unsold books and Betjeman's habit of giving away copies. After much trouble with James, John Murray published Betjeman's second book, *Continual Dew* (1937), which contains the 'Slough' poem, with the famous lines 'Come, friendly bombs, and fall on Slough! / It isn't fit for humans now ...'

Heywood Hill and Nancy Mitford • 10 Curzon Street

G. Heywood Hill, a bookseller who had been a contemporary at Eton of Anthony Powell and James Lees-Milne, opened his own shop first at No. 7 and later at No. 10 Curzon Street in 1936. The bookshop was a favourite haunt of a generation of writers, including Osbert Sitwell, Graham Greene, Anthony Powell and Evelyn Waugh who, in 1944, described the bookshop as 'the one centre of old world gossip left'.

Author Nancy Mitford worked behind the counter as an assistant, until the huge financial success of her novel *The Pursuit of Love* (1945) enabled her to move to Paris – precisely for the purpose of pursuing love, in the form of 'the Colonel', Gaston Palewski. *Love in a Cold Climate* (1949) followed. After two less well-received novels she took to writing historical biographies, and enjoyed even greater success. Her second biography *The Sun King* (1966) sold a quarter of a million copies in two years, earning more than £350,000.

Throughout her Paris years she maintained a regular correspondence with Heywood Hill and other former colleagues at the bookshop.

Heyward Hill Bookshop

A Mayfair Dance • 9 Shepherd Market

Novelist Anthony Powell chose to live in Mayfair as it was the setting of Michael Arlen's novel *The Green Hat* (1924) – the novel of sexual liberation that scandalised his parents' generation and was cult reading for the Bright Young Things. He lived here from 1928 to 1929 and gave Nicholas Jenkins, the narrator of his twelve-novel series *A Dance to the Music of Time* (1951–75), a Shepherd Market address.

Powell had an affair with artist Nina Hamnett, who introduced him to the bohemian world of the Cavendish Hotel in Jermyn Street, and to the pubs and clubs of Fitzrovia and Soho. Along with many of his friends, such as Peter Quennell and Evelyn Waugh, Powell became a member of the Gargoyle Club [see SOHO].

A Time of Gifts • Shepherd Market

Travel writer Patrick Leigh Fermor set out on a rainy day in 1933 from Shepherd Market for his epic journey on foot to Constantinople. The first part of the journey – from the Hook of Holland, where he started walking, to Hungary – is recounted in magical detail in *A Time of Gifts* (1977). The first paragraphs provide a virtuoso evocation of London (rivalled only by the opening to *Bleak House*) as his taxi threads its way through the rain-soaked 'flux of traffic' from Half Moon Street where 'all collars were up', down Piccadilly where 'a thousand glistening umbrellas were tilted over a thousand bowler hats', past the clubmen of Pall Mall scuttling for sanctuary 'with tea and anchovy toast in mind' and on past the 'dark complexes of battlements' of the Tower to the 'stone steps that descended to Irongate Wharf' where his ship awaited.

Fermor's sense of history and place, combined with a lyrical and erudite evocation of youth, has made *A Time of Gifts* a modern classic. The second part of the journey, through Hungary, Transylvania and middle Europe, is contained in *Between the Woods and the Water* (1985).

Romantic Revolutionary • 120 Mount Street

Drama critic Kenneth Tynan lived here from October 1955 until May 1966, during which time he rose to prominence as *Observer* drama critic. He used his columns to advocate radical change, calling on dramatists to make words 'put on flesh, throng the streets and bellow through the buses.' He was able to witness precisely the kind of transformation he had advocated and celebrate remarkable developments in British theatre which, in the single year from August 1955 to August 1956, saw the premieres of Samuel Beckett's *Waiting for Godot* and John Osborne's *Look Back in Anger*, the flowering of Joan Littlewood's Theatre Workshop with Brendan Behan's *The Quare Fellow*, and the arrival of the Berliner Ensemble with a three-play Brecht season.

Through his writing, Tynan inspired John McGrath, Trevor Griffiths and Tom Stoppard to become playwrights, and effectively campaigned for the creation of a National Theatre, with Laurence Olivier as its Artistic Director. He was appointed Literary Manager of the National Theatre when it opened at the South Bank, and was responsible for the repertoire from 1963 to 69; his role changed to the less influential Literary Consultant from 1970 to 73.

With a big international reputation as a drama critic, often working in New York and other parts of the world, Tynan was also a prominent campaigner on behalf of many

causes associated with the 1960s, such as nuclear disarmament, sexual liberation and the abolition of theatrical censorship. He had a wide circle of friends that included Doris Lessing, Norman Mailer, Gore Vidal, Albert Finney, Peter Brook, George Melly, Edna O'Brien, John Osborne, Laurence Olivier, Joan Plowright, Jonathan Miller, Peter Cook, Marlon Brando and Princess Margaret. His election night party of 31 March 1966 is said to have inspired the orgy scene in Michelangelo Antonioni's film about 'swinging' London, *Blow-Up* (1966).

Dedicated to breaking taboos, Tynan was the first person to say the word 'fuck' on British television, on 13 November 1965, and devised *Oh! Calcutta!*, a stage revue which, in his words, was designed to provide 'civilized erotic stimulation'. Containing in its title a phonetic French pun ('Oh! Quel cul t'as!' or, freely translated, 'Oh! What a lovely arse you have!'), the show featured plenty of on-stage nudity (often involving spanking), as well as contributions from distinguished writers and

No. 120 Mount Street celebrities, including Edna O'Brien, Jules Feiffer, John Lennon and Samuel Beckett – who was not amused when he discovered what the rest of the show contained.

The revue debuted in New York off-Broadway in 1969, and was revived on Broadway in 1976, where it ran for 13 years, briefly becoming the longest-running play in Broadway history. In London *Oh! Calcutta!* opened at the Roundhouse in Chalk Farm on 27 July 1970, transferring to the Royalty Theatre in the West End on 30 September 1970, then on to the Duchess Theatre, where it remained from 1974 to 1980.

Both Tynan and his wife, Elaine Dundy, had numerous affairs within a turbulent and often sado-masochistic relationship. They decided to separate in March 1964 after he found Elaine in the kitchen with poet and BBC producer George MacBeth, who was naked, apart from a necktie. In 1966 Tynan moved to Thurloe Square *(see p216)*.

Queer Visionary • Dalmeney Court, 8 Duke Street St James's

American novelist William S. Burroughs used a flat here as his London base from 1966 to 1974. He found the flat well placed to enjoy both the rent boys of Piccadilly Circus and the burgeoning counter-cultural scene that could be found nearby at Indica Books, Gallery (in Mason's Yard, off Duke Street), where John Lennon met Yoko Ono, and the Robert Fraser Gallery (at No. 69 Duke Street). Jeff Nuttall, J.G. Ballard and Michael Horovitz were among those who visited Burroughs in Duke Street.

Burroughs' first novel, *Junkie* (1953), was a semi-autobiographical account of his time as a drug addict. He established his reputation with his next book *The Naked Lunch* (1959), which contained graphic descriptions of sexual sadism, heroin abuse and black comedy about a totalitarian state. It famously ends with the words of the Chinese dealer – 'No glot … C'lom Fliday'.

The nature of power and the dynamics of control were a constant theme in Burroughs' work, underscored by visionary research into language, information and the pre-recorded universe. His work presages cultural phenomena of today such as e-viruses and the wired society.

Coffee and Cigars • St James's Street

St James's Street, the main thoroughfare between Piccadilly and Pall Mall, dates from the 1660s and became an increasingly fashionable location as St James's Palace expanded. The gatehouse of St James's Palace is visible in the background of Plate 4 of William Hogarth's *The Rake's Progress* (1732–34), in which Tom Rakewell is thrown out of his sedan chair and arrested.

Notable early residents included Nell Gwyn, who was given No. 79 St James's Street by Charles II, the architect Sir Christopher Wren (who is thought to have died here in 1723), diarist John Evelyn and the poet Alexander Pope.

Following the introduction of Turkish coffee to England in 1652, many of London's most significant coffee houses were established on St James's Street. These later developed into the gentlemen's clubs for which the area is still known today. Members of the political parties tended to adopt one or other coffee house as a regular meeting place: The Whigs frequented St James's at No. 60; the Tories went to the Cocoa-Tree at No. 64, or round the corner to Ozinda's or Pall Mall (both sited in Pall Mall).

St James's Coffee House • 60 St James's Street

Jonathan Swift wrote some of his letters to Esther Johnson, published posthumously as *Journal to Stella* (1766), at St James's Coffee House, and used the address for his mail. He also claimed that more truth and light were available in the coffee houses than from any man in power. Addison and Steele regularly visited on Sunday evenings to gather political news for *Tatler* and *The Spectator*. These folio sheet newspapers, comprising fluent essays on current moral or political issues, were published more or less daily from 1709 to 1711 and sold in the coffee houses. They also contained advertisements for noteworthy publications and events including, for example, the latest books by Alexander Pope.

Later on, Oliver Goldsmith and David Garrick became habitués. In response to Garrick's proposal that they write each other's epitaph, Goldsmith wrote 'Retaliation: A Poem' (1774) at St James's. In the poem Goldsmith sets out to provide epitaphs for ten friends – including himself and Garrick – all of whom he imagines gathered around a table. He died before completing the poem.

Lady Mary Wortley Montagu, proto-feminist, poet and wit, wrote one of her six *Town Eclogues* (1747) about St James's, evoking the drinking and womanising for which the coffee houses had become notorious. She advised Addison on his tragedy *Cato* (1712) and wrote an issue of *The Spectator* for him in 1714. In 1722 she rejected Alexander Pope's declaration of love with an amused laugh, and so became his enemy for life.

White's • 37–38 St James's Street

An Italian, Francesco Bianco, opened White's Chocolate House at No. 28 St James's Street in 1693. Over the years he moved premises several times, before finally relocating to Nos. 37–38 in 1755. In the first issue of *Tatler*, Steele described White's as renowned for 'accounts of Gallantry, Pleasure and Entertainment'. Plate 6 of Hogarth's *The Rake's Progress* shows a distraught man just having lost his fortune in the gaming room at White's. Swift referred to White's as the 'bane of half the English nobility', shaking his fist in the direction of the club every time he passed, while in *The Dunciad* (1728) Pope describes White's as a place where one 'may teach oaths to youngsters and to nobles wit'. A fire destroyed the coffee house in 1773; it re-opened in 1775 as White's Club and continues to this day.

The printshops and bookshops of St James's and Bond Street competed with the coffee houses as centres of conversation, scandal and intrigue. In the attic above Hannah Humphrey's bookshop at No. 27, the caricaturist James Gillray etched and printed his work. In July 1811 he attempted to kill himself by jumping out of the window (his eyesight had been failing since 1806), but survived and lived on until 1815.

John Cleland was living at No. 37 St James's Place when, in 1748, he published (anonymously) the risqué *Memoirs of a Woman of Pleasure*, better known as *Fanny Hill*. Enormous sales brought its publisher £10,000, but its author only 20 guineas.

Fame and Notoriety • 8 St James's Street

From 1808 to 1814, Lord Byron owned No. 8 St James's Street. He was in residence in March 1812 when the first cantos of *Childe Harold's Pilgrimage* were published. The first five hundred copies sold out within three days, and Byron found himself the most famous man in London. His poetry continued to sell in record quantities, but his fame soon turned into notoriety following disclosure of his affair with Lady Caroline Lamb during April and May 1812. Lady Caroline lived at Melbourne House (later Dover House and Scotland Office), Whitehall, with her husband, William Lamb, a Whig politician and future Prime Minister. It was Lady Caroline who declared Byron 'mad, bad and dangerous to know'.

After Byron broke off the affair she pursued him, arriving outside the house one day dressed as a pageboy, and even, on 9 August 1812, sending him her pubic hair as a gift. She was finally persuaded to desist by her father-in-law, Lord Melbourne.

However, he could not prevent her from writing *Glenarvon* (1816), a bestselling 'apology' to Byron, containing barely concealed portraits of the poet and Society figures. By publicising their relationship in this way, she had shown greater disregard for convention than Byron himself and was sent from London in disgrace. Her subsequent novels *Graham Hamilton* (1822) and *Ada Reiss* (1823) sold less well.

Meanwhile, Byron moved on to Jane Elizabeth, countess of Oxford, an older woman with six children and a veteran of the discreet affair. He eventually married Lady Caroline's cousin, Annabella Milbanke. The office block that now stands at No. 8 St James's is named Byron House.

Spymasters • 5 St James's Street

Novelist Graham Greene lived at No. 5 in 1947–48. He depicted the spymaster Colonel Daintry living in a flat above a restaurant at No. 5 in his novel *The Human Factor* (1978). During the Second World War Colonel Claude Dansey had run MI9, the Government's escape and evasion unit, from a room at the house.

Greene's *The End of the Affair* ,1951 *(see p325)* was based on his relationship with Catherine Wolston, who also lived in St James's Street.

St James's
Street

St James's
Park

Courtly Playground • St James's Park

The Mall bounds St James's Park to the north and Birdcage Walk to the south, with Horse Guards' parade ground its eastern border and the Queen Victoria memorial its western limit. Charles II renovated the park by planting new trees and constructing the Mall. Nell Gwynne's house stood on the south side of Pall Mall, with its garden in the park. The Earl of Rochester, John Wilmot, wrote 'A Ramble in St James' Park' (1672), which captures an aspect of the Park:

> *Much Wine had pass'd, with grave Discourse*
> *Of who fucks who, and who does worse ..*
>
> *And nightly now, beneath their shade*
> *Are Buggeries, Rapes and Inceasts made ..*
> *Great Ladies, Chambermaids and Drudges*
> *The Rag-picker and the Heiress trudges.*
>
> *Carmen, Divines, Great Lords and Taylors*
> *Prentices, Poets, Pimps and Jayles,*
> *Footmen, fine Fopps do here arrive*
> *And here – promiscuously – they swive ..*

Sexual activity in the park also caught the attention of Alexander Pope in the second book of Horatian Satires, *Imitations* (1735):

My Lord of London, chancing to remark
A noted Dean much busy'd in the Park
'Proceed' he cry'd, 'proceed my Reverend Brother
'tis Fornicatio Simplex and no other;
Better than lust for Boys, with Pope and Turk
Or other Spouses like my Lord of York'.

While living nearby in Downing Street, James Boswell recorded in his diary on 20 March 1763 that he felt a carnal desire and so went into the park to pick up a whore.

London Library • 14 St James's Square

Thomas Carlyle founded the London Library in 1841 with the purpose of enabling members to borrow books to read at home. 'The good of a book,' he announced at a public meeting, 'is not in the facts that can be got out of it, but the kind of resonance it awakens in our own minds! … For this purpose I decidedly say that no man can read a book well with the bustle of three or four hundred people about him! … Even forgetting the mere facts which a Book contains, a man can do more with it in his own apartment, in the solitude of one night, than in a week in such a place as the British Museum!'

The Library moved to its present location in 1845, after a brief initial period during which it occupied the first floor of the Travellers Club at 49 Pall Mall. Many of the country's most notable writers and scholars have been members or served on the committee, including Dickens (who was among the founder members), Henry James, George Eliot and Virginia Woolf. T. S. Eliot and Lord (Kenneth) Clark have been among the library's presidents; Sir Harold Nicolson, Sir Rupert Hart-Davis and the Hon Michael Astor have served as chairmen. The library remains an independent subscription library, with membership open to all.

On Your Soapbox • Speaker's Corner, Hyde Park

Since 1872 any individual has had the democratic right to stand and speak on any subject they like at Speaker's Corner, situated close to where the Tyburn gallows once stood. Speakers – of almost every religious and political persuasion – gather to debate here, and face down their hecklers, every Sunday morning. Among those who have spoken publicly at Speaker's Corner are Karl Marx, William Morris, the Pankhursts, C.L.R. James, Marcus Garvey, George Orwell and Lord Soper.

The dramatist and poet Heathcote Williams captured the atmosphere and spirit of the place in his documentary novel *The Speakers* (1964), which portrays four orators, MacGuinness, Axel Ney Hoch, Webster and Van Dyn, and their struggling milieu.

KENSINGTON

THE JOINT MONARCHS William III and Mary Stuart moved their Court to Nottingham House (now Kensington Palace) in 1690. In this era contemporary accounts describe Kensington as 'inhabited by Gentry and Persons of Note: There is also an abundance of Shopkeepers and all sorts of Artificers in it, which makes it appear rather like part of London, than a Country Village'. The presence of royalty stimulated development and by the 19th century Kensington had indeed become part of London, linked to Buckingham Palace and Westminster by the smaller localities of Brompton and Belgravia.

Since the 19th century Kensington has grown into a large, sprawling area with a fairly transient population and a varied level of affluence, from the relative grandeur of South Kensington to the bedsits of Earls Court.

The literary history of the area encompasses writers as English as they come, such as Matthew Arnold and Thackeray for example, as well as French poets seeking to escape the eyes of God under the capital's famously grey skies. And over the years a succession of American writers, including Henry James, Ezra Pound, T.S. Eliot and H.D. (Hilda Doolittle) lived in the area.

Literary salons held by wealthy patrons in the area have provided important meeting places and entry to London literary life for numerous writers. In the 19th century Countess Blessington held gatherings that were attended, at various times, by Lord Byron, Bejamin Disraeli, Thackeray and Dickens.

In the early 20th century, Violet Hunt's salon drew writers such as Ford Madox Ford, Ezra Pound, H.D. and Richard Aldington. In the more cramped surroundings of their lodgings on a small lane at the back of St Mary Abbot's Church, these same writers were engaged in feuds raging over adherence to different '–isms', out of which modernist poetics emerged.

Many houses in Kensington began to be converted into multi-unit dwellings from the mid-20th century on, giving rise to the quiet desperation of the bedsit. In different ways Patrick Hamilton, in *Hangover Square*, George Lamming, in *The Emigrants*, and Muriel Spark, in *A Far Cry from Kensington*, plotted small worlds of isolation in the land of cheap rented accommodation.

Doris Lessing came to the same subject from a different angle, entering the 'world of the lost' through the lodgers she took in to help pay the rent.

Kensington

Key

① Campden Hill Square
② Palace Gardens Terrace
③ Campden Grove
④ Campden Hill Road
⑤ Phillimore Place
⑥ Kensington Church Walk
⑦ St Mary Abbot's
⑧ Young Street
⑨ Kensington Court Place
⑩ De Vere Gardens
⑪ Hyde Park Gate
⑫ Royal Albert Hall
⑬ Brompton Square
⑭ Thurloe Square
⑮ Queen's Gate Gdns
⑯ Cornwall Gdns
⑰ Ashburn Gdns
⑱ Old Brompton Rd
⑲ Earls Court Square
⑳ Warwick Road
㉑ St Barnabas's Church

Marguerite Gardiner • Gore House (site of Royal Albert Hall)

Marguerite Gardiner, Countess of Blessington lived here from 1836 until her death in 1849. She was at the centre of London literary life for thirty years and ran a literary and political salon that, over time, was attended by Dickens, Forster, Thackeray, Byron, Disraeli, Louis Napoleon and Wellington among many others. She wrote novels, poems, short stories, travel books and edited the *Keepsake Annuals* from 1841 to 51.

An Irish beauty, she had been hired by the Earl of Blessington from a landed Hampshire man (for whom she had been a kept mistress). They were married in 1815. The earl died in 1828 leaving the Countess with little income, thus requiring her to live off her literary earnings.

Her first novel, *Grace Cassidy, or the Repealers* (1833), was a satire on Anglo-Irish society. She gained success and fame with her *Journal of Conversations of Lord Byron* (1834), about their six-week friendship in Genoa, and was able to support her live-in lover Alfred, Count d'Orsay, as well as a number of younger women writers, such as Letitia Landon and Emma Roberts. Her most admired novel, *The Victims of Society* (1837), examines themes of marriage and female virtue and attacked the hypocrisy of London society. As editor of the very popular *Keepsake Annual* and *Heath's Book of Beauty*, she was an arbiter of public literary and moral taste – an odd position for someone who was ostracised by respectable society on account of her morality.

Poetry Olympics • Royal Albert Hall

Hubert Parry's choral version of Blake's *Jerusalem* was premiered at the Royal Albert Hall in 1918 to celebrate women being granted the vote.

On 11 June 1965 7,000 people attended the Poets of the World/Poets of Our Time festival here, which featured Allen Ginsberg, Lawrence Ferlinghetti, Gregory Corso, Stevie Smith, Ernst Jandl and Adrian Mitchell. In 1980 poet Michael Horovitz held the first international 'Poetry Olympics' here. A 25th anniversary event was held in October 2005.

Driven • 16 Young Street

William Makepeace Thackeray lived here from 1846 to 1853 while establishing his literary career (he had initially worked in journalism, *see p40*). While in Young Street he wrote and illustrated *Vanity Fair* (1847), *Pendennis* (1848–50), and *The History of Henry Esmond* (1852), as well as writing for *Punch* (until 1854) and other magazines.

Following the success of *Vanity Fair* he became a celebrity, and was much discussed in both literary and social circles. He hosted a reception here for Charlotte Brontë after the success of *Jane Eyre*. Finding the formidable Charlotte and the after dinner atmosphere too much, he quietly left for his club.

Thackeray had a wide variety of literary, theatrical and publishing friends, including the Carlyles, the Kembles, the Proctors, Dickens and his wife, and Countess Blessington. He became a prominent member of the Garrick and Reform clubs, was friends with prominent Whig politicians and also knew the young Disraeli.

After a reading tour of America in 1853 Thackeray moved to 36 Onslow Square, where he wrote *The Newcomes* (1853–55) and *The Virginians* (1857–59), and in 1860 became the first editor of, and a regular contributor to, the *Cornhill Magazine*. His prodigious output was driven by an obsession to earn sufficient money to provide for his family after his death. In 1862 he bought and redesigned a dilapidated Queen Anne house at 2 Kensington Palace Green where, worn out by work and beset by illness, he died on Christmas Eve 1863. He was buried at Kensal Green *(see p249)*.

God Cannot See You • 6 Brompton Square

The late 19th century saw a steady stream of French poets crossing the channel in pursuit of love – and, like Monet, being inspired by the London fog. First was the leading Symbolist poet Stéphane Mallarmé in 1862, followed by Rimbaud and Verlaine in the 1870s *(see p123)*. Jules Laforgue made the journey in 1886 and, at the beginning of the 20th century, came Guillaume Apollinaire.

Mallarmé's best-known work includes 'Hérodiade' (c.1864), 'L'après-midi d'un faune' (The Afternoon of a Faun, c.1865), which inspired a composition by Debussy, and 'Un coup de dés jamais n'abolira le hasard' (A Throw of the Dice Will Never Eliminate Chance, 1897), which made innovative use of typography. He spent a year in London shortly after leaving school. In a quasi-elopement, he married his German lover Marie Gerhard at the Brompton Oratory, and between April and August 1863 lodged at Brompton Square. In 1862 he wrote to a friend 'I love this perpetually grey sky. God cannot see you.'

What Maisie Knew • 34 De Vere Gardens

American novelist Henry James lived in a fourth-floor apartment here from early 1886 until 1898, when he moved to Rye. While here he contributed to *The Yellow Book (see p190)* and wrote *The Aspern Papers* (1888), *The Tragic Muse* (1890), *The Spoils of Poynton* (1897) and *What Maisie Knew* (1897). The ambitious *What Maisie Knew* is a first person narrative from the point of view of a girl caught between warring parents. His elaborate prose style was not entirely suited to that of a child, but his attempt to tell a story entirely from the child's perspective was a significant literary development.

His writing style was arguably better suited to the themes of later books such as *The Wings of the Dove* (1902) and *The Golden Bowl* (1904). James developed the theme of the corruption of innocence in his seminal ghost story *The Turn of the Screw* (1898), about two children haunted by the ghosts of former household servants.

Although a popular novelist, his plays were not favourably received. Colm Toibin's biographical novel *The Master* (2004) begins in January 1895 on the first night of James's play *Guy Domville*. James arrived after the performance to catcalls and booing. He was later informed that when the actor playing Domville had uttered his final lines – 'I'm the last, my lord, of the Domvilles' – someone in the gallery had called out, 'It's a damned good thing you are!'

Robert Browning • 29 De Vere Gardens

After moving out of Warwick Crescent *(see p174)*, Robert Browning lived here from June 1887 until his death on 12 December 1889. He completed and proofed *Asolando: Fancies & Facts* (1889), published on the day of his death. Although De Vere Gardens had electric cables, Browning chose not to use the new facility.

Violet Hunt • South Lodge, 80 Campden Hill Road

Novelist Violet Hunt lived here from 1908 until her death in 1942. Wyndham Lewis decorated the house and Ford Madox Ford (Ford Hueffer until 1919), the editor of the *English Review* 1908–10, was a frequent guest, along with Ezra Pound, H.D. (Hilda Doolittle), Richard Aldington and others. Together, this group of friends would play tennis and attend lavish teas here. When Violet and Ford became lovers and he moved into South Lodge in 1913, their affair became a newspaper scandal.

Violet Hunt was a member of the suffragette movement and from 1909 to 1914 held regular literary and artistic gatherings attended by many of the more radical writers and artists of the day, including Amy Lowell, Madame Strindberg, Jacob Epstein, Kate Lechmere, Rebecca West and Henri Gaudier-Brzeska. She published her autobiography *The Flurried Years* in 1926.

While at South Lodge, Ford wrote *The Good Soldier* (1915), one of the finest English novels of the 20th century. In this story of adultery and deceit, Ford pioneered the use of narrative flashbacks, and attempted to recreate the patterns of thought through his use of an unreliable and sometimes confused narrator.

T.S. Eliot considered Ford's poem 'Antwerp' the only worthy poem about the First World War. After the war Ford moved to Paris and founded *The Transatlantic Review*, publishing James Joyce, Ernest Hemingway, Gertrude Stein, Ezra Pound, Jean Rhys and E.E. Cummings.

Birth of Modernism
10 Kensington Church Walk

Poet and critic Ezra Pound moved here from Marylebone *(see p178)* in August 1909 to what was described by writer Richard Aldington as 'an awful slum courtyard' behind St Mary Abbot's Church. Here Pound, who had taken to wearing an open-necked black shirt, straw hat and a single turquoise earring, dispensed his idiosyncratic hospitality – burning incense, serving dried apricots and singing Hebridean songs – to friends and visitors who included Aldington, Ford Hueffer (later Ford Madox

No. 80 Campden Hill Road

Ford), Violet Hunt, D.H. Lawrence, Robert Frost , F.S. Flint and H.D. (Hilda Doolittle). One evening, after a late party, Pound let Lawrence (who was living and teaching in Croydon at the time) have half his bed for the night. Lawrence, however, was unable to sleep owing to a combination of the church bells and Pound's snoring.

While at Church Walk Pound wrote *Canzoni* (1911), *Ripostes* (1912) – which includes 'The Complete Poetical Works of T.E. Hulme' as an appendix and contains the

first mention of 'Imagiste' – and *Lustra* (1916). He also edited *Des Imagistes* anthology (1914), which featured members of the Poet's Club *(see p125)*.

Pound was a tireless networker and promoter of poetry. As editor and co-ordinator of the Imagist anthology he was able to link his American poet friends, such as William Carlos Williams, H.D., Amy Lowell and John Cournos (who took over Pound's tenancy at Kensington Church Walk in 1914), with Hulme, Flint, Ford, Aldington and Lawrence.

Pound was also London correspondent of the American magazine *Poetry*, published by Harriet Munroe. The March 1913 issue contained the three tenets of Imagism:

1. Direct treatment of the 'thing', whether subjective or objective 2. To use absolutely no word that does not contribute to the presentation 3. As regarding rhythm: to compose in the sequence of the musical phrase, not in the sequence of a metronome.

No. 10 Kensington Church Walk

As T.S. Eliot later wrote, this marked the starting point of modern poetry. Pound married artist Dorothy Shakespear at St Mary Abbot's in 1914 and they moved into 5 Holland Place Chambers. Here he wrote *Qui Pauper Amavi* (1919), containing 'Homage to Sextus Propertius', his free verse defence of the private and erotic against war and jingoism. Shortly afterwards, however, Pound grew disillusioned with the factional in-fighting of London literary life. Having fallen out with Flint over the history and aims of Imagism and in the process of losing his battle with Amy Lowell over the group's leadership, he left for Paris in 1920.

From Hulme and Flint Pound had learned the need for economy, and from Wyndham Lewis and the Vorticists that poetry could be made of juxtaposed masses and planes. Pound left London having materially helped develop the later work of W.B. Yeats *(see p149)* and T.S. Eliot's *The Waste Land (see p66)*.

Schisms • 6 & 8 Kensington Church Walk

Poets H.D. (Hilda Doolittle) and Richard Aldington lived at No. 6 and No. 8 Kensington Church Walk, respectively, from August to October 1913. They married at Kensington Registry Office, with Pound and Helen Doolittle (Hilda's sister) as witnesses, then lived across the landing from Pound at No. 5 Holland Place Chambers until December 1914.

At this time the squabbles and intrigues surrounding Pound's struggle with Amy Lowell over the leadership and direction of the Imagist group became intense. On 17 July 1914 the Imagists held a dinner party at the Dieudonne Restaurant in Ryder Street, St James's. In attendance were Lowell, Aldington and H.D., Ford, Hunt, Flint, Cournos, Allen Upward, Ada Russell and Gaudier-Brzeska among others.

Here Pound attempted to change the group's name from 'imagiste' to 'nageiste' (derived from the French verb 'nager', to swim), proclaiming that its symbol would be a bathtub. At this point he began to lose his battle with the aristocratic Lowell, while H.D., more interested in poetry than labels, started to forge friendships with Lawrence and others on the periphery of the group.

St Mary Abbot's

St Mary Abbot's Church has a 278-foot spire that is visible throughout Kensington. The current church building dates from 1872, but retains the 17th-century pulpit. G.K. Chesterton, who lived at 11 Warwick Gardens from 1877, married here in 1901.

No. 6 Kensington Church Walk

Thackeray and the historian Thomas Macaulay, when he lived at Holly Lodge on Campden Hill, worshipped in the previous building between 1856 and 1859.

Lewis • 61 Palace Gardens Terrace

Wyndham Lewis lived here from May 1923 until March 1926, and sublet a studio at 44 Holland Street, where he provided various services for society ladies, of which portraiture was but one. He had liaisons with, among others, Nancy Cunard, whom in his notebook he called Messalina after Emperor Claudius's promiscuous wife, and Gladys Hoskins, whom he later married.

While here he wrote *The Lion and the Fox* (1927) about the role of the hero in Shakespeare and an essay, 'The Apes of God' (published in Eliot's *Criterion* in April 1924), in which he complained of hordes of wealthy pseudo-artists renting studios in London to 'daub and dabble' to the exclusion of 'genuine painters'. It was not long before he fell out with his wealthy patrons, the painters Fanny and Edward Wadsworth, who felt used and abused.

Securing the Inheritance • 28b Campden Grove

James Joyce and his family moved here from Paris in 1931 for what they thought would be an indefinite stay. Joyce was concerned to live closer to his ailing father and to regularise his marriage to Nora Barnacle, which was not recognised under English law. The Registry Office wedding took place on 4 July 1931, and for two days afterwards reporters camped outside the Campden Grove flat. Kensington proved too dull for Joyce though, and he complained that their street was full of mummies and should be renamed 'Campden Grave'. He and his family returned to Paris that winter.

No. 23 Campden Hill Square

Mad Jack • 23 Campden Hill Square

Poet Siegfried Sassoon lived here from 1925 to 1932. He had made his name as an officer in the First World War, during which he had won the nickname 'Mad Jack' and been awarded the Military Cross – which he later threw in the river Mersey. The poems for which he is principally remembered express contempt for the war leaders, and compassion for his comrades. At the time, however, neither his campaign against the war, nor the poems, garnered much success. At Campden Hill Square he embarked on writing semi-fictional autobiographies, including *Memoirs of A Foxhunting Man* (1928) and *Memoirs of an Infantry Officer* (1930). His spare and muted poems in *Vigils* (1935), dating from the late 1920s, are concerned with spiritual growth. After the publication of *Sequences* (1956), Mother Margaret Mary, Superior of the Convent of the Assumption at 23 Kensington Square, wrote to him in Wiltshire (to where he had moved). The correspondence led to his conversion to Roman Catholicism in 1957.

The Emigrants • The Balmoral Hotel, 191 Queen's Gate Gardens

Here Trinidadian novelist, playwright and short-story writer Samuel Selvon *(see p242)* and Barbadian novelist and poet George Lamming stayed when they first came to London from the Caribbean. They arrived on the same boat in April 1950. Lamming's first novel, *In the Castle of the Skin* (1953), is set in Barbados, but his second book, *The Emigrants* (1954), focuses on experiences of exile and describes the voyage to, and arrival in, London of a group of West Indians.

Politics and History • 28 Hyde Park Gate

Winston Churchill made this his London home after the Tories lost the 1945 General Election. He later bought No. 27 and merged the two buildings.

Keen to establish his version of the war years, he immediately embarked, with a team of researchers and writers, on a six-volume history *The Second World War* (1948–56). In 1953 he was awarded the Nobel Prize for Literature *(see also p18)*.

Churchill vacated the house after becoming Prime Minister in 1951, returning in 1955 when he wrote *A History of the English-Speaking Peoples* (1956–58). Crowds gathered to celebrate his 90th birthday in 1964. He died here and was given a state funeral in 1965.

Ivy Compton-Burnett • 5 Braemer Mansions, Cornwall Gardens

Novelist Ivy Compton-Burnett lived here from 1934 until her death in 1969, sharing the flat with interior decorator and furniture historian Margaret Jourdain until the latter's death in 1951. Ivy Compton-Burnett's fiction examines the corruption of power within the domestic environment, exposing the disruptive forces – such as adultery, incest or abuse – that lie, concealed, beneath a seemingly calm and well-ordered society. Her work is highly condensed, relying heavily upon dialogue, and demands close attention from the reader. It has been compared to post-impressionist painting. Her most important novels include *A House and Its Head* (1935), *A Family and A Fortune* (1939), *Manservant and Maidservant* (1947) and *Mother and Son* (1955).

The Pope of Gloucester Road

3 Kensington Court Gardens, 37 Kensington Court Place

T.S. Eliot moved here from Carlyle Mansions, Chelsea in 1957 after marrying Valerie Fletcher *(see pp 216 & 221)*. On 14 May 1960 the couple entertained poets Stephen and Natasha Spender, Ted Hughes and Sylvia Plath. Plath wrote to her mother in America: The Eliots 'live in a surprisingly drab brick building on the first floor – yet a comfortable lavish apartment. His Yorkshire wife, Valerie, is handsome, blond and rosy …'

After the break-up of his first marriage in 1933 *(see p179)*, Eliot had lived briefly in a boarding house at 33 Courtfield Road in South Kensington. There Bubbles, the cat of his neighbour Miss Bevan, became the inspiration for *Old Possum's Book of Practical Cats* (1939), which was later adapted as the musical *Cats* in 1981.

From Courtfield Road, Eliot moved to 9 Grenville Place, and became churchwarden of the Church of St Stephen, Gloucester Road, from 1940 to 1965. There is a commemorative tablet in the church. From his devotion to religious duties he gained the nickname 'Pope'. The *Four Quartets* (1935–42), the supreme expression of his Anglo-Catholic vision, were originally called 'The Kensington Quartets'.

Since Eliot's death in 1965, Valerie Eliot has remained at Kensington Court Gardens, managing the Eliot estate, fending off enquiries from academics, and editing his correspondence for publication. Volume 1 of *T.S. Eliot Letters* – containing the years 1898 to 1922 – was published in 1988, the centenary of Eliot's birth.

Driven By Demons • 13 Ashburn Gardens

Antonia White lived here from 1942 to 1959, having formerly lived in Chelsea *(see p226)*. While in Ashburn Gardens she wrote *The Lost Traveller* (1950) after undergoing psychoanalysis, *The Sugar House* (1952), *Beyond The Glass* (1954), and a short story collection *Strangers* (1954). She also translated Guy de Maupassant's *A Woman's Life* (1948) and many novels by Colette, whose love of the sensuous and unconventional can be seen in Antonia White's own work.

Perhaps as a consequence of her complex relationship with her possessive father, Antonia White was driven by demons. She was grandly unconventional, as well as being exceptionally strong-minded. Her work employs elements of autobiography and often features the heroine Clara Batchelor, named after Clara Middleton, from George Meredith's *The Egoist*, her father's favourite novel.

When working for the Special Operation Executive during the Second World War she met poet Kathleen Raine, whom she inspired to become a Catholic. In 1959 White moved to 42D Courtfield Gardens, where she lived until 1979. There she wrote an account of her re-conversion to Catholicism, *The Hound and The Falcon* (1966).

Talking Bronco • 17 Campden Grove

Poet Roy Campbell and his wife Mary lived here from 1944 to 1952, when they moved to Portugal, where Campbell died in a car crash in 1957.

Campbell's pro-Fascist *Flowering Rifle* (1939) had been given a hostile review entitled 'The Talking Bronco' by Stephen Spender in the *New Statesman*. Campbell's riposte was to name his fiery 1945 collection *Talking Bronco* and resume his attacks on the self-promoting left-wing poets of the 1930s, whom he labelled MacSpaunday:

> *... joint MacSpaunday shuns the very strife*
> *He barked for loudes, when mere words were rife,*
> *When to proclaim his proletarian loyalties*
> *Paid well, was safe, raked in the heavy royalties,*
> *And made the Mealy Mouth and Bulging Purse*
> *The hallmark of Contemporary verse.*

In the spring of 1946 Campbell sought out his adversaries and confronted them with his fists at the George Inn *(see p180)* and at a Poetry Society reading at the Ethical Church *(see p243)*. An habitué of Fitzrovia, Soho and Portland Place, Campbell worked as a BBC Talks producer, working with Dylan Thomas, George Orwell, John Arlott and enemy-turned-friend Louis MacNeice.

He edited the Catholic literary magazine *The Catacomb* from 1949 to 1951, publishing his own translations of Lorca, Baudelaire, Rimbaud and Apollinaire. His *Collected Poems* were published in 1949, and he won the 1952 Foyle Prize for Poetry for his translations of the poems of St John of the Cross.

Campbell's basement parties became legendary, drawing guests from all walks of life – from the Spanish Ambassador and South African High Commissioner to the local butcher and ex-servicemen. T.S. Eliot, the Sitwells, Evelyn Waugh, Dylan Thomas, George Orwell and Laurie Lee were among the literary contingent.

The Wind in the Willows • 16 Phillimore Place

Kenneth Grahame lived here from 1901 to 1908. During this time he wrote T*he Wind in the Willows*, which began as a bedtime story for his son Alistair. Published in 1908, the story of Rat, Mole, Badger and Toad by the river was not an immediate success. It was only after A.A. Milne's 1929 dramatisation, *Toad of Toad Hall*, that the story began to be established as a children's classic. By this time Grahame, previously a contributor to Harland and Beardsley's *The Yellow Book (see p190)*, had more or less given up on literature and was employed as a secretary at the Bank of England.

The popularity of *The Wind in the Willows* was further enhanced by E.H. Shepherd's illustrations in editions of the book from 1930 onwards.

Girls of Slender Means • Sussex Mansions, Old Brompton Road

Poet and novelist Muriel Spark moved to a bedsit in Vicarage Gate, off Kensington Church Street, in 1949 after her dismissal as Secretary of the Poetry Society and editor of *The Poetry Review*. She was the victim of Poetry Society in-fighting, ousted for being too sympathetic to modern poets. While at Vicarage Gate she wrote 'Elegy in a Kensington Churchyard' (1949) about the old garden at St Mary Abbot's. She then moved to Sussex Mansions with poet Derek Stanford, and the couple lived here throughout the 1950s.

After winning the 1951 *Observer* short story competition, she concentrated on fiction. She wrote her first novels, including *The Comforters* (1957) and *Memento Mori* (1959), a comic and macabre study of old age, here at Sussex mansions. She drew upon her experiences of the world of 1950s bedsits for her tragicomic novels *The Girls of Slender Means* (1963) and *A Far Cry from Kensington* (1988), in which the Hector Bartlett character was inspired by her former lover Derek Stanford.

The Troubadour • 263-7 Old Brompton Road

The Troubadour Coffee House in Earl's Court has hosted poetry events since it opened in 1954, and still presents poetry on Monday evenings. The satirical magazine *Private Eye* was first produced and distributed here in 1961. This was also the place where Bob Dylan first performed in London. Paul Simon, Jimi Hendrix, Joni Mitchell, Charlie Watts, Tom Robinson and Elvis Costello have also played here.

Oh! Tynan! • 20 Thurloe Square

Kenneth Tynan moved here from Mount Street, Mayfair *(see p197)* in May 1966, and stayed until 1975 when he moved to America. His writing for the *Observer, New Yorker* and other periodicals championed the plays of Brecht, Joe Orton, John Osborne and Harold Pinter, as well as the performances of Laurence Olivier.

His various collections of reviews and essays include *Curtains* (1967), *The Sound Of Two Hands Clapping* (1975) and *A View of the English Stage* (1976), which paid tribute to the work of the English Stage Company at the Royal Court Theatre. After his death in 1980, his second wife, novelist and screenwriter Kathleen Tynan, published his *Letters* (1994) and *Diaries* (2001).

Hangover Square • Earl's Court Square

Novelist and playwright Patrick Hamilton, keen observer of the English boarding house and the twilight world of pubs, lived in the White House Hotel, Earl's Court Square in the early 1920s. The hotel features in his novels *Monday Morning* (1925) and *Hangover Square* (1941), where it is the home of protagonist George Harvey Bone.

In 1932 Hamilton and his wife Lois stayed with his sister in her flat at 134 Earl's Court Road. *Hangover Square*, a thriller set in the furnished flats and boozy pubs of Earl's Court, concerns lonely and unstable George Harvey Bone's fatal passion for destructive Netta, with her 'drunken, lazy, impecunious, neurotic, arrogant, pub-crawling cheap lot of swine …' Subsequently made into a film and play, it built on his London trilogy *Twenty Thousand Streets Under The Sky* (1935), which deals with the interlocking lives of a waiter, prostitute and barmaid. As ever in Hamilton's novels, there is much about the pleasures and perils of alcohol, and concern for the social plight of his characters.

St Barnabas's Church • Addison Road

On 31 December 1886 the French poet Jules Laforgue married the Englishwoman Leah Lee here. Within seven months he was dead from TB, having first returned to Paris. Laforgue was a formative influence on T.S. Eliot – the languorous quality of Laforgue's verse finds a clear echo in the Eliot of *Prufrock and Other Observations* (1917). In 1957 Eliot and his second wife, Valerie, were married at St Barnabas's.

World of the Lost • 58 Warwick Road

Novelist Doris Lessing lived here from 1954 to 58, having previously lived in Kensington Church Street from 1950. Here she wrote *A Ripple From The Storm* (1958), which used Warwick Road as a setting, and continued her sequence of novels tracing the history of 'Martha Quest' from childhood in Rhodesia through post-war London. She also wrote the stage play *Play For A Tiger* (1962).

To help pay the rent she took in lodgers, and entered 'the world of the lost, the lonely, the misfits, the waifs and strays that drift from one let room to another ...' She had a wide variety of friends, including Joan Rodker, who introduced her to the haunt of BBC regulars The George *(see p180)*; Fitzrovians such as John Sommerfield, who introduced her to the Soho pubs and clubs; John Deakin, who photographed her for *Vogue*; playwright Arnold Wesker; literary agent Tom Maschler; the historians Dorothy and Edward Thompson (author of *The Making of the English Working Class*, 1968); critic Kenneth Tynan; and writers such as Colin Wilson.

Despite an active social and political life, she was ill-at-ease in London and would walk the streets of Earl's Court and Kensington late at night:

> I did not care where I was, though when I moved from one little knot of streets, or even one street, into another, it was moving from one territory to another, each with its own strong atmosphere and emanations, bestowed by me and by my need to understand this new place.

Six to eight years after her arrival from Rhodesia (Zimbabwe since 1980), she was still dismayed by London's size:

> A practised dweller in London learns to subdue it by living – that is, with heart and mind and senses – in one part of it, making that a home, and says, 'London is a conglomeration of villages,' and chooses one ...

CHELSEA & BELGRAVIA

CHELSEA DEVELOPED FROM a fishing village into a fashionable area in the 1520s when Sir Thomas More built a house near Cheyne Walk. The area was popular among courtiers and aristocrats in the 16th and 17th centuries owing to its proximity to Westminster and the river. Chelsea expanded between 1680 and 1850 thanks to its easy access by water or coach to the Court and the City. Daniel Defoe in his *Tour through the Whole Island of Great Britain* (1724) described Chelsea as a 'Town of Palaces' promising soon to become part of London.

A road was built between Kensington and Chelsea in 1693, and in the 18th century Chelsea developed as a riverside pleasure resort. The Ranelagh Gardens opened in 1742 and visitors came by boat to enjoy concerts and balls and its many coffee houses and taverns. From 1750 the riverside views, picturesque old buildings and stately mansions attracted artists. Chelsea lost its fashionable status, as the courtiers moved away, and by the early 1800s the fashionable set abandoned Chelsea entirely.

The subsequent low demand for property enabled artists to rent houses and studios cheaply, and in the 19th century Chelsea became a bohemian and artists' quarter. Painters such as Rossetti, Turner, Whistler and Hunt, and writers Leigh Hunt, Thomas Carlyle, George Meredith and Algernon Swinburne all lived and worked here. Arthur Ransome's *Bohemia in London* (1907) gives a somewhat romanticised and partly fictional account of the area at the turn of the 19th/20th century.

Artists and writers, such as Augustus John and Dylan Thomas, continued to be attracted to Chelsea in the first half of the 20th century, The Chelsea Arts Club becoming a convenient meeting place. Chelsea was the epicentre of swinging London in the 1960s, and where Elvis Costello didn't want to go in the 70s. Following the 1980s property boom Chelsea was more luxurious than bohemian, the Goths having departed to Camden Town and the hippies to Notting Hill. It has since become one of the most expensive and desirable parts of London.

Belgravia was developed in the 1820s by Lord Grosvenor. With its central location and terraces of white stucco houses, it was fashionable from the beginning, and has since remained a bastion of wealth and exclusivity.

Chelsea and Belgravia

Key

1 Redcliffe Square
2 Harcourt Terrace
3 Redcliffe Road
4 Elm Park Gdns
5 Old Church Street
6 Chelsea Arts Club
7 Mallord Street
8 World's End
9 Apollo Place
10 Paultons Square
11 Chelsea Old Church
12 Cheyne Walk
13 Oakley Street
14 Manresa Road
15 Tite Street
16 Markhouse Square
17 Royal Avenue
18 Royal Court Theatre
19 Cadogan Square
20 Hans Place
21 Eaton Square
22 Chester Square
23 Ebury Street
24 Victoria Square

Sir Thomas More • Chelsea Old Church

Sir Thomas More built a riverside manor house at Danvers Street, near Cheyne Walk, in 1524. He was living in retirement when Henry VIII sent him to the Tower of London for refusing to recognise the break from Rome which would allow Henry to divorce Catherine of Aragon *(see p15)*.

More reconstructed the south chapel of Chelsea Old Church, at Old Church Street, for his private use. A tomb, which he designed, and a large seated statue outside the church commemorate his life. The garden to the west is named after More's daughter, Margaret Roper, whose husband, William, was More's first biographer.

The church also contains a memorial to playwright and poet laureate Thomas Shadwell, who died in 1692. Shadwell wrote fourteen comedies, including *The*

Virtuoso (1676), *Epsom Wells* (1672) and *Bury Fair* (1689). These offer a scurrilous portrait of contemporary manners, and were famously ridiculed by Dryden in *Absalom and Achitopel* (1681). There is also a wall plaque to Henry James, whose memorial service took place here in 1916.

Henry James • 21 Carlyle Mansions
Novelist Henry James lived in this block of flats overlooking the river from January 1913 until his death on 28 February 1916. Having previously lived in Mayfair *(see p190)* and Kensington *(see p208)*, James rented a room at the Reform Club for more than ten years before coming to Carlyle Mansions; he found the L-shaped apartment here 'just the thing for me.' There is a bust of James in the library on Manresa Road.

T.S. Eliot • 19 Carlyle Mansions
T.S. Eliot lived here from 1946 to 57, sharing the apartment with John Hayward. Hayward kept Eliot's archive, helped edit some of his poetry and shared Eliot's passion for Sherlock Holmes. During his time here Eliot wrote *Notes towards the Definition of Culture* (1948), *The Cocktail Party* (1950) and *The Confidential Clerk* (1954). He was awarded the Nobel Prize for Literature and the Order of Merit in 1947.

Statue of Sir Thomas More, Chelsea Old Church

Without confiding in Hayward or other friends, Eliot married his secretary Valerie Fletcher on 10 January 1957 and moved to Kensington Court Place. As a schoolgirl, Fletcher had slept with Eliot's poems under her pillow – a fact that hadn't escaped the notice of a fellow student, the future Henrietta Moraes, muse to Francis Bacon and Lucian Freud *(see pp114 & 224)*.

Ian Fleming briefly used flat 23 of Carlyle Mansions in 1952. Back in London and recently married, Fleming kept it as a quiet refuge away from his wife and her children from previous marriages while he continued to write the first of the James Bond novels, *Casino Royale (see also p236)*.

Cheyne Walk
In addition to the bust of Dante Gabriel Rossetti holding a quill and palette, Cheyne Walk has many literary connections. Novelist Elizabeth Gaskell was born at No. 93 Cheyne Walk in 1810. Her mother died a month after giving birth and Elizabeth was sent to her aunt's in Cheshire. Civil servant and future author of *Dracula* Bram Stoker lived at No. 27 Cheyne Walk in the 1870s and George Eliot moved to No. 4 with her

young husband, John Cross, after the death of her long-term partner, George Lewis. Eliot died of kidney failure after only three weeks living here in December 1880.

Hilaire Belloc lived at No. 104 Cheyne Walk from 1900 to 1905 before he became Liberal M.P. for Salford and a prolific poet and essayist. Virginia Woolf set her novel *Night and Day* (1919) in Chelsea, where Mrs Hilbery has a Cheyne Walk address.

Don Saltero's Coffee House • 59 & 18 Cheyne Walk

Don Saltero's Coffee House was originally opened at No. 59 Cheyne Walk by James Salter, former barber and valet to Sir Hans Sloane. It moved to No. 18 Cheyne Walk in 1718 and remained a tavern until 1867 when it became a private residence. Among its customers were Dr Johnson and essayists Addison and Steele. Don Saltero's is mentioned in the *Tatler* in 1709, Fanny Burney's *Evalina* (1778) and Benjamin Franklin's *Autobiography* (1793).

Carlyle's House • 5, later 24, Cheyne Walk

Scottish philosopher and historian Thomas Carlyle lived here from 1834 until his death in 1881. The house became a museum in 1896 and contains many original furnishings.

Carlyle's *Life of Schiller* had been serialised in John Scott's *London Magazine* in 1823–4. Here he completed the novel *Sartor Resartus* (1834), inspired in part by Sterne's *Tristram Shandy*, and a *History of the French Revolution* (1837). These works established his reputation as 'the Sage of Chelsea'. He became involved in the 'Condition of England question', attacking laissez-faire economics and heralding the new novels of social consciousness by Mrs Gaskell and Disraeli in the 1840s.

Carlyle's evocation of medieval conditions in *On Heroes Past and Present* (1843) provided a new perspective on machinery and craftsmanship that was later developed by John Ruskin and William Morris. Despite embracing anti-democratic and racist views, which outraged some of his friends, Carlyle retained his influence as a cultural prophet and critic until the 20th century. He was painted by James Whistler in *Arrangement in Grey and Black No 2: Portrait of Thomas Carlyle* (1873) and by John Everett Millais in a fiery portrait now hanging in the National Portrait Gallery.

Jane Carlyle, Thomas's wife, was a famous literary hostess. Among her wide circle of friends were Tennyson, Browning, Dickens, Forster, Ruskin, Rossetti and Geraldine Jewsbury. Jane, who humoured her temperamental husband, was immensely popular among their circle. Her letters to relatives, writers and, indeed, Carlyle (during their periods of separation) vividly portray a Chelsea household with recalcitrant servants and the difficulties of their marriage.

Leigh Hunt lived next door to the Carlyles at No. 4 Cheyne Walk (later 22 Upper Cheyne Row) when he was struggling to survive as a full-time writer and editor from 1833 to 1840. Despite disagreements and the Carlyles' distaste at Marianne Hunt's lack of housekeeping – Thomas described the Hunts' children as 'beautiful, strange, gypsy-like' – the neighbours got along. Carlyle appeared in Leigh Hunt's *London Journal* 1834–5 with W.S. Landor and the remnants of the Lamb-Hunt circle.

Rossetti's Menagerie • 16 Cheyne Walk

When his wife Elizabeth Siddal died from an overdose of laudanum in 1862, Dante Gabriel Rossetti buried a collection of his poems with her at Highgate Cemetery. Rossetti then moved to 16 Cheyne Walk, where he lived until 1882 with a menagerie of poets and pets, including a wombat, peacocks, hedgehogs, a deer, armadillos and a kangaroo; the poets included George Meredith and Algernon Swinburne.

Meredith had married Mary Ellen Nicolls, a widowed daughter of Thomas Love Peacock, in 1849, abandoning the law and becoming a writer. She left him for another man in 1858 and died in 1861. He was still coming to terms with his loss when he entered Rossetti's bohemian household. He stayed for a year and completed *Modern Love* (1862) and *Poems of the Roadside* (1862) here. His early novels such as *The Ordeal of Richard Feverel* (1859) – banned by Mudie's library for its 'low moral tone' – and *Evan Harrington* (1861) did not sell well. He finally gained critical and commercial success with *The Egoist* (1879) and *Diana of the Crossways* (1885).

Swinburne stayed until 1863 and was often seen by visitors reciting his poetry naked. While here he wrote his verse dramas, such as *Atalanta in Calydon* (1865) and *Chastelard* (1866), which helped establish his reputation for rhythmic invention and irreverence. He was concerned with challenging accepted moral codes of behaviour, and despite heavy drinking and drug taking remained a prolific poet and critic, later writing about Blake, Chapman, Marlowe and Middleton.

Rossetti painted his new muse, the former model and 'Cockney prostitute' Fanny Cornforth, in a series of erotic paintings, including *Venus Verticordia* and *The Blue Bower* (1865). Fanny became his mistress, although she putatively lived in a nearby street.

In 1869 Rossetti retrieved his poems from Highgate cemetery and published them with 'The House of Life' sonnets in *Poems* (1870), which attracted accusations of obscenity. Rossetti and the Morrises rented Kelmscott Manor in Oxfordshire until, convinced that enemies stalked him and haunted by

No. 16 Cheyne Walk

the ghost of his former wife, he returned to Fanny in Chelsea and started taking even larger quantities of laudanum. By their example and works, Rossetti and Swinburne inspired subsequent aesthetes, most notably Oscar Wilde.

King's Head and Eight Bells • 50 Cheyne Walk

The King's Head and Eight Bells was created by the amalgamation of two adjacent pubs in 1580. The pub was rebuilt in early 19th century, since when its patrons have included Whistler, Thomas Carlyle, Augustus John, Dylan Thomas, John Davenport, Philip Lindsay and Laurie Lee. During the 1940s writers met here on Sunday mornings to read the newspaper book reviews. No longer a pub, it has recently been turned into the Cheyne Walk Brasserie.

Henrietta Moraes • 9 Apollo Place

Between 1954 and 57, this studio house belonged to Johnny Minton. One of the most admired and influential illustrators of the mid-20th century, Minton designed book and magazine covers for Grey Walls Press, *Penguin New Writing*, the *Listener*, *Radio Times* and *Tribune*. When he commited suicide in 1957, he left No. 9 Apollo Place to Henrietta Law, despite the fact that his partner, the actor Norman Bowler, had left him a few years earlier to marry her.

Henrietta moved in and lived here until 1966, sharing the house with her third husband, Indian poet Dom Moraes from 1961 to 63. She was a muse to Francis Bacon, Lucian Freud and *Vogue* photographer John Deakin, who famously photographed her naked for Bacon and sold the prints to sailors in Soho.

Henrietta dropped out of the Chelsea/Soho scene in the mid-1960s to join a group of upper-class hippies. She eventually returned to Chelsea, changing her lifestyle to become a gardener and writer. She lived in a first-floor flat at 18 Edith Grove from 1989, publishing a memoir *Henrietta* in 1994. In the last year of her life she became the muse and lover of artist Maggi Hambling. Hambling's book *Maggi and Henrietta* (2002) charts their relationship in a series of drawings.

Oscar Wilde • Tite Street

Irish poet and playwright Oscar Wilde lived at 44 Tite Street, which he renamed Keats House, in 1881 while advocating aestheticism and the central importance of art in life. His flamboyant lifestyle attracted scorn and helped make him a prominent London personality. Here he completed his first volume of poetry *Poems* (1881). His belief in 'art for art's sake' was mocked in Gilbert and Sullivan's *Patience* (1881), but this only served to enhance his reputation.

After a lecture tour in America he married Constance Lloyd in 1884 and moved to 16 (later, 34) Tite Street, and became an art critic known for his wit. During this period he worked for the *Pall Mall Gazette* and wrote the fairy story *The Happy Prince and Other Tales* (1888). He had the house painted white and redesigned by 'aesthetic architect' Edward Godwin (who had designed Whistler's house at 35 Tite Street). Here Wilde wrote his novel *The Picture of Dorian Gray* (1891) and the shrewdly observed society comedies *Lady Windermere's Fan* (1892), *A Woman Of No Importance* (1893) and *An Ideal Husband* (1895), as well as his satirical masterpiece, *The Importance of Being Earnest* (1895). All were great theatrical successes.

Wilde became an habitué of the Café Royal *(see p192)*, the Savoy Hotel and Kettner's *(see p117)*. *Salomé*, written in French, was refused a licence, but performed in Paris by Sarah Bernhardt in 1896. The English translation, with illustrations by Aubrey Beardsley, was published in 1894 by Lord Alfred Douglas and formed the basis of Richard Strauss's opera *Salomé* (1905).

When Wilde was found guilty of 'gross indecency' (a euphemism for homosexuality) in 1895, following an unwise libel action provoked by Lord Alfred Douglas's father, the house was looted and later sold to help pay court costs. He wrote his apologia, *De Profundis* (1905), while in Reading prison. When released in 1897 he moved to Paris, where he wrote *The Ballad of Reading Gaol* (1898), inspired by his prison experience. Oscar Wilde died of cerebral meningitis in 1900.

Dylan and Chelsea

Welsh poet Dylan Thomas was introduced to Chelsea in the 1930s by Richard Rees and Ruth Pitter who lived at 33 Cheyne Walk, where Rees ran *Adelphi* magazine. Thomas had almost certainly met Pitter drinking at The Fitzroy or The Wheatsheaf in Fitzrovia *(see p127 & 129)*. He also made at least two visits (in April and August 1934) to No. 6 Cheyne Walk, where his girlfriend of the time, novelist Pamela Hansford Johnson, lived with her mother. Pamela wrote *This Bed Thy Centre* (1935), a title suggested by Thomas, drawing upon her experience of growing up in Clapham. In 1950 she married the novelist C.P. Snow.

Thomas shared his first London address with artist friend Alfred Janes at 5 Redcliffe Street, near Brompton Cemetery, from November 1934 to June 1935. Here he lived 'amid poems, butter, eggs, mashed potatoes' and canvases, while frequently travelling back and forth between Swansea and London. Thomas's entrance into literary London was smoothed through friendships with Rayner Heppenstall, Norman Cameron, Edwin Muir and Geoffrey Grigson, and favourable reviews of his *18 Poems* (1934).

Dylan and Caitlin • Flat 3 Wentworth Studios

Dylan and Caitlin Thomas, who had married in 1937, lived in Wentworth Studios, just off Manresa Road, from September 1942 to August 1944. Here, against a backdrop of the Blitz, he worked on documentary film scripts for Strand Films and the celebrated poems that went into *Deaths and Entrances* (1946). He had numerous one-night stands and gave local readings of his poetry while attempting to deal with his fear and disgust at the death and destruction of World War II.

From the 1930s until the time of his death, in New York in 1953, Dylan Thomas was a notable figure in the pubs and clubs of Fiztrovia, Soho and Chelsea.

Geraldine Jewsbury • 3 Oakley Street

Novelist Geraldine Jewsbury lived at No. 3 Oakley Street from 1855 to 60 and at No. 43 Markham Square from 1860 to 67. She was a publisher's reader for Bentley's and a prolific reviewer for *The Athenaeum* and *Westminster Review* in which she advocated a woman's right to education and independence. An important mid-Victorian commentator on women's issues, she is now remembered more for her letters to Jane Carlyle *(see p222)* and for her fighting spirit than for her novels, which include *The Half-Sisters* (1848) and *The Sorrows of Gentility* (1856).

Antonia White • 105 Oakley Street

The first Chelsea address of novelist and fashion writer Antonia White was No. 38 Glebe Place, where she lived from 1921 to 25 with her first husband, Reggie Green-Wilkinson. She described their tiny house in *The Sugar House* (1952). His drinking and homosexuality drove her to despair, but no sooner had she parted from Green-Wilkinson than she married another homosexual (and much older) man, Eric Earnshaw Smith, with whom she lived at No. 55 Paultons Square from 1925 to 1930.

Publication of her first and most successful novel, *Frost in May* (1933), based on her experiences at convent school, brought Antonia White American literary friends, including art collector Peggy Guggenheim and Djuna Barnes, who wrote the surrealist novel *Nightwood* (1936).

White's third marriage was to journalist and future editor of *Picture Post* Tom Hopkinson. The couple had lived at No. 18 Cecil Court, off the Fulham Road, where they gave famous Sunday tea parties for writers and friends. However, in 1934 Tom had an affair with Geoffrey Grigson's wife, Frances. After breaking up with Tom, Antonia moved to No. 105 Oakley Street in 1935. While there she underwent psychoanalysis and befriended the young Fitzrovian poets. She had been introduced to them by Emily Holmes Coleman, who was living upstairs at No. 7 Oakley Street and having an affair with the ground-floor occupant, civil servant and authority on Rimbaud, Sir Samuel Hoare.

Over the following year White and Coleman formed a close bond and exchanged literary ideas with George Barker, Humphrey Jennings, Dylan Thomas, David Gascoyne and Norman Cameron *(see p129)*.

In 1936 she returned to Cecil Court, without her now estranged husband, and her diary entries record long, intense discussions about all aspects of art and life. She confided that she was sceptical but learning from the young, non-established poets. The entry for 18 September 1936, for example, describes 'the feeling I like the best – of flow and communication between people', as she sat up through the night talking with Emily and Hoare, Jennings and Gasgoyne, and being amused by Jennings's 'constant images – the horse, the electric light bulb, the train, Byron, the prism…'

From January 1938 until September 1939 she lived at Cornwall Gardens, Kensington, with Ian Henderson and her children and worked on *The Lost Traveller* (1950). During the War, Antonia White lived near Notting Hill Gate, working as a publicist for the BBC and later the Foreign Office, helping the Free French movement.

Paultons Square Poets

Kathleen Raine lived at No. 9 Paultons Square from 1944 to 58, having previously lived in Percy Street, Fitzrovia. Raine leased the house and let out rooms to Dolly Donn Byrne, widow of Irish writer Donn Byrne, writer and critic John Davenport and later Ruthven Todd.

Tambimuttu had published Raine's first book *Stone and Flower* (1943) with illustrations by Barbara Hepworth. Here she started her Sunday evening poetry readings attended by a mixture of Fitzrovians linked by Tambimuttu's *Poetry London* and friendships made at Cambridge. Among the many poets who read were George Barker, Dylan Thomas, Bernard Gutteridge, Bernard Spencer, Humphrey Jennings and David Gascoyne.

Tambimuttu introduced her to painter Gavin Maxwell, with whom she formed a tempestuous relationship. Later, during the 1950s, he lived on the first two floors of the house. Maxwell took the title of his best-known work *Ring of Bright Water* (1960) from Raine's poem 'The Marriage of Psyche' (1952):

> *He has married me with a ring, a ring of bright water*
> *Whose ripples travel from the heart of the sea …*

Kathleen Raine moved to 47 Paultons Square in 1959 and lived here until her death in July 2003. A prolific writer celebrating spiritual values, she also wrote extensively on Blake and Yeats and published three volumes of autobiography.

The Poet's Kitchen • 39 Markham Square

Elizabeth Smart lived in the basement flat here from October 1945 to July 1946, while her lover and father of her children, George Barker, stayed with his parents at nearby 23A Stanhope Gardens. Her passionate prose poem *By Grand Central Station I Sat Down And Wept* (1945) is an account of her love for Barker. Her flat became known as the Poet's Kitchen due to her hospitality for destitute poets. One of her guests was fellow Canadian poet Paul Potts, who introduced her to his Soho drinking friends, the painters Robert MacBryde and Robert Colquhoun – known as 'the two Roberts'.

Smart returned to Chelsea in 1951 from Tilty Mill, Duton Hill, Essex, subletting 1 Rossetti House, Flood Street, from Sir Caspar John. While here she had an affair with Scottish poet W.S. Graham, author of *The White Threshold* (1949) and *The Nightfishing* (1955). He urged her to return to writing. She eventually produced the novel *The Assumption of the Rogues and Rascals* (1978).

P. G. Wodehouse • Markham Square

P.G. Wodehouse, creator of *Jeeves and Wooster*, lived at Markham Square in 1900 while working at the Hong Kong and Shanghai Bank in the City by day and writing by night. In 1902 he gave up his day job for literature and moved across the King's Road to No. 23 Walpole Street. There he wrote stories for *The Globe* and *Punch* and his first books, *The Pothunters* (1902) and *Love Among the Chickens* (1906), which features the amoral rogue Uckridge. His friend Herbert Westbrook – who had all the egotistical temperament of an artist but none of the talent and was always borrowing money from Wodehouse – inspired the character of Uckridge.

Laurie Lee • 49 Elm Park Gardens

Laurie Lee first lived in Chelsea in 1941, when he lodged with portrait painter Anthony Devas and his wife Nicolette – sister of Caitlin Thomas – in the top floor flat at No. 6 Markham Square. There he wrote poems for *The Sun My Monument* (1944), his first collection of poems, and *The Bloom of Candles* (1947), his second. He also embarked upon a number of relationships following his break-up with Lorna Wishart (née Lorna Garman), who left him for Lucian Freud. He eventually married Wishart's niece, 18-year-old Kathy Polge, in May 1950.

When he returned to Chelsea in 1951 he lived at Elm Park Gardens, where sculptor Elisabeth Frink was a neighbour. Here Lee wrote *Cider With Rosie* (1959), an evocative, fictionalised account of his Cotswold childhood. It was an instant success and has remained in print ever since. Two years after its publication, he moved his family to Slad in Gloucestershire, while using the Elm Park Gardens house as a base during his visits to London. The second volume of his 'fictional autobiography', *As I Walked Out One Midsummer Morning* (1969), chronicling his walk from Slad to London and his time in Spain before the Spanish Civil War, was also a huge success.

He moved across the square in 1980, buying the top floor flat at 40 Elm Park Gardens, where he wrote *A Moment of War* (1991), an account of his Spanish Civil War experiences. It was criticised by some veterans for its lack of accuracy and subsequently revised for the paperback edition. He became a noted drinker with an eye for a short skirt at the Chelsea Arts Club.

William De Morgan • 127 (now 125) Old Church Street

Ceramicist, designer and novelist William De Morgan and wife Evelyn lived here from 1909 until their deaths in 1917 and 1919 respectively. De Morgan designed pottery, glass and tiles, and collaborated with William Morris from a studio at No. 1 Upper Church Street. He began writing novels in his retirement. His first was *Joseph Vance* (1906), the story of a drunken builder's son who becomes an engineer and inventor. It was hugely popular and was followed by others, such as *When Ghost Meets Ghost* (1914). His last two novels were completed by Evelyn after William's death.

Katherine Mansfield • 141a Old Church Street

Short story writer Katherine Mansfield lived here in 1917–18, when she was beginning to be recognised as a talented and original writer. Her stories were the first in English to show the influence of Anton Chekhov, whom she venerated. Her success aroused the jealousy of Virginia Woolf, who described her work as 'hard' and 'shallow'. Mansfield was suffering from tuberculosis and spent part of every year in the south of France. She then moved from Chelsea to Hampstead *(see p291)* for the better air.

Chelsea Arts Club • 143 Old Church Street

Artists Thomas Stirling Lee, James McNeill Whistler, James Elder Christie and others founded the Chelsea Arts Club at 118 King's Road in 1890. It moved to two cottages on Old Church Street in 1901, by which time it had become a second home for local artists. Portrait artist Augustus John, who joined the club in 1909 when he was living at 153 Old Church Street, sculptor Jacob Epstein and composer Philip Heseltine, who lived at 30 Tite Street, were instrumental in linking Chelsea, Bloomsbury and Fitzrovia in the 1920s. For a succession of artists and writers, the Chelsea Arts Club became part of a regular circuit of drinking and womanising in the pubs and clubs of Chelsea, Fitzrovia and Soho. Dylan Thomas even managed to get himself banned from the club in 1941. Laurie Lee joined in 1949, as did Henry Moore.

Women were admitted in 1966, and the Liverpool poets Roger McGough and Brian Patten joined in 1974, McGough becoming Chairman in 1984 and 1985.

The Chelsea Arts Club

Poky, Dark and Cramped • 53 Old Church Street

John Betjeman lived here from 1917 to 24 while at private school. In *Summoned by Bells* (1960) he remembered the house as 'poky, dark and cramped / Haunted by quarrels

The former Queen's Elm pub

and the ground floor ghost', and whenever possible would escape to explore London on the Underground's Metropolitan line. Towards the end of his life he returned to Chelsea, living at No. 29 Radnor Walk from 1977 until his death in 1984.

The Queen's Elm • Corner of Old Church Street and Fulham Road
The charismatic Sean Treacy ran The Queen's Elm from the late 1950s. He attracted a lively mix of artists, writers, actors and musicians, including James Cameron, Jeffrey Bernard, Oliver Reed, Sean Connery, Virginia McKenna, Bill Travers, Eric Sykes, Laurie Lee, Julian Bream, Elizabeth Frink and Gerald Scarfe. Laurie Lee described the Elm as 'more like a club than a pub' in a 1975 article for the *Telegraph* magazine, while novelist Mavis Cheek – whose works include *Three Men on a Plane* (1998) and *The Sex Life of My Aunt* (2002) – was at one time a barmaid here. The Queen's Elm building remains, its name still visible in the plasterwork above the ground-floor windows, but the premises are now occupied by a shop.

The House at Pooh Corner • 13 Mallord Street
After A.A. Milne relinquished the post of assistant editor at *Punch*, he became a full-time writer. He lived in this three-storey Arts and Crafts house from 1914 to 42. Although a prolific writer of plays, novels, poetry and short stories, he is best known for his children's books, most of which he wrote here, including *When We Were Very Young* (1924); the phenomenally successful *Winnie-the-Pooh* (1926); *Now We Are Six* (1927); *The House at Pooh Corner* (1928); and *Toad of Toad Hall* (1929), a dramatisation of Kenneth Grahame's *The Wind in the Willows (see p215)*.

Granny Takes A Trip • 488 King's Road, World's End
At the height of 1967's 'Summer Of Love', 20-year-old Salman Rushdie rented a room here, above the then highly fashionable hippie boutique Granny Takes A Trip. The author of *Midnight's Children* (1981) and *The Satanic Verses* (1988) among other

books recounts this period in an essay in *Step Across This Line: Collected Non Fiction 1992–2002* (2002).

You Can't Always Get What You Want • Chelsea Drug Store

The Chelsea Drug Store, on the corner of Royal Avenue and the King's Road, with a bar, restaurant, discotheque, and boutiques, attracted a large following, including 60s musicians such as Jimi Hendrix, Mick Jagger (who in the early 1960s lived in Edith Grove) and Ray Davies. The Chelsea Drug Store featured in songs of the period, notably the Rolling Stones' 'You Can't Always Get What You Want', with its reference to sharing a soda with 'Mr Jimmy', a reference to Hendrix. The site of the Drug Store is now occupied by a branch of McDonalds.

Wartime Pepys, Peacetime Hippie • Redcliffe Road

Bohemian London is brought vividly to life in Joan Wyndham's four volumes of diaries and memoirs, comprising *Love Lessons* (1985), *Love Is Blue* (1986), *Anything Once* (1992) and *Dawn Chorus* (2004). The books chart the progress of a life lived to the full, from coming of age in London during wartime, through the 1960s as a middle-aged hippie, to the 1980s when she had to cope with the suicide of a friend and her own, finally successful, battle with cancer in *Anything Once*.

By turns moving and hilariously funny, *Love Lessons* (covering the period August 1939 and May 1941) finds her just 17, eager to escape her prudish mother and throw herself at the first unsuitable man she comes across. 'What a life,' I said, 'never knowing if you're going to be bombed or seduced from one moment to the next!'

Love Is Blue continues the story from April 1941 to September 1945 when she was in the WAAF and features her visits to Soho, Fitzrovia and Chelsea and her encounters with Dylan Thomas, Julian MacLaren-Ross, Augustus John and Quentin Crisp, written with irresistible charm and humour.

November 1945 and the beginning of *Anything Once* finds her demobbed from the WAAF and living at No. 32 Cadogan Street, determined to be 'gloriously, totally and dangerously free' – a resolution she steadfastly maintains. It encompasses everything from a short affair with Lucian Freud to being arrested for vagrancy on the Scilly Isles, researching rent boys for women in Amsterdam's red-light district to her first acid trip at the age of 50. While publication of the full diaries awaits, *Dawn Chorus* provides the prequel to the trilogy.

Lowell's Mermaid • 80 Redcliffe Square

Writer and journalist Lady Caroline Blackwood – who had been married to Lucian Freud from 1953 to 59 – moved to No. 80 Redcliffe Square in February 1970. In the same year she accepted an invitation to Faber & Faber's welcoming party for Robert

Lowell, recently appointed visiting professor at All Souls Oxford. Lowell wasted no time – he moved into her home on the night of the party and, despite still being married to Elizabeth Hardwick, attempted to conduct a clandestine affair with Caroline.

In July of 1970 Caroline experienced the fearful intensity of Lowell's manic depressive illness when he locked her in the upstairs flat for three days. He was hospitalised and subsequently rented a flat at 33 Pont Street, Knightsbridge, during the autumn. There he began writing the poems that went into *The Dolphin* (1973).

He determined to marry Caroline, however, and by March 1971 was back in the upstairs flat at Redcliffe Square and Caroline was pregnant. Fearing a return of his illness, Caroline moved her family to the country, while keeping the Redcliffe Square house as a London base. Lowell stayed here in the summer of 1972, agonising over his use of telephone conversations and letters in poems about the dissolution of his marriage. Having divorced Elizabeth Hardwick in September 1972, Lowell married Caroline in October. For Lowell their affair and marriage was a renewal, and their relationship is charted in the 'Mermaid' and 'Redcliffe Square' poems from *The Dolphin*, which won the 1974 Pulitzer Poetry Prize.

In 1972 Caroline published *For All That I Found There*, consisting of short stories, journalism and memoirs of her Ulster childhood, a novella entitled *The Stepdaughter* (1976) and *On the Perimeter* (1984), an account of the Greenham Common anti-nuclear protest. Her best work is perhaps *Great Granny Webster* (1977), a notable addition to the decaying country house theme in Anglo-Irish fiction – a trend that was started by Elizabeth Bowen *(see p179)*.

The Good Apprentice • 59 Harcourt Terrace

Novelist and philosopher Iris Murdoch moved here in 1963, soon after she had resigned her Fellowship at St Anne's College (in 1962). She lived here until 1967, during which time she lectured at the Royal College of Art.

While here she completed *The Unicorn* (1963), *The Italian Girl* (1964) and *The Red And The Green* (1965), collaborated with J.B. Priestley to turn *A Severed Head* (1964) into a play, and wrote *The Sovereignty Of Good And Other Moral Concepts* (1967), one of the most widely read English books on moral philosophy. Chelsea features as a backdrop to characters in many of her novels, especially *An Unofficial Rose* (1962) and *The Good Apprentice* (1985), her allegory about good and evil.

Royal Court Theatre • Sloane Square

The Royal Court established its reputation as London's most controversial and innovative theatre in May 1956 with its production of John Osborne's *Look Back in Anger*. George Devine, the Royal Court's first artistic director, aimed to create a writers' theatre, 'a place where the dramatist is acknowledged as the fundamental creative force'. *Look Back in Anger* heralded the arrival of a new generation of dramatists, including Arnold Wesker, whose *Chips With Everything*, 1962 *(see also p304)* was a huge success, Ann Jellicoe, N.F. Simpson, John Arden and Edward Bond.

Major productions over the years have included a series of Samuel Beckett's plays, directed by the author who, during the engagement, stayed next door at the Royal Court Hotel. Caryl Churchill, who was resident dramatist in 1974–5, emerged as one of the country's leading playwrights. Among her many Royal Court successes have been *Top Girls* (1982), about five historical female characters at a dinner party in a London restaurant; *Serious Money* (1987), which satirised the stock market after the 1987 crash; *Mad Forest* (1990), about Romania; and *A Number* (2002) which addressed the issue of human cloning.

During the 1990s the Royal Court was instrumental in developing the careers of a new generation of dramatists, foremost among them Sarah Kane, whose uncompromising work included *Blasted* (1995), *Phaedra's Love* (1996), *Cleansed* (1998), *Crave* (1998) and *4.48 Psychosis* (2000). A fierce young talent, Kane hanged herself on 20 February 1999.

Royal Court Theatre

BELGRAVIA

The Improvisatrice • 22 Hans Place

Letitia Elizabeth Landon (L.E.L) was born at No. 25 Hans Place in August 1802; the family remained here until 1809. Her first poem was published in *The Literary Gazette* (issue 164) when she was aged just 17. After the death of her father she lodged here at Hans Place, from January 1826 until 1837, supporting her mother, her invalid sister and brother, who lived elsewhere, through her writing. Although her first book, *The Fate of Adelaide* (1821), sold few copies, her second collection, *The Improvisatrice* (1824), was internationally successful and established her career. She went on to write several volumes of poetry, including *The Troubadour* (1825), *The Golden Violet* (1827) and *The Venetian Bracelet* (1829), novels such as *Romance and Reality* (1831) and *Francesa Carrar* (1834) and most of the eight volumes of *Fisher's Drawing Room Scrap Book* in the 1830s.

Chester
Square

Mary Shelley • 24 Chester Square

After the death of Shelley in 1822, Mary Shelley (daughter of William Godwin and Mary Wollstonecraft) returned to England from Italy, and lived here in Chelsea with her son Percy Florence from 1846 until her death in February 1851.

In May 1816 Shelley had gone to Geneva with Mary and her step-sister Claire, Byron's lover. Mary, Byron and Shelley each agreed to write a supernatural tale. Mary was the only one to complete the task. *Frankenstein, or The Modern Prometheus* (1818) was the result. Told through the letters of Walton, an English explorer in the Arctic, *Frankenstein* concerns an idealistic Genevan natural philosophy student who constructs a human-like creature that turns against him. This story of the corruption of an essentially good nature by ill treatment is regarded as the origin of modern science fiction and retains an iconic status in both literary and popular culture to this day.

Mary also wrote biographies, poetry for the *Keepsake* annual, and a number of other novels including *Valperga* (1823), a romance set in 14th-century Italy, *The Last Man* (1826), a novel set in the future, and *Ladore* (1835), which has a 'Noble Savage' motif. Her children's story *Maurice*, written in 1820, was rediscovered in 1997 and published in 1998. She also edited her husband's poems, essays and letters, keeping Shelley's work in print and ensuring that his reputation endured.

Culture and Anarchy • 2 Chester Square

Essayist and poet Matthew Arnold lived here from 1858 to 1868 when he was an inspector of schools. Here he wrote *New Poems* (1867), which included his most famous early poems, 'Rugby Chapel', 'Thyrsis' and 'Heine's Grave', *Essays on Criticism* (1865) and his social criticism *Culture and Anarchy* (1869).

A man of ideas, he was elected Oxford Professor of Poetry in 1857. He was critical of Victorian materialism and an advocate for the improvement of secondary education. He maintained that the critic should be free of prejudice, aiming to see the object as it really is. Arnold had a resigned dissatisfaction with Victorian society and in 'Dover Beach' the certainties of faith ebb away. In a poem that is unusually intimate for Arnold, the narrator sees a world that 'seems / To lie before us like a land of dreams, / So various, so beautiful, so new', yet in reality 'Hath really neither joy, nor love, nor light, / Nor certitude, nor peace, nor help for pain'.

Unlike his contemporaries Tennyson and Browning, Arnold had to earn a living through means that took him away from writing and into direct experience of English social conditions, in which he saw the vast unrealised potential of the working poor.

The Return of Shelley • 41 Hans Place
On their return to England from Switzerland in late 1816 the Shelleys, together with Claire Clairmont, stayed here. Mary gave birth to a daughter, Clara, who lived for ten days in February 1817. Shelley's friend, Thomas Hogg, who had been expelled from Oxford on the publication of the latter's *Necessity of Atheism* (1811), as infatuated with Mary as he had previously been with Shelley's first wife, Harriet Westbrook, briefly augmented their experimental household. Hogg later wrote *Life of Shelley* (1858).

Edward Trelawny • 17 Eaton Square
Edward Trelawny lived here in the late 1830s. Part of Shelley's entourage at the time of his death in Italy and later with Byron in Greece in 1823, Trelawny was encouraged by Mary Shelley to publish his autobiographical novel *Adventures of a Younger Son* (1831) and *Recollections of the Last Days of Shelley and Byron* (1858), which he expanded into *Records of Shelley, Byron and the Author* (1878). He eventually eloped with Lady Augusta Goring and settled in Monmouthshire.

Brief Encounters • 111 Ebury Street
Actor, dramatist and composer Noël Coward lived here with his mother from 1917 to 1930. He first achieved fame with his drama *The Vortex* (1924), in which he played a young drug addict tormented by his mother's adulterous affairs. The money he received enabled Coward to rent ground-floor rooms from his mother.

More success followed with comedies such as *Hay Fever* (1925), about the eccentric, theatrical, self-regarding Bliss family; *Private Lives* (1933), about two disastrous interconnected second marriages; *Design For Living* (1933), about a successful ménage à trois, and *Blithe Spirit* (1941).

These sophisticated and, for the time, morally daring plays brought the spirit of the Roaring Twenties to the stage and were hugely successful. From 1930 until 1956

Coward lived at No. 17 Gerald Road. There he wrote the sentimental *Cavalcade* (1931) and screenplays *This Happy Breed* (1943) and *Brief Encounter* (1944).

King's Daughter • 182 Ebury Street

Poet and novelist Vita Sackville-West lived here in the late 1920s with her husband, the diplomat and diarist Harold Nicolson. Their 'open' marriage allowed both partners to enjoy same sex liaisons, and Vita attempted to seduce both Roy and Mary Campbell (née Mary Garman) in the summer of 1927, succeeding with Mary in September. She published a series of sonnets about her short affair with Mary in *King's Daughter* (1928). Unamused, Roy Campbell in *The Georgiad* (1931) expressed his contempt for Bloomsbury in general and Vita's literary set in particular.

Vita's most successful novel, *The Edwardians* (1930), concerns illicit entanglements, very much reflecting the author's life. Sackville-West provided the inspiration for Virginia Woolf's *Orlando* (1928) – the motivation partly arising from Virginia's sexual jealousy of Vita and Mary's affair (Vita and Woolf also had an intimate and sexual relationship). Nigel Nicolson, son of Harold and Vita, describes his parents' unorthodox marriage in *Portrait of a Marriage* (1973).

The Name is Bond • 16 Victoria Square

Ian Fleming was born into a wealthy family at No. 27 Green Street in Mayfair. His father was killed in the First World War, while mother and sons went on to become fixtures within London Society of the inter-war period. After working as a journalist with Reuters, Fleming joined a banking firm and moved to 22B Ebury Street, where he lived from 1936 to 39. He amassed an important collection of first editions and Surrealist art, while leading an elegant life of dinner parties and love affairs. His circle of friends included Noël Coward, Peter Quennell, Patrick Leigh Fermor and Cyril Connolly.

Shortly after the Second World War – in which he served in Naval Intelligence – Fleming built Goldeneye, his famous house on the north coast of Jamaica. In 1952 he married his long-time lover Ann Charteris (formerly Lady Rothermere), and the following year the couple purchased No. 16 Victoria Square as a London base. Here Fleming completed his first novel, *Casino Royale* (1953), which introduced the supremely suave secret agent James Bond 007. *Live and Let Die* followed in 1954, with a new Bond novel appearing every year until the short stories *Octopussy and the Living Daylights* in 1966. Highlights included *Diamonds Are Forever* (1956), *From Russia With Love* (1957), *Goldfinger* (1959), *On Her Majesty's Secret Service* (1963) and *You Only Live Twice* (1964).

In an article in 1962 Fleming summed up his work in this way: 'My contribution to the art of thriller-writing has been to attempt the total stimulation of the reader all the way through, even to his taste buds…'

Arnold Bennett • 75 Cadogan Square

Novelist Arnold Bennett lived here from 1923 to 1930. He edited *Woman* from 1896 to 1900 and was Director of Propaganda at the Ministry of Information during the First Word War, by which time he was a famous novelist. He refused a knighthood in 1918. Bennett worked his way up to Belgravia, with income from the success of *Anna of the Five Towns* (1902), *The Old Wives Tale* (1908) and the *Clayhanger* series of novels, enabling him to lease this red brick house. While here he wrote *The Riceyman Steps*, 1923 *(see p156)*, the story of a miserly second-hand bookseller in Clerkenwell.

Witness to the Century • 72 Cadogan Square

American journalist and novelist Martha Gellhorn lived here in the attic flat on the 6th floor of the building from 1964 until her death in 1998. Radiantly beautiful as a young woman, she had been pursued by an aging H.G. Wells in 1935 before becoming Ernest Hemingway's second wife from 1940 to 1944.

She was one of the 20th-century's greatest war correspondents. Motivated by a concern for social justice, she reported on every major conflict from the Spanish Civil War to the US invasion of Panama. She reported on the American Depression, witnessed the liberation of Dachau, and covered the Vietnam War for the *Guardian* and *Atlantic Monthly*. Her war correspondence is collected in *The Face of War* (1959) and her peacetime journalism in *The View From The Ground* (1988). Her novels include *The Stricken Field* (1940), about Prague before its fall to Germany; *Liana* (1944), about the French Caribbean; and *The Lowest Trees Have Tops* (1967), about McCarthyism.

As a self-proclaimed 'student of disaster', in *Travels With Myself and Another* (1978) she provides penetrating and hilarious accounts of, among others, her journey to the front line of the Sino-Japanese war in 1941 (accompanied by the 'Another' of the book's title, the never directly identified Ernest Hemingway). She also describes a visit to Moscow to meet 'Mrs M' (Nadezhda Mandelstam, author of *Hope against Hope* (1970) and *Hope Abandoned* (1974), profoundly moving and incisive accounts of life in Stalinist Russia.

At Cadogan Square in the 1990s she would meet her 'chaps' – journalists such as John Pilger, Rosie Boycott, John Simpson and Jon Snow, with whom she would dissect the news.

No. 72 Cadogan Square

WEST LONDON

WEST OF MAYFAIR AND MARYLEBONE and north of Kensington Gardens are the largely residential and cosmopolitan areas of Paddington, Bayswater and Notting Hill. The area developed from a rural base after the opening of an extension to the Grand Junction Canal in 1801 and the building of Paddington Station in 1838. In the mid-20th century the area attracted bohemian writers and artists who wished to avoid or move away from Bloomsbury, Fitzrovia, Soho and Chelsea.

Notting Hill has fascinated writers throughout the last century. It is featured in G.K. Chesterton's bizarre fantasy *The Napoleon of Notting Hill* (1904), about a small community's attempts to resist progress, and in studies of London, such as Jonathan Raban's *Soft City* (1974) and Nicholas Shakespeare's *Londoners* (1986). It is also very much associated with the works of Martin Amis, particularly *London Fields*, which centres on Trellick Tower on the Golborne Road. The area is also pivotal in Michael Moorcock's *Mother London* (1988) and his Colonel Pyatt books, *Byzantium Endures* (1981), *The Laughter of Carthage* (1984) and *Jerusalem Commands* (1992), which concern a Russian émigré living on the Portobello Road in the 1970s.

The borough of Hammersmith and Fulham lies to the west of Kensington, further along the central western route out of London, described by Leigh Hunt in 1855 as the 'pleasantest route out of town'; few would describe it as such today. Its riverside proximity, however, has brought attractive townhouses, boating and many popular inns dating back to the 17th century. The Dove provided lodgings for the Scottish poet James Thomson in the 18th century; in the 19th William Morris lived next door at Kelmscott House; and in the 20th Graham Greene and A.P. Herbert drank there.

The riverside suburbs of Richmond and Twickenham became increasingly fashionable retreats for writers and actors in the early 18th century, and they remain leafy and picturesque today. Alexander Pope lived in the area as, at varying times, did Francis Bacon, Alfred Lord Tennyson and, occasionally, Charles Dickens. While living in Richmond, Marian Evans adopted the *nom de plume* George Eliot, and wrote the first chapters of *The Mill on the Floss*.

When Virginia and Leonard Woolf moved out to Richmond in 1913 it was with the purpose of finding some tranquillity. Before long, they had acquired a hand printing press and founded the Hogarth Press.

Around Notting Hill

Key

1 Paddington Station
2 Westbourne Terrace
3 Bayswater Road
4 Queensway
5 Ossington Street
6 Leinster Square
7 Chepstow Villas
8 Portobello Road
9 Holland Park Avenue
10 Blenheim Crescent
11 Ladbroke Grove
12 Powis Square
13 Leamington Road Villas
14 Harrow Road
15 Delamere Terrace
16 Westbourne Park Villas
17 Westbourne Grove

An Intriguing Mind and a Finely Chiselled Face • Delamere Terrace, Paddington

Peter Watson – described by the artist and writer Michael Wishart as 'a dandy and dilettante par excellence' – provided the funds for Cyril Connolly's literary magazine *Horizon*, as well as support for a number of artists (including Graham Sutherland).

Horizon published drawings by a 17-year-old Lucian Freud in 1939, and in 1943 Watson set up Freud and another young painter, John Craxton, in a studio by the canal on Delamere Terrace. The distinctly down-at-heel area appealed to Freud's louche side and, according to the art critic John Richardson, 'permeates Freud's painting as deeply as Tahiti permeates Gauguin's … the funkiness of the place … and its slightly shabby light seep into virtually all his work, and Londonize it.'

The Paddington studio was described by Waldemar Hansen, one of Peter Watson's friends, as having 'a zebra-head on the wall, an old-fashioned phonograph with a huge horn, and a live falcon which swoops around the room and alights on the master's wrist!' Here Joan Wyndham 'in an icy bed … made love to an intriguing mind and a finely chiselled face', before being replaced in Freud's affections by Kitty Garman, daughter of Kathleen Garman and Jacob Epstein. Kitty and Lucian married in 1948 and lived in St John's Wood, but he kept the studio in Paddington; four years later, when the marriage ended in divorce, Freud returned to live in the studio, where shortly afterwards he was joined by Caroline Blackwood *(see pp112 & 231)*.

Open House • 9 Westbourne Terrace, Paddington

Elizabeth Smart lived here from 1955 to 64, with her four children by the poet George Barker. Smart kept an open house for Soho and Fitzrovian writers and artists. Poets David Gascoyne, David Wright and Patrick Kavanagh were frequent guests; the painters Robert MacBryde and Robert Colquhoun ('the Two Roberts') were the children's nannies. Smart's former lover W.S. Graham, who had just published *The Nightfishing*, stayed with her during 1955 and subsequent London visits. He maintained a lively correspondence with her, David Wright, 'the two Roberts', and other Soho friends. Smart worked as a copywriter for Crawford's Advertising Agency and freelanced as a writer for *Vogue* and *House and Garden*. She eased her working life by spending afternoons and evenings at the French House and The Colony Room in Soho *(see pp111 & 114)*, where she met Bacon, Freud, John Deakin, David Archer and others. George Barker remained an intermittent visitor.

From 1964, Smart wrote for *Queen* (later *Harper's & Queen* and now *Harper's Bazaar*) promoting women's literature. Her son, Sebastian, is an accomplished poet and currently editor of *The London Magazine*, based in west Kensington.

Crome Yellow • 155 Westbourne Terrace

Aldous Huxley lived here from October 1921 until December 1922. While here, he published his first novel, *Crome Yellow* (1921), which included a caricature of Lady Ottoline Morrell and Garsington Manor, where he had been a guest during the First World War. The book also explores themes that he would more fully develop in 1931 with *Brave New World* (1932).

Crome Yellow earned Huxley a reputation for precocious brilliance and cynicism. He also deeply offended Lady Ottoline *(see p139)*. Success enabled him to become a full-time writer and, contracted to write two novels a year, he was able to divide his time between London and Europe throughout the 1920s. His next novel *Antic Hay* (1923) is set in bohemian London shortly after the First World War.

Dr Finlay's Casebook • 152 Westbourne Grove

Scottish novelist and physician A.J. Cronin had a medical practice in Westbourne Grove from 1925 to 1930. It was here that he wrote his first novel, *Hatter's Castle* (1931), which was sufficiently successful to allow him to move to Harley Street. He became a popular novelist, combining realism with social criticism. His novels *The Stars Look Down* (1935) and *The Citadel* (1937), which draw on his experiences as a doctor in a mining community, contributed to the demands for a National Health Service.

Cronin's short story collection *The Adventures of a Black Bag* and his autobiography *Adventures in Two Worlds* (1953) formed the basis of the popular television and radio series *Dr Finlay's Casebook*, which began in 1959.

To One Day Lean Against the Wind • Bayswater Road

Samuel Selvon, who supported himself by working in hostels and hotels in Bayswater, wrote a number of bittersweet comedies of black immigrant experience in and around Earl's Court, Notting Hill and Bayswater. These include *The Lonely Londoners* (1956), *Ways of Sunlight* (1958), *The Housing Lark* (1965) and *Moses Ascending* (1975).

Bayswater Road

The Lonely Londoners is notable for its use of patois, or creolised English, and its descriptions of, and ruminations on, London from an outsider's perspective. His characters – Moses, Sir Galahad, Captain, and Big City – are a mix of wide boys, chancers and grafters. They tread the Bayswater Road, 'wondering if in truth the streets of London are paved with gold', while everyday experiencing the problems of integration, racism, discrimination, isolation and homesickness.

To one day lean against the wind walking up the Bayswater Road (destination unknown), to see the leaves swirl and dance and spin on the pavement (sight unseeing), to write a casual letter home beginning: "Last night in Trafalgar Square ..."

Selvon's naturalistic use of language inspired a subsequent generation of black writers, including Grace Nicholls, James Berry, Fred D'Aguiar, David Dabydeen and Linton Kwesi Johnson *(see p322).*

Rotting Hill • 33 Ossington Street

Percy Wyndham Lewis moved across the Bayswater Road from Palace Gardens Terrace *(see p211)* to Ossington Street in March 1926, remaining here at No. 33 until August 1931. Here he published three issues of *The Enemy: A Review of Art and Literature.* Issue one consisted largely of his own long essay 'The Revolutionary Simpleton', in which he attacked Gertrude Stein, Ezra Pound and James Joyce for their belief in the Bergsonian idea of the flux of time. He also published poems by Roy Campbell and work by the American poet and critic Laura Riding.

While at Ossington Street Lewis wrote several books, including *The Lion and The Fox* (1927), *Time and Western Man* (1927) and the long novel *The Apes of God* (1930). From November 1928 until May 1932 Lewis rented the ground floor of No. 53 as 'a sort of studio' – which he used more for seduction than for work. *The Apes of God* lost Lewis useful patronage by satirising aristocratic bohemian writers and artists such as Dick Wyndham, Edward Wadsworth, and Osbert, Sacheverell and Edith Sitwell.

From October 1937 Lewis, now married, lived at 29A Notting Hill Gate, on and off, until his death in March 1957. Here he painted his celebrated and often reproduced portrait of Ezra Pound in November 1938, using Ruthven Todd to keep the sitter awake. Returning from a trip to America in 1946, Lewis found fungus in the building's wood. The incident features in *Rotting Hill* (1951), his collection of stories, as does a surreal walk through the 'Rotting Hill' locale, where he encounters friends, such as 'the two Roberts', Roy Campbell and Augustus John. He was art critic of the *Listener*, and a keen supporter of the young Francis Bacon.

Ivy Compton-Burnett • 59 Leinster Square

Ivy Compton-Burnett lived here from 1916 to 1929. Here she wrote the two books that established her literary career: *Pastors and Masters* (1925) and *Brothers and Sisters* (1929). Her witty and ironic style eschews Bloomsbury modernism for an impressionism informed by George Eliot and Greek tragedy, using dialogue as a central element in the narrative.

A Bloody Nose • Ethical Church, Queensway

A long-running dispute between poets Roy Campbell and Stephen Spender *(see p214)* finally boiled over into physical action and abuse at a Poetry Society reading at the Ethical Church on Queensway on 14 April 1949. As far back as 1934 Campbell had been incensed by unfavourable comments Spender had made about his work. He, in turn, accused Spender of vulgar self-promotion.

When Spender took to the podium at the Poetry Society event, Campbell bellowed that he wished to 'protest on behalf of the Sergeants' Mess of the King's African Rifles' and accused Spender of cowardice for not fighting in the Second World War. Not content with that, he then climbed on to the stage and bloodied Spender's nose with his right fist. Pandemonium broke out, while Campbell, still swearing at Spender, was dragged away by his family and friends. For his part, Spender refused to involve the police, saying, 'He is a great poet. He is a great poet. We must try to understand.' Order restored, Spender then went on to give his reading.

Thomas Hardy • 16 Westbourne Park Villas

Novelist Thomas Hardy lived here from 1865 to 67 while working for architect Arthur Blomfield. He read incessantly, took French classes at King's College, and went to readings by Dickens at the Hanover Square Rooms. He wrote his first poems here, and his first novel *The Poor Man and the Lady*, a social satire. Unable to find a publisher for the novel, he used parts of it in *Under The Greenwood Tree* (1872). He also published a long section of it, as a short story, in *The New Quarterly* of July 1878. This piece was eventually re-published as *An Indiscretion In The Life Of An Heiress* (1976).

The 4.50 from Paddington
Paddington Station

Paddington Station, which opened in 1854, has extensive literary connections. It is where Dylan Thomas arrived in London from Wales in 1932, and Laurie Lee from the Cotswolds, as he described in *As I Walked Out One Midsummer Morning* (1969).

Paddington Station

Arthur Conan Doyle's Sherlock Holmes story *The Adventure Of The Engineer's Thumb* (1892) features the station, and Graham Greene's novel *The Ministry of Fear* (1943) ends at a blacked-out Paddington Station, where 'the season-ticket holders were making a quick get-away from the nightly death'. Agatha Christie's *The 4.50 From Paddington* (1957) has the character Mrs McGillicuddy catch a train from platform three and witness a murder taking place on another train as the two carriages pass one another.

Michael Bond's children's series about Paddington Bear, starting with *A Bear Called Paddington* (1958), features the station as well as Paddington and Notting Hill locations.

The English Review • 84 Holland Park Avenue

The maisonette here above a poultry and fishmonger's shop doubled as the living quarters of Ford Hueffer (later Ford Madox Ford) and the offices of *The English Review* from 1907 to 1910. *The English*, as it became known, was founded by Ford, Joseph Conrad, H.G. Wells and others in the summer of 1908 and quickly became established as the leading magazine of new writing. Tolstoy, Henry James, Thomas Hardy, John Galsworthy and W.H. Hudson all had work appear in its pages, and in November 1909 *The English* was the first to publish work by D.H. Lawrence – four poems sent to the magazine by Jessie Chambers, Lawrence's closest friend back in Eastwood, Nottinghamshire.

At the time Lawrence was a schoolteacher in Croydon, but it was not long before he was invited to Holland Park Avenue. His opening remark may have caused a degree of consternation – 'This isn't my idea, Sir, of an editor's office' – but nevertheless the meeting proved to be his entrée into London's literary society.

The miner's son from Nottingham was introduced and welcomed as a rare find – Ford, to Lawrence's intense embarrassment, singing his praises and declaring him 'a genius'. On one packed day the itinerary included lunch at South Lodge, the Campden Hill villa of Ford's mistress, the glamorous suffragette novelist Violet Hunt *(see p209)*, tea in Hampstead with Ernest Rhys, an editor of literary classics, and then on to visit H.G. Wells. Ford was instrumental in getting Lawrence's first novel *The White Peacock* (1911) published, but the friendship was effectively ended when Ford declared the second novel, *The Trespasser* (1912), 'one-fourth masterpiece, the rest rotten'.

The Outsider • 24 Chepstow Villas

Writer Colin Wilson lived here in close to slum conditions from January 1956 to summer 1957 while revising his novel *Ritual in the Dark* (1960). He divided his time between meetings in coffee bars with anarchist friends and the British Museum Reading Room, where he befriended novelist Angus Wilson.

His seminal study of the literary wanderer and outsider, *The Outsider* (1956), which was dedicated to Angus Wilson, catapulted him to fame and critical success. In *The Outsider* Wilson examined the philosophical position of the wanderer in literature and life, differentiating the romantic from the existentialist and the visionary. He drew upon the works of Hemingway, Hesse, Nietzsche, T.E. Hulme, Camus, Sartre, Blake and Traherne. Favourably reviewed by Cyril Connolly in *The Sunday Times*, he was critically linked with the plays of John Osborne and the genre of the 'Angry Young Men'. In Soho Wilson mixed with Daniel Farson, Francis Bacon and others at David Archer's Bookshop and The Colony Room *(see pp114 & 116)*. However, after some damaging publicity involving his girlfriend's family misinterpreting his diary notes concerned with sexual deviation, he was forced to leave London for Cornwall.

Returning to London in February 1960, Wilson shared the rental of a room at No. 25 Chepstow Road with John Braine, author of *Room at the Top* (1957), and critic and playwright Stuart Holroyd. Here he completed his novel *Adrift in Soho* (1961). Subsequently Wilson has written further novels, as well as works on mysticism, existentialism and the occult.

No. 22 Portobello Road

Freezing Garret • 22 Portobello Road

Having quit his job as a policeman in Burma in disgust, Eric Blair (later George Orwell) arrived in London in 1927 determined to be a writer. Poet Ruth Pitter found him lodgings in the unheated attic here in Portobello Road, next to the pottery studio at No. 24 where she worked. He set to, and wrote a story about a writer in a freezing garret who has to warm his hands over a candle before he can pick up a pen.

Resolved to experience something of the life of London's outcasts, he would change into tramp's clothing and walk to Limehouse Causeway and back. In spring of 1928 he left for Paris and the experiences that would inform *Down and Out in Paris and London*, 1933 *(see p302)*.

Mother London • 87 Ladbroke Grove

Novelist and editor Michael Moorcock lived here from 1962 to 1972. He then lived at No. 51 Blenheim Crescent until moving to Texas in the 1990s. Moorcock edited the science-fiction magazine *New Worlds* from May 1964 until March 1971, and again in 1978, publishing J.G. Ballard, Brian Aldiss, D.M. Thomas and Tom Disch. He was very much part of the late 60s and early 70s hippie scene in this area, collaborating with space-rock group Hawkwind, supporting the underground press and writing science fiction.

Alongside the sci-fi, however, he has produced a series of novels that are imbued with London – Notting Hill in particular. Of the latter, his most successful work is *Mother London* (1988), a novel that celebrates the adaptability and vitality of London's people, landscape, history and mythology through a non-linear narrative following the lives of a group of psychiatric outpatients, its scope stretching from the Blitz to the 1980s. The book's hero, Joseph Kiss, criss-crosses and transcends the city, both geographically and through time, narrating his story through a rather fractured psychological state. The book mixes optimistic regret for the loss of London's community spirit with contempt for the gentrification of working-class areas. Its influence can be seen in the work of Peter Ackroyd, Martin Amis, J.G. Ballard and Iain Sinclair.

Performance • 25 Powis Square

The exterior of No. 25 Powis Square (re-numbered No. 81 in the film) provides the location of the Notting Hill home of reclusive rock star Turner (played by Mick Jagger) in the cult movie *Performance* (1970). Into Turner's decadent universe steps Chas (played by James Fox), a London gangster who's on the run from his own mob.

Written by Donald Cammell and co-directed by Cammell and Nicolas Roeg, the film explores the collision of two of London's most topical 'demi-mondes' of the late 1960s – gangsters and rock stars.

In an interview with the trade paper *Daily Cinema*, Cammell cited his initial inspiration for the film as 'Borges and Vladimir Nabokov's *Despair*, a story which makes a kind of ecstatic exploration of a character's fatal encounter with his double or alter ego – as in *Performance*. I was fascinated by the idea of murder which might also be suicide.' In the film Turner reads aloud from a Borges story, *The South*, as he awaits his murderer. In one of the film's most remarkable scenes, the camera tracks the bullet fired into Turner's skull and momentarily a photograph of Borges appears in a shattered mirror. In another memorable and indeed pivotal scene, Turner remarks: 'The only performance that makes it, really makes it, that makes it all the way is the one that achieves madness.'

Notoriety and legend became attached to *Performance* from the outset. Warner Bros were appalled on two counts: by the apparent realism of the sex scenes (which gained added spice as they principally involved Jagger and Anita Pallenberg, who at the time was Keith Richards' girlfriend); and by the graphic violence of the gangster sequences (which were informed by David Litvinoff, reputedly an associate of the Kray twins, and credited as 'Dialogue Consultant and Technical Adviser'). Extensive cuts were demanded before the film's eventual release in 1970.

In 1996 Cammell committed suicide by a gunshot into the top of his head, with the result that he did not die instantly. He allegedly requested that his wife hold up a mirror so he could watch himself die, and asked her, 'Do you see the picture of Borges?'

Bananas • 2 Blenheim Crescent

Novelist Emma Tennant edited *Bananas* literary magazine here from 1975 to 78. Tennant, who lived nearby in Elgin Crescent, published new work by Angela Carter, J.G. Ballard, Beryl Bainbridge, Bruce Chatwin, Ted Hughes, Alan Sillitoe and Heathcote Williams. She had an affair with Ted Hughes, revealed in her memoir *Burning Diaries* (2000), and her magical realist novels of this period, such as *Hotel de Dream* (1976), *The Bad Sister* (1978) and *Wild Nights* (1979), written in poetic prose, show the influence of both Hughes and *Bananas* contributor Angela Carter. Tennant was later commissioned to write a sequel to Jane Austen's *Pride and Prejudice*, out of which came *Pemberley* (1993) followed by *An Unequal Marriage* (1994).

The War Against Cliché • 54A Leamington Road Villas

For many years Martin Amis, novelist, critic and son of Kingsley Amis, lived at Leamington Road Villas – in his 'sock', as he referred to his flat. Situated on the fringes of the Paddington/Notting Hill/Holland Park triangle, this is where much of his work is set, from his first novel, *The Rachel Papers*, 1973 (which recounts the story of precociously intelligent 19-year-old Charles Highway in his quest to bed an older woman before he reaches 20) to *The Information*, 1995 (which revolves around the mid-life crisis of a writer living in, er … Notting Hill).

Amis has stated 'I don't want to write a sentence that any guy could have written', and indeed his prose is immediately recognisable – a combination of hypnotic, layered repetition and outlandish vocabulary peppered with freshly coined words, colloquialisms and street argot. Lines such as 'When Keith left I sacked out immediately' or 'It was fixed. It was written. The murderer was not yet a murderer. But the murderee had always been a murderee.' (from *London Fields*, 1989) or 'She reeked of spinst … like unmarried men reek of batch' (from *The Information*) are unmistakably Martin Amis. Likewise the names of his characters, such as Keith Talent, Guy Clinch and Nicola Six (from *London Fields*). Amis's work tends to provoke wildly polarised reactions. At its best, the prose reverberates with muscular energy, like the city itself as described in *London Fields*: 'taut and delicate as a cobweb'.

The Rachel Papers is centred in and around the smart houses of Campden Hill Square; *London Fields* in the area where the Portobello Road gutters out at its northern end, at a time when the Trellick Tower – 'the lone tower block at the end of Golborne Road' where Keith Talent lives – generally represented everything that was dysfunctional about Modernist architecture. In *The Information* geography helps to define the contrasting fortunes of its two central characters, both writers turning 40. The wealthy, shallow Gwyn Barry occupies a large residence in Holland Park Avenue, while his would-be nemesis, Richard Tull, lives at the decidedly downmarket '47 Calchalk Street' and 'tubes' to his day job at the 'Little Magazine'.

Crime Fiction • Site of Kensal Lodge, Harrow Road

William Harrison Ainsworth, prolific author of romance and popular historical fiction, lived here from 1838 to 1841. He made his name with *Rockwood* (1834), a Gothic romance in the style of Sir Walter Scott that famously includes an account of highwayman Dick Turpin's flight from London to York on his mare Black Bess – an event that never actually happened. On the back of the novel's success, however, Ainsworth entered London literary circles, mixing with Carlyle, Thackeray, Coleridge and Southey. At Kensal Lodge (and the adjoining Kensal Manor House, to which he moved in 1841), he established a salon for writers and fashionable figures of the day. Ainsworth introduced Charles Dickens, at the time a little known reporter, to publisher Richard Bentley and artist George Cruikshank, who later illustrated *Oliver Twist*.

In 1839 Ainsworth published *Jack Sheppard, A Romance*, an immediate and even greater success than *Rockwood*. It was first serialised by Richard Bentley in his magazine *Miscellany*, then issued in book form by Bentley, with illustrations by

Cruikshank. It established the genre now termed the 'Newgate Novel', which offered sensationalised versions of the lives and exploits of criminals – the facts of which were generally derived from *The Newgate Calendars*, a compilation of notorious crimes.

Historically Jack Sheppard carried out a daring series of robberies and caught the public's imagination by managing to escape repeatedly from London's most notorious jails, including Newgate. Finally, however, he was betrayed and taken, and hanged at Tyburn on 16 November 1724 in front of a reported crowd of 200,000.

Notoriously, the murderer Francois Courvoisier, whose public hanging at Newgate in 1840 was witnessed by Dickens and Thackeray *(see p61)*, claimed at his trial that he had been driven to his crime by reading Ainsworth's tale of Jack Sheppard. Ainsworth's reputation as a literary novelist never fully recovered. In 1868 Ainsworth left London for Brighton. He died at Reigate in 1882 and is buried in Kensal Green Cemetery.

Paradise – by Way of Kensal Green • Kensal Green Cemetery

G.K. Chesterton's poem 'The Rolling English Road' makes reference to the Kensal Green cemetery in the couplet: 'For there is goodness yet to hear and fine things to be seen / Before we go to paradise by way of Kensal Green.'

Opened in 1832, Kensal Green Cemetery is described by its Friends as 'the doyen of British cemeteries'. It has seen over 700,000 interments in 250,000 graves, and has been a popular choice as a last resting place for writers. Thackeray, Wilkie Collins, Anthony Trollope, Leigh Hunt, Thomas Hood and George Dyer are all buried here. It also provides the resting place for Lord Byron's wife, Oscar Wilde's mother, Charles Dickens's sister-in-law and Winston Churchill's daughter. John Diamond, journalist, broadcaster and author of *C: Because Cowards Get Cancer Too...* (1999), is buried here too.

Kensal Green
Cemetery

Hammersmith & Fulham

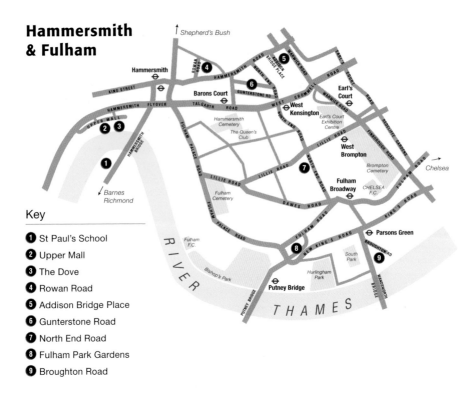

Key

1. St Paul's School
2. Upper Mall
3. The Dove
4. Rowan Road
5. Addison Bridge Place
6. Gunterstone Road
7. North End Road
8. Fulham Park Gardens
9. Broughton Road

HAMMERSMITH & FULHAM

Trouble in Mind • 7 Addison Bridge Place (formerly 7 Portland Place)

Samuel Taylor Coleridge lived here from November 1810 until October 1811 with lawyer John Morgan and his family, who had to put up with drunken scenes, periods of extreme depression and opium-confused nights as the poet attempted to deal with his troubled personal, financial and family situation.

Under the protective eyes of Morgan and Charles and Mary Lamb, Coleridge made a return to public literary life in spring 1811, writing for the *Courier* newspaper on the Strand. His anxieties – over his relationships with Wordsworth, with whom he had quarrelled, and 'Asra' (Sara Hutchinson), with whom he was infatuated yet estranged – lessened, and he moved in with the Lambs, beginning his Shakespeare lectures at the Crown & Anchor tavern near Fleet Street *(see p29)*, in November 1811.

Visited by Pilgrims • 7 Cornwall Road, later 16 Rowan Road

Leigh Hunt moved to Hammersmith from Kensington, where he had lived at No. 32 Edwards Square from 1840–51, during which time he had written *The Town* (1848), a literary guide to London, and *Autobiography* (1850). After a short stay in Phillimore Terrace (later Allen Street) from 1851, Leigh Hunt moved to Cornwall Road in 1853, remaining here for the last six years of his life. While in Hammersmith Hunt wrote *The Religion of the Heart* (1853), *The Old Court Suburb* (1855), about the suburb of Kensington, and *Stories in Verse* (1855). He also continued to edit, write plays and biographies, and to promote the lives and work of Shelley and Keats.

Leigh Hunt's household was devoted to books and literature, and his connections with, and writings on, Byron, Shelley, Keats and Hazlitt drew many visitors. The American essayist Ralph Waldo Emerson visited him at his Kensington home in 1848, and American novelist Nathaniel Hawthorne, author of *The Scarlet Letter* (1850), visited Hunt in Hammersmith in 1855. The significance of Leigh Hunt's life and role in the Lamb-Hunt circle of poets has increasingly been recognised since his death.

The Retreat • 26 Upper Mall

Scottish novelist and poet George Macdonald lived here, from 1868 to 77, calling his house The Retreat. Here he wrote his popular children's stories *At The Back of the North Wind* (1871) and *The Princess and the Goblin* (1872), which provided inspiration for C.S. Lewis, author of the *Narnia Chronicles*.

Kelmscott House • 26 Upper Mall

William Morris lived here from 1879 until his death in 1896. Morris and his daughter May were among Britain's first socialists, and organised the Hammersmith branch of the Socialist League from 1884. He published a manifesto advocating revolutionary international socialism in 1885, but gained negligible support. Eleanor Marx, Edward Carpenter, Walter Crane, W.B. Yeats, George Bernard Shaw and others attended their meetings. In 1888 Morris published the socialist fantasy *A Dream of John Ball* (1888).

In 1890 he founded the Kelmscott Press with the aim of raising standards in printing and book design. He designed the Golden Roman and Troy Gothic typefaces, employed decorative borders and reduced the space between words to create a distinct design approach. He published his own work, including his utopian novel *News From Nowhere* (1891), and work by others including editions of Caxton's *The Golden Legend* and Chaucer's *Canterbury Tales*. His historical romances set in a Germanic past – for example *The House of the Wolfings* (1889), *The Roots of the Mountains* (1890), *The Wood Beyond the World* (1894) and *The Sundering Flood* (1898) – inspired C.S. Lewis's *Narnia Chronicles* and J.R.R. Tolkien's *Lord of The Rings*.

Greatly revered by early socialists and writers, such as Shaw and Yeats, Morris made lasting contributions to design, the Arts and Crafts movement, and the labour movement. He was able to unify his literary, artistic and political aspirations, making people think about work, time and value in a new way.

The Dove Inn • 19 Upper Mall

The Dove dates from the 17th century and has been the site of an inn since 1430. Scottish poet James Thomson, author of the poem 'Rule Britannia', lodged here. He wrote *The Seasons* (1726–30), one of the most popular and illustrated of English poems. It marked a departure in style and subject from Alexander Pope and the wits. Thomson died from a cold caught after taking an evening boat trip from Hammersmith to Kew. Thomson's writing about his experience of landscape was much admired by Coleridge, Wordsworth, John Clare, artist J.M.W. Turner and composer Joseph Haydn.

Neighbour William Morris, as well as writers Graham Greene, A.P. Herbert and, on at least one occasion, Ernest Hemingway, also drank here. A.P. Herbert's novel *The Water Gypsies* (1930) features a pub called the Pigeon, which is based on the Dove.

The Dove, Upper Mall, Hammersmith

Man of Letters

The Grange, 49 North End Road

Samuel Richardson, one of the founders of the English novel *(see p32)*, lived here from 1739 to 1754, and at a villa in Parson's Green from 1754 to 61 in a house once inhabited by Catherine of Aragon. While in Fulham he remained active in his business and continued to revise his novels. He published *A Collection of the Moral and Instructive Sentiments … in the Histories of Pamela, Clarissa and Sir Charles Grandison* (1755), which in his consideration contained his pithiest writing.

In 1867, Pre-Raphaelite painter Edward Burne-Jones moved from No. 41 Kensington Square to Samuel Richardson's former home in North End Road, remaining there until his death in June 1898. He worked with Morris, Rossetti and Madox-Brown in their various businesses, preparing ceramic, stained-glass and tapestry designs, and producing illustrations for the Kelmscott Press.

An active member of the Arts and Crafts movement, he was visited here by Ruskin, Whistler and Wilde. His wife Georgiana wrote *The Flower Book* and a two-volume memoir of her husband. His granddaughter and Kipling's cousin, novelist Angela Thirkell, wrote *Three Houses* (1931), a memoir of her parental home at No. 27 Young Street, Kensington and her grandfather's homes at The Grange in North End Road and at Rottingdean, West Sussex. She set her popular novels, such as *Ankle Deep* (1933) and *The Brandons* (1939), in Trollope's fictional county Barsetshire. Thirkell's son by her first marriage was writer Colin MacInnes, author of *Absolute Beginners (see p118)*. He disliked her writing and was left out of her will.

King Solomon's Mines • 69 Gunterstone Road

Adventure novelist H. Rider Haggard, a close friend of Kipling, lived here between 1885 and 1888 while writing his most celebrated novels – *King Solomon's Mines* (1886) and *She* (1887). Both novels are set in Africa and convey the continent's landscape, wildlife and history. He had a worldwide readership that included Sigmund Freud – in fact Freud cited the imaginative qualities of Haggard's work and their effect on his dreams in *The Interpretations of Dreams*; while Carl Jung used *She* as an example of the anima concept (the characteristics of an image in the mind).

Arnold Bennett • 9 Fulham Park Gardens

Novelist and playwright Arnold Bennett, who wrote mainly about life in the Potteries (around Stoke-on-Trent), lived here from 1897 to 1900. Here he wrote *Anna of the Five Towns* (1901) and *The Grand Babylonian Hotel* (1902), and became a partner in the management of the Lyric Theatre, Hammersmith.

The Singing Detective • Hammersmith

Dennis Potter, one of the most original writers of television drama, grew up in Hammersmith and the Forest of Dean. He moved between the two locations – as does his fictional hero, Philip Marlow, in *The Singing Detective* (1986). He drew on his Hammersmith memories and his own experience of psoriasis for this moody thriller set partly in the 1940s that, like the earlier *Pennies From Heaven* (1978), incorporated popular songs and fantasy sequences as a narrative device.

As a child he lived with his mother's family on and off from 1945, and attended St Clement Danes School, Du Cane Road, from September 1949 to July 1953. After studying at Oxford he returned to Hammersmith, living at No. 11 St Paul's Mansions from September 1960 before moving to No. 15 Fairway Avenue, Kingsbury, where he lived between May 1963 and May 1965.

Potter's work explores themes of class, childhood trauma, sexual exploitation and social mores. His two television plays about a working-class, Oxford-educated politician, *Vote, Vote, Vote for Nigel Barton* (1965) and *Stand Up, Nigel Barton* (1965) brought him immediate acclaim. His work in the 1970s included *Brimstone and Treacle* (1978), a play about disability and Satanism which was banned days before transmission, and *Blue Remembered Hills* (1979), the title referencing A.E. Housman's *A Shropshire Lad* (1896) and its 'land of lost content' *(see p297)*. His later work included *Black Eyes* (1989), and *Lipstick On Your Collar* (1993), a musical black comedy drawing on Potter's National Service experience. His final works were two serialised plays, the nightmarish thriller *Karaoke* and a study of the meaning of memory, *Cold Lazarus*, completed just before he died from cancer in 1994.

The Ginger Man • 40 Broughton Road

Novelist and painter J.P. Donleavy lived here from 1953 to 66. Born in Brooklyn of Irish parents, he studied microbiology at Trinity College, Dublin and led a bohemian life as a painter. After failing to gain entry into the London gallery scene, he became a writer, producing his most famous work, *The Ginger Man*, in 1955. Written while living in Broughton Road, this comic and bawdy Joycean novel is set in Dublin and concerns hapless law student Sebastian Dangerfield.

The Ginger Man was originally published in Paris by The Olympia Press. Owned by Maurice Girodias, The Olympia published a mixture of erotica and avant-garde literature – including *The Story of O* by Pauline Reage (although originally published anonymously), William S. Burroughs' *Naked Lunch* and works by Samuel Beckett, Raymond Queneau, Jean Genet and Georges Bataille. Girodias was also the first to publish Vladimir Nabokov's *Lolita*.

The Ginger Man quickly went into several printings, but its continued availability was threatened by a crackdown against The Olympia's erotic publications, forcing Donleavy to arrange a UK edition. He adapted the novel for the stage in 1961 and also wrote *A Singular Man* (1963), adapted as a play in 1965. In 1966 Donleavy applied to become an Irish citizen and moved to Ireland.

St Paul's School • Lonsdale Road, Barnes

St Paul's School, founded in the City in 1509 *(see p53)*, was sited in Hammersmith, between the Talgarth and Hammersmith Roads, from 1884 to 1968, before moving to its present site just over the bridge in Barnes.

Literary alumni since 1884 include G.K. Chesterton, Leonard Woolf, Compton Mackenzie, Edward Thomas, Paul Nash, E.H. Shepard, Laurence Binyon, Eric Newby, Jonathan Miller, and twin brothers Peter and Anthony Shaffer who, in the late 1940s, wrote detective stories under the name Peter Anthony. Anthony Shaffer dropped out of the world of commercial advertising after experimenting with LSD in the late 1960s; he wrote the play *Sleuth* (1970) and the screenplay of the cult film *The Wicker Man* (1973). Peter Shaffer wrote *Equus* (1973), a play that delves into the mind of a 17-year-old stable boy who is obsessed with violently injuring horses, and *Amadeus* (1979), a play and later a highly successful film about the competitive relationship between composers Wolfgang Amadeus Mozart and Antonio Salieri. The screenplay adaptations for both *Equus* and *Amadeus* were written by Shaffer.

RICHMOND & TWICKENHAM
And at Mine Eyes, and at Mine Ears • Twickenham Park, St Margaret's

Statesman and essayist Francis Bacon lived in a Tudor villa (demolished in 1817) within 87 acres opposite the Queen's Richmond Palace from 1594 until 1606. He established a Scriptorium, or writing centre, to disseminate new and useful philosophical knowledge. Here he wrote *Essays, Colours of Good and Evil and Mediationes Sacrae* (1597) and *Promus of Formularies and Elegances* (1594), a collection of phrases and witty aphorisms from different languages.

Lucy, Countess of Bedford, expanded the villa and lived here from 1608 to 1617. She was a poet and patron to Ben Jonson, John Donne, Michael Drayton, George Chapman and Samuel Daniel, among other poets and playwrights. A Lady of the Queen's Bedchamber, renowned for her wit, beauty and horticultural skills, she was sufficiently independent to cultivate writers from the Sidney-Spenser circle. She performed in Court masques that were written by Jonson and designed by Inigo Jones.

Jonson wrote 'To Lucy, Countesse of Bedford, with Mr Donnes Satyres':

> *Lucy, you brightnesse of our spheare, who are*
> *Life of the Muses day, their morning Starre!*
> *If works (not th' authors) their own grace should look,*
> *Whose poems would not wish to be your book?*

Donne was a frequent visitor here between 1608 and 1610, after being imprisoned, and wrote 'Twicknam Garden':

> *Blasted with sighs, and surrounded with tears,*
> *Hither I come to seek the spring*
> *And at mine eyes, and at mine ears,*
> *Receive such balms as else cure every thing.*

Cross Deep Grotto • St Catherine's Convent, Grotto Road, Strawberry Hill

The Cross Deep Grotto, an ornamental cave, marks the site of Alexander Pope's home from 1719 until his death in 1744. He built the grotto in his gardens that ran down to the river. In the grotto he translated Homer's *The Illiad* (1720) and wrote *The Dunciad* (1728). His visitors included John Gay, William Congreve, Jonathan Swift and Voltaire. When Pope finished the grotto he wrote:

> *I have put the last hand to my works ... happily finishing the*
> *subterraneous Way and Grotto: I then found a spring of the clearest*
> *water, which falls in a perpetual Rill, that echoes thru' the Cavern day*

and night ... When you shut the Doors of this Grotto, it becomes on the instant, from a luminous Room, a Camera Obscura, on the walls of which all the objects of the River, Hills, Woods, and Boats, are forming a moving Picture ... And when you have a mind to light it up, it affords you a very different Scene: it is finished with Shells interspersed with Pieces of Looking-glass in angular Forms ... at which when a Lamp ... is hung in the Middle, a thousand pointed Rays glitter and are reflected over the place.

Strawberry Hill House • Waldegrave Road

Downstream from Pope – and the object of his ridicule – actor and dramatist Colly Cibber lived in the 'cottage in the woods' that would become Strawberry Hill. Cibber became the subject of Pope's *The Dunciad (see p45)* after becoming poet laureate in 1730, though their enmity stemmed from Pope's attack on Cibber's *The Non-juror* (1717), a comedy based on Molière's *Tartuffe* (1664), and Cibber's primary concern with theatrical effect above literary merit. While here Cibber wrote *The Refusal* (1721).

Horace Walpole later developed Cibber's house, beginning in the mid-18th century and continuing until his death in 1797. He added battlements, arches and two towers, creating the Gothic building of Strawberry Hill House (now home to St Mary's College). He wrote the Gothic novel *The Castle of Otranto* (1764) at Strawberry Hill, a work that was later parodied by Jane Austen in *Northanger Abbey*. Walpole established the Strawberry Hill Press in 1757, publishing Thomas Gray's *Odes* (1757), work by playwright Hannah More and his own *Essay on Modern Gardening* (1785).

Strawberry Hill
House

St Mary's Church • Ferry Road, Teddington
Mystical poet and priest Thomas Traherne lived at Bridgeman House on Teddington High Street from 1672 to 1674, the last two years of his life; his tomb is at St Mary's Church. The poems in Traherne's *Centuries of Meditations* – which lay forgotten in a notebook until rediscovered in 1897 – express a rapturous joy in creation. Traherne urged mankind to regain the wonder and simplicity of childhood and asserted the boundless potential of man's mind and spirit.

St Mary of the Virgin • Church Street, Twickenham
There are memorial plaques here to Alexander Pope and actress Peg Woffington, who was also buried at the church. Alfred, Lord Tennyson baptised his son, Hallam, here on 5 October 1852, with his friend Robert Browning among the congregation.

Summer Retreat • 4, later 2, Ailsa Park Villas, St Margaret's
Dickens lived here from June 1838 until early 1839, commuting to his Doughty Street home *(see p139)*, while his wife, Catherine, recovered from post-natal depression. Here he wrote parts of *Nicholas Nickleby* (1839), which was being serialised in *Bentley's Miscellany*. In the story Kenwigs dines, as did Dickens, on 'a cold collation – bottled beer, shrub, and shrimps' on Eel Pie Island, approached by a footbridge (now private) from the river bank. Talfourd and Thackeray visited him here.

Second Summer Retreat • Elm Lodge, Sudbrook Lane, Petersham
From spring to late summer 1839 Dickens came here for a summer retreat, continuing with *Nicholas Nickleby*, returning to *Barnaby Rudge* (1841) and planning a new periodical, *Master Humphrey's Clock*. Dickens regularly returned to Richmond, and in 1850 stayed at the old Star and Garter Hotel on Richmond Hill with Tennyson and Thackeray to celebrate the publication of *David Copperfield*.

Poet Laureate • Chapel House, Montpelier Row, Twickenham
Alfred, Lord Tennyson lived here from March 1851 until November 1853, not long after being made poet laureate. Here he wrote 'Ode on the Death of the Duke of Wellington' which begins with the lines:

> *Bury the Great Duke*
> *With an empire's lamentation;*
> *Let us bury the Great Duke*
> *To the noise of the mourning of a mighty nation;*

The famous photograph of Tennyson by Julia Margaret Cameron was taken here.

Southend House, Montpelier Row, Twickenham

Walter de la Mare

Southend House, Montpelier Row, Twickenham

The poet and children's writer Walter de la Mare lived here from 1940 until his death in 1956. Here he completed *The Burning Glass* (1945) and two long poems, 'The Traveller' (1946) and 'The Winged Chariot' (1951). During the war a policeman rowed across the river to rebuke him for leaving his windows uncurtained. His inventive and skilful verse has remained popular and unaffected by fashion.

Doone Country • Doone Close, Teddington

Novelist and horticulturalist R.D. Blackmore taught classics at Welleseley Grammar School, later Fortescue House, Hampton Road in 1853. He also published two volumes of poetry anonymously: *Poems by Melanter* (1853) and *Epullia* (1853). Posterity remembers him, however, for one novel, set in 17th-century Exmoor: *Lorna Doone* (1869), an epic story of love, outlaws, retribution and farming folk. Blackmore's garden, which supplied fruit to London, occupied the area between Station Road and Field Lane. His home, Gomer House, was situated at the end of Doone Close. Blackmore's Grove, Gomer Gardens and Gomer Place are named in the writer's memory.

Leading Novelist • 8 Parkshot, Richmond

George Eliot and her partner George Henry Lewes lived at Parkshot in Richmond from 1855 to 59. And it was here that Marian Evans adopted the pseudonym George Eliot to protect herself from possible ridicule and social ostracism if critics discovered that she was living with a man still married to another, albeit adulterous, woman.

A series of her stories was published in *Blackwood's Magazine* in 1857. These appeared the following year in two volumes as *Scenes of Clerical Life* (1858), and helped to establish her as a leading writer. They were praised for their domestic realism, pathos and humour. She wrote *Adam Bede* (1858), notable for its realistic and humorous portrayal of rural life, and the first chapters of *The Mill on the Floss* (1860) while here in Richmond.

In 1859 she and Lewes moved to Holly Lodge, at No. 31 Wimbledon Park Road. There she completed *The Mill on the Floss*. Upon its publication in 1860, she moved to Blandford Square, Marylebone *(see p176)*, then left for Florence the following year.

The Return of the Native • 1 Arundel Terrace, later 172 Trinity Road, Richmond
After publication of *The Return of the Native* (1878), which established his reputation, Thomas Hardy made his London base here from March 1878 until May 1881. He quickly fell into the swing of literary London, joining the Savile Club *(see p195)*, the Rabelais Club and Hanover Square Club, where he met such diverse figures as Matthew Arnold, Barry Cornwall's widow Mrs Proctor (who had been on the fringes of the Lamb-Hunt circle), Tennyson and George Du Maurier. While in Richmond Hardy wrote *The Trumpet Major* (1880), set during the Napoleonic wars, and *A Laodician* (1881), about the vacillating Paula Power, for *Harper's* magazine.

The Hogarth Press • Hogarth House, Paradise Road, Richmond
Writers Virginia and Leonard Woolf moved here from 17 The Green, Richmond in March 1915. Anxious to find some therapeutic literary diversion for his physically and mentally ailing wife, Leonard bought a hand printing press. Together they founded the Hogarth Press, named after the house, and published *Two Stories*, one by each of them, in July 1915.

They hand printed half of the Hogarth Press's output here between 1917 and 1924, and published a collection of Virginia's short stories, *Monday or Tuesday* (1921), and her novel *Jacob's Room* (1922), set in the First World War. With its indirect narration and poetic impressionism, *Jacob's Room* was widely hailed as a significant development in fiction, but was also attacked by the literary editor John Middleton Murry for its lack of plot.

In her diary entry for 20 July 1918 Virginia described the celebrations in Richmond that marked the end of the First World War:

> *After sitting through the procession and the peace bells unmoved, I began after dinner to feel that if something was going on, perhaps one had better be in it ... The doors of the public house at the corner were open and the room crowded; couples waltzing; songs being shouted, waveringly, as if one must be drunk to sing. A troop of little boys with lanterns were parading the Green, beating sticks ... A woman of the upper classes was supported dead drunk between two men partially drunk.*

The Woolfs moved to No. 52 Tavistock Square in March 1924 *(see p142)*.

NORTH LONDON

AROUND THE NORTHERN PERIMETER of Regent's Park are the wealthy areas of St John's Wood and Primrose Hill and the grittier neighbourhoods of Camden Town and Kentish Town. In the 20th century, after significant rebuilding, St John's Wood has become a bastion of moneyed respectability and fragrant Jewish delis; in the mid-19th century, however, the area had a reputation for high-class brothels, providing a convenient location for the mistresses of politicians.

In Galsworthy's *The Forsyte Saga* (1922) St John's Wood is an area where 'no Forsyte liked to be seen'. However, it was where Katherine Mansfield discovered a new approach to story telling following her brother's death in the First World War, and where Dorothy Richardson pioneered the 'stream of consciousness' technique from a woman's perspective, also in the early 20th century.

It is even less likely that any Forsyte would have wished to be seen in the decidedly (at the time) low rent Camden or Kentish Town, where the liaison between Rimbaud and Verlaine finally fell apart in the summer of 1873, a drunken Rayner Heppenstall fought with George Orwell in 1935 and, in more recent times, the resting actors 'Withnail' and 'Marwood' staggered through a haze of drink and drugs in Bruce Robinson's cult classic *Withnail and I*.

Situated between St John's Wood and Camden, Primrose Hill is where W.B. Yeats lived as a child. When she returned to London from Devon in 1962, Sylvia Plath moved into this same house with a feeling of hope that slowly drained away over the following cold winter.

Beyond this inner ring of north London neighbourhoods lie Highbury and Stoke Newington to the northeast and Palmers Green, Kilburn and Willesden to the northwest. While still a country village, distant from the city, Stoke Newington offered a haven for dissenters such as Daniel Defoe and Mary Wollstonecraft in the 17th and 18th centuries; it is also where Edgar Allan Poe attended boarding school from 1817 to 1820.

Areas such as Stoke Newington, and equally Willesden, Kilburn and Highbury, have long since been subsumed by the sprawling metropolis. Now in something of a hinterland, they seemingly fit into no clear category such as country, city or suburbia. More urban than suburban in character, yet adrift from the fashionable centre of the city, they are places where writers of recent years, such as Nick Hornby and Zadie Smith, have found both alienation and vibrant life.

Around Regent's Park

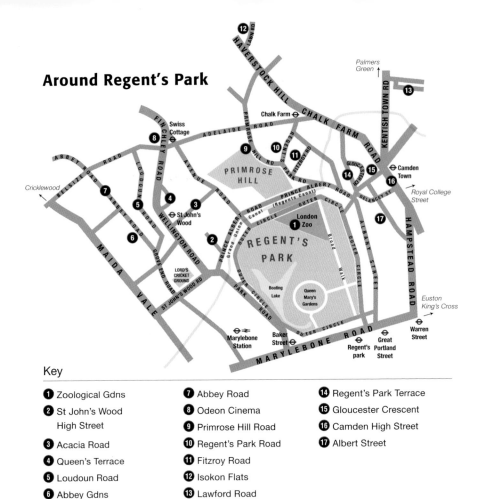

Key

1. Zoological Gdns
2. St John's Wood High Street
3. Acacia Road
4. Queen's Terrace
5. Loudoun Road
6. Abbey Gdns
7. Abbey Road
8. Odeon Cinema
9. Primrose Hill Road
10. Regent's Park Road
11. Fitzroy Road
12. Isokon Flats
13. Lawford Road
14. Regent's Park Terrace
15. Gloucester Crescent
16. Camden High Street
17. Albert Street

Keats and Leigh Hunt • 13 Mortimer Terrace, Kentish Town

Leigh Hunt lived here from April 1820 until September 1821 when he and his family left to join Shelley and his wife in Pisa, Italy. Here he edited *The Examiner* and his popular literary supplement *The Indicator*, which ran from October 1819 until March 1821, and featured the work of Coleridge, Lamb, Shelley and Keats.

It was to the Hunt household that Keats, suffering from tuberculosis and missing his love, Fanny Brawne, came to be nursed between June and August 1820. Keats had rented 2 Wesleyan Place, just around the corner, for the previous seven weeks. Taylor and Hussey published *Lamia, Isabella, The Eve of St Agnes and Other Poems* in July and Keats helped assemble *The Indicator*. Keats responded to Shelley's invitation to visit him in Italy and left in September, only to die the following February (1821) in Rome.

Edward Lear • The Zoological Gardens

Situated to the north of Regent's Park, the Zoological Gardens opened in 1828. Artist and writer Edward Lear lived at 30 Seymour Street in 1831 when he occupied the position of official draughtsman to the Zoological Society. Here he drew the zoo's parrots for an ornithological guide. These came to the attention of the Earl of Derby, who asked Lear to paint his private menagerie at Knowsley Hall, near Liverpool. While working at Knowsley Hall, Lear wrote and illustrated *A Book of Nonsense* (1845), ostensibly for the Earl's grandchildren.

Deux Gentlemen Parisiens • 8 Royal College Street

After a brief return to France following their first foray into London life *(see p123)*, Rimbaud and Verlaine returned on 27 May 1873 and this time found lodgings here in two tiny attic rooms at No. 8 Great College Street (since 1940, Royal College Street).

To support themselves, they advertised in *The Daily Telegraph* of 21 June 1873 offering 'LECONS de FRANCAIS, en francais – perfection, finesses – par deux Gentlemen parisiens.' At least one *Telegraph* reader parted with the 'half a pound' necessary to be taught French by Rimbaud and Verlaine, who had had a book of his poems sent over as credentials.

However, Rimbaud never lost an opportunity to ridicule and taunt his partner, who could never quite decide whether he wanted to live the life of a scandalous bohemian poet or that of a bourgeois family man, and it was not long before this ever-volatile relationship reached its final denouement.

No. 8 Royal College Street

On 3 July Verlaine could take no more, and walked out after hitting Rimbaud around the face with a fish he had just bought for their supper. Pursued by Rimbaud, Verlaine took the first boat for Brussels. Here he purchased a revolver and, after first threatening to shoot himself, fired at Rimbaud, wounding him in the wrist.

Changed Utterly • 5 Acacia Road
Writers and lovers John Middleton Murry and Katherine Mansfield moved here in 1915 to be near Hampstead and the Lawrences, with whom they were writing and publishing *Signature* magazine. They left when news came that Katherine's brother had been killed in action at the front in Belgium in October. This had a profound effect on Mansfield's writing: 'the [short story] form that I would choose has changed utterly. I feel no longer concerned with the same appearance of things.' She began to completely rearrange the structure of her stories, the first example of which was *Prelude*, a pared-down revision of an earlier story *The Aloe* (which was not published in her lifetime). First published in 1918 in a hand-printed edition of 300 copies by Virginia and Leonard Woolf, *Prelude* was the second publication of the Hogarth Press.

Stream of Consciousness • 32 Queen's Terrace
Novelist Dorothy Richardson lived here from 1916 until 1938. Here she wrote *Honeycomb* (1917) and the third of her autobiographical novels, *Pilgrimage*. The final volume in the series, *March Moonlight* (1967), appeared posthumously.

Dorothy Richardson pioneered the stream of consciousness technique, narrating the action through the mind of her heroine, Miriam. She believed in 'unpunctuated' female prose, citing James Joyce in support. Virginia Woolf credited her with creating 'the psychological sentence of the feminine gender'. Angus Wilson wrote in the *Listener*, October 1968, that she 'enters more fully than any novelist I know into the material and spiritual struggles of a young, very gifted, but at the same time utterly underprivileged woman in a world made by men, for men'. Virago Press reissued *Pilgrimage* in four volumes in 1979.

Air of Decay • 50 Lawford Road, Kentish Town
Writers Rayner Heppenstall and Michael Sayers, together with their mutual friend Mabel Fierz, persuaded George Orwell to share rooms here in this 'road with an air of decay about it' in July 1935. Their memoirs contain fascinating portraits of Orwell. Heppenstall and Sayers regarded Orwell as a writer of popular fiction who sought a wider audience, whereas they, by comparison, were concerned with writing and reviewing more 'serious' art and literature.

In December 1935 a drunken Heppenstall disturbed Orwell and an altercation ensued. This developed into a fight which left Heppenstall battered and locked in

Sayers' room. Demanding to be released, Heppenstall was then confronted with Orwell armed with a shooting stick; he had raised a chair over his head, ready to strike in defence, before two other tenants appeared and Orwell left. In the morning Orwell lectured Heppenstall about his behaviour and demanded that he leave.

Orwell's arguable over-reaction has been variously interpreted as 'a disappointed homosexuality' and jealousy of the attention Heppenstall paid to his girlfriend, Jo Atterbury. Certainly Orwell dropped Atterbury and pursued Eileen O'Shaughnessey, whom he later married.

In the New Year Orwell greeted Heppenstall as if nothing had happened, and the two remained close friends until Orwell's death. Later that January, at the suggestion of his publisher, Victor Gollancz, Orwell left for a tour of the industrial North, which formed the basis of *The Road To Wigan Pier* (1937).

Stephen Spender • **15 Loudoun Road**
Poet Stephen Spender lived here from March 1945 until his death in July 1995. W.H. Auden stayed here when he was over from America, and friends such as Louis MacNeice, Cecil Day Lewis, Cyril Connolly, Lucian Freud, John Craxton, Angus Wilson and the American novelist Reynolds Price visited. Spender published *Poems of Dedication* (1947), which included elegies for his sister-in-law; his autobiography *World with World* (1951); a work of criticism, *The Creative Element* (1953), in which he stressed the creative power and resistance of the individual; and *Collected Poems 1928–53* (1955). He was co-editor of *Encounter* magazine (1953–67), a periodical later revealed to have been covertly funded by the CIA.

Encounter's most celebrated and successful contribution was Nancy Mitford's essay 'The English Aristocracy' (1955), in which she developed a glossary of 'U and Non-U' terms. The phrase was coined by British linguist Alan Ross to describe the difference social class makes in usage of the English language, where U stands for Upper class and non-U, non-upper class. Examples included: luncheon and dinner, lavatory and toilet, house and home.

Spender wrote much about the public and social role of the poet, which informed both his political poems and his subsequent work for *Index on Censorship* magazine. After years of making a career out of direct, public political poetry, he declined all requests for an authorised biography. The first authorised biography, written by his teaching colleague John Sutherland, finally appeared in 2004.

House of Books • **36 Abbey Gardens**
Novelist Olivia Manning lived at this four-storey Edwardian house, filled with thousands of books, from July 1951 until 1973, when she moved to a flat at 10 Marlborough Place (which remained her address until her death in July 1980).

While at Abbey Gardens she wrote the *Balkan Trilogy* – comprising *The Great Fortune* (1960), *The Spoilt City* (1962) and *Friends and Heroes* (1965) – inspired by her experiences with her husband Reggie Smith working for the British Council in Bucharest, Greece and the Middle East during the Second World War. The novels are a tragicomic portrait of war and its effects on civilian life. When they returned to London, Reggie became a BBC Radio producer and Olivia resumed her literary career.

Before the war Olivia Manning had published *The Wind Changes* (1937) and in 1942 wrote an important essay 'Poets in Exile' for *Horizon* in which she discussed English poets, such as Lawrence Durrell and Keith Douglas, who she had encountered abroad. In 1946 she published a collection of short stories, *Growing Up*, and resumed friendships with poets and writers such as Stevie Smith (who was a bridesmaid at her wedding), Ivy Compton-Burnett, Rose Macaulay and David Gascoyne.

She later wrote the Levant Trilogy *The Danger Tree* (1977), *The Battle Lost and Won* (1978) and *The Sum of Things* (1980) here. Reggie was a close friend of Louis MacNeice, the best man at their wedding, and composer Elizabeth Lutyens, an habitué of the George Inn *(see p180)*. Among their various lodgers in the 1950s were novelist and dramatist Julian Mitchell, and the film and theatre director Tony Richardson.

Abbey Road

George Orwell and his wife, Eileen, lived in a 5th-floor flat at No. 111 Langford Court, Abbey Road, from April 1941 to June 1942. From June 1941 Orwell worked as a BBC Talks producer for the India service; Room 101, the torture chamber in *Nineteen Eighty-Four* (1949), was borrowed from the Eastern Service committee meeting room at Room 101, 55 Portland Place.

While in Abbey Road, Orwell was a member of the St John's Wood Home Guard and regularly contributed to *Horizon* magazine, where he met Sonia Brownell, the model for Julia in *Nineteen Eighty-Four (see p130)*.

In the 1960s Abbey Road became famous for the EMI studios (at No. 3) where the Beatles recorded most of their music. The photograph of the band walking across the pedestrian crossing to the south of the studios for the cover of the *Abbey Road* album sparked long-running conspiracy theories that Paul McCartney, pictured barefoot, had died and been replaced by a lookalike.

A Fine Powdering of Extravagance • St John's Wood High Street

The fragrant delis and cafés of St John's Wood High Street provide the life-changing treat that re-awakens Henry, the eponymous hero of Howard Jacobson's *The Making of Henry* (2004) and, hitherto, miserable middle-aged man.

The restaurant in which a key moment in his burgeoning love life takes place is based loosely on the Oslo Court, situated just behind the High Street and described elsewhere by Jacobson as 'an out-of-time and even out-of-the-body establishment that serves you cuts of meat of a grandeur not usually seen outside Budapest or Bratislava, in a wonderful operetta ambience of lilac arches, sugar-pink table linen and preposterously helpful and toupéed waiters.'

Autumn Journal • 16A Primrose Hill Road

Louis MacNeice lived here from May 1938 to March 1939. He made protests against the 1938 Anglo-Italian pact and wrote *Autumn Journal* (1939), his epic and personal meditation on the events leading up to the Second World War:

> *A smell of French bread in Charlotte Street, a rustle*
> *Of leaves in Regent's Park*
> *And suddenly from the Zoo I hear a sea-lion*
> *Confidently bark.*
> *And so to my flat with the trees outside the window*
> *And the dahlia shapes of the lights on Primrose*
> *Hill*
> *Whose summit once was used for a gun emplacement*
> *And very likely will*
> *Be used that way again. The bloody frontier*
> *Converges on our beds*
> *Like jungle beaters closing in on their destined*
> *Trophy of pelts and heads.*

MacNeice's narrator drives around Southern England, criss-crossing through time and place, probing the nature of his Irishness, before returning to Primrose Hill.

MacNeice and his wife, the singer and actress Heidi Anderson, lived at No. 10 Wellington Place, St John's Wood, from January 1943 until March 1945, while they both worked for the BBC. Here he wrote the *Springboard* (1944) book of poems, radio documentaries and parable plays such as *Christopher Columbus* (1944), and the powerfully dramatic *The Dark Tower* (1947).

In July 1952 the MacNeices took over the tenancy of No. 2 Clarence Terrace, on the southwest edge of Regent's Park, from Elizabeth Bowen. They lived there until spring 1961, when Heidi had finally had enough of his philandering and asked him to leave. While at Clarence Terrace, he completed *Autumn Sequel* (1954), concerning autumn 1953 and written in *terza rima* (ABA, BCB, CDC etc) form, drawing upon sketches of friends such as Auden, Nancy Spender, W.R. Rodgers and Dylan Thomas.

MacNeice and Mary Wimbush, his lover at the time, lived at No. 10 Regent's Park Terrace from June 1961 until his death in September 1963. Here he completed the poems that went into the posthumously published *The Burning Perch* (1963). His funeral took place at St John's Wood Church, his wife and lover occupying separate camps in the wake afterwards.

The Old Men at the Zoo • 2 Regent's Park Terrace

Novelist Angus Wilson lived here, close by London Zoo, from 1962. His novel *The Old Men at the Zoo* (1961) – about the evacuation of zoo animals and the doomed attempt to establish a nature reserve for them – revolves around a conflict between the disciplined and free, and ends with a portrayal of Europe at war.

Absolute Beginners • 4 Regent's Park Terrace

Novelist and journalist Colin MacInnes, son of Angela Thirkell *(see pp252–3)*, lived here from May 1946 to March 1958. Here he wrote two of his London novels, *City of Spades* (1957), depicting the lives of contemporary black immigrants in London, and *Absolute Beginners* (1959), about teenagers and the bohemian world of coffee bars and jazz clubs in Notting Hill and Soho.

His experimental realism – incorporating street slang in episodic rather than plot-driven narrative – gave voice to 1950s black and youth cultures with sharp social detail. MacInnes sought to represent the lifestyles of those excluded from contemporary literature and journalism, including 'working-class child mothers, ageing semi-professional whores, the authentic agonies of homosexual love, and the new race of English-born coloured boys … the millions of teenagers … the Teds … the multitudinous Commonwealth minorities in our midst.'

Mainstream readers are the absolute beginners in a novel that attempts to warn society of its implicit prejudices against youth and blacks. Those prejudices surfaced in the Notting Hill 'race riots' of 1958. MacInnes moved to the East End to complete his third London novel, *Mr Love and Justice* (1960), about the world of prostitution.

The Twilight Bark • Primrose Hill

Primrose Hill offers a vantage point with extensive views over London – the sightline to St Paul's, for example, is a protected view. In 1842 an Act of Parliament secured the land as public open space, and this has been enjoyed for many years by Londoners as a place from which to survey their city and take stock. It is also here, in H.G. Wells's *The War of the Worlds* (1898), that the Martians made their seventh 'final and largest' base for their assault on the city.

During the Blitz, Primrose Hill provided a location from which to defend the city, as described in Aldous Huxley's wartime novel *Time Must Have a Stop* (1944): A man meditates in his flat during an air raid in which 'the guns on Primrose Hill were banging away in a kind of frenzy'.

Primrose Hill

The location has featured in many works, including *Father and Son* (1907) by Edmond Gosse, in which the author recounts how he arrived at Primrose Hill with his father and, sitting down on a bench, burst into tears and asked to go home. In Dodie Smith's children's novel *The Hundred and One Dalmatians* (1956) Pongo and his wife, Missis, escape from Regent's Park and run to Primrose Hill. Here they stand on the hill's summit and bark out a message across London asking for help in tracing their missing puppies. And Helen Falconer's *Primrose Hill* (1999) concerns late 20th-century adolescents chilling out on the hill during summer.

Ariel • 23 Fitzroy Road

After the breakdown of her marriage to Ted Hughes, Sylvia Plath took an upstairs flat here in December 1962, attracted by the fact that W.B. Yeats had lived here as a child from 1867 to 1872.

Previously, in 1960–61, she and Ted Hughes had lived around the corner at No. 3 Chalcot Square, where Sylvia had enjoyed one of the most productive and happy periods of her life: she wrote *The Bell Jar* (1963), published *The Colossus* (1960) and gave birth to her first child, Frieda. In 1961 they moved to the small rural town of North Tawton in Devon.

Sylvia Plath first came to London in 1955 as a Fulbright scholar on her way to Cambridge University. In a letter to her mother on 25 September she wrote 'London is simply fantastic …' and over the following months frequently visited the capital. Reporting for *Varsity*, the University magazine, she attended a reception for Bulganin and Khrushchev where 'at the posh Claridge Hotel [sic], with the hammer and sickle waving over the door, your daughter shook hands with Bulganin! … ' (letter to her mother 21 April 1956).

By this time she had met and fallen in love with Ted Hughes. On 16 June 1956, the two were married in a 'secret wedding' – secret because a married woman was not eligible to be a Fulbright scholar or to attend the women-only Newnham College, Cambridge. The marriage took place in The Church of St George the Martyr in Bloomsbury. In a letter to her brother, 18 June 1956, Sylvia recalls '… standing with the rain pouring outside in the dim little church, saying the most beautiful words in the world as our vows, with the curate as second witness and the dear Reverend, an old, bright-eyed man (who lives right opposite Charles Dickens' house!) kissing my cheek, and the tears just falling down my eyes like rain – I was so happy with my dear, lovely Ted.'

In late 1962, happy to be moving from Devon back to Primrose Hill, Sylvia's letters home speak of a new confidence and happiness 'in my favourite house, in my favourite neighbourhood, happy as a clam!' However, the onset of an extraordinarily cold winter, combined with illness and exhaustion, rapidly began to sap her morale. She committed suicide on 11 February 1963, leaving on her desk a manuscript of 40 poems in a black spring binder with a cleanly typed title page: *Ariel and Other Poems*. A selection of these poems (edited by Ted Hughes) was published by Faber and Faber in 1965 under the title *Ariel*. A facsimile edition, comprising all the poems in the order she had planned, was published in 2004 by Faber and Faber.

Chalk Farm Bridge

Epiphany • Chalk Farm Bridge

> *London. The grimy lilac softness*
> *Of an April evening. Me*
> *Walking over Chalk Farm Bridge*
> *On my way to the tube station.*

The opening lines of 'Epiphany', one of the central poems in Ted Hughes's autobiographical collection *Birthday Letters* (1998). The poem recounts Hughes's chance encounter on the hump of Chalk Farm Bridge with a young man who has a fox cub buttoned into the top of his jacket.

The incident comes to represent a pivotal moment in his relationship with Sylvia Plath, to whom all but two of the poems in Birthday Letters are addressed. Offered the little fox for a pound, Hughes is instinctively drawn towards the animal, but suddenly turns away – only to immediately regret his decision: 'Then I walked on / As if out of my own life.' The poem concludes:

> *If I had grasped that whatever comes with a fox*
> *Is what tests a marriage and proves it a marriage –*
> *I would not have failed the test. Would you have failed it?*
> *But I failed. Our marriage had failed.*

Beryl Bainbridge • Albert Street, Camden Town

The novelist and playwright Beryl Bainbridge first lived in Albert Street from 1962 until 1965, before moving to Hampstead and then returning to Camden Town in 1973. Her early novels drew upon her Liverpool upbringing, as in *A Quiet Life* (1976), and experiences as an actress, as in *An Awfully Big Adventure* (1989).

She established her reputation with unsettling and comic novels that included *The Dressmaker* (1973), *The Bottle Factory Outing* (1974), *Injury Time* (1977) and *Winter Garden* (1980), where violence and absurdity lurk beneath urban domesticity. Her later work often deals with historical themes. *Master Georgie* (1998), her fifth novel to make the Booker Prize short-list, is set in the Crimean War; *According to Queeney* (2001) is an account of Samuel Johnson's last years, narrated by Hester Thrale's daughter Queeney *(see p78)*.

The Folks that Live on the Hill • 194 Regent's Park Road

Novelist and poet Kingsley Amis shared this house with his first wife, Hilly, and her third husband, Lord Kilmarnock, from July 1985 until Amis's death. The *ménage à trois* began for a few weeks in a temporary Hampstead flat and continued from early

1982 at No. 186 Leighton Road, Kentish Town. In 1984 Amis sold his literary archive to enable the move to the larger Primrose Hill house. The house was designed so that all parties, including visiting children, could live their own lives interacting as and when they wanted. Amis worked as a newspaper and magazine columnist and constructed a life that was as much like being married to Hilly as possible.

Here he wrote Booker-Prize-winning *The Old Devils* (1986), *Difficulties with Girls* (1988), *You Can't Do Both* (1994), his *Memoirs* (1991) and *The Folks that Live on the Hill* (1990). Amis was knighted in 1990.

The life of retired librarian and twice-married Harry Caldecote in *The Folks that live on the Hill* – looking out of his window at a wine emporium, going to his gentleman's club, visiting his local (the King's Arms), and thinking about the state of marriage – closely resembles Amis's own life at the time. His local pub, at No. 49 Regent's Park Road, was The Queen's; in his later years he would travel to and from it by taxi.

The Lady in the Van • Gloucester Crescent

In 'The Lady in the Van', writer and dramatist Alan Bennett (born 1934) wrote about Miss Shepherd, an elderly, eccentric tramp who resembled Vanessa Bell and lived in a succession of vans in Gloucester Crescent. This was published in his collection of reminiscences and reviews *Writing Home* (1994) and later made into a play. Alarmed by the bullying and vandalism she received from passers-by, Bennett gave her sanctuary in his front garden.

Site of Compendium Bookshop • 240, 281 Camden High Street

In August 1968 Compendium Bookshop first opened its doors, offering the most comprehensive range of imported American and new English literature in London. Originally specialising in the Beat movement, the bookshop quickly became a meeting place for writers and poets, and grew to encompass departments specialising in the women's movement, new psychology, philosophy and politics. The bookshop closed in September 2000.

I Demand to Have Some Booze! • 171 & 174 Camden High Street

Bruce Robinson originally wrote *Withnail and I* over the winter of 1969/70 as a novel. However, 'after some positive feedback from friends', in 1980 he turned this semi-autobiographical study of two aspiring, out of work actors into a screenplay, eventually filmed, with Robinson as director, in 1986.

Sharing a disintegrating flat in Camden Town in 1969 and living off a diet of tobacco, booze and drugs, Withnail and Marwood (the 'I' of the title, though never actually named on screen) decide they need a holiday 'to rejuvenate', and set off for a disastrous weekend in the Lake District. But before that – they need a drink ('Two

The World's End,
Camden

pints of cider. Two large gins. Ice in the cider') at The Old Mother Black Cap. This is a
conflation of two local pubs, The Black Cap at No. 171 Camden High Street and The
Old Mother Red Cap (now The World's End) at No. 174 Camden High Street. (The
scene was actually filmed at Babushka's Wine Bar, Tavistock Crescent, Notting Hill.)

Full of brilliant exchanges and one-liners – I: 'If my father was loaded I'd ask him
for some money.' Withnail: 'If your father was my father you wouldn't get it' – the film
was released in 1987 to little notice, but has since become a cult classic.

The Body in the Library • Isokon Flats, 22 Lawn Road

In notable contrast to the country house setting of some of her best-loved novels,
Agatha Christie lived in this 1934 Bauhaus-inspired building designed by Wells Coates
from 1940 to 46. Here she combined voluntary work at University College Hospital
with a prolific output as a writer. Her writing included the Hercule Poirot detective
novels *One Two, Buckle My Shoe* (1940), *Evil Under The Sun* (1941), *Five Little Pigs*
(1942) and *The Hollow* (1946), and two Miss Marple mystery novels, *The Body in the
Library* (1942) and *The Moving Finger* (1942).

Christie, who lived alone as her husband Max was working for the Air Ministry in
Cairo, was a popular member of this close-knit community. Her neighbour, Professor
Stephen Glanville, provided scholarly information about ancient Egypt for her novel
set in 2000 BC, *Death Comes At The End* (1946). She in turn lent a sympathetic ear
to his complicated and disastrous love life. She also found time to write for the stage
and an autobiographical work, *Come, Tell Me How You Live* (1946), as a 'welcome
home' present for her husband.

Arsenal
Stadium

Other tenants at this time included the writer Nicholas Monsarrat, author of *The Cruel Sea* (1951); artist Henry Moore; Walter Gropius, founder of the Bauhaus, and other designers and architects who had escaped Nazi Germany.

Odeon Cinema, Swiss Cottage

Poet, film critic and novelist Gilbert Adair's *Love and Death on Long Island* (1990) concerns a Hampstead novelist who is so unfamiliar with multiplexes that he wanders into the wrong auditorium at the Swiss Cottage cinema. Instead of watching *A Room With A View*, he sits through *Hotpants College II* and, to his consternation, becomes hopelessly infatuated with the film's young star, Ronnie Bostock. With semi-satirical echoes of Thomas Mann's *Death in Venice*, the elderly writer obsessively tracks down Bostock's back catalogue on video and details of his private life before flying to America to try to meet him.

Fever Pitch • Avenell Road

The Arsenal Football Club, in their final year at Avenell Road at the time of writing, is the focus and spiritual home of Nick Hornby's *Fever Pitch* (1992), a rite of passage novel in which he explores his all-consuming obsession with the club. This influential novel has been widely imitated and spearheaded a new trend in male confessional writing. One of Britain's best-known and most successful writers, he edited *My Favourite Year* (1993), an anthology of football pieces and followed *Fever Pitch* with a succession of entertaining novels – many of which have been made into equally successful films – that speak for a generation of emotionally bewildered young men. They include *High Fidelity* (1995), *About a Boy* (1998) and *How to be Good* (2001).

Internal Exile: Stoke Newington

Stoke Newington, meaning new town in the wood, was originally a farming community. In certain parts it has retained some of the quality of a 'dream-like and spirit-soothing place', as described by Edgar Allen Poe, who went to school here.

Elsewhere the titles of Ernest Raymond's *We The Accused* (1935) and Alexander Baron's *The Lowlife* (1963) – both set locally – suggest a bleaker character, underlined by Iain Sinclair's description of Stoke Newington in *Lights Out For the Territory* (1997) as 'Limboland. London's Interzone. Large shabby properties that ask no questions. Internal exile with a phoney rent-book'.

The True-Born Englishman • Newington Green

In the 17th century Newington Green was a sanctuary for religious dissenters. Daniel Defoe was educated for the Presbyterian Ministry at the Nonconformist Academy at Newington Green in the 1670s. However in 1682 he abandoned this plan and became a hosiery merchant in Cornhill. He travelled extensively in Europe, and took part in Monmouth's rebellion and, in 1688, joined the advancing troops of William III. He wrote the satirical poem *The True-Born Englishman* (1701), attacking the prejudice against the Dutch king. Defoe was imprisoned *(see p61)* for writing *The Shortest Way with Dissenters* (1702), in which he ridiculed the Tory government by demanding the suppression of dissent. While in prison his *Hymn to the Pillory* (1703), a mock-Pindaric ode, was sold on the streets to sympathetic crowds.

Robert Harley, the Tory politician, bibliophile and friend of Pope and Swift, arranged a pardon and employed Defoe as a secret agent from 1703 to 1714. A prolific pamphleteer and journalist, Defoe lived at No. 95 Stoke Newington Church Street from 1708 to 30. He is best known for *Robinson Crusoe* (1719), *Moll Flanders* (1722) and the ingenious and innovative *A Journal of the Plague Year* (1722), a fiction which is presented as a first-hand account of the 'Great visitation' in 1665 by a citizen 'who continued all the while in London'. At the time of the Great Plague, however, Defoe was just five years old. Defoe also wrote *Tour through the Whole Island of Great Britain* (1724–26), a vivid account of the country in three volumes.

Dissenters

Mary Wollstonecraft ran a school by Newington Green from 1783 to 1785 while she gathered material for her *Thoughts on the Education of Daughters* (1787). She led a quintessentially bohemian life, and was part of a group of Dissenters that included Dr Richard Price, the minister at Newington Green, and publisher Joseph Johnson.

She fell passionately in love with the painter Henry Fuseli and defied convention by living with, but refusing to marry, the writer Gilbert Imlay. In 1795, when he eloped with an actress, Wollstonecraft attempted suicide by throwing herself off Putney Bridge.

She married philosopher and publisher William Godwin, but within two years was dead from septicaemia after giving birth to their daughter, the future Mary Shelley. Her most famous work is the seminal *A Vindication of the Rights of Women* (1792). She also wrote *A Vindication of the Rights of Men* (1790) in riposte to Edmund Burke.

William Wilson • Stoke Newington Church Street

A plaque marks the site of Manor House boarding school (demolished in 1880), at which the American writer Edgar Allan Poe was a pupil from 1817 to 1820. The principal, the Reverend Dr John Bransby, described Poe as 'a quick and clever boy,' who 'would have been a very good boy had he not been spoilt by his parents' – by which he meant Poe's foster parents, the Allans, who 'allowed him an extravagant amount of pocket-money, which enabled him to get into all manner of mischief.'

Little else is known of this period in Poe's life except as fictionalised in his tale *William Wilson* (1839). An early version of the story describes the school building (probably quite accurately) as an 'old, irregular, and cottage-built' dwelling. In the final published version it is 'a large, rambling, Elizabethan house' with a 'long, narrow, and dismally low' school room. In a remote and terror-inspiring angle was a square enclosure of eight or ten feet, comprising the sanctum, 'during hours,' of our principal, the Reverend Dr Bransby.' The school as described contains many features that would be familiar to generations of pupils at English public schools, from the 'innumerable benches and desks, black, ancient, and time-worn, piled desperately with much-bethumbed books', to the 'many little nooks or recesses' which 'the economic ingenuity of Dr Bransby had [also] fitted up as dormitories.'

In the story Wilson, 'prey to the most ungovernable passions' and distinguished by his 'evil propensities' leaves Bransby's school for Eton, and then on to Oxford before a final disastrous confrontation with his doppelganger. Poe himself, after five years at Manor House, returned to Virginia with his foster parents. In 1826 he registered at the University of Virginia but left after a year, having run up large gambling debts that his foster father refused to pay.

The Secret Agent • 6 Dynevor Road, Stoke Newington

Joseph Conrad, who worked as a merchant seaman, lived at Dynevor Road in Stoke Newington from 1881 to 1886, when not at sea. He used his landlord Adolf Krieger and his wife as the basis for Mr and Mrs Verloc in *The Secret Agent* (1907).

Not Waving But Drowning • 1 Avondale Road, Palmers Green

Poet and novelist Stevie Smith lived here, with her aunt Margaret, for most of her adult life, making few modifications to the interior over the years. When she won the Queen's Medal for Poetry in 1969, journalists and photographers who entered her home felt as if they were stepping into a previous era. For her visit to Buckingham Palace to receive the medal, she bought a hat from a local jumble sale.

Smith's witty and idiosyncratic work – which includes the poetry collection *A Good Time Was Had By All* (1936) and the semi-autobiographical novel written on yellow paper she obtained while working as a publishing secretary, *Novel on Yellow Paper* (1936) – achieved great popularity before the Second World War, after which it fell out of fashion.

Her book of poems *Not Waving But Drowning*, published in 1957, began to reawaken readers to the quality of her work, and in the 1960s she was a popular poetry reader, broadcaster and reviewer, famously appearing at the Royal Albert Hall in June 1965 *(see p207)*. Her *Collected Poems* appeared in 1975.

White Teeth • Cricklewood Broadway

This is where Zadie Smith's invigorating and dynamic first novel *White Teeth* (2000) begins, in the early hours of 1 January 1975, with the attempted suicide of Alfred Archibald Jones. But 'Life is about to say Yes to Archie Jones', hapless veteran of the so-called Buggered Battalion in World War II with Samad Iqbal who, 'after a year of mercilessly hard graft' had been able to make the move from 'the wrong side of Whitechapel to the wrong side of Willesden.' Here, Samad's wife Alsana notes, 'there was just not enough of any one thing to gang up against any other thing and send it running to the cellars while windows were smashed.'

White Teeth embraces issues such as the legacy of history and questions of assimilation, and is at once a celebration and examination of the multicultural landscape of London. Ranging across northwest London, the novel charts ethnicity along the route of the No. 52 bus: from the 'Willesden kaleidoscope', west through Kensal Rise, to Portobello and Knightsbridge (in which direction 'the many colours shade off into the bright white lights of town'); or east to Willesden, Dollis Hill and Harlesden, watching 'as white fades to yellow, fades to brown, and then Harlesden Clock … standing like Queen Victoria's statue in Kingston – a tall stone surrounded by black'.

In Smith's second book, *The Autograph Man* (2002), a wrestling match at the Albert Hall provides the background for the pivotal events in 12-year-old Alex-Li Tandem's life: he meets Joseph Klein, a boy whose fascination with autographs proves infectious; two key friendships are firmly established; and his father drops dead.

Both *White Teeth* and *The Autograph Man* were launched at the Willesden Bookshop, at No. 95 High Road, NW10.

THE LAST STRAW
LAST ✕ MEWS HOUSE✕

HAMPSTEAD

NORTH AND WEST OF PRIMROSE HILL and Camden Town are Hampstead and Highgate, with their winding hills, narrow streets and windswept heath separating the two. They developed as villages surrounded by farmland in the early 18th century.

Dr Johnson, Fanny Burney and other 18th-century literary figures visited Hampstead, but it was not until the 19th century that writers and artists came to live here, in search of cleaner air and various medicinal waters. Leigh Hunt, the central figure in literary London at the time, lived here in the 1810s.

Leigh Hunt was visited by friends such as Shelley, Hazlitt, Lamb and Keats, who, moved to the area in 1817. While in Hampstead Keats met and fell for his neighbour Fanny Brawne, so beginning one of the most famous love affairs in English literature. Keats celebrated his love for her in poems and letters. Fanny agreed to marry Keats but, with the onset of Keats's tuberculosis, it became clear to both that their love was doomed.

The open space of the heath and village atmosphere also attracted the next generation of writers, including Charles Dickens, Wilkie Collins and George Du Maurier. Dickens has Bill Sikes make an erratic journey across Hampstead Heath after murdering Nancy in *Oliver Twist* (1837–38). He also features the famous Spaniards Inn in *The Pickwick Papers* (1838) and *Barnaby Rudge* (1841). Writers from each subsequent generation have been drawn to the area, from A.E. Housman, H.G. Wells and John Galsworthy to Compton Mackenzie, John Fowles and Kingsley Amis.

The early 20th century saw Hampstead's bohemian period at its peak. Aldous Huxley, Katherine Mansfield and D.H. Lawrence lived here on and off in the 1920s, while in the 30s and 40s William Empson, Roland Penrose, Lee Miller, Stephen Spender, Geoffrey Grigson and many others established Hampstead as the intellectual and bohemian heart of London. The novelist E.M. Forster called Hampstead 'the intellectual suburb'.

By the 1950s the poet Edwin Muir could write in his autobiography that Hampstead is 'filled with writing people and haunted by young poets'. This has been replaced by what the novelist Doris Lessing described in *The Golden Notebook* (1962) as a world of 'political intellectuals, reformers, therapists and feminists'. It has a reputation for attracting moneyed socialists – though that association perhaps peaked in the 1990s.

With such rich literary heritage, it may come as no surprise that Hampstead and Highgate have the highest concentration of blue plaques in London.

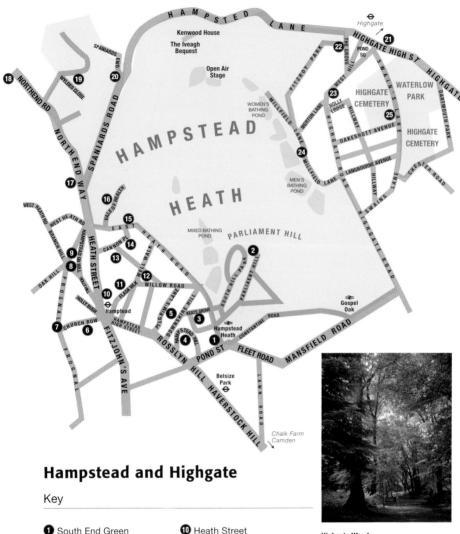

Hampstead and Highgate

Key

1. South End Green
2. Parliament Hill
3. Keats Grove
4. Hampstead Hill Gdns
5. Downshire Hill
6. Church Row
7. Frognal
8. Admiral's Walk
9. Hampstead Grove
10. Heath Street
11. Flask Walk
12. Well Walk
13. Christchurch Passage
14. Cannon Place
15. East Heath Road
16. Vale of Health
17. Jack Straw's Castle
18. The Old Bull & Bush

Highgate Woods

19. Wyldes Close
20. Spaniards Inn
21. Highgate High Street
22. The Grove
23. West Hill
24. Millfield Lane
25. Highgate Cemetery

Left **Flask Walk** Right **Wells Tavern**

The Kit-Kat Club • 124 Heath Street, site of Upper Flask Tavern
This group of influential Whigs *(see p35)* visited Hampstead every summer from the late 1690s until the 1710s. Tonson, Congreve, Addison, Steele, Garth and Vanbrugh were among the literary members of a club described by Dr Johnson as the best that ever existed. The Inn featured in scenes in Samuel Richardson's *Clarissa* (1748).

Jake's Thing • Gardnor House, Flask Walk
Kingsley Amis lived here from 1976 until 1982. Here he wrote *Jake's Thing* (1978), his examination of middle-aged impotence and its causes, and the less-successful futuristic melodrama *Russian Hide-and-Seek* (1980) that is set in a 21st-century England ruled by Russians.

Amis lived here with his second wife, the novelist Elizabeth Jane Howard, author of the Cazalet family saga and a highly regarded memoir *Slipstream* (2002). She gained an intimate knowledge of the effects of heavy drinking during this period of their marriage. They consulted doctors and therapists who prescribed routines – comically presented in *Jake's Thing* – to revive Amis's sex drive. However, they proved ineffective, Amis continued drinking, and Howard left him in 1980. For several days Amis failed to find the note she left explaining her departure. He unsuccessfully appealed to her to return before eventually moving to Primrose Hill *(see p271)*.

Images • 7 Christchurch Passage
Hilda Doolittle (H.D.) and husband Richard Aldington lived here from January 1915 to February 1916 to escape infighting within the Imagist group *(see p211)*. The poetry anthology *Some Imagist Poetry* (1915), edited by Amy Lowell, included their work and that of their neighbour, D.H. Lawrence. Aldington's first book *Images 1910–1915* (1915) was published by the Poetry Bookshop during their time here.

Forsyte Saga • Grove Lodge, Admiral's Walk

Writer John Galsworthy lived here from 1918 until his death in 1933. Although primarily a playwright and poet, he is best known as the novelist of *The Forsyte Saga* (1922), which consists of *The Man of Property* (1906), *In Chancery* (1920) and *To Let* (1921). A second series of Forsyte novels was published collectively as *A Modern Comedy* (1929), and a further collection of stories, *On Forsyte Change*, appeared in 1931. He was awarded the Nobel Prize for Literature in 1932.

Jamaica Inn • Cannon Hall, Cannon Place

In 1916 novelist Daphne Du Maurier moved into this sprawling mansion (dating from the 1730s) with her parents. Her father, Sir Gerald Du Maurier, was a leading actor-manager and son of George Du Maurier *(see p284)*. It was not until her family bought a second home in Cornwall that Daphne was able to escape the social life she disliked so much and find the solitude to write. Her first novel, a romantic saga called *The Loving Spirit* (1931), was an immediate success.

Daphne wrote a frank memoir of her father, *Gerald* (1934), before moving permanently to Cornwall in 1935. There, encouraged by her publisher Victor Gollancz, she wrote *Jamaica Inn* (1936).

I Stood Tip-toe Upon a Little Hill • Site of 1 Well Walk

John Keats lived here, in the local postman's house, next to the Green Man (now a gastropub called Wells Tavern) from March 1817 until February 1818, in search of clean air and walks on the heath. Here he completed *Endymion* (1818), met his publisher, John Taylor, and worked briefly as theatre critic of *The Champion* newspaper (in John Hamilton Reynolds's absence). He also attended Haydon's 'Immortal Dinner' *(see p171)* and Hazlitt's lectures.

He returned here in August 1818 to nurse his brother, Tom, who died of tuberculosis. Fearful for his own life, and in need of cheaper lodgings, he moved to Wentworth Place *(see p288)*.

The History of Mr Polly • 17 Church Row

H.G. Wells, successful and prolific both as a novelist and a lover, lived here between 1909 and 1915. Renowned for his independence of thought and highly imaginative novels, such as *The Time Machine* (1895) and *The War of the Worlds* (1898), Wells entertained many of the leading writers and intellectuals of the day, including Arnold Bennett, David Garnett, D.H. Lawrence, Katherine Mansfield and John Middleton Murry. When the Lawrences and Murrys attended a dinner party here in August 1914, Mansfield teased Lawrence that the attention of the ladies present had been lavished on Wells and not on him.

At Church Row Wells wrote *The History of Mr Polly* (1910), about an inefficient shopkeeper's quest for freedom, *The New Machiavelli* (1911), about a politician involved in sexual scandal, and *Marriage* (1912), which sparked an outspoken review by Rebecca West, with whom he had had a ten-year love affair.

Come, Come, Come and Make Eyes at Me • The Old Bull and Bush

Dating from 1721, rebuilt in 1924 and immortalised in Florrie Ford's music hall song *Down at the Old Bull and Bush* (1903), this pub has associations with painter William Hogarth, who lived nearby and laid out the gardens, as well as Joshua Reynolds, David Garrick, Dr Johnson, Thomas Gainsborough, Wilkie Collins, George Du Maurier and Charles Dickens, who all drank here at one time or another. It also inspired George and Weedon Grossmith's Cow and Hedge pub in *Diary of a Nobody*, 1892 *(see p163)*. Music hall entertainments, utilising a large back garden, began here in 1867 and became a popular attraction for Londoners out for the day.

Old Wyldes • Wyldes Close, North End Road

This early 17th-century farmhouse was once a retreat for artists and writers. William Blake was a frequent visitor when his friend the artist John Linnell rented the house from 1824 to 30. Linnell commissioned Blake to engrave illustrations to the *Book of Job* (1826). Here Blake met and inspired several artists, including Samuel Palmer, John Varley and William Mulready. Blake most probably met John Constable who lodged most summers in Hampstead from 1819, before leasing No. 40 Well Walk in 1827. Later visitors to the retreat included Charles Dickens, Wilkie Collins, Walter Besant and George Bernard Shaw.

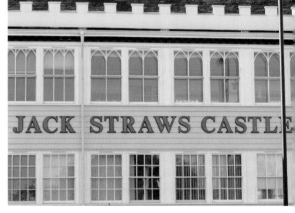

Jack Straw's Castle

Jack Straw's Castle
12 North End Way

Although rebuilt in 1964, Jack Straw's Castle dates from 1713 and was where Wilkie Collins, Charles Dickens, John Forster, Thackeray and friends came to drink. The pub is named after one of the leaders of the Peasants' Revolt (1381) who sought refuge here, but was later hanged nearby. The pub, recently refurbished as apartments, features in Bram Stoker's *Dracula* (1897).

Hampstead Grove

George Du Maurier
28 Hampstead Grove

George Du Maurier, writer and illustrator for *Punch*, moved to Hampstead's bohemian community in 1869, living first at No. 4 Holly Mount and then from 1870–74 at No. 27 Church Row; he lived at Hampstead Grove from 1874–95.

Du Maurier had established a reputation as a satirical cartoonist – notably ridiculing the Aesthetic movement – while working for *Punch*, *Cornhill* and other magazines. He was neighbours and friends with artist Kate Greenaway and novelist Walter Besant. The Pre-Raphaelite artist John Millais, novelist George Eliot and her lover George Henry Lewis (editor of *The Westminster Review*) visited him here.

To widen his circle of contacts Du Maurier joined the Rabelais Club, a literary dining club founded in 1879. Members included Henry James, Thomas Hardy, Besant and Millais. Through the club he gained commissions to illustrate Hardy's *The Hand of Ethelberta* for *Cornhill* magazine (1875–76) and *A Laodicean* for *Harper's New Monthly* (1880–81). He also illustrated novels for Wilkie Collins, Elizabeth Gaskell, Thackeray, George Meredith and Henry James.

Du Maurier wrote three novels himself: *Peter Ibbetson* (1889), *Trilby* (1894) and, published posthumously, *The Martian* (1897). *Trilby*, the story of a vivacious French girl and a satanic hypnotist (Svengali), sets the theme of the 'fallen woman' against the romantic backdrop of Paris's Latin Quarter. It was the bestseller of 1894, and gave rise to a wide range of *Trilby* merchandise (mostly shoes and boots); the 1922 Hollywood film *Svengali* is based upon the book. Du Maurier is buried in Hampstead cemetery.

Spaniards Inn • Spaniards Road

Originally dating from 1585 and rebuilt several times since, this house became the country residence for the Spanish Ambassador to King James I and was opened as an inn in the 1750s. Anti-Catholic protesters were cunningly plied with drinks here during the 1780 Gordon Riots, allowing time for soldiers to arrive and arrest them. A portrayal of this event is featured in Charles Dickens's *Barnaby Rudge* (1841). The inn also features in the tea party scene in *The Pickwick Papers* (1837).

Keats, Shelley, Byron, William Blake, John Constable, Charles Dickens, Robert Louis Stevenson (who lodged at Abernethy House, No. 7 Mount Vernon between 1873 and 1879), A.E. Housman and Evelyn Waugh have all drunk here.

Frognal Pamphlets • 10 Frognal

Stephen Spender, son of distinguished liberal journalist Edward Harold, lived here from 1919 to 1933. He studied at nearby University College School, where he published his first poems, before going on to Oxford where he met W.H. Auden, Christopher Isherwood, Cecil Day Lewis and Louis MacNeice.

While here he printed and published the Frognal pamphlets, including W.H. Auden's *Poems* (1928), dedicated to Isherwood, and his own *Nine Experiments* (1928). His critical reputation was swiftly established with *Twenty Poems* (1930) and *Poems* (1933), published by T.S. Eliot at Faber. His name is forever linked with Auden and Day Lewis as one of the 'poets of the Thirties'.

After living and travelling with Tony Hyndman in the mid-1930s, Spender married Inez Pearn, who later eloped with Kathleen Raine's husband, Charles Madge. Madge, also a poet, was the founder of Mass Observation, an organisation that recruited observers to collect sociological information about daily life and popular culture *(see also p130)*. Spender was then introduced to musician Natasha Litvin while in Bloomsbury. They began to meet daily at the Café Royal, and soon fell in love.

Spaniards Inn

Stephen Spender and Litvin lived at Flat 4, No. 2 Maresfield Gardens, owned by Lucian Freud's father, Ernst, from January 1942 until March 1945. Spender made his study in the largest room of the attic suite, which was full of dead birds and still being used as a studio by Lucian. He was by now much less involved with *Horizon* magazine *(see p151)* and more engaged with John Lehmann's magazine *Penguin New Writing*.

He worked part-time at the Maresfield Gardens Fire Service station and completed his autobiographical *Ruins and Visions* (1942), with its uneasy mixture of public and private poems. The book is divided into four sections – separation, ironies of war, deaths and visions – and moves from personal breakdown, through public upheaval, to personal reintegration. In 1945 Spender moved to Loudoun Road in St John's Wood *(see p265)*, where he remained for the rest of his life.

The Collector • 55 Frognal

Novelist John Fowles lived here with Elizabeth Christy from February 1955 until spring 1959. He worked at St Godric's Secretarial College, bought books from Norman's second-hand bookshop off Heath Street, and wrote in his spare time. They married in April 1957 after Elizabeth had secured a divorce from her first husband.

In 1959 the couple moved to No. 28 Church Row (which in 1910 had been occupied by Compton McKenzie), where Fowles was able to resolve the problems with his early writing. He was Head of English at St Godric's from 1959 to 62, but gave up teaching in April 1963 after his psychological thriller *The Collector* (1963) was published. He continued working on the various drafts of his collection of philosophical notes and aphorisms, *The Aristos* (1968), and his Greek island-based magical and mythological novel *The Magus* (1966, revised 1977). Throughout this period he kept a *Journal*, which was published in 2004 and described his earlier literary struggle.

Instant success with *The Collector*, which was made into a film, propelled Fowles into the world of film and literary celebrity. He and his wife became part of the Hampstead literary set of Edna O'Brien, Doris Lessing, Tom Maschler, Elizabeth Jane Howard, Kingsley Amis and playwright Arnold Wesker.

In April 1964 the couple moved to No. 44 Southwood Lane, Highgate, where Fowles continued to revise *The Magus* and worked on an angry, unpublished novel, *The Fucker*. In October 1965 they left London for Lyme Regis in Dorset – the setting for *The French Lieutenant's Woman* (1969).

Metamorphosis • 7 Downshire Hill

Scottish poet Edwin Muir and his wife, Willa Anderson, lived here from 1932 to 35. Together they translated Kafka's *Metamorphosis* (1935). Edwin published his poems in *New Verse*, completed his novel *Poor Tom* (1932) and wrote *Scottish Journey* (1935) here. A recurrent theme in his work is the dream journey through time and place. His employment of the myth of Eden threatened by various forms of catastrophe or expulsion struck a chord with the younger poets of the 1930s.

The Muirs were habitués of the pubs of Fitzrovia. In his *Autobiography* (1954), Muir described Hampstead as 'filled with writing people and haunted by young poets despairing over the poor and the world, but despairing together, in a sad but comforting communion'.

Surrealist International • 21 Downshire Hill

Artist and writer Roland Penrose lived here from 1936 to 47. He was attracted to Hampstead by the large number of his artistic and literary friends already living locally, including sculptors Henry Moore, Barbara Hepworth and Naum Gabo; painters Paul Nash, Ben Nicholson and Piet Mondrian; and writers Geoffrey Grigson and Herbert Read.

Almost immediately, with the help of poet David Gascoyne, he began planning the First International Surrealist Exhibition. Additional help came from poets Humphrey Jennings and Ruthven Todd, from critics Hugh Sykes Davies and Henry Read, and from artists Man Ray, Henry Moore, Paul Nash and Eileen Agar. The event opened at the New Burlington Galleries on 11 June 1936, with 1150 people crowding into the gallery. André Breton, Hans Arp, Max Ernst, Salvador Dalí and other overseas artists exhibited. Poets Paul Eluard, Gascoyne, Jennings and Dylan Thomas gave readings. In 1938 Penrose bought the London Gallery in Cork Street and ran it with Belgian Surrealist E.L.T. Mesens until the war forced its closure in 1940.

Vogue photographer Lee Miller joined him at Downshire Hill in January 1940. Miller photographed London during the Blitz and, after D-day, became a war correspondent with the U.S. Army advancing through Europe. Her photographs of the liberation of Buchenwald and Dachau are among the most searing war documents. *Time-Life* magazine photographer David E. Scherman famously photographed Miller in Hitler's bath at the end of the conflict.

Penrose and Miller were renowned for their hospitality, and during the war provided a home from home for many friends. Mesens and his wife Sybil, journalist Kathleen McColgan and photographer David E. Scherman lodged here at various times during the war. Penrose and Fred Uhlman also ran the Artists Refugee Committee here, enabling more than thirty artists to escape from Nazi Germany.

Penrose and Miller married in 1947 and moved down the road to No. 36 Downshire Hill. Here Penrose, Mesens, Read, Grigson and others founded the Institute of Contemporary Arts (ICA) as a space for new and experimental art of all kinds.

New Verse • 4a Keats Grove

Poet Geoffrey Grigson lived here in the garden flat from 1932 to 36. He worked as book reviews editor of the *Morning Post* and edited the influential bi-monthly poetry magazine *New Verse* from February 1933 until May 1939. *New Verse* was the leading poetry magazine of the 1930s, publishing W.H. Auden, Louis MacNeice, Stephen Spender, Cecil Day Lewis, George Barker, William Empson, Herbert Read, Edwin Muir, Norman Cameron, David Gascoyne, Dylan Thomas and Kathleen Raine, helping to establish and enhance their reputations.

When the *Morning Post* collapsed and Grigson lost his job, he was forced to move to Wildwood Terrace. He sublet the flat to his friend, poet Louis MacNeice, who lived here from November 1936 until May 1938. MacNeice completed *Letters from Iceland* (1937) here, written in collaboration with W.H. Auden, who lived nearby in Upper Park Road with the artists Nancy and Bill Coldstream. During this period MacNeice also wrote *The Earth Compels* (1938), which featured the love poem 'The Sunlight on the Garden' (1937), warning of the effects of war on relationships.

MacNeice, recently divorced, embarked on an affair with Nancy Coldstream. This gave him a fresh burst of creative energy and inspired several poems. She illustrated *Zoo* (1938) and *I Crossed The Minch* (1938), his travel book about the Hebrides. In 1938 Nancy fell in love with poet Stephen Spender's older brother, Michael, whom she eventually married. Her portrait of Louis MacNeice is in the National Portrait Gallery.

Keats House

Keats House • Keats Grove (formerly Wentworth Place)

John Keats lived at Lamb Bank, Wentworth Place, later renamed Keats Grove, from December 1818 until May 1820. He then moved to be near Leigh Hunt *(see p262)*. Keats House is now a small museum. It combines the house next door, where Keats may have first met and fallen in love with 18-year-old Fanny Brawne. Here Keats wrote 'The Eve of St Agnes', 'The Eve of St Mark', 'The Fall of Hyperion: A Dream', his series of Odes, and other poems.

'Ode on a Grecian Urn', with its Catullan wordplay and erotic classicism, was part of the Cockney School's attempt to define the classic as pagan, passionate and politically radical, associating Greece with the struggle for liberty. 'Ode to a Nightingale', inspired by walking on the Heath with Coleridge and written in May 1819, evokes the work of Horace. Redolent with death and wine, it equates the bird's flight and song with the freedom of poetry and explores the relationship between poetry's power and life's mortal hardships. It begins:

> *My heart aches, and a drowsy numbness pains*
> *My sense, as though of hemlock I had drunk,*
> *Or emptied some dull opiate to the drains*
> *One minute past, and Lethe-wards had sunk:*

One of the first visitors to the House when it opened to the public in 1925 was novelist Thomas Hardy. After the visit he was inspired to write the poem, 'At a House in Hampstead' (1925).

I am Dying, but Otherwise Quite Well • **20 Keats Grove**

Poet Dame Edith Sitwell – renowned for her theatrical dress and manner almost as much as for *Façade* (1923), her poetic collaboration with composer William Walton – lived here from June 1964 until her death in December of the same year. She moved here from No. 42 Greenhill, Prince Arthur Road, where she had lived since 1961. While at Keats Grove she wrote to a friend, 'I am dying, but otherwise quite well.'

The Examiner • **Vale Lodge, Vale of Health**

Leigh Hunt lived here, near a row of white cottages in a marshy hollow on the edge of the heath, from October 1815 until September 1817, editing *The Examiner* and hosting parties with his literary and political friends. Dubbed the 'Cockney School of Poets' by the Tory press, this extended group of friends maintained a commitment to writing literature for social, cultural and political reform. They held weekly meetings here or at the Lambs' *(see p36)* or Haydon's *(see p171)*, keeping up a continual round of discussion, praise and censure. The group held informal writing competitions and continually exchanged manuscripts with, and dedicated poems to, one another. Hunt emerged as the group's figurehead, and dedicatee of much of their literary output.

While living here Hunt published the influential poem *The Story of Rimini* (1816), which Byron had helped edit and to whom it is dedicated. It is a joyous celebration of Paolo and Francesca, derived in part from Dante's *Inferno*. During this period Hunt also published a collection of his own essays, with contributions from Lamb and Hazlitt, under the title *The Round Table*. In *The Examiner* he published poetry by Byron and Keats – including 'On Solitude' and 'On First Looking into Chapman's Homer' (1816) – and Shelley's 'Hymn to Intellectual Beauty' (1817).

Shelley visited frequently in December 1816 and January 1817, and both he and Mary stayed with Hunt through most of February 1817. They discussed ideas on the nature of love, derived from the dialogues in Plato's *Symposium*, and plans for a Spenserian epic set in Greece.

Hunt, a meticulous host, arranged for his guests to dine with Keats, Hazlitt, Lamb, Haydon, Reynolds, Crabb Robinson and Shelley's future publisher Charles Ollier. Keats and Shelley famously walked together on the Heath, during which they discussed the way Shelley was being attacked in the Tory press. Fearing that Keats would also be subjected to such attacks, Shelley attempted to persuade Keats not to publish *Poems*, but Keats was unmoved.

Winds of Love • **Woodbine Cottage, Vale of Health**

Scottish writer and novelist Compton Mackenzie lived here from 1937 to 43. He wrote his first novel *The Passionate Elopement* (1911) at No. 28 Church Row in 1910. He served at Gallipoli and worked for British Intelligence in Greece.

Vale of Health

He became a prolific writer of novels, travel books, biography, war memoirs, poetry and journalism. His *Extraordinary Women* (1928), in which various absurd lesbian entanglements are set against a brittle hedonistic society, caused a controversy. Here he wrote the sextet *The Four Winds of Love* (1947), his most ambitious work, tracing the life of Scot John Ogilvie from the Boer War to the emergence of Scottish nationalism in 1945.

Rabindranath Tagore • 3 Villas on-the-Heath, Vale of Health

Bengali poet Rabindranath Tagore lived here in 1912, publishing his free-verse revisions of his Bengali poems modelled on medieval Indian devotional lyrics, *Gitanjali: Song Offering* (1912), for which he became the first Asian writer to win the Nobel Prize for Literature, in 1913.

In a series of lectures in London he presented an image of ancient India with its guiding principle that 'Man must realise the wholeness of his existence, his place in the infinite'. Tagore was a tireless campaigner for Indian literature and Indian vernacular writers, and was fiercely opposed to insular nationalism and war.

The Rainbow • 1 Byron Villas, Vale of Health

D.H. Lawrence and wife Frieda lived here from 4 August to 21 December 1915. Always on the move and frequently short of money, their life together was both passionate and stormy.

While here, Lawrence and Middleton Murry's magazine *Signature*, originally envisaged as six issues devoted to essays on social and personal freedom, failed to pay its way and closed after the third issue.

Further setback awaited on publication of *The Rainbow* (1915), which was savagely attacked by reviewers and did not even find favour with close friends such as Murry and Katherine Mansfield. The book was seized by the police from the publishers and prosecuted under the Obscene Publication Act of 1837.

The Lawrences left for Cornwall, but returned to Hampstead in October 1918, staying at poet Dollie Radford's home at No. 32 Well Walk while she was away visiting her son. Lawrence's *New Poems* (1918) was published at this time.

Cold Comfort • Vale Cottage, Vale of Health

Novelist and poet Stella Gibbons lived here from 1927 to 30 when she worked for the *Evening Standard* and was given the job of writing a synopsis of Mary Webb's *The Golden Arrow* (1916). Gibbons found the novel so absurd that she began a parody that became *Cold Comfort Farm* (1932). She left the *Evening Standard* for *The Lady* magazine, writing poetry in her spare time. Her parody of the earthy, primitive school of regional fiction proved so witty and successful that she was able to give up journalism. Her Hampstead novel *The Charmers* (1965) registers local changes from the early 1960s, when terraced houses began to be replaced by Council blocks, large houses converted into flats and a greater social and inter-racial mix engendered.

Bliss and Other Stories • 2 Portland Villas, 17 East Heath Road

New Zealander Katherine Mansfield and her lover, the editor John Middleton Murry, lived here from 1918 to 1921, between winters in the south of France.

After years of publishing his own short-lived modernist periodicals – such as *Rhythm*, *Blue Review* and *Signature* (the last of these with D.H. Lawrence) – Murry became editor of the *Athenaeum*, which dated back to 1828. In it, he published T.S. Eliot, Virginia Woolf, Robert Graves and Paul Valéry. In 1915 and 1916 D.H. Lawrence and his wife Frieda lived in Zennor, Cornwall, close to Mansfield and Murry. The intense and tempestuous relations between the couples inspired Lawrence's *Women in Love* (1920), where Gerald and Gudrun are partly based upon Murry and Mansfield.

At Portland Villas Mansfield completed the short stories in *Bliss and Other Stories* (1920) and wrote *The Garden Party and Other Stories* (1922). Her stories present intangible moments of decision, defeat and triumph. Her emphasis on the authenticity of the interior life came at a time when the First World War replaced the sense of a static world with one subject to violent flux. Her portrayal of the elusiveness of life reached new heights in the sixty-page story *Prelude* (1918), which depicts a New Zealand family moving house from the town to the countryside. It employs twelve sections of impressionistic insights without a plot, mediated by a narrative that moves from character to character – all of whom experience their own small crises. Her work probes matters of identity, belonging and desire.

Mansfield noted in her *Journal* how like Lawrence she was becoming, with the fits of temper she associated with the tuberculosis from which she died.

Aldous Huxley in *Point Counter Point* (1928) modelled Burlap and Beatrice on the couple, and satirised Murry's enthusiasm for publishing the remnants of his wife's work.

On The Heath

Coleridge, Lamb, Hazlitt, Hunt and Keats all loved to take walks at Millfield Lane – so much so that it was called Poet's Lane in the 1830s and 40s.

On 11 April 1819 Keats, having walked across Highgate Ponds until he reached the point where Millfield Lane begins to climb towards Highgate, met Coleridge in conversation with surgeon J.H. Green, his supervisor at Guy's Hospital. They walked for about two miles together. Coleridge spoke about nightingales, poetical sensation, metaphysics, the classification of dreams and nightmares and different levels of consciousness. Returning home, Keats took opium for his throat and, falling into a deep sleep, had an extraordinary dream that inspired the haunting sonnet 'A Dream, after reading Dante's Episode of Paolo and Francesca' and 'La Belle Dame sans Merci', his vision of the mysterious knight-at-arms wandering over the heath, 'alone and palely loitering'. Hunt published both poems in the *Indicator* in 1820.

Wilkie Collins lived in Pond Street (later, South End Green) during his childhood from 1826 to 29. Walter Hartright in *The Woman in White*, 1860 *(see p174)* strolls home 'across the lonely heath' to approach London 'through its most open suburb by striking into the Finchley Road, and so getting back, in the cool of the new morning, by the western side of the Regent's Park':

> *I wound my way down slowly over the heath, enjoying the divine stillness of the scene, and admiring the soft alternations of light and shade as they followed each over the broken ground on every side of me.*

Galsworthy has Old Jolyon Forsyte in *Man of Property* (1906) reflect on 'those Sunday afternoons on Hampstead Heath, when young Jolyon and he went for a stretch along the Spaniard's Road to Highgate, to Child's Hill, and back over the heath again to dine at Jack Straw's Castle – how delicious his cigars were then! And such weather! There was no weather now.'

Contemporary poet and novelist Jeremy Reed has written several Hampstead poems, including 'Hampstead Ponds', with 'their prolonged meditations on a sky / backfloating into a frame'.

The Contemplative Quarry • 68 Parliament Hill

Poet Anna Wickham lived here from 1919 until she hanged herself in April 1947. Born in Wimbledon and raised in Australia, Anna Wickham is the pseudonym of Edith Harper. In 1906 she married solicitor Patrick Hepburn and lived in Tavistock Square in Bloomsbury. There she began writing poetry, to which her husband objected, finding it a threatening pursuit. In 1913 he had Anna committed to a mental hospital, where she continued to write poetry. Released after four months, she joined the suffrage movement and wrote *The Contemplative Quarry* (1915) and *The Man with a Hammer* (1916). She became friends with Edward Garnett, his son David, D.H. Lawrence, whom she regularly visited when he was in Hampstead, and Harold Monro.

Anna became a regular at the Fitzroy Tavern *(see p127)*, and after the death of her husband in 1929 dismissed the cook and maid and began to take in lodgers as a source of income. At the Fitzroy she befriended Malcolm Lowry, who was about to publish his first novel, *Ultramarine* (1933). She also became friends with Lawrence Durrell, John Davenport and Dylan Thomas, all of whom lodged with her at various times. Thomas wrote part of *Adventures in the Skin Trade* (1955) in her bathroom, which he describes as being filled with birds in cages. She wrote *The Little Old House* (1921) and *Thirty Six New Poems* (1936), charting her struggle to become a poet and to fulfil herself as a wife and mother.

Aldous Huxley • 18 Hampstead Hill Gardens

Aldous Huxley lived here from June 1919 until December 1920. He had lived with his father and stepmother at No. 16 Bracknell Gardens from April until July 1917 before taking up a post as a master at Eton College. In July 1919 he married Belgian Marie Nys, whom he had met at Garsington Hall, home of hostess Lady Ottoline Morrell.

Huxley left Eton to work as a writer and reviewer with Middleton Murry at the *Athenaeum* magazine. He worked with Murry from April 1919 until October 1920 and was a prolific contributor to the magazine. After Marie gave birth to their son and went to convalesce at Garsington Hall, he regularly dined at the White Tower Restaurant *(see p130)* with friends Tommy Earp, T.S. Eliot, Iris Tree, Marie Beerbohm, Nancy Cunard and others. Here the conversation revolved around 'the cubists of literature' – poets such as Aragon, Tzara, Picabia and Breton, whom Huxley had met in Paris in January 1920. His book of short stories, *Limbo* (1920), was successful among young literate aristocrats. However, his volume of poetry, *Leda* (1920), did not impress Eliot, who advised him to concentrate on fiction.

The Gathering Storm • 1 Hampstead Hill Gardens

Poet and critic William Empson lived here from 1946 until his death in 1984. Before the Second World War he lived at No. 160 Haverstock Hill, where he wrote his collection *The Gathering Storm* (1940). Empson had made his critical reputation with *Seven Types of Ambiguity* (1930) which, based on a close reading of poetic texts, illustrated how uncertainty or overlap of meaning enriches poetry.

Empson worked as Chinese editor at the BBC during the Second World War, coming into contact with George Orwell, Tambimuttu, Mulk Raj Ananad, Dylan Thomas, Louis MacNeice and other Fitzrovian poets and writers.

His wife Hetta, a sculptor, was renowned for hosting flamboyant and generous parties, with or without her husband, who from 1953 was often away teaching at Sheffield University. Guests comprised a mixture of Hampstead intellectuals and habitués of the Gargoyle and The George *(see pp110 & 180)*. At one party in 1961 Hetta's occasional lover Josh Avery chinned writer Charles Osborne – causing Empson to apologise on behalf of his wife's lover.

Empson's rational, metaphysical poetry, brought together in *Collected Poems* (1955), inspired members of 'the Movement' (such as John Wain, Donald Davie and Elizabeth Jennings), who wrote in a witty, rational and anti-romantic style.

Keep The Aspidistra Flying • 3 Warwick Mansions, South End Green

Novelist and essayist George Orwell lived here from October 1934 until February 1935 above the Booklovers' Corner, where he worked as an assistant in the mornings. In those days it was a social borderland between Kentish Town and Hampstead.

The Booklovers' Corner sold a broad range of new and second-hand books, and inspired the description of the bookshop in *Keep The Aspidistra Flying* (1936), which he started writing here. The novel recounts the literary aspirations, financial humiliations and shotgun wedding of Gordon Comstock, bookseller's assistant. Comstock can be read as forerunner to the 'Angry Young Man' of the 1950s. The bookshop satisfied Orwell's interest in popular culture and gave him time to write

upstairs. During this time Orwell frequented the Fitzrovian pubs *(see pp128–9)*, meeting Rayner Heppenstall, Dylan Thomas and others.

In February 1935 he moved to No. 77 Parliament Hill and completed *Keep The Aspidistra Flying*. In March *A Clergyman's Daughter* appeared, followed by the British publication of *Burmese Days* in June. He was visited here by Cyril Connolly, who was 'appalled by the ravaged grooves that ran down [his face] from cheek to chin.' From then on, Connolly supported Orwell through *Horizon* magazine. In July 1935 Orwell

Site of the Booklovers' Corner   moved to No. 50 Lawford Road *(see p264)*.

Left **No. 3 The Grove** Right **Pond Square**

HIGHGATE

Site of Andrew Marvell's Cottage • Opposite 112 Highgate High Street

A plaque on the west side of Hampstead High Street reads: 'Four feet below this spot is the stone step, formerly the entrance to the cottage in which lived Andrew Marvell, poet, wit, satirist, colleague of John Milton in the Foreign or Latin secret service during the Commonwealth and for about twenty years M.P. for Hull'. Marvell lived here in the 1670s. His *Miscellaneous Poems* (1681) were printed from papers found in his rooms by his housekeeper Mary Palmer, who claimed authorship and signed the preface, 'Mary Marvell' in order to gain income. They were not identified as wholly his work until a century later. Marvell's reputation as a lyric poet was developed by Charles Lamb, and enhanced by T.S. Eliot. His oblique and sometimes enigmatic approach, as in 'To His Coy Mistress' *(see p16)*, appealed to the modern mind.

Sage of Highgate • 3 The Grove

Samuel Taylor Coleridge lived at Moreton House, South Green, with Dr James Gillman and his family, from 15 April 1816 until September 1823. There is a memorial flagstone in the nave of St Michael's Church close by. Coleridge had retired to the Highgate medical practice in an attempt to control his opium addiction. From October 1823 until his death on 25 July 1834, Coleridge lived here with the Gillmans, occupying the finest upper room and large attic bedroom with views looking westwards.

Lord Byron had encouraged him to publish the unfinished 'Christabel' and his opium poems, 'Kubla Khan' and 'The Pains of Sleep' *(see p188)*. They appeared in *Christabel and Other Poems* (1816) and cemented his legendary status among the younger generation of Romantic poets, writers and readers. Coleridge went on to publish *Biographia Literaria* (1817), a philosophical work of poetic criticism and humorous autobiography, and *Sibylline Leaves* (1817), the first edition of his collected poems, expanded in 1828 and 1834.

Memorial stone to Coleridge, St Michael's Church

In July 1824 Coleridge watched Byron's funeral cortège pass slowly up Highgate Hill from outside the chemist's shop where he obtained his illicit supply of opium, and gave a spontaneous and heartfelt funeral oration to the chemist's assistant.

Lamb described Coleridge as 'an Archangel a little damaged', an apt description for the drug-ravaged, grey-haired man who took to religion in his retirement years. His last major work, *Aids to Reflection* (1825), a collection of commentaries and aphorisms in which he stressed the importance of Christianity as a 'personal revelation', inspired the Christian Socialists.

Thomas Carlyle, who named him 'the Sage of Highgate', Gabriel Rossetti, John Stuart Mill, Ralph Waldo Emerson, Thomas Hood and Harriet Martineau were among those who visited Coleridge here.

Novelist and playwright J.B. Priestley lived in this house from 1935 until 1939. Here he wrote his 'Time' plays *I Have Been Here Before* (1937) and *Time and the Conways* (1937) and the West Riding farce *When We Are Married* (1938). His plays, especially *An Inspector Calls* (1947), remain popular and are regularly revived.

Priestley had been able to move to Hampstead following the success of his novel *The Good Companions* (1929), an account of theatrical adventures on the road. He lived at No. 27 Well Walk from 1929 until 1931, and there he wrote his London novel *Angel Pavement* (1930).

A Shropshire Lad • Byron Cottage, 17 North Road

Poet and classicist A.E. Housman lived here from 1886 until 1905, attracted by the atmosphere of rural seclusion. He became Professor of Latin at University College, London in 1892 and in 1896 self-published *A Shropshire Lad*. This sequence of spare and nostalgic verse, based largely on ballad forms and principally set in an imagined Shropshire, a 'land of lost content', is addressed to, or spoken by, a farm boy, who becomes a soldier. The book made almost no impact upon publication, but became hugely popular during the First World War and established Housman as a poet.

Summoned by Bells • 31 West Hill, Highgate

Poet John Betjeman was born at No. 52 Parliament Hill Mansions. He lived here 'safe in a world of trains and buttered toast' from 1907 until 1917. During the First World War Betjeman was a pupil at Highgate Junior School, 3 Bishopswood Road. Here he was taught Latin, French, German and arithmetic by T.S. Eliot. Hearing that the American master liked poetry, Betjeman, aged ten, presented Eliot with a volume of verse. He received little encouragement and Eliot soon left teaching to work in a bank.

As a child, Betjeman would take his pencil and writing pad to Hampstead Heath and stand 'tip-toe upon a little hill, awaiting inspiration from the sky'. His collection *Summoned by Bells* (1960) recounts his Highgate childhood and his dismay when, returning from school one day, he finds that 'we'd moved – 53 Church St [Chelsea]. Yes, the slummy end' (see p229).

Highgate Cemetery
Swain's Lane

The cemetery was consecrated in 1839. Dickens buried his parents, brother, sister and one of his daughters here. Dante Gabriel Rossetti buried his beloved wife, Elizabeth Siddall, in 1862 and seven years later had the coffin dug up in order to retrieve the poems he had buried with her (see p223).

The East wing contains the graves of Karl Marx and George Eliot. Others buried here include Christina Rossetti, Radclyffe Hall, Sir Leslie Stephen and Sir John Betjeman's parents.

Highgate Cemetery

THE EAST END

LIFE IN THE EAST END – comprising for the purposes of this book Whitechapel, Spitalfields, Bethnal Green, Hackney, Shadwell, Stratford, Stepney and Wapping – has been shaped by successive waves of immigration, the growth and decline of heavy industry and extreme levels of hardship. Writers such as Jack London and George Orwell have had a tendency to regard the East End as a discrete subject, reporting on the area as if it were a foreign land. It is still regarded as the most pliable part of London, in which whole areas can be torn down to make way for new buildings or redeveloped en masse.

Like much of East London, 17th-century Hackney was a popular destination to take the country air. Samuel Pepys recorded many visits to destinations east of the City, including one to Bethnal Green on 3 September 1666 to store his possessions as the Great Fire approached his home. Daniel Defoe's novels of the 1720s, *Roxana* and *Moll Flanders*, refer to the 'villages' of Stepney and Hackney. However, by the early 19th century increasing industrialisation and the construction of the docks saw rapid expansion eastwards.

Hackney became almost completely urbanised, with railways, houses and factories. Breweries, sugar refineries, gasworks, glue making and other 'stink' industries along the Mile End Road contributed to the East End's image as a place where life was nasty, brutish and short. Arthur Morrison's *Tales of Mean Streets* and *A Child of the Jago* capture the grim realities of East End life at its toughest at the end of the 19th century.

Located one mile east of the City, Whitechapel's history includes the Jack the Ripper Murders of 1888–91, the Sidney Street siege of 1911 and the gangland murders of the 1960s. The area's lurid past has fascinated local writers such as Iain Sinclair, whose *White Chappell, Scarlet Tracings* (1987) deals with the mythology of Jack the Ripper.

From 1860 Whitechapel and Bethnal Green provided refuge for thousands of Jews fleeing pogroms in Eastern Europe: at its peak, in 1914, the Jewish community here numbered around 200,000 people. The Jewish East End produced such celebrated playwrights as Arnold Wesker, Bernard Kops, Harold Pinter and Steven Berkoff.

Since 1950 the area has been the centre of the city's Bangladeshi community, and Asian writers such as Farrukh Dhondy (author of *East End at Your Feet*, 1976) and Monica Ali have come to the fore, drawing inspiration from the rich culture of this area.

East End

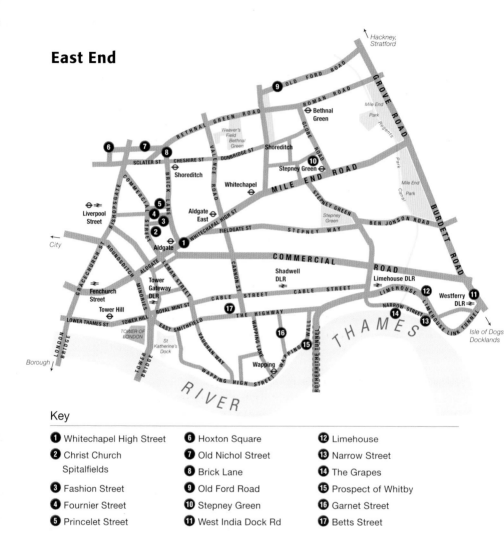

Key

1. Whitechapel High Street
2. Christ Church Spitalfields
3. Fashion Street
4. Fournier Street
5. Princelet Street
6. Hoxton Square
7. Old Nichol Street
8. Brick Lane
9. Old Ford Road
10. Stepney Green
11. West India Dock Rd
12. Limehouse
13. Narrow Street
14. The Grapes
15. Prospect of Whitby
16. Garnet Street
17. Betts Street

The Old Nichol

Novelist Arthur Morrison wrote stories about the bleak conditions of East End life for *Macmillan's Magazine*. These were later collected as *Tales of Mean Streets* (1894). His novel *A Child of the Jago* (1896) concerned violent crime in the area. The Jago was a fictionalised version of a small district of half a dozen streets, courtyards and alleyways immediately to the Northeast of the junction of Shoreditch High Street and Bethnal Green Road called the Old Nichol. Apart from the change of name Morrison made no attempt to disguise the identity of the district. Even in his modifications of street names within the Nichol, he deliberately stayed very close to the originals, with Boundary Street becoming Edge Lane, Chance Street becoming Luck Row, and Mead Street becoming Honey Lane. The novel was not intended as pure fiction as much as a dramatised documentary. In particular Morrison introduced into the story a parish priest, Father Sturt, whose attitudes he based squarely on those of the Reverend Arthur Osborne Jay, a Vicar of Holy Trinity, Shoreditch, whose parish included the Old Nichol. He dedicated the book to Father Jay, who first introduced him to the district and whose hints he followed in surveying it. The Reverend Jay showed Morrison the Old Nichol area, having thought that *Tales of Mean Streets* wasn't hard enough.

Children of the Ghetto • 288 Old Ford Road

Journalist, novelist and playwright Israel Zangwill is commemorated by a plaque here. Prominent in Jewish cultural circles, his popular novel *Children of the Ghetto* (1892) established his reputation through its critical yet sympathetic portrayal of East End Jewish life at a time when immigration was a major issue. *Ghetto Tragedies* (1899) and *Ghetto Comedies* (1907) offer humorous and realistic stories of Jewish life. Zangwill's plays were often adaptations of his novels and used as vehicles for ideas. His play *The Melting Pot* (1908), which coined the phrase, concerns immigrants in America. Literary friends such as Jerome K. Jerome and W.W. Jacobs visited him here.

Isaac Rosenberg • 80 Whitechapel High Street

Poet and painter Isaac Rosenberg lived in Whitechapel from 1897 and went to school in Stepney Green until he was 14. He studied at the Whitechapel Art Gallery and Library, where there is a commemorative plaque. Rosenberg took evening art classes at Birkbeck College and went on to the Slade School of Art thanks to the patronage of three Jewish women. He became part of a group of avant-garde artists that included David Bomberg and Mark Gertler. He self-published *Night and Day* (1912) and *Youth* (1915) and was encouraged in his writing by Ezra Pound. Enlisting in the Army in 1915, Rosenberg was killed in April 1918.

His modernist poems explore Jewish life in the East End in vivid and striking language. 'A Ballad of Whitechapel' concerns one of the area's streetwalkers:

Arnold Circus in the Old Nichol Street neighbourhood

I watched the gleams
Of jagged warm lights on shrunk faces pale.
I heard mad laughter as one hears in dreams,
Or Hell's harsh lurid tale.

His lyrics on biblical themes are rich, spare and incisive, and he is now regarded as one of the finest poets of the First World War.

People of the Abyss

In his exploration of the East End, George Orwell followed in the footsteps of American writer Jack London, whose *The People of the Abyss* (1903) recorded his experiences of the 'lowest of the low'.

Orwell started his London tramping in spring 1928 with short trial runs *(see p246)*. He then moved to Paris, living as a 'down and out' for 18 months. He returned home to Suffolk for Christmas 1929 and resumed his tramping by going to the East End in April 1930. Before setting out, he would leave his better clothes at Mabel Fierz's house in Hampstead Garden Suburb, or else at Ruth Pitter's Chelsea studio or Richard Rees's Cheyne Walk flat (where Rees ran the *Adelphi* magazine and published Orwell's work written under his real name, E.A. Blair).

Having donned his rags, he would walk to the poorest parts of London, spending nights sleeping rough or in doss houses *(see p313)*. His experiences formed the basis of *Down and Out in Paris and London* (1933).

All day I loafed in the streets, east as far as Wapping, west as far
as Whitechapel. It was queer after Paris; everything was so much
cleaner and quieter and drearier.

Orwell learned about the street beggars, those who sold matches, bootlaces or sang hymns, the pavement artists and the organ grinders, who worked the coffee shops and pubs around Whitechapel and Commercial Road. He identified words distinct to the East End, such as a 'judy', meaning woman, and to 'bawl', meaning to suck or swallow.

From the East End he went to Southwark and tramped to Sevenoaks, following the route taken by Dickens's David Copperfield when he walks to his aunt's house in Dover. On his return, Orwell took lodgings in Tooley Street, near Tower Bridge, and attempted to spend Christmas 1931 in prison by spending all his money getting drunk on the Mile End Road. He was duly arrested, and released after two nights in the cells.

Down and Out in Paris and London was published as a 'travel book' with an epigraph from Chaucer, 'O scathful harm, condition of poverte.' Blair adopted the name of Orwell so that the book might more readily be accepted as an authentic account of a man living at the lowest ebb, as opposed to an experiment being conducted by an Old Etonian. This subtle move contributed to the novel's success and allowed Blair to continue his double life.

That's How It Was • Whitechapel High Street

The novelist, playwright and poet Maureen Duffy drew upon her East End childhood in her autobiographical novel *That's How It Was* (1962), which examines her relationship with her mother, who died of tuberculosis when she was 14. Duffy returned briefly to her East End roots in *Capital* (1975), part of her trilogy, featuring *Wounds* (1969) and *Londoners* (1983), a sardonic view of the writer's lot in an Earl's Court bedsit. She also wrote a play about Virginia Woolf, *A Nightingale in Bloomsbury Square* (1974).

The Freedom Bookshop • 84b
Whitechapel High Street at Angel Alley

This bookshop is associated with the Freedom Press, publishers of *Freedom*, an anarchist fortnightly newspaper founded in 1886 by a group of friends including Prince Peter Kropotkin and Charlotte Wilson, and *Raven*, a quarterly journal of anarchism. On the alley wall is a mural containing portraits of prominent East End anarchists, such as Kropotkin and Rudolf Rocker.

The Freedom Bookshop

The Hamlet of Stepney Green
23 Stepney Green Buildings

Dramatist, novelist and poet Bernard Kops, born in 1926 to unemployed Dutch Jewish parents, lived at No. 23 Stepney Green Buildings until it was bombed in 1940. He became associated with the Angry Young Men of the late 1950s with his first play *The Hamlet of Stepney Green* (1959). It is often linked with another play set in the East End, Arnold Wesker's *Chicken Soup with Barley* (1958).

Kops's writing was shaped by, and drew inspiration from, his life within the Jewish community in the East End – and the kind of gallows humour that accompanies the reflection that the family had avoided the Holocaust principally because they had lacked the money to return to Holland.

In the 1950s he was selling second-hand books off a barrow at Cambridge Circus, when, unimpressed by John Osborne's *Look Back In Anger* (1956), he vowed to write something better. *The Hamlet of Stepney Green* was completed quickly and accepted, although not staged, by Joan Littlewood at the Theatre Royal, Stratford. It premiered at the Oxford Playhouse and was a huge success. He became a rags-to-riches media story, but his subsequent plays did not replicate this early commercial success.

Nevertheless, Kops continued to write and be published, including an autobiography, *The World is a Wedding* (1963), and novel *By the Waters of Whitechapel* (1969). It was not until the 1990s that his work, including *Dreams of Anne Frank* (1993) and *Sailing With Homer* (1995), began to win awards and his career become fully established. His other plays include *Playing Sinatra* (1992), *Café Zeitgeist* (1997) and *Houdini* (1998).

Chicken Soup With Barley
43 Fashion Street, Spitalfields

Dramatist Arnold Wesker, born in May 1932 to unemployed eastern European Jewish immigrants, grew up in Fashion Street. He was educated at the Jews Free School, at 43a Commercial Street, and later at Upton House Central School, just round the corner from Hackney Downs, from which he was temporarily expelled in 1947. He tried but failed to get into RADA and took various menial jobs, including working as a hotel kitchen porter, before embarking on a writing career.

Inspired by Osborne's *Look Back In Anger*, Wesker wrote *Chicken Soup With Barley* in six weeks. The play concerns his communist background and the impact on his family of the Soviet invasion of Hungary in 1956. *The Wesker Trilogy*, including *Roots* (1959) and *I'm Talking About Jerusalem* (1960), enjoyed huge success at the Royal Court Theatre and sold more than half a million copies as a book. Prominent drama critics such as Kenneth Tynan and Bernard Levin championed his work.

The Kitchen (1959) evoked the stresses and conflicts in a restaurant kitchen and won praise for its dramatisation of labour. It stimulated interest in other plays of domestic realism known as 'kitchen sink drama', as distinct from the drawing-room comedies of Noël Coward and Terence Rattigan. *Chips With Everything* (1962) studied class attitudes in the RAF during National Service and was described by Harold Hobson in *The Times* as 'left-wing drama's first real breakthrough'. Wesker's subsequent plays, however, received hostile criticism, and his work in the 1970s was beset with difficulties and the premature closures of his productions. Subsequently he has found more interest in his work internationally.

His autobiography *As Much As I Dare* (1994) attacked the cult of the director and led to him being called 'The Angry Old Man of British Theatre'. His most recent plays include *Groupie* (2002) and *Longitude* (2002). He was knighted in 2006.

Dramatist and screenwriter Wolf Mankowitz was also born in Fashion Street, and set some of his work here. He wrote many original plays and screenplays, including *The Bespoke Overcoat* (1954), *A Kid For Two Farthings* (1955) – which includes the line 'Unicorns can't grow in Fashion Street, but boys have to' – *Expresso Bongo* (1958) and *The Long and the Short and the Tall* (1960), as well as adaptations of *Casino Royale* (1961), *Black Beauty* (1971) and *Treasure Island* (1973).

The X Press • 6 Hoxton Square
Founded by Dotun Adebayo and Steve Pope in 1991, the X Press published the acclaimed and explosive *Yardie* trilogy by Jamaican-born Victor Headley, consisting of *Yardie* (1992), *Excess* (1993) and *Yush!* (1994).

The *Yardie* trilogy, written with extensive use of Jamaican patois, provides a powerful portrayal of London's Jamaican immigrant criminal subculture. In 1987 'Yardie' gangs of Jamaican criminals had begun establishing strongholds in Brixton, Harlesden, Clapham and Stoke Newington, and quickly gained notoriety through their gun-toting violence.

The strong cover design and innovative promotional techniques, such as the use of flyers and selling at clubs, brought *Yardie* strong sales within the black community and mainstream publication (with Pan). Headley has subsequently published *Fetish* (1995), *The Best Man* (1999), *Off Duty* (2001) and *Seven Seals, Seven Day* (2002).

In 1994 the X Press itself gained some notoriety by sending a bullet out with the press release for the pulp fiction book *Cop Killer* by Donald Gorgon.

Dividing Lines • Brick Lane
Brick Lane was originally the centre of brick and tile manufacturing from the 1680s until the early 19th century. The other significant industry in the area was brewing – The Truman Black Eagle Brewery opened here in 1669. The building remains, but has been converted into artists' studios, workshops, retail outlets and cafés.

Over the centuries Brick Lane has been home to successive waves of immigrants, beginning with the Huguenots in the late 17th century who specialised in silk weaving. It was the heart of the Jewish community from 1880 to 1950 and since then has been the centre of the city's Bengali-speaking community. Jeremy Gavron's *An Acre Of Barren Ground* (2005) details the history of Brick Lane.

Amitav Ghosh's *The Shadow Lines* (1988) concerns the history of an Indian family living in Calcutta, with roots over the border in Dhaka and connections in London's East End. It employs the symbolism of geographical, cultural and imaginary lines to explore differing social realities and cultural identities in India and the East End. The story juxtaposes the lives of Jewish people in 1940s Brick Lane with that of Indian people in the Brick Lane of 1979.

No. 19 Princelet Street

Monica Ali's debut novel *Brick Lane* (2003), short-listed for the 2003 Booker Prize, chronicles the life of Nazneen, a girl from Bangladesh, who has an arranged marriage with Chanu, a Bangladeshi immigrant twenty years her senior, living in Tower Hamlets. At the heart of the book is Nazneen's adulterous affair with Karim, who wants to radicalise the Muslim community, in contrast to Chanu, who dreams of closer social integration. Beyond this intimate domestic setting, the novel is alive to the wider political world as it impinges on the Bangladeshi community, with the 'Bengal Tigers' arguing whether they should engage with global jihad or local injustices.

Rodinsky's Room • 19 Princelet Street

Artist Rachel Lichtenstein recorded her re-engagement with Judaism, and her attempts to understand and preserve the mysteriously abandoned room of David Rodinsky, caretaker/tenant of the former synagogue at No. 19 Princelet Street, in *Rodinsky's Room* (1999), written in collaboration with Iain Sinclair.

For Sinclair, this was a return to one of the central episodes in *Downriver* (1991), in which he had written 'Rodinsky's room was left as he had abandoned it: books on the table, grease-caked pyjamas, cheap calendar with the reproduction of Millet's 'Angelus', fixed forever at January 1963.'

The narrative, propelled by the search for Rodinsky's identity, and to discover what lay behind his sudden disappearance, is inter-cut by Sinclair's ruminations on East London history and mythology.

From its beginnings in the cramped, abandoned room in Spitalfields, the search extends into the diaspora of European Jewish history in the 20th century before the quest is finally resolved in the footprint of the M25, an area Sinclair had just begun to walk and explore for his next book, *London Orbital* (2003).

City of the Mind • Jamme Masjid Mosque, Fournier Street and Brick Lane

Penelope Lively's *City of the Mind* (1991), a multi-layered vision of London seen through the eyes of architect Matthew Holland, has him fascinated by the Jamme Masjid Mosque, Fournier Street. Dating from 1742, the building was originally a Huguenot church, before becoming first a synagogue and then a mosque. In this way, it has become a potent symbol for the population changes in this part of London.

Gilbert and George's Studio • 12 Fournier Street

This has been the studio of artists Gilbert and George since 1968. They also own houses nearby. According to Gilbert Proesch, when they moved into the area 'it was like walking into a book in the 19th century: amazing light, and a few people in the street, more like literature than reality'. Since then gentrification and an influx of artists have changed the character of the area. Gilbert and George have remained largely aloof, maintaining their outsider status and formal tailoring.

Christ Church Spitalfields

The towering Christ Church Spitalfields (built 1714–29) was designed by architect Nicholas Hawksmoor, whose churches have gripped the imaginations of Iain Sinclair in *Lud Heat* (1975) and Peter Ackroyd in *Hawksmoor* (1985).

Both Sinclair and Ackroyd see Hawksmoor's churches as centres of malevolent energies that are connected with the Ratcliff Highway and Whitechapel murders. Note, as Sinclair has done, the curious detail of the Venetian window at Christ Church. The house at No. 2 Fournier Street was also designed and built by Hawksmoor between 1726 and 1728 for the incumbent of Christ Church.

Site of Page One Bookshop and Café • 53 West Ham Lane

The performance poet Benjamin Zephaniah worked here from 1979 and started giving poetry readings locally. His first book, *Pen Rhythm* (1980), was published by Page One and quickly went into three editions. He later wrote *City Psalms* (1992) and the first rap play, *Job Rocking* (1989). Page One closed in 1987.

Theatre Royal, Stratford East • Gerry Raffles Square

Theatre director Joan Littlewood and actor-manager Gerry Raffles rented the dilapidated Victorian Theatre Royal at Angel Lane, Stratford East in February 1953 as a permanent base for their Theatre Workshop troupe.

An advocate of community and political theatre, Littlewood believed that theatre drew energy from its location and gave it back as *joie de vivre*. In the midst of urban decay, and without public subsidy, she developed a theatre and audience in East London. She trained her company on a mixture of ideas from Konstantin Stanislavski (originator of the 'method' school of acting), Bertolt Brecht and Rudolf Laban (the dance movement theorist). Littlewood eschewed decoration in favour of realism. Her production of *Volpone* was hugely successful, representing Britain at the Paris International Theatre Festival in 1955.

Success brought larger audiences and critics to Littlewood's performances. She staged a combination of English classics, such as John Marston's comedy *The Dutch Courtesan* (1605); new work by Brendan Behan and Shelagh Delaney, whose *A Taste of Honey* was performed in 1958 and hailed as a landmark in 'kitchen sink' realism; and popular musicals, such as Lionel Bart's *Fings Ain't Wot They Used T'Be* and Stephen Lewis's *Sparrers Can't Sing*. Her crowning achievement was the self-penned *Oh, What A Lovely War!* (1963), in which all of her techniques were brought together in one celebrated production. It counter-pointed the futility of the Battle of the Somme with the affirmative popular songs of the period. She was fined twice for allowing her actors to deviate from the script approved by the Lord Chamberlain's office.

Over the years many of her company went on to develop successful careers in film and television, including Harry H. Corbett, Michael Caine, Richard Harris, Barbara Windsor, Victor Spinetti and Youtha Joyce. In 1974 Angel Lane was redeveloped and renamed Gerry Raffles Square in honour of the theatre's former manager.

HACKNEY

The Birthday Party • Hackney Downs Grammar School, Downs Park Road

Harold Pinter, one of the most influential dramatists of the post-Word War II era, was born in Hackney in 1930 and educated at Hackney Downs Grammar School – now Mossbourne Community Academy. At school he discovered the works of Hemingway and Franz Kafka, whose work inspired his first full-length play, *The Birthday Party* (1957), in which two intruders, an Irishman and a Jew, mysteriously threaten an unemployed pianist in a seaside boarding house with an indictment of unexplained crimes. This air of menace pervades Pinter's major plays, which include *The Caretaker* (1960), *The Lover* (1963), *The Homecoming* (1965) and *No Man's Land* (1975). Distinctive use of pauses and the nuances of colloquial speech are the hallmarks of his work.

As a screenwriter, he has adapted L.P. Hartley's *The Go-Between* (1969) and John Fowles's *The French Lieutenant's Woman* (1982). His later plays include *Mountain Language* (1988), *Party Time* (1991) and *Ashes to Ashes* (1996), a short drama about the Holocaust.

Steven Berkoff • 25 Anthony Street

Kafka was also an inspiration for Steven Berkoff, who was born in Stepney in 1937 and grew up at No. 25 Anthony Street. Like Pinter, he too was educated at Hackney Downs Grammar School. He was downgraded to the 'C' stream, bullied and isolated.

His discovery of Kafka in 1954 helped him make sense of his outsider position. He formed the London Theatre Group in 1968, which became renowned for its physicality and use of choruses to comment, illustrate and clarify the actions of other characters.

He adapted and staged Kafka'a *Metamorphosis* (1969) and *The Trial* (1970), *Agamemnon after Aeschylus* (1973) and Poe's *The Fall of the House of Usher* (1974). His plays include *East* (1975), *Sink the Belgrano* (1986), *Brighton Beach Scumbags* (1991), *Massage* (1997), *Messiah* (2000) and *Sit and Shiver* (2004). *East* is a loosely structured play composed of nineteen scenes with a minimal plot. It employs Cockney songs, comic sketches and a mimed 'silent movie' sequence. In his use of improvisation and movement exercises, his work can be seen as an extension of Joan Littlewood's legacy, particularly with the concepts of the chorus and ensemble acting. Berkoff employs stillness as movement in the same way that Harold Pinter employs silence as language.

White Chappell, Scarlet Tracings • Albion Drive

Novelist, essayist, poet and filmmaker Iain Sinclair has lived in Albion Drive, Hackney since 1968 and uses it as a base for his walks across and around London.

Hackney, Whitechapel and Bethnal Green feature in his early trilogy, *Lud Heat* (1975), *Suicide Bridge* (1979) and *White Chappell, Scarlet Tracings* (1987), and resurface as a consistent theme throughout his subsequent work. *White Chappell, Scarlet Tracings* concerns the mythology of Jack the Ripper and the psycho-geography of East London. Self-critical and imaginatively experimental, the book blazed a trail which others have followed.

Sinclair's background as a book dealer – recalled in John Baxter's *A Pound of Paper* (2002) – underlies his analysis of the economics of culture. He uses his interests in film, pulp fiction, the Beats, the poetry of place, and mythology to subvert conventional notions of the novel form. *Radon Daughters* (1994) posits literature as both a stock exchange and a dialogue with the reader, who is invited to go on a journey.

Hackney is the base for *Lights Out for the Territory* (1997), a diary of nine walks that provide the reader with a virtual psychopathology of East London, replete with the graffiti and political subculture of Dalston; half-forgotten novelists such as Alexander Baron, who wrote *The Low Life* (1963) and Emanuel Litvinoff, who wrote *Journey Through a Small Planet* (1972); and endless dog associations, eventually leading to a re-mapping of aesthetic London.

Downriver (1991) examines the changing face of the city as seen from its evolving rail and waterways. Through a blistering narrative combining political satire and black comedy – echoing earlier writers such as Charles Dickens and Joseph Conrad, Sinclair dissects the squalor, greed, criminality and madness at the heart of London's chaotic boom and bust economy of the 1980s:

A man, a hunched solitary, is standing at the far end of the long platform, beneath a bank of television screens that play back an idealised version of the necropolis junction: pearly, dim, soft. These pictures have the quality of transmissions from a diving bell in the deepest ocean trench. Eel-grass fronds of morbid light flare from the black hole of the tunnel: an extinct monster's last breath.

Subjective, paranoid and prophetic, *Downriver* registers urban decay and terror with a glowing immediacy, and established Sinclair as a major writer. A searing indictment of the Thatcher era, with its extremes of wealth and poverty, it is one of the most potent novels of the late 20th century.

In 2003 Sinclair published *London Orbital*, a book that traces the new outer limit of the city through a circular walk shadowing the M25.

Heart of Darkness • Wapping

Located southeast of the Tower of London, Wapping grew around the Port of London and was where sailors disembarked on arrival in London. During his days as a merchant seaman, 1874–94, novelist Joseph Conrad would end his voyages here.

Anchored a little further downriver, awaiting the turn of the tide on the cruising yawl 'Nellie', the narrator of Conrad's *Heart of Darkness* (1902) reflects on the vastness that lies to the east – 'What greatness had not floated on the ebb of that river into the mystery of an unknown earth! … The dreams of men, the seed of commonwealths, the germs of empires.' – while 'farther west on the upper reaches the place of the monstrous town was still marked ominously on the sky, a brooding gloom in sunshine, a lurid glare under the stars.' As if reading his mind, Marlow, seaman and wanderer who is sitting apart from the others, in 'the pose of a Buddha preaching in European clothes', suddenly speaks out of the fading light, 'And this also … has been one of the dark places of the earth' – the thought that sets in motion his tale of 'the fascination of the abomination'.

In Iain Sinclair's *Downriver*, the bibliophile Todd Sileen obsessively collects Conrad's complete works. Sileen appears in the churchyard of St John's Church, Scandrett Street which, as Sinclair writes, was once inhabited by exotic pets that had escaped after being brought to Wapping by sailors and sold at riverside inns.

The writer, W.W. Jacobs was born in Wapping, the son of a wharf manager. He became a Post Office Savings Bank clerk and began to publish stories of dockers, bargees and retired sailors in the *Idler* and *Strand Magazine* in the 1890s. His stories, characterised by a dry humour, were collected in *Many Cargoes* (1896), *Light Freights* (1901), *The Lady of the Barge* (1902) and *Night Watches* (1914), and were often serialised on BBC radio between the world wars.

View from
The Prospect
of Whitby

Prospect of Whitby • 57 Wapping Wall

London's oldest surviving riverside pub, the Prospect of Whitby dates from 1520 and, over the centuries, has been frequented by Pepys, Dickens and Thackeray. The Pepys Society is based here and there is a Pepys Room upstairs.

In P.D. James's novel *Original Sin* (1994) an object is found floating in the Thames, 'like the domed head of a gigantic insect, its million of hairy legs stirring gently in the tide'. It turns out to be the head of a drowned body.

Ratcliff Highway Murders

The Ratcliff Highway Murders of 7 December 1811 (at No. 29, near the junction with Betts Street) and 19 December 1811 (at the King's Arms Inn, No. 81 New Gravel Lane – now Garnet Street) have fascinated writers since Thomas De Quincey wrote his famous essay 'On Murder, Considered as One of the Fine Arts' (1827).

De Quincey wrote of the 'perilous region' filled with 'manifold ruffianism', starting a trend, which many writers have followed. According to Dickens, Ratcliff Highway (now known as The Highway) was a 'reservoir of dirt, drunkenness and drabs' (*Sketches by Boz*, 1837) 'where [the] accumulated scum of humanity seemed to be washed from higher ground' (*Our Mutual Friend*, 1865).

P.D. James, with T.A. Critchley, brought Home Office forensics to bear on the Ratcliff Highway case in *The Maul and the Pear Tree*, 1972 (and later returned to Wapping for *Original Sin*, 1997). The murderer in the case, John Williams, hanged himself while in prison, and the Home Secretary allowed his body to be paraded through the streets

The Grapes

to placate the public hysteria for vengeance. He was buried with a stake through his heart at the crossroads of Cannon Street Road and Commercial Road.

Peter Ackroyd features the murders in both *Hawksmoor* and *Dan Leno and the Limehouse Golem* (1994).

Limehouse

Limehouse was named after the lime kilns that proliferated in the area, serving the shipbuilding industry in the 18th century. In *Limehouse Days* (1991) Daniel Farson provides a good introduction to the area's history.

The Grapes Inn • 76 Narrow Street

The Grapes Inn was the basis for the Six Jolly Fellowship Porters Tavern in Dickens's *Our Mutual Friend*. It is still the most 'Dickensian' of Thameside inns, with its tiny bar and narrow upstairs dining room 'a crazy wooden impending over the river… with a bar to soften the human breast'. Novelist Angus Wilson's father was born at the inn. Wilson, coincidentally or not, wrote extensively on Dickens.

Opium • West India Dock Road

After the opening of the 'Strangers' Home for Asiatics' (now called simply 'The Strangers' Home') at West India Dock Road in 1856, the area became notorious for its opium dens, an exoticism that intrigued numerous writers.

Dickens begins his last (unfinished) novel, *The Mystery of Edwin Drood* (1870), with a description of an opium den in the Docks in which:

> *Shaking from head to foot, the man whose scattered consciousness has thus fantastically pieced itself together, at length rises, supports his trembling frame upon his arms, and looks around. He is in the meanest and closest of small rooms. Through the ragged window-curtain, the light of early day steals in from a miserable court. He lies, dressed, across a large unseemly bed, upon a bedstead that has indeed given way under the weight upon it. Lying, also dressed and also across the bed, not longwise, are a Chinaman, a Lascar, and a haggard woman. The two first are in a sleep or stupor; the last is blowing at a kind of pipe, to kindle it. And as she blows, and shading it with her lean hand, concentrates its red spark of light, it serves in the dim morning as a lamp to show him what he sees of her.*

Oscar Wilde in *The Picture of Dorian Gray* (1890) has the eponymous hero visit a Limehouse opium den in an attempt to cure his soul. And in Joseph Conrad's *Chance* (1913) a sea captain, staying at the Eastern Hotel on West India Dock Road, describes the passers-by 'in their shabby garments, with sallow faces, haggard, anxious or weary, or simply without expression'.

Daniel Farson • 92 Narrow Street

Writer and biographer Daniel Farson lived here from 1958 to 64, and gives an account of his experiences in his autobiography, *Never A Normal Man* (1997). He was one of the links between the Soho bohemians and East End gangsters. He arranged for Joan Littlewood to film a scene from *Sparrows Can't Sing* (1962) at one of the Krays' clubs. He owned the Waterman's Arms, on the Isle of Dogs, from 1962 to 64. Francis Bacon, John Deakin, William Burroughs and Claudette Colbert were among those who mingled with the locals.

Down and Out • Limehouse Causeway

George Orwell, in his guise as a tramp in *Down and Out in Paris and London (see also pp246 & 302)*, secured a bed in a doss house in Limehouse Causeway. Here he saw an impromptu religious service, conducted by 'a grave and reverend seignior', being ignored by the lodgers.

You Don't Crucify People! Not on Good Friday! • Docklands

As sharp as one of his anti-hero's suits, playwright Barrie Keefe's screenplay for *The Long Good Friday* (1980) traces the downfall of gangland boss Harold Shand, who, in the middle of planning a major property development with the Mafia, finds his East End organisation under attack.

In this intricately plotted thriller Shand, brilliantly played by Bob Hoskins, discovers that he has unwittingly crossed rivals whose connections, expertise and dedication to violence outclass his own. Filmed in pre-development Docklands, *The Long Good Friday* fills the screen with images of a violent and corrupt London and, with a vibrantly sexy performance by Helen Mirren and an excellent supporting cast, retains an iconic status.

The Thames at Wapping

SOUTH LONDON

FOR MANY CENTURIES the area south of London, beyond the compact settlement of Southwark, consisted of villages and farmland. When, for example, the ailing Pepys moved out of the City in 1701 to see out the remainder of his days in the house of his former servant Will Hewer, Clapham consisted of little more than a few houses gathered around a church. By 1904, however, the French poet Guillaume Apollinaire was taking the Tube down to the distinctly suburban Clapham in a last ditch attempt to win the love of one Annie Playden.

There are more open spaces and parks south of the Thames than to the north, and perhaps this is why, despite the spread of Victorian urban- and suburbanisation, several of South London's hubs still retain the village constituents of church, green and pub. In Wimbledon, Clapham, Dulwich and, arguably, Deptford, it is not hard to peel back the centuries. The poet and writer Edward Thomas was inspired by the natural history of southwest London, and it is still possible to visualise his walks and cycle rides over the commons of Clapham, Wandsworth and Wimbledon.

There are several writers associated with the Clapham environs, most notably Graham Greene and his novel *The End of the Affair*, which is suffused with the social and geographical landscape of Clapham Common. For the most part, however, the story of literature in South London is a fractured tale of disparate elements – Marlowe stabbed in Deptford; Blake seeing angels on Peckham Rye; John Ruskin eulogising the Pre-Raphaelite painters from a house on Denmark Hill; Émile Zola exiled to a small hotel in Upper Norwood; Hanif Kureishi soaking up the peccadillos of suburban life in Beckenham and Bromley. Dulwich College has produced many writers, including P.G. Wodehouse, Raymond Chandler, Michael Ondaatje and Graham Swift.

Brixton, probably the most urban, vibrant and diverse neighbourhood of South London, has produced or influenced writers as varied as Wendy Cope, Linton Kwesi Johnson, C.L.R. James and Geoff Dyer. The area was developed as a suburban retreat following the opening of Brixton railway station in 1862. It soon became a popular place to lodge for actors and music hall performers. Angela Carter drew upon this heritage for her final novel, *Wise Children*, which mixes theatrical traditions with the celebratory aspects of Caribbean culture that imbue the neighbourhood today.

South London

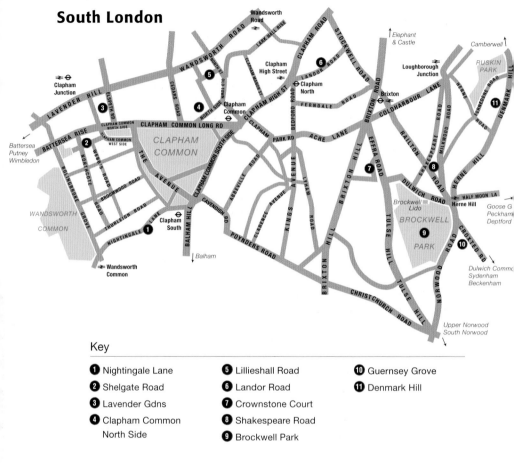

Key

1. Nightingale Lane
2. Shelgate Road
3. Lavender Gdns
4. Clapham Common North Side
5. Lillieshall Road
6. Landor Road
7. Crownstone Court
8. Shakespeare Road
9. Brockwell Park
10. Guernsey Grove
11. Denmark Hill

St Nicholas's Church • Deptford Green

St Nicholas's has a memorial tablet to playwright Christopher Marlowe, who was buried here in an unmarked grave on 1 June 1593. Marlowe's death, by fatal stabbing on 30 May 1593, has long been a matter of conjecture and argument.

The churchman and author Francis Meres – whose commonplace book *Palladis Tamia* (*Wits Treasury*, 1598) is an important source for establishing the chronology of Shakespeare's plays – wrote that Marlowe was 'stabbed to death by a bawdy serving-man, a rival of his in his lewd love' as punishment for his 'epicurism and atheism'. Over the years, however, the opinion that he was killed accidentally in a drunken fight gained greater currency, and this is how his death was recorded in the 1917 edition of the *National Dictionary of Biography*.

In 1925 the scholar Leslie Hotson discovered the coroner's report on Marlowe's death. This reported that Marlowe, following an argument over a bill, had started a fight in which he was fatally stabbed 'above his right eye'. Ingram Frizer is named as the man who (accidentally) caused Marlowe's death.

However, a wealth of circumstantial evidence suggests Marlowe was not killed accidentally, but murdered. Park Honan's very thorough biography *Christopher Marlowe: Poet & Spy* (2005) outlines and analyses the known facts.

Marlowe and Frizer, Thomas Walsingham's business agent, had spent the day at Eleanor Bull's guesthouse, together with government agent Robert Poley and Frizer's friend, the state hireling and thug Nicholas Skeres. At this time Marlowe was on bail from the Queen's Council.

Marlowe had been at Walsingham's home at Scadbury Manor, in Kent, when the Queen's Council had put him under arrest. Although no specific reference was made to charges of blasphemy and atheism within the text, the warrant effectively altered Marlowe's relationship with his patron, Walsingham, who at this time was scheming against Elizabeth (and for James of Scotland). Frizer, it is argued, invited Marlowe to a 'feast' at Mrs Bull's, the outcome of which was the poet's death. Frizer was pardoned by the Queen's Council within a month, and through his work for Walsingham he later gained property and sufficient income to retire.

The suspicion, controversy and mystery surrounding Marlowe's life and death have provided inspiration for a number of novelists, notably Anthony Burgess, whose *A Dead Man in Deptford* was published in 1993.

Marlowe's work has proven no less controversial – even to this day. In 1599 his translation of *Ovid* was banned and copies publicly burned as part of the ongoing suppression of material that transgressed the policy of religious uniformity that had been adopted by Elizabeth I and continued to be enforced by her Archbishop, John Whitgift (who had attended Elizabeth on her deathbed and crowned James I).

In November 2005 the director of a production of Marlowe's *Tamburlaine*, which transferred from the Bristol Old Vic to the Barbican Arts Centre in London, was accused of censorship by excising the original text's disparaging references to Mohammed, and by having Tamburlaine defile books representing all religions, as opposed to specifically burning the Koran.

St Nicholas Church, Deptford

Shakespeare's early histories are strongly influenced by Marlowe, and Shakespeare paid tribute to him as the 'dead shepherd' in *As You Like It* (1599). The poet Michael Drayton, a near contemporary, praised him thus:

> *Next Marlow, bathed in the Thespian Springs,*
> *Had in him those brave translunary things,*
> *That the first poets had.*

Dulwich College • Dulwich Common

Actor and entertainment entrepreneur Edward Alleyn founded Dulwich College on 21 June 1619 with letters patent from King James I.

Alleyn had bought the manorial estate of Dulwich in 1605. The estate extended from Denmark Hill to the Crystal Palace grounds on Sydenham Hill, in between Lordship Lane on the east and Croxted Road on the west. William Blake and his disciple Samuel Palmer – who called it 'the Gate into the world of vision' – frequented this valley of fields and surrounding wooded hillside. P.G. Wodehouse, who was educated at Dulwich College and retained a lifelong affection for the school, named the estate 'Valley Fields' in his books. His school novels, such as *Mike*, *The Gold Bat*, and *The White Feather* include thinly disguised portraits of Dulwich College figures.

Though born in Chicago, Raymond Chandler spent most of his formative years in London. He attended Dulwich College and later worked as a freelance journalist for *The Westminster Gazette* and *The Spectator*. During the First World War he served in France, returning to the United States in 1919. He settled in California and pursued a career in the oil business, eventually becoming Vice-President of the Dabney Oil Syndicate. However, in 1932 he was fired for drinking and absenteeism and turned to writing fiction. His short story *Blackmailers Don't Shoot* was published in *Black Mask* magazine in December 1933, and thereafter he enjoyed increasing success. His first novel, *The Big Sleep* (1939), introduced his wisecracking detective narrator, Philip Marlowe, named in part after playwright Christopher Marlowe.

Novelists Michael Ondaatje, Graham Swift and several younger Asian dramatists and writers including Chiwetel Ejiofor were also educated at Dulwich.

Ondaatje, a Canadian writer, born in Sri Lanka of Dutch-Tamil-Singhalese extraction, won the Booker Prize with his novel *The English Patient* (1992). Graham Swift's *Last Orders* (1996) was another Booker winner. The story revolves around the journey of four Bermondsey pub regulars who are intent on fulfilling the last wish of their friend Jack – that his ashes be scattered in the sea at Margate. Employing a multiplicity of narrative voices, *Last Orders* has echoes of *The Canterbury Tales*.

In Charles Dickens's *The Pickwick Papers* (1836) the eponymous hero retires to Dulwich, where he contemplates the paintings in the Dulwich Picture Gallery.

By contrast, the sex-obsessed, middle-aged TV critic at the centre of Howard Jacobson's *No More Mr Nice Guy* (1998) decides that Dulwich is not the place for him.

John Ruskin • Denmark Hill

Art critic John Ruskin lived at No. 163 Denmark Hill, opposite Ferndene Road, from 1842 to 1852 and from 1854 to 1872. The property included a stable, farmyard, pigsty and a porter's lodge. Here Ruskin completed the second volume of *Modern Painters* (1848), in which he championed the work of J.M.W. Turner.

Ruskin began the first volume of *Modern Painters* (1843) in his parents' house at No. 28 Herne Hill. The family lived there from March 1823 until October 1842. In 1851 his father secured the lease of No. 30 Herne Hill for his son and wife, Effie Gray, to occupy. Following the collapse of his marriage, Ruskin returned to Denmark Hill in 1854.

Ruskin was a mentor and supporter of Rossetti, Millais and Holman Hunt, and his letter to *The Times* in 1851 marked a turning point in appreciation of the Pre-Raphaelites. The ideas of this artist, philosopher, poet, environmentalist and social commentator inspired the Arts and Crafts movement as well as the founding of the National Trust and Society for the Protection of Ancient Buildings. A Christian Socialist, he taught at the Working Men's College, London, until he became Slade Professor of Art at Oxford. He endowed the Ruskin School of Art, where draughtsmanship is still taught, and the Guild of St George.

The Arts Man • Peckham Rye

The Ballad of Peckham Rye (1960) by Muriel Spark charts the mayhem let loose following the arrival in Peckham of Dougal Douglas M.A., self-professed 'devil', with the ability 'to drive devils out of people.'

Hired as 'Arts Man' by two local textile factory owners to 'bring vision into the lives of the workers', his interventions have the effect of unleashing the latent aggression and hostility within the tightly class-based environment of the factory, resulting in fraud, blackmail, violence and finally murder.

At the beginning of this circular structured novel, Humphrey Place embarks on a pub crawl at the Rye Hotel (which stood at No. 31 Peckham Rye), crosses the road to the White Horse (No. 29), proceeds to the Morning Star (No. 231 Rye Lane), the Heaton Arms (No. 249 Rye Lane) and the Harbinger, which is probably based on the Hope Inn, at the corner of Elm Grove in Rye Lane.

The Hope, Rye Lane

Blake mural at
Goose Green

Walking with Elaine, a process controller at one of the textile factories, to Camberwell, Douglas quotes Ruskin on his doomed relationship with Charlotte Wilkes – 'I walked with her to Camberwell Green, and we said good-bye rather sorrowfully at the corner of New Road; and that possibility of meek happiness vanished for ever.'

A Tree Filled with Angels • Goose Green, East Dulwich

There is a mural to William Blake's 1767 vision of 'a tree filled with angels, bright angelic wings bespangling every bough like stars' (the mulberry trees of Peckham Rye) at Goose Green, which was originally a village green connected to Peckham Rye common. It is on a wall at the junction of Ady's Road and Hinckley Road.

Enid Blyton was born very close to the green, in a flat above a shop on Lordship Lane. A teacher and journalist, she was the most prolific children's writer of the 20th century, publishing more than 600 books. She wrote *Noddy Goes to Toyland* (1949), the *Famous Five* series and was the first children's author to be published in paperback.

The novelist and art historian Anita Brookner, who won the Booker Prize with *Hotel du Lac* (1984), attended James Allen's Girls School (JAGs), East Dulwich Grove, in the 1940s. She was the first woman to be named Slade Professor of Art at Cambridge University in 1967. From 1904 to 1920 Gustav Holst was music master at JAGs.

Alleyn's School, at Townley Road, was founded by Edward Alleyn in 1619 and established as a boys' school in 1882. The writers V.S. Pritchett and C.S. Forester, author of the *Hornblower* series of novels, both attended the school. Pritchett left in 1915 to work in the leather trade, but went on to become one of the acknowledged masters of the 20th-century short story. His first collection was *The Spanish Virgin* (1930); other notable collections include *When My Girl Comes Home* (1961) and *The Camberwell Beauty* (1974).

Forester's work has seen something of a revival in recent years, culminating in a television series based on the *Hornblower* novels. He also wrote *The African Queen* (1935), filmed in 1951 starring Humphrey Bogart and Katharine Hepburn. More recently, actors Julian Glover, Simon Ward and Jude Law were educated at Alleyn's.

English Poetry Renaissance • 40 Guernsey Grove, Herne Hill

Poet and critic Eric Mottram lived here from September 1972 until his death in 1995. He was editor of *The Poetry Review* (1971–77) and coined the phrase 'The English Poetry Renaissance' for those poets who, between 1960 and 1975, had reacted against the insularity of the Movement group, which was hostile to Modernism and Internationalism. The Movement group included poets such as Philip Larkin and Kingsley Amis. Mottram became Professor of English and American Literature at King's College, London in October 1982.

He wrote extensively on William Burroughs, Allen Ginsberg, Ezra Pound and Basil Bunting, and published thirty-six collections of poetry, including *A Book of Herne: 1975–81* (1981) and *Selected Poems* (1989). His home was a centre for a generation of 1960s poets, including Jeff Nuttall, Allen Fisher and Bill Griffiths.

Making Cocoa for Kingsley Amis • Brockwell Park

A gifted parodist, Wendy Cope sprang to fame with her first collection *Making Cocoa for Kingsley Amis* (1984) which, in addition to the celebrated title poem, contained the 'Strugnell Sonnets' – Strugnell being a benignly hopeless suburban would-be poet who inhabits an enjoyably seedy 1970s world of pubs, joints and 'birds':

> *Here with a bag of Crisps beneath the Bough,*
> *A Can of Beer, a Radio – and Thou*
> *Beside me half-asleep in Brockwell Park*
> *And Brockwell Park is Paradise now*

A second, much darker, volume followed in 1992 – *Serious Concerns*, which expresses the sense of isolation she felt at the time as a freelance writer living alone in London without a partner. In her latest book, *If I Don't Know* (2001), domestic contentment has replaced that earlier angst, echoing a happier change in circumstances and a move to Winchester.

Brockwell
Park

What a Joy It is to Dance and Sing!

Novelist and poet Angela Carter set her final novel, *Wise Children* (1991), in Brixton, drawing on the area's associations with music hall and cultural resistance. The book's many Shakespearean references imply a congruence between Caribbean culture and Elizabethan revelry. This novel of renewal and regeneration – with its refrain 'What a joy it is to dance and sing!' – revolves around the history of two theatrical families, the Hazards and the Chances. The Chances live at No. 49 Bard Road, a reference to Brixton's 'poets corner' – a grouping of roads between Brockwell Park and Railton Road named after Chaucer, Shakespeare, Milton and Spenser.

Inglan is a Bitch • Junction of Railton Road and Shakespeare Road, Brixton

Jamaican reggae poet and performer Linton Kwesi Johnson contributed to the radical publication *Race Today*, which had its office and advice centre here, in an old kitchen utensil shop, from the early 1970s until 1991 (an advice centre is still there today).

Railton Road, known locally as 'the frontline' during the 1970s and 80s, was at the fulcrum of the April 1981 Brixton Riots. *Race Today* published Johnson's first book, *Voices of the Living and the Dead* (1974), in which disaffection and dissent find a powerful voice. In 1975 he released *Dread Beat An' Blood*, in book and album form, followed in 1980 with *Inglan Is A Bitch* and *Tings An' Times* (1991).

In 1977 Johnson held the post of writer in residence for the Borough of Lambeth. A selected poems, *Mi Revalueshanay Fren*, was published in 2002.

No. 165
Railton
Road,
Brixton

Beyond a Boundary • 165 Railton Road, Brixton

The Trinidadian historian, novelist, critic and cricket writer C.L.R. James lived here in
a one-bedroom flat in the 1980s, the last decade of his life. He had first come to
Britain in the 1930s and in the intervening years had lived and worked in the USA and
Caribbean. His many works include *Minty Alley* (1936), about the intrigues of mixed-
race lodgers in a West Indian boarding house, and *Beyond a Boundary*, essays on the
socio-historical and political context of cricket. Like those other great cricket writers,
Neville Cardus and John Arlott, James wrote for the *Manchester Guardian* on cricket,
extolling the virtues of George Headley, Garfield Sobers and socialist politics.

Brixton Rock

In *Brixton Rock* (1999) and *East of Acre Lane* (2001), novelist Alex Wheatle recreates
the sights, sounds and flavours of 1980s Brixton: the fruit and vegetables piled high in
the market, the chaos of the crowds milling around the Tube station, the ever-present
soundtrack of reggae – details shored against the tide of hopelessness and violence
that threatens to overwhelm his youthful protagonists.

Ⅰ *Checkers* (2002), co-written with Mark Parham, is a tale of gangland turf wars
raging across South London and the East End, while in *The Seven Sisters* (2003)
Wheatle, who was brought up in care himself, tells the story of four boys on the run
from a life of abuse in a children's home. The novel is set in the hinterland between
rural Surrey and suburban Croydon.

Morrissey meets George Steiner • Crownstone Court, Brixton

Novelist and essayist Geoff Dyer's semi-autobiographical first novel, *The Colour of Memory* (1989), is a wistful and joyous celebration of friendship in Brixton in the early 1980s. The characters, including aspiring writer and occasional spectacle-wearer Freddie ('My new affectation … one part Morrissey to one part George Steiner') and painter Steranko are D.H.S.S. bohemians – slackers *avant la lettre*. They drift in and out of work, pubs and love affairs, sunbathe and party on the roof of the building where they live ('the single best thing about the block') and watch afternoons turn into evenings discussing Callas, Coltrane and Nietzsche.

Dyer's subsequent work includes *But Beautiful* (1991), a series of semi-fictional portraits of jazz greats; *Out of Sheer Rage* (1998), a study of D. H. Lawrence that's every bit as quirky and original as Lawrence's own *Studies in Classic American Literature*; and *Yoga For People Who Can't Be Bothered To Do It* (2003), the self-help book he couldn't be bothered to write. In 2005 he published *The Ongoing Moment*, a characteristically idiosyncratic contemplation of photography.

Song of the Poorly Loved • 75 Landor Road

In May 1904 the French poet Guillaume Apollinaire, whose real name was Willhelm de Kostrowitzky, came to London in pursuit of Annie Playden, a young Englishwoman he had fallen in love with in Germany, where she had been working as a governess. She had bright blue eyes and, he noted in a letter to a friend 'great tits, and a behind.' Annie had declined his marriage proposal to her on a German mountainside and returned to Clapham. Undaunted, he pursued her and threatened to break the door down here. Her parents forbade his entry.

While in London Apollinaire stayed with the Albanian writer, scholar and diplomat Faik Bey Konitza *(see p162)*, and travelled down to Clapham by Tube. In fear of his jealous rages, Annie left to take up a governess post in California, never to return. An Apollinaire scholar tracked her down in New York in 1951. She had no idea that the 'Kostro' she had known had become Apollinaire, one of the most celebrated French poets of the 20th century, and that the poems he had written about their affair – such as 'Annie' and 'L'Emigrant de Landor Road' – included one of his greatest works: 'La Chanson du Mal-Aime' ('Song of the Poorly Loved'). It begins:

> *One foggy night in London town*
> *A hoodlum who resembled so*
> *My love came marching up to me –*
> *The look he threw me caused my eyes*
> *To drop and made me blush with shame*

Greeneland • 14 Clapham Common North

Graham Greene lived here from 1935 until 1940 with his first wife Vivien Dayrell-Browning and their children. He worked as a book and film reviewer for *The Spectator* as well as co-editing the weekly periodical *Night and Day*. However, his review of *Wee Willie Winkie* (1937) and criticism of Hollywood's exploitation of child star Shirley Temple led to a messy lawsuit and the closure of *Night and Day*.

A prolific writer, Greene began to travel abroad in search of new material. A 400-mile trek through the jungles of Liberia provided the substance for *Journey Without Maps* (1936). *Brighton Rock* (1938), set among the criminal underworld of that seaside town, became his first big success and fuelled a desire to live on the edge. With its murders, corruption, and probing examination of justice, *Brighton Rock* foreshadows the religious complexity and ambiguities of his later work.

His trip to Mexico to investigate alleged atrocities against Catholics led to *The Lawless Roads* (1939) and, arguably his masterpiece, *The Power and the Glory* (1940). It was in *Horizon* that the critic Arthur Calder-Marshall described the atmosphere of his novels as 'Greeneland', and the epithet has stuck.

In *Memoirs of the Forties* (1965), Julian Maclaren-Ross describes visiting Greene in Clapham in July 1938 to discuss the dramatisation of Greene's *A Gun For Sale*. Greene was amazed that Maclaren-Ross combined writing with a job as a vacuum-cleaner salesman; this became Wormald's occupation in *Our Man in Havana* (1958).

At the outbreak of the Second World War his family was evacuated to the country and Greene joined the Ministry of Information. In 1940, during the Blitz, his Queen Anne home was hit by a bomb. Greene escaped harm because he was with his lover, the illustrator Dorothy Glover, at the time. His wartime novel *The End of the Affair* (1951) draws on this experience (as well as that of a later affair with Catherine Wolston, *see p201*), and is set in and around Clapham Common. It is with 'the sight of Henry Miles slanting across the wide river of rain' that the story begins, on that 'black wet January night on the Common, in 1946'.

After numerous affairs, Greene finally left his wife in 1948, declaring himself 'a bad husband and fickle lover'.

No. 14 Clapham Common North Side

Home • 34 Lillieshall Road, Clapham

A Victorian terraced family house in a typical Victorian suburb – and the subject of Julie Myerson's *Home: The Story of Everyone Who Ever Lived In Our House* (2003), in which Myerson explores the history of her house and the lives of those who have lived there.

Working from 1877 when the house was built, Myerson introduces the reader to previous occupants, such as Charlotte and Henry Hayward (1881–93) and their three children, who were the same ages as Myerson's own children, and Mavis Jones-Wohl, who in 1948 holds her wedding reception in her room on the first floor. Excavating and imagining the lives of her predecessors in vivid detail, she evokes the extraordinary character of every 'ordinary' life.

Roving reporter • 33 Lavender Gardens, Battersea

Novelist and Crimean war correspondent G.A. Henty lived here. Henty's life as a roving war reporter provided the settings for his popular adventure stories for boys mainly based on military history. His stories include *The Young Buglers* (1880), *Under Drake's Flag* (1883), *With Clive in India* (1884) and *With Buller in Natal* (1901). He was a prolific writer, sometimes producing three or four books a year, many of which ran into several editions.

Edward Thomas • 61 Shelgate Street, Battersea

Poet, critic and travel writer Edward Thomas lived at his parental home from 1888 until 1900. His only novel, *The Happy Go Lucky Morgans* (1913), is partly set in the area. He had been born to Welsh parents at what is now No. 14 Lansdowne Gardens in March 1878. His family moved in and around Wandsworth Common until settling here. Edward was fascinated by birds, especially pigeons, and went fishing in ponds and canals, studied butterflies and moths, and explored rural south London, walking long distances southwards.

In Pursuit of Spring • Nightingale Lane, Clapham

On 21 March 1913 Edward Thomas set off on bicycle from Clapham through Wandsworth Common southwards en route to Salisbury and, eventually, the Quantock Hills in a quest for signs of spring and renewal along the way. His poetic account of the journey through south London and rural England, *In Pursuit of Spring* (1914), written against the backdrop of impending war, is a classic of English travel writing.

> *The suburban by-streets already looked rideable; but they were false prophets. For example, the surface between the west end of Nightingale Lane and the top of Burntwood Lane was fit only for fancy cycling-in and out among a thousand lakes a yard wide and three inches deep.*

Rose & Crown, Wimbledon

His friend, the American poet Robert Frost, was so impressed by the poetic nature of the book that he persuaded Thomas to start writing more poetry. Thomas was killed in the First World War, his death coming during the Arras offensive on Easter Day, 1917. His poetry was published posthumously and includes a *Collected Poems* published in 1978.

Algernon Swinburne • The Pines, 11 Putney Hill

Algernon Swinburne lived here, in a joint tenancy with Theodore Watts-Dunton (who gradually weaned him away from excessive drinking), from 1879 until his death in 1909. Rossetti's pictures covered the walls of the house. Ford Hueffer (later Ford Madox Ford), William Morris and Max Beerbohm, who described the tamed Swinburne in his 1899 essay 'No. 2 The Pines', visited him.

Swinburne wrote many works here, including his studies of *Shakespeare* (1880), *Marlowe* (1883) and *Ben Jonson* (1889), *Poems and Ballads: Third Series* (1889) and his last subdued volumes, such as *Astrophel* (1894), *A Tale of Balem* (1896) and *A Channel Passage* (1904). Such was Swinburne's fame in the 1890s that crowds would gather to watch him drinking at the Rose & Crown pub in Wimbledon.

No Direction Home • Lynton Cottage, Mount Gardens, Sydenham

Robert Shelton moved to this tiny cottage off Sydenham Hill in the early 1970s to concentrate on writing his biography of Bob Dylan, *No Direction Home*. Shelton, a journalist for the *New York Times*, had been the first person to review a gig by Dylan, and had been with him from the early years to the motorcycle crash of 1966. He left New York to escape the music industry and any pressures that might issue from Dylan's office. In New York he had been at the centre of a thriving social and cultural scene, whereas in Sydenham he found himself increasingly isolated and out of touch.

Notes and background material for the book took up an entire room of which few visitors were allowed even a glimpse for fear that the uncirculated tapes and other rarities might go missing. He spent years writing and re-writing some 300,000 words for a planned two-volume biography. In the end, he had to cut the length by a third to meet his American publisher's revised demands. The book was published in 1986 to mixed reviews, but provides the most complete account of Dylan's early years. Shelton died in 1995, aged 69, in his adopted home town of Brighton.

A big modern villa of staring brick • 12 Tennison Road, South Norwood

Sir Arthur Conan Doyle, creator of Sherlock Holmes, lived here with his family from 1891 to 1894, during which time he wrote twenty-one of the sixty adventures of the world's most famous consulting detective – though ironically *The Norwood Builder* was written after he had left the area. Conan Doyle's happiness in Norwood is recorded in the novel *Beyond the City*, a tale of suburban romance. He received many visitors here, including J.M. Barrie (with whom he wrote an operetta), Jerome K. Jerome and Bram Stoker (author of *Dracula* and the agent of actor Henry Irving). In 1894 when his wife Louise was diagnosed with tuberculosis, they left for Switzerland for her to convalesce.

J'Accuse • 122 Church Road, Upper Norwood

Émile Zola's first visit to London was in 1893 at the invitation of the Institute of Journalists. He hesitated before accepting as only five years earlier his English publisher Henry Vizetelly had been fined and imprisoned for publishing what had been judged an obscene libel – Zola's *The Soil* (*La Terre*). However, the visit went well. He was put up at the Savoy, fêted at the Athenaeum Club and taken on a trip by river down to Greenwich by novelist George Moore.

Zola returned to London on 19 July 1898 in an effort to avoid imprisonment following his intervention into the Dreyfus case in France. The case centred on Alfred Dreyfus, a Jewish officer who had been convicted for spying. Zola had denounced the conviction in an open letter to the President entitled *J'Accuse* and published in the *L'Aurore* newspaper. For this, Zola had been found guilty of libel and sentenced to a year's imprisonment.

Vizetelly helped Zola evade the press and the French spies. He ended up on 15 October at the Queen's Hotel (later Quality Hotel), where he spent most of his exile, from October 1898 to June 1899, receiving occasional visits from his wife, Alexandrine, and his mistress, Jeanne. Zola used the eight months he spent in Norwood working on his novel *Fécondité* (1899) and took more than one hundred photographs in and around Norwood and Crystal Palace.

The Buddha of Suburbia • Beckenham High Street
Novelist and screenwriter Hanif Kureishi's *The Buddha of Suburbia* (1990) is set in and around Bromley, where the author grew up and attended Technical College. Kureishi's screenplays include *My Beautiful Laundrette* (1986), *Sammy and Rosie Get Laid* (1987) and *My Son The Fanatic* (1997). *The Buddha of Suburbia*, resonantly narrated by bisexual Karim Amir, 'an Englishman, born and bred, almost', offers a comic portrayal of multicultural south London life – sex, drugs, rock 'n' roll and yoga.

Questions of culture and identity are key themes in Kureishi's work, often explored through gay, lesbian or bisexual characters. The relationship between Omar and Johnny is central to *My Beautiful Laundrette* as is Karim's bisexuality in *The Buddha of Suburbia*.

Kureishi returned to Bromley as a setting in his memoir of his father, *My Ear at His Heart* (2004). Kureishi's father, Rafiushan, came to London in 1947, married an Englishwoman and moved to Bromley. He worked as a civil servant in the Pakistani embassy, but throughout his life wrote novels and plays, none of which were published.

Kureishi's other works include *The Black Album* (1995), a novel examining themes of race and religion in contemporary London, and a confessional novella *Intimacy* (1998), narrated by a man about to leave his partner and sons.

Selected Bibliography

Ackroyd, Peter – *Dickens* Sinclair Stevenson 1990
Ackroyd, Peter – *Blake* Sinclair Stevenson 1995
Ackroyd, Peter – *London: The Biography* Chatto & Windus 2000
Ackroyd, Peter – *Albion* Chatto & Windus 2002
Baker, Deborah – *In Extremis: The life of Laura Riding* Hamish Hamilton 1993
Barbera, Jack & McBrien, William – *Stevie* Heinemann 1985
Barrow, Andrew – *Quentin & Philip: A Double Portrait* Macmillan 2002
Bate, Jonathan – *The Genius of Shakespeare* Picador 1997
Bate, Jonathan – *John Clare* Picador 2003
Baxter, John – *A Pound Of Paper* Bantam 2004
Bedford, Sybille – *Aldous Huxley: A Biography Vol. 1* Paladin Books 1987
Bell, Quentin – *Virginia Woolf* Hogarth Press 1972
Benedetti, Jean – *David Garrick* Methuen 2001
Bentley, G.E. Jr. – *Blake Records/Blake Records Supplement*
    The Clarendon Press 1969/1989
Bernard, Jeffrey – *Reach For The Ground: The Downhill Struggle of Jeffrey Bernard*
    Duckworth 1996
Betjeman, John – *Summoned By Bells* John Murray 1960
Blunden, Edmund – *Leigh Hunt* Cobden-Sanderson 1930
Bowen, Elizabeth – *The Death of the Heart* Penguin 1962
Bowker, Gordon – *George Orwell* Little Brown 2003
Braybrooke, Neville & June – *Olivia Manning: A Life* Chatto & Windus 2004
Brooker, Peter – *Bohemia in London* Palgrave 2004
Burford, E.J. – *Royal St James's* Robert Hale 1988
Burgess, Anthony – *Little Wilson and Big God* Weidenfeld & Nicolson 1986
Burney, Fanny – *Journals And Letters* Penguin 2001
Burton, Sarah – *A Double Life* Viking 2003
Butler, Marilyn – *Romantics, Rebels & Reactionaries* OUP 1981
Carpenter, Humphrey – *Dennis Potter* Faber & Faber 1998
Chilcott, Tim – *A Publisher And His Circle* RKP 1972
Chisholm, Kate – *Fanny Burney* Chatto & Windus 1998
Chitty, Susan Ed. – *Antonia White Diaries 1926-57* Virago 1992
Clark, Alan – *Diaries: Into Politics* (Ed. Ion Trewin) Weidenfeld & Nicolson 2000
Clark, Alan – *The Last Diaries: In and Out of the Wilderness* Weidenfeld & Nicolson 2002
Coe, Jonathan – *Like a Fiery Elephant: The Story of BS Johnson* Picador 2004
Cook, Elizabeth (Ed) – *John Keats: The Major Works* OUP 1990
Cope, Wendy – *Making Cocoa for Kingsley Amis* Faber & Faber 1986
Cox, Jeffrey N. – *Poetry and Politics In The Cockney School* Cambridge University Press 1998
Crick, Bernard – *George Orwell: A Life* Penguin 1982
Cross, Tom – *Artists and Bohemians* Quiller Press 1992
Davin, Dan – *Closing Time* OUP 1975
Devas, Nicolette – *Two Flamboyant Fathers* Collins 1966
Donne, John – *The Complete English Poems* Penguin 1986
Drabble, Margaret – *The Oxford Companion to English Literature* OUP 2000
Dun, Aidan Andrew – *Vale Royal* Goldmark 1995
Dunn, Jane – *Antonia White: A Life* Virago 2000

Duffy, Maureen – *The Passionate Shepherdess: The Life of Aphra Behn* Phoenix Press 1989

Dyer, Geoff – *The Colour of Memory* Cape 1989

Erdal, Jennie – *Ghosting* Canongate 2004

Farson, Daniel – *The Gilded Gutter Life of Francis Bacon* Vintage 1994

Farson, Daniel – *Never A Normal Man* Harper Collins 1997

Fisher, Clive – *Cyril Connolly* Macmillan 1995

FitzGibbon, Constantine – *Life of Dylan Thomas* Dent 1965

FitzGibbon, Theodora – *With Love* Century Press 1982

Feinstein, Elaine – *Ted Hughes* Weidenfeld & Nicolson 2001

Ferguson, Robert – *The Short Sharp Life of T.E. Hulme* Allen Lane 2002

Ferris, Paul – *Dylan Thomas: The Biography* Dent 1999

Foreman, Amanda – *Georgiana Duchess of Devonshire* Harper Collins 1998

Foster, R.E. – *W.B. Yeats: A Life Vol. I The Apprentice* Magi OUP 1997

Foster, R.E. – *W.B.Yeats: A Life Vol. II The Arch Poet* OUP 2003

Fraser, Robert – *The Chameleon Poet: A Life of George Barker* Cape 2001

Frewin, Leslie – *The Café Royal Story* Hutchinson Benham 1963

Gascoyne, David – *Collected Journals 1936-1942* Skoob Books 1991

Gellhorn, Martha – *Travels With Myself and Another* Allen Lane 1978

Gittings, Robert – *John Keats* Penguin 2001

Glinert, Ed – *A Literary Guide to London* Penguin 2000

Gould, Tony – *Insider Outsider* Allison & Busby 1993

Gray, Michael – *Song & Dance Man III: The Art of Bob Dylan* Continuum 2000

Greene, Graham – *The Ministry of Fear* Heinemann 1943

Greene, Graham – *The End of the Affair* Heinemann 1951

Greene, Graham – *The Human Factor* Bodley Head 1978

Grundy, Isobel – *Lady Mary Wortley Montagu* OUP 1999

Grayling, A.C. – *The Quarrel of the Age* Weidenfeld & Nicolson 2000

Grigson, Geoffrey – *Recollections* Chatto & Windus 1984

Grove, Valerie – *Laurie Lee: The Well-Loved Stranger* Viking 1999

Hamilton, Ian – *Robert Lowell: A Biography* Faber 1983

Hardy, Florence Emily – *Life of Thomas Hardy* Macmillan 1962

Hartnoll, Phyllis Ed. – *Oxford Companion To The Theatre* OUP 1951

Hawkins, Desmond – *When I Was* Macmillan 1989

Heppenstall, Rayner – *Four Absentees* Barrie & Rockliff 1960

Heppenstall, Rayner – *The Intellectual Part* Barrie & Rockliff 1963

Heppenstall, Rayner – *Portrait of the Artist As A Professional Man* Peter Owen 1969

Hewison, Robert – *Under Siege: Literary Life In London 1939-45* Weidenfeld & Nicolson 1977

Hollinghurst, Alan – *The Swimming-Pool Library* Chatto & Windus 1988

Holmes, Richard – *Shelley the Pursuit* Weidenfeld & Nicolson 1974

Holmes, Richard – *Coleridge: Early Visions* Hodder & Stoughton 1989

Holmes, Richard – *Coleridge: Darker Reflections* Harper Collins 1998

Holroyd, Michael – *Augustus John* Vintage 1997

Honan, Park – *Christopher Marlowe: Poet & Spy* OUP 2005

Hooker, Denise – *Nina Hamnett* Constable 1986

Hope, Warren – *Norman Cameron* Greenwich Exchange 2000

Hopkins, Justine – *Michael Ayrton* Andre Deutsch 1994

Hughes-Hallett, Penelope – *The Immortal Dinner* Penguin 2001

Jackson, Kevin – *Humphrey Jennings* Picador 2004

Jacobs, Eric – *Kingsley Amis* Hodder & Stoughton 1995

Jones, Nigel – *Through A Glass Darkly* Scribners 1991

Jones, Terry – *Who Murdered Chaucer?* Methuen 2003

King, James – *William Blake: His Life* Weidenfeld & Nicolson 1991

Kinkead-Weekes, Mark – *D.H. Lawrence 1912–1922* CUP 1996

Konitza, Faik – *Selected Correspondence 1896–1942* Centre for Albanian Studies 2000

Kops, Bernard – *The World is a Wedding* MacGibbon & Kee 1963

Kureishi, Hanif – *Buddha of Suburbia* Viking 1990

Lessing, Doris – *London Observed* Harper Collins 1992

Lessing, Doris – *Under My Skin* Harper Collins 1994

Lessing, Doris – *Walking in the Shade* Harper Collins 1997

Lewis, Jeremy – *Cyril Connolly: A Life* Cape 1997

Luke, Michael – *David Tennant and the Gargoyle Years* Weidenfeld & Nicolson 1991

Lycett, Andrew – *Dylan Thomas* Weidenfeld & Nicolson 2003

Maclaren-Ross, Julian – *Memoirs Of The Forties* Penguin 1984

MacNeice, Louis – *Collected Poems* Faber & Faber 1966

Maddox, Brenda – *The Married Man: A Life of D.H. Lawrence* Sinclair-Stevenson 1994

McEwan, Ian – *Saturday* Cape 2005

Mitchell, Adrian – *Heart on the Left: Poems 1953–1984* Bloodaxe 1997

Moorehead, Christine – *Gellhorn: A Twentieth Century Life* Henry Holt 2003

Moraes, Henrietta – *Henrietta* Penguin 1995

Motion, Andrew – *Keats* Faber & Faber 1997

Neville-Sington, Pamela – *Robert Browning: A Life after Death* Weidenfeld & Nicolson 2004

Norbrook, David – *Poetry And Politics In The English Renaissance* OUP 2002

Norman, Frank & Bernard, Jeffrey – *Soho Night & Day* Secker & Warburg 1966

Orwell, George – *Nineteen Eighty-Four* Secker & Warburg 1949

Orwell, George – *Orwell and the Dispossessed* Penguin Classics 2001

O'Connor, Philip – *Memoirs Of A Public Baby* Faber & Faber 1958

O'Keefe, Paul – *Some Sort of Genius: Wyndham Lewis* Cape 2000

O'Toole, Finlan – *A Traitor's Kiss: Life of Richard Brinsley Sheridan* Granta Books 1999

Pearce, Joseph – *Bloomsbury and Beyond* Harper Collins 2001

Pepys, Samuel – *The Shorter Pepys* (Ed. Robert Latham) Penguin 1987

Plath, Sylvia – *Letters Home* (Ed. Aurelia Schober Plath) Faber & Faber 1976

Pound, Ezra – *The Cantos* Faber & Faber 1975

Powell, Anthony – *A Question of Upbringing* Heinemann 1951

Powell, Anthony – *To Keep The Ball Rolling* Penguin 1983

Raine, Kathleen – *William Blake* Thames & Hudson 1970

Raine, Kathleen – *The Land Unknown* Hamish Hamilton 1975

Raine, Kathleen – *The Lion's Mouth* Hamish Hamilton 1977

Reed, Jeremy – *Duck and Sally Inside* Enitharmon Press 2004

Remy, Michel – *Surrealism in Britain* Ashgate 1999

Rhodes, James Robert (Ed) – *Chips: The Diaries of Sir Henry Channon*
        Weidenfeld & Nicolson 1967

Robb, Graham – *Rimbaud* Picador 2000

Robinson, Bruce – *Withnail and I* Bloomsbury 1998

Rowse, A.L. – *William Shakespeare* MacMillan 1963

Rowse, A.L. – *The Tower of London* Weidenfeld & Nicolson 1972
Sandhu, Sukhdev – *London Calling* Harper Collins 2003
Schmidt, Michael – *Lives of the Poets* Phoenix Press 1999
Schoenberger, Nancy – *Dangerous Muse: a life of Caroline Blackwood* Weidenfeld & Nicolson 2001
Selvon, Sam – *The Lonely Londoners* MacGibbon & Kee 1956
Sinclair, Andrew – *War Like A Wasp* Hamish Hamilton 1989
Sinclair, Iain – *Downriver* Paladin 1991
Sinclair, Iain – *Lights Out For the Territory* Granta 1997
Sisman, Adam – *Boswell's Presumptive Task* Hamish Hamilton 2000
Sheldon, Michael – *Friends of Promise* Minerva 1990
Skelton, Barbara – *Tears Before Bedtime* Hamish Hamilton 1987
Smith, Zadie – *White Teeth* Hamish Hamilton 2000
Spalding, Francis – *Dance till the Stars Come Down: A Biography of John Minton* Hodder & Stoughton 1991
Spark, Muriel – *The Ballad of Peckham Rye* Macmillan 1960
Stallworthy, Jon – *Louis MacNeice* Faber & Faber 1995
Stanford, Derek – *Inside the Forties* Sidgwick & Jackson 1977
Stedman Jones, Gareth – *Outcast London* OUP 1971
Stock, Noel – *The Life of Ezra Pound* RKP 1970
Spurling, Hilary – *The Girl From The Fiction Department: A Portrait of Sonia Orwell* Hamish Hamilton 2002
Sullivan, Rosemary – *Elizabeth Smart* Lime Tree 1991
Sutherland, John – *Stephen Spender* Viking 2004
Swinnerton, Frank – *The Bookman's London* Wingate 1951
Tatchell, Molly – *Leigh Hunt and his family in Hammersmith* Hammersmith Local History Group 1969
Taylor, D.J. – *Thackeray* Chatto & Windus 1999
Thomas, R. George – *Edward Thomas: A Portrait* OUP 1985
Thompson, E.P. – *The Making of the English Working Class* Pelican 1968
Todd, Ruthven – *Fitzrovia And The Road To The York Minster* Parkin Gallery 1973
Tomalin, Claire – *Samuel Pepys: The Unequalled Self* Penguin 2003
Tynan, Kathleen – *The Life of Kenneth Tynan* Weidenfeld & Nicolson 1987
Vannsittart, Peter – *In The Fifties* John Murray 1995
Warburton, Eileen – *John Fowles: A Life in Two Worlds* Cape 2004
Wart, Alice Van Ed. – *The Second Volume of the Journals of Elizabeth Smart* Flamingo 1995
Wilson, Colin – *Dreaming To Some Purpose* Century 2004
Wooolley, Benjamin – *The Queen's Conjuror* Harper Collins 2001
Wood, Michael – *In Search of Shakespeare* BBC 2003
Yates, Frances A. – *The Art of Memory* Routledge & Kegan Paul 1966
Yates, Frances A. – *Theatre of the World* RKP 1969
Yates, Frances A. – *The Occult Philosophy in the Elizabethan Age* Routledge & Kegan Paul 1979
Yorke, Michael – *The Spirit of Place* Constable 1988
Wheen, Francis – *Karl Marx* Fourth Estate 1999
Willets, Paul – *Fear & Loathing in Fitzrovia* Dewi Lewis 2003
Wishart, Michael – *High Diver* Blond & Briggs 1977
Wyndham, Joan – *Love Lessons* Heinemann 1985
Wyndham, Joan – *Love is Blue* Heinemann 1986
Wyndham, Joan – *Dawn Chorus* Virago 2004

Index of People

Index of Places

Copyright Permissions

For the quotations used in this book every effort has been made to trace the holders of copyright and to acknowledge the permission of authors and publishers where necessary. If we have inadvertently failed in this aim, we will be pleased to correct any omissions in future editions of the book.

We would like to thank the following authors, publishers and agents for allowing us to use their quotations:

The quotations from the poems 'Autumn Sequel', 'The Streets of Laredo' and 'Autumn Journal' by Louis MacNeice, published in *Collected Poems* by Faber & Faber, are printed here with the kind permission of David Higham Associates Ltd.

The quotation from *Saturday* by Ian McEwan, published by Jonathan Cape, is reprinted by kind permission of The Random House Group Ltd.

The quotation from *The Diary of Virginia Woolf* by Virginia Woolf, published by Hogarth Press, is used by kind permission of the executors of the Virginia Woolf Estate and The Random House Group Ltd.

The quotation from *A Question of Upbringing* by Anthony Powell, published by William Heinemann Ltd, is reprinted by kind permission of The Random House Group Ltd.

The quotation from *The Swimming Pool Library* by Alan Hollinghurst, published by Chatto & Windus, is reprinted by kind permission of The Random House Group Ltd.

The quotation from *The Guilded Gutter Life of Francis Bacon* by Dan Farson, published by Century, is reprinted by kind permission of The Random House Group Ltd.

The quotation from *A Time of Gifts* by Patrick Leigh Fermor is reproduced by kind permission of John Murray Publishers.

The quotation from *Under My Skin* by Doris Lessing is reprinted by kind permission of HarperCollins Publishers Ltd.

The quotation from *London Observed* by Doris Lessing is reprinted by kind permission of HarperCollins Publishers Ltd.

The quotation from *White Teeth* by Zadie Smith, published by Hamish Hamilton, is reprinted by kind permission of the author and the Penguin Group (UK).

The quotation from *Birthday Letters* by Ted Hughes is reprinted by kind permission of Faber & Faber Ltd.

The quotation from *The Death of the Heart* by Elizabeth Bowen is published by Penguin.

The quotation from the 'Strugnell Sonnets' by Wendy Cope is published in her collection *Making Cocoa for Kingsley Amis* by Faber & Faber Ltd.

The quotation from *Letters Home: Correspondence* by Sylvia Plath is published by Faber & Faber Ltd.

The quotation from *The Waste Land* by T.S. Eliot is published by Faber & Faber Ltd.

The quotation from 'Annus Mirabilis' by Philip Larkin is published in *High Windows* by Faber & Faber Ltd.

The quotation from 'Bar Italia' by Hugo Williams is published in *Billy's Rain* by Faber & Faber Ltd.

The quotation from 'Sestina Altaforte' by Ezra Pound is published in *Selected Poems* by Faber & Faber Ltd.

The quotation from *The Alan Clark Diaries* is published by Weidenfeld & Nicolson.

The quotation from *The Diaries of Henry Channon* is published by Weidenfeld & Nicolson.

The quotation from *The Lonely Londoners* by Samuel Selvon was published by Longman.

The quotation from *Downriver* by Iain Sinclair was published by Granta.

The quotation from *Albert Angelo* by B.S. Johnson is published in the *B.S. Johnson Omnibus* by Picador.

The quotation from the poem 'Celia Celia' by Adrian Mitchell was published in 1991 by Bloodaxe Books.

Photography Permissions

For allowing us to photograph on their premises, we would like to thank:

The manager and staff at Bar Italia
The manager and staff at the French House
Nigel Harris at St Margaret's Church
Susie Symes at No. 19 Princelet Street, an international historic site of conscience
(www.19princeletstreet.org.uk)
The visitor staff at Southwark Cathedral
The manager at the John Calder Bookshop

If you liked this book, you might also like to try:

The annual *Londoner's Diary*, published by Blue Island. The 2007 edition will be available from August 2006 (ISBN: 0-9552324-0-6).